Game Theory and the Humanities

Game Theory and the Humanities

Bridging Two Worlds

Steven J. Brams

The MIT Press
Cambridge, Massachusetts
London, England

First MIT Press paperback edition, 2012
© 2011 Massachusetts Institute of Technology

For information about special quantity discounts, please email special_sales@mitpress.mit.edu

This book was set in Syntax and Times Roman by Toppan Best-set Premedia Limited. Printed and bound in the United States of America.

Library of Congress Cataloging-in-Publication Data

Brams, Steven J.
Game theory and the humanities : bridging two worlds / Steven J. Brams.
   p. cm.
Includes bibliographical references and index.
ISBN 978-0-262-01522-6 (hardcover : alk. paper)—978-0-262-51825-3 (paperback)
1. Game theory. 2. Humanities—Mathematical models. I. Title.
HB144.B73   2011
300.1'51932—dc22

                          2010030323

10 9 8 7 6 5 4 3

Contents

Preface

Game theory models are ubiquitous in economics, common in political science, and more and more used in psychology and sociology. In the natural sciences, game theory provides a theoretical foundation for evolutionary biology, offering compelling explanations of competition in nature.

By comparison, game theory has only sporadically been applied to the humanities, broadly conceived. Disciplines in the humanities represent a world we do not normally associate with mathematical calculations of strategic interaction and rational choice. Nonetheless, a key aspect of our humanity is our ability to think rationally about alternative choices, selecting the one that best satisfies our goals. Game theory provides a calculus for this selection when we face other players, often with conflicting goals, in strategic situations.

The applications of game theory I make in this book are to philosophy and political philosophy, religion (as illustrated by stories in the Hebrew Bible), theology, law, history, and literature—including short stories, plays, epic poems, and novels—to which game theory offers important, and sometimes startling, new insights. As for the other humanities, game theory has little to say about the visual arts, such as painting, or music, with the exception of the strategic insights it offers into the choices characters make in operas and musicals. Likewise, game theory has not contributed much to cultural studies by anthropologists and other scholars, although the misperceptions of players in two historical situations analyzed here (the 1962 Cuban missile crisis and the 1979–1981 Iranian hostage crisis) might be attributed in part to the cultural differences of the players.

Neither has game theory shed much light on the learning of languages, but there are important applications of game theory to linguistics.

Although some may not consider law a humanities subject, I devote a chapter to law-related situations that involve palpably human choices. In addition, I touch upon the corruption of law in my discussion of medieval witch trials as catch-22s and in my analysis of fair-division paradoxes, which raise questions about equity and jurisprudence.

By and large, I use game theory to interpret *texts*, whether they be historical documents, fictional accounts, or some mixture, such as the Bible. This strategic exegesis of texts helps one relate the goals of characters to their choices and their consequences.

While I use standard game theory in several cases to explicate the connection between a character's goals and the means he or she chooses to achieve them, much of the analysis is based on the theory of moves (TOM), a theory grounded in game theory that I develop gradually, and apply systematically, throughout the book. Coupled with standard game theory, TOM helps to unify and render coherent the diverse contents of this book.

TOM is especially useful in illuminating the *dynamics* of player choices, at least insofar as players think ahead when contemplating their moves. It also facilitates the analysis of misperceptions and deception by players, the exercise of different kinds of power, and the use of threats and related stratagems.

More than using TOM to elucidate player choices and explain game outcomes in specific historical and fictional situations, I derive propositions about "generic games," which subsume several specific games and are applicable to a broad class of situations. These games offer a strategic perspective of a larger playing field, providing conditions under which different outcomes may occur in *classes* of games.

This is the role, I believe, that a theory should play. Admittedly, it makes harder reading than the application of TOM to a specific story, but the reward is that the theory enables one to think beyond this story, describing what, in general, is likely to occur in similar, but not identical, situations. To help the reader, there is a glossary of more technical terms at the end of the book.

Applications of game theory and TOM are not without controversy. It is sometimes alleged, for example, that these theories are cold-blooded and lifeless, suitable only for cool, cerebral thinkers who calculate rather than feel. By contrast, characters in both history and fiction have intense feelings and strong emotions, which some critics claim mathematical theories, austere and remote, are incapable of capturing.

I agree that emotions play a central role in the decisions humans make at all levels, from interpersonal to international. But how they arise is not so mysterious. Indeed, rather than covering up emotions, TOM enables one to identify the games in which feelings such as anger are likely to be expressed and, moreover, are rational responses to trying situations.

Pleasingly, TOM shows that anger and other negative emotions need not exacerbate conflict but may, in fact, ameliorate it. Indeed, as people struggle to attain acceptable, if not perfect, outcomes, knowledge of game theory and TOM may, in practical terms, help them achieve happier and more productive lives.

Acknowledgments

I am grateful to several people who read an early version of this book, or some of its chapters, and provided me with valuable comments: Gustavo Camilo, Shamarah J. Hernandez, Brian Hopkins, Jenna Kefeli, Theodora Koullias, Shilpika Lahri, Mira Rapp-Hooper, and Fan Wei. I also benefited from the helpful suggestions of anonymous reviewers.

I thank the publishers, acknowledged in footnotes in each chapter, who kindly permitted me to adapt material from previous publications for this book. I also thank my coauthors of these publications—Morton D. Davis, Paul H. Edelman, Peter C. Fishburn, Marek P. Hessel, Christopher B. Jones, D. Marc Kilgour, Ben D. Mor, Douglas Muzzio, and Donald Wittman—for their important contributions, as well as Edward W. Larroca for a student paper on which part of chapter 6 is based. Finally, I thank John S. Covell of the MIT Press, who provided strong support for this project and offered excellent advice, and Kathleen A. Caruso and Julia Collins for their expert editing of the manuscript.

1 Game Theory and Literature: An Overview

1.1 Introduction

Fiction has been one of the most fertile grounds for humanistic applications of game theory. Novels, short stories, plays, narrative poems, and even the librettos of operas—all have been subject to game-theoretic exegesis, as have stories in the Bible. It is these applications, all of which involve noncooperative game theory, that I survey in this chapter.[1]

I will sketch but not present technical details of several models, in part because my primary purpose is to emphasize literary themes amenable to game-theoretic treatment, and in part because I will model in depth the choices of characters in specific literary works later. This survey is meant to be reasonably comprehensive, but it is only a survey: Those interested in the modeling details will need to consult the sources cited, which I hope to encourage by stimulating interest in literature as a fruitful source of ideas worthy of strategic analysis.[2]

Game theory provides a parsimonious framework and an important set of tools for the literary theorist. Although there are no rigorous tests to determine what the "right" interpretation of a work of fiction is, some interpretations are clearly more tenable than others. Game theory

1. This chapter is adapted from Brams 1994a with permission. Some specialized terms (e.g., *noncooperative game theory* in the present sentence) often will not be defined in this chapter but can be found in the glossary and will be discussed later in the book.

2. I have excluded from this survey work that originally appeared in movies and television. This is not because I think that writing for these popular media is superficial or otherwise unworthy of game-theoretic treatment. On the contrary, some of the plots, such as for the popular TV series *The Sopranos*, reflect game-theoretic reasoning par excellence. But this enormous body of work, in my opinion, requires its own book-length treatment.

explicates the strategic choices of characters by illuminating the linkage between their motives and their actions. It also offers insight into certain interpretive questions, such as whether the ordinary calculations of literary characters can explain their extraordinary actions in some of literature's great tragedies.

My review of applications of game theory to literature has both a critical and a historical dimension. In an attempt to gain an understanding of how and why the applications evolved as they did, I asked several people who have applied game theory to fiction three questions, which are given in section 1.2. I also give in this section a chronological listing (table 1.1) of the literary works and opera librettos to which game theory has been applied.

In later sections, I make use of the respondents' answers to see what inspired them to tackle a particular literary work and what they think a game-theoretic perspective brings to the understanding and interpretation of that work. I also asked them whether this work, in turn, stimulated them to probe new theoretical questions.

In discussing fictional works analyzed by game theorists, I begin in section 1.3 by showing how two authors (Arthur Conan Doyle and Edgar Allan Poe), instead of confronting the consequences of the so-called minimax theorem in their fiction, sidestepped them. I then present in some detail an application that illustrates how one writer (William Faulkner) captured the spirit of the theorem, even invoking a fictitious "Player" to make seemingly random choices, which, according to the minimax theorem, are optimal under certain conditions.

In section 1.4, problems of coalition formation in zero-sum games take center stage in a play (by Harold Pinter); they also pervade a political novel (by C. P. Snow), arguably to the detriment of character development. One analyst, in fact, contends that emotions tend to be submerged when there are clear-cut winners and losers, whereas ambivalence is better expressed in literary plots with nonzero-sum elements.

Several works of fiction that may be interpreted as nonzero-sum games are reviewed in sections 1.5 and 1.6—some quite critically, because of what I believe are some misuses of game theory in these applications. Contrary to the views of some, I argue in section 1.5 that great tragedies—such as Shakespeare's *Othello*, Puccini's *Tosca*, and Shakespeare's

Richard III (usually classified as a history but certainly a tragedy for many of its characters)—can be well understood in rational-choice terms: Their high drama is less a product of irrational behavior than a train of events, and rational choices in response to them, that spiral out of control. Joseph Heller's *Catch-22* illustrates the frustration that may burden characters who see no way out of their predicaments.

What start out as rather mundane calculations may become anything but routine in their consequences for the players. These include a classic coordination problem (in an O. Henry story), compounded by incomplete information that also plagues Portia's suitors in a game they play with her father in Shakespeare's *The Merchant of Venice*. But incomplete information also creates opportunities for signaling and credible commitments, which are prominent in works by Homer, Shakespeare, Joseph Conrad, George V. Higgins, and Richard Wagner that are briefly discussed in section 1.6.

In section 1.7, I consider game-theoretic analyses of the devil in Johann Wolfgang von Goethe's *Faust* and of God in the Hebrew Bible. *Faust* is modeled as a differential game (described later), whereas in chapter 2 two stories in the Hebrew Bible are viewed as simple ordinal games, in which players can order or rank outcomes from best to worst but cannot attach cardinal utilities, or numerical values, to them. The latter games and a biblical story in chapter 5 are interconnected by the continuing presence of God, who exhibits an abiding interest in using threats to cement His reputation and thereby tries to deter future untoward actions, including some by His chosen people, the Israelites.

Sir Gawain and the Green Knight, a medieval narrative poem that has been explicitly modeled as a game of incomplete information, is discussed in section 1.8. In the model, reputation plays a prominent role in explaining the actions of the main characters. Also modeled is the dual character of Sir Gawain, who, in an intrapsychic game between his two natures, has only incomplete information about the Green Knight.

In section 1.9 I offer some observations on the state of the art—an apt phrase, because game theory, as applied to literature, is still more an art than a science. I also discuss possible new uses of the theory, such as the exploration of games played between the author and the reader that incorporate the expectations of each player. I conclude that game theory offers a structure for clarifying strategic issues in plot design and character development that literary theories often ignore.

1.2   Method of Inquiry

Besides considering the merits of different applications, it is useful to inquire how game theory has gained the foothold that it has in literary analysis.[3] For this purpose, I wrote several game theorists who at some time had applied game theory to literature and asked them the following questions:

1. What inspired you to make the application(s) you did? Are there other humanistic works that you considered?

2. Does game theory offer unique insights into these works? Or does it offer more a framework for elucidating strategic conflict that these works illustrate?

3. Do these applications make a contribution to game theory, viewed as an applied field? What kind?

A number of respondents did not confine themselves just to these questions but went on to express wide-ranging views, replete with examples, of what benefits game theory can bring to the study of the humanities and vice versa.

To organize this rather open-ended information, I have grouped applications partly in terms of the theory (e.g., zero-sum games, games of coordination) and partly in terms of literary motifs (e.g., the role of emotions, the rational foundations of tragedy). At the same time I try to give a historical perspective to the applications by reporting what influenced game theorists, told mostly in their own words, to make the applications they did, and what they see as their benefits to both literature and game theory.

Because many readers will not be familiar with all the applications that have been made, I have included some information about the applications themselves, especially if they seemed representative or unique in

---

3. I use the word *foothold* with care: Game theory has hardly taken literary analysis by storm, perhaps in part because the theory is often misunderstood by humanists.

their approaches. In one instance, I describe in some detail how one writer (William Faulkner), in a grim tale of pursuit and mayhem, better captured the unpredictability of strategies in two-person zero-sum games without a saddlepoint—in which mixed or randomized strategies are optimal—than the usual authors cited on this subject.

The examples I discuss illustrate how game theory can enhance one's understanding of the strategic elements of fiction. The feedback may also go in the other direction, whereby a story, for example, may force the theorist to rethink how game theory may need to be extended or refined to mirror the strategic situation that it describes.

Before discussing some of the applications and looking at responses to the questions I posed, a chronological listing of literary works to which game theory has been applied is worth perusing (see table 1.1). Game-theoretic exegeses of these works range from a few sentences to lengthy articles. They also vary greatly in technical level, from relatively informal strategic descriptions to sophisticated mathematical analyses.

In applying game theory to literary works, it is useful to bear in mind the admonition of Howard (1971, 146) that "skillful authors often conceal certain essential motivations of their characters in order to reproduce the mystery we often feel in real life as to why people behave in the way they do." Game theory helps one unravel the mystery, at least in literary works in which there is a plot and the characters indicate reasons for acting the way they do. Plotless or surrealistic works, while they may have aesthetic appeal, are least amenable to this kind of analysis.

1.3 Avoidance and Acceptance of the Minimax Theorem

A number of conflicts in the literary works I assay can be viewed as zero-sum, in which what one player wins the other players lose. If there are only two players, the fundamental theorem of game theory or minimax theorem—proved in von Neumann (1928), sixteen years before the appearance of the first edition of his monumental treatise on game theory with Morgenstern (von Neumann and Morgenstern 1944/1953)—established that there is always a solution that guarantees the players at least a particular value, whatever the opponent does. However, it may be in mixed strategies, which are randomized choices designed to keep an opponent guessing.

Table 1.1
Literary works and operas to which game theory has been applied

The listing below is given in the order in which the first application was made. If I have quoted from a work in the text, the source used is given in the References. Not included in this listing are works analyzed by the literary scholars mentioned in note 16.

1. Arthur Conan Doyle, *Sherlock Holmes* (several books in a series) (Morgenstern 1935; von Neumann and Morgenstern 1944/1953; Vorob'ev 1968)—mystery

2. William Shakespeare, *The Merchant of Venice* (Williams 1954/1966)—play

3. William Shakespeare, *Othello* (Rapoport 1960; Teodorescu-Brinzeu 1977)—play

4. William Shakespeare, *Measure for Measure* (Schelling 1960)—play

5. O. Henry (William Sidney Porter), "The Gift of the Magi" (Rapoport 1960; Vorob'ev 1968; Rasmusen 1989)—short story

6. Giacomo Puccini, *Tosca* (Rapoport 1962)—opera

7. William Shakespeare, *Henry V* (Schelling 1966; Dixit and Nalebuff 1991)—play

8. Joseph Conrad, *The Secret Agent* (Schelling 1966)—novel

9. Alexander Pushkin, *Eugene Onegin* (Vorob'ev 1968)—novel

10. William Shakespeare, *Hamlet* (Vorob'ev 1968; Brams 1994; Howard 1996)—play

11. Edgar Allan Poe, "The Purloined Letter" (Davis 1970)—short story

12. Harold Pinter, *The Caretaker* (Howard 1971)—play

13. William Shakespeare, *Richard III* (Lalu 1977)—play

14. Agatha Christie, *The Mousetrap* (Steriadi-Bogdan 1977)—play

15. Homer, *The Odyssey* (Elster 1979; Mehlmann 2000)—mythology

16. *Bible* (Brams 1980/2003; Dixit and Nalebuff 2008; Brams and Kilgour 2009)—religious work

17. C. P. Snow, *The Masters* (Riker 1986)—novel

18. Boris Pasternak, *Dr. Zhivago* (Howard 1988)—novel

19. Johann Wolfgang von Goethe, *Faust* (Mehlmann 1990, 2000)—play

20. *Sir Gawain and the Green Knight* (anonymous) (O'Neill 1991)—medieval poem

21. *The Feast of Bricriu* (anonymous) (O'Neill 1991)—medieval tale

22. William Faulkner, *Light in August* (Brams 1994a, 1994b)—novel

23. William Shakespeare, *Hamlet* (Brams 1994b)—play

24. William Shakespeare, *King Lear* (Chami 1996; Dixit and Nalebuff 2008)—play

25. Aristophanes, *Lysistrata* (Brams 1997a)—play

26. William Shakespeare, *Macbeth* (Brams 1997a)—play

27. Joseph Heller, *Catch-22* (Brams and Jones 1999; Dixit and Nalebuff 2008)—novel

28. William Goldman, *The Princess Bride* (Dixit and Nalebuff 2008)—novel

29. Giuseppe Verdi, *Rigoletto* (Dixit and Nalebuff 2008)—opera

30. Friedrich von Schiller, *Wallenstein* (Holler and Klose-Ullman 2008)—play

31. Richard Wagner, *Lohengrin* (Huck 2008)—opera

32. Richard Wagner, *Tannhäuser* (Harmgart, Huck, and Müller 2008, 2009)—opera

33. William Shakespeare, *Much Ado about Nothing* (Chwe 2009)—play

34. Richard Wright, *Black Boy* (Chwe 2009)—novel

Mixed strategies introduce an element of uncertainty into the play of a game and turn a certain guarantee into a guarantee of an average amount, or an expected value. In *Sherlock Holmes*, Conan Doyle portrayed this element in the difficult choice that he gave to Sherlock Holmes, pursued by the notorious Professor Moriarty, of whether to get off his train at Dover or at Canterbury, an intermediate stop. He chose Canterbury, anticipating that Moriarty would take a special faster train to Dover to try to catch him if he got off there. Holmes's anticipation was correct, but Morgenstern (1935, 174) asks the critical question: "But what if Moriarty had been still more clever, had estimated Holmes's mental abilities better and had foreseen his actions accordingly?"

Morgenstern originally posed this question in his first book (Morgenstern 1928), which coincidentally was published the same year as von Neumann's proof of the minimax theorem. Unaware of the minimax theorem, Morgenstern saw the Holmes-Moriarty story as an illustration of a paradox in which "an endless chain of reciprocally conjectural reactions and counter-reactions . . . can never be broken by an act of knowledge but always only through an arbitrary act—a resolution" (Morgenstern 1935, 174). Although prescient in recognizing the arbitrariness of the resolution, Morgenstern did not yet know its mixed-strategy form—which involves randomly choosing among pure strategies according to some probability distribution—that had actually been calculated for specific games before the minimax theorem was proved (Dimand and Dimand 1990).[4]

Conan Doyle's resolution, on the other hand, was to make Holmes one whit more clever than Moriarty, ignoring that Moriarty himself might have been able to make an anticipatory calculation similar to Holmes's. Moreover, the matter does not end there: Holmes could have anticipated Moriarty; Moriarty, Holmes; and so on, leading to Morgenstern's "endless chain of reasoning."

In the short story "The Purloined Letter," Edgar Allan Poe broke this chain by assuming that an extremely clever boy could always calculate exactly how far ahead his less clever opponents would reason. Then, in a game in which this boy guessed whether an opponent was concealing

---

4. But in von Neumann and Morgenstern 1944/1953, 177–178, the authors proposed a 2×2 payoff matrix for the Holmes-Moriarty game and found the mixed-strategy solution, pointing out that Holmes's "complete victory" is "somewhat misleading."

an odd or an even number of marbles in his hand, the clever guesser would be able to anticipate his opponent, and whether the opponent was a "simpleton" or someone of great cunning (but not greater than his own). Here is how the clever boy, according to Poe, was able to do this:

When I wish to find out how wise, or how stupid, or how good, or how wicked is any one, or what are his thoughts at the moment, I fashion the expression of my face, as accurately as possible, in accordance with the expression of his, and then wait to see what thoughts or sentiments arise in my mind or heart, as if to match or correspond with the expression. (quoted in Davis 1970, 26–27)

Labeling this reasoning "tortuous," Davis points out that "the adversary can undo all the boy's labor by simply randomizing, in which case it will take nothing short of the Delphic Oracle to gain an edge." This is also true in William Goldman's *The Princess Bride* (1973), in which the two antagonists try to outguess each other about which of two cups of wine has been poisoned. Goldman's clever twist is that both cups have been poisoned, but one person has made himself immune to the poison, so it doesn't matter which cup he takes (Dixit and Nalebuff 2008, 141–143).

To return to "The Purloined Letter," Davis wrote that he chose this example "because of the irony of Poe's comment: 'As poet and mathematician, he would reason well; as mere mathematician, he could not have reasoned at all'" (quoted in Davis 1970, 27). On the contrary, Davis argues, "as mathematician (using the minimax theorem) *he need not reason at all*—random play is sufficient to confound the boy" (italics in original).

Hence, it is the mathematician—who, according to Poe, "could not have reasoned at all"—who can play this game at least to a draw, even against an incredibly clever opponent.[5] By randomizing, the mathematician robs the opponent of any control over the outcome and so ensures the value of the game.

This is a fundamental insight of the minimax theorem that neither Conan Doyle nor Poe seems to have understood. (To be sure, the cunning

---

5. Of course, knowing *exactly* how clever an opponent is, the boy can always win, but this cleverness is better characterized as omniscience, which even the biblical God did not possess (Brams 1980/2003, 1983/2007). Moreover, it can lead to a "paradox of omniscience" (section 9.7), which hurts the omniscient player.

these writers attributed to their characters may make for better fiction than resolving each game with the flip of a coin.) But just the opponents' *knowledge* of this greater cunning would have been sufficient for them to even the score by choosing mixed strategies, because it protects them from being outsmarted. Apparently, however, they did not have even this knowledge—or, more accurately, the writers did not choose to give it to them.

Not all writers portray their characters in such a one-sided fashion. For example, knowledge is more shared, and calculations more even-handed, in the climactic scene of William Faulkner's novel *Light in August* (first published in 1932), in which Percy Grimm pursues Joe Christmas, a prisoner who has just escaped his captors. Though hand-cuffed in front, Christmas, like Grimm, has a gun. Grimm thinks, as the pursuit by bicycle and on foot nears its end, like a game theorist: "He can do two things. He can try for the ditch again, or he can dodge around the house until one of us gets a shot" (Faulkner 1950, 404).

Grimm runs for the ditch, but soon he realizes that "he had lost a point. That Christmas had been watching his legs all the time beneath the house. He said, 'Good man'" (Faulkner 1950, 405).

The pursuit continues until it reaches the house of Reverend Hight-ower, who, though knocked down and injured by Christmas when Christ-mas burst in, refuses to tell Grimm in which room Christmas has run to hide. But a fictitious "Player"—a literary device in the novel—guides Grimm. Grimm storms into the kitchen, where Christmas has overturned a table to protect himself, and Grimm fires his revolver. Before Christmas dies, Grimm castrates him with the butcher knife he finds in the kitchen.

This, the most gruesome scene in the novel, contrasts sharply with Grimm's pursuit of Christmas, which is all cool calculation. Faulkner seems to have invented Player to epitomize the calm and deliberate mind of the fanatic; Grimm, who is "moved," as in a parlor game, by Player, is utterly devoid of emotion, except when he explodes with savagery in the end. The beast in Grimm coexists with the cerebral Player, which is a juxtaposition that game theory normally does not entertain when it posits a player with one set of preferences.[6]

6. If more than one type of player is allowed, as in games of incomplete information, only one type is actually the true type—there are not different types embodied in a single player (e.g., with multiple personalities), though in section 1.8 I discuss intrapsychic games.

Grimm seems genuinely in the dark after he rushes into Hightower's house, repeatedly asking where Christmas went: "'Which room?' Grimm said, shaking him. 'Which room, old man?'" (Faulkner 1950, 406). After Grimm asks once again, Hightower attempts to exonerate Christmas for the alleged murder he committed, but Grimm "flung the old man aside and ran on" (at random?) into the kitchen (Ibid.).

Unlike Conan Doyle and Poe, Faulkner beautifully captures the uncertainty inherent in mixed strategies—and how to act in the face of this uncertainty. And act Grimm does: first, to his own disadvantage when he discovers that Christmas could follow his movements as he ran toward the ditch; second, to his advantage when, "waiting for Player to move him again" (Faulkner 1950, 406), he rushes into the kitchen. Faulkner has little to say about the motivations behind Christmas's choices, but it seems they were essentially arbitrary, as if Christmas, as well as Grimm/Player, was randomizing.

Faulkner does *not* assume that one player had superior calculational abilities. True, Grimm has Player on his side, so to speak, but this device, in my view, reinforces the desultory character of Grimm's choices. Calculated they may have been, but because Grimm, at each stage of the pursuit, has only imperfect information, he can never be sure what his best choice is. Grimm "won," finally, not because of sheer cleverness but because the game was unfair—the odds were heavily stacked against the fugitive, Christmas, whom Grimm so relentlessly hunted down.[7]

I have offered this analysis of a scene from *Light in August* to suggest that Faulkner is one fiction writer who had an astute if implicit understanding of mixed strategies in two-person zero-sum games of imperfect information. Doubtless, other examples could be found. While the scenes that Morgenstern and Davis discussed in *Sherlock Holmes* and "The Purloined Letter" have the earmarks of games in which mixed strategies are optimal, both Conan Doyle and Poe shrank from making their protagonists' opponents as smart as the protagonists themselves. They got tidy results that way, but the minimax solution in games of imperfect information shows that not all conflicts can be resolved by outguessing. Faulkner understood this, even if the formal calculations eluded him.

---

7. I assume that once Christmas is cornered, Grimm has the upper hand. Until then, however, the players seem evenly matched.

1.4   Are Zero-Sum Games Emotionless?

Zero-sum games with more than two players raise entirely new theoretical questions, chiefly related to what coalitions are likely to form and be stable. Nigel Howard (1990) reports that when he went to a performance of Harold Pinter's *The Caretaker*, he was struck by its similarity to the game of split-the-dollar—where a dollar (or better 99¢) is divided equally among three people unless at least two agree on another way of dividing it. This zero-sum game has no stable solution, because however the dollar is divided, there are always two players who can do better by agreeing on another split that excludes the third.

In the case of *The Caretaker*, there is a pecking order of respect, such that the least-respected character can always suggest to one of the other two a deal in which they give each other greater mutual respect at the expense of the third. Each of the play's three acts deals with the formation of one of the three two-person coalitions.

Howard (1971) describes the formation and disintegration of each coalition in the three acts, involving two brothers who share a house and a third man who might become their caretaker. The play ends with "no relationships," but with the possibility that new relationships will form once again, "causing the three acts to be repeated in sequence again and again" (Howard 1971, 145). Although *The Caretaker* "is almost classically austere and simple from a game-theoretic point of view" (Ibid.), Howard argues that "Pinter's view is however interesting in that at least he has risen to the level of dramatizing a three-player interaction" (Howard 1990).[8]

In analyzing C. P. Snow's *The Masters*, William H. Riker (1986) examines the more complex interactions of thirteen fellows in a Cambridge (UK) college, who must vote on a new master of their college in a zero-sum game (there are two candidates among the thirteen fellows, and only one can win). The novel is about the election campaign, in which "pride and ambition and humiliation and failure are displayed against a background of political bitterness" (Riker 1986, 52).

There are four switches in support for the two candidates as they vie for the votes of the eleven other fellows of the college. Riker shows how

8. It is worth noting that coalitional cycles of the kind that Howard identified can occur in nonzero-sum games; they are not exclusive to zero-sum games like split-the-dollar.

the maneuvers of one fellow, in particular, who abandons his original favorite the day before the election, ultimately succeed. Although Riker's analysis stresses social-choice theory rather than game theory (e.g., Riker shows that no logrolling is possible, based on the positions of the fellows on two dimensions), it is evident that the campaign is suffused with game-theoretic calculations.

The leaders of the two factions constantly plot to hold their coalitions together, and draw in new members, against opposition efforts to woo away potential defectors. Riker in fact explored this idea in an earlier game-theoretic model (Riker 1962); its best-known prediction—that only minimal winning coalitions will form under certain assumptions (the so-called size principle)—is exactly what happens in Snow's story.

Riker regards *The Masters* as uniquely political: It "is, so far as I know, the only one [novel] in which politics is not mere background but the very plot itself" (Riker 1986, 52); "all other novels concern character development, love affairs, hurried journeys, family history, etc." (Riker 1990). Riker admits that building coalitions is "hardly the stuff to release readers' adrenalin as do seductions, quarrels, or chases," but he believes "political ambition, and indeed political success, uniquely reveal tragic flaws in character," as demonstrated by Greek dramatists and Shakespeare (Riker 1986, 52).

To Howard (1990), by contrast, the most interesting conflicts are not zero-sum:

Such a zero-sum view is a common one, as shown by the frequent comparisons of politics or war with chess, poker, or football. I think it is unrealistic; all my experience with applying game theory leads me to think that people are both more clever than this (they don't see things as zero-sum when they aren't) and more stupid (the simplest game-theoretic model of their situation often shows them simple, gross, obvious things they have entirely failed to see).

For Howard, "Pinter's view is the bleak, cynical one obtained by supposing that adults do not grow out of the 'zero-sum' mentality of children," which he disdains:

In fact, I would think this mistaken view is a rare, sophisticated aberration of the 20th century elitism. In a two-person game, zero-sumness means absence of emotion, deceit, preference change, etc.—all the things that artists have traditionally been most interested in. (In the three-person case, zero-sumness no longer excludes these—it merely means that they are necessarily exercised at the expense of a third party, as in *The Caretaker*). (Howard 1990)

In depicting *n*-person games of coalition formation, Pinter and Snow illustrated the fragility of coalitions in zero-sum games, which Howard (1971) and Riker (1986) explicated by showing how alliances may unravel. From a literary point of view, however, the question is not the stability of coalitions but whether such works are only plot and calculation—or something more. And if the latter, does the something more require that characters transcend their own rationality? I argue not: In an appropriate game, rationality—with respect to some plausible goals—perfectly well explains the choices of most characters we find compelling in literature.

In section 1.5, I turn to applications of game theory that have been made to nonzero-sum games. Whether game theory can illuminate emotions in such games, as Howard maintains, or is better suited to elucidating purely political plots and stories, as Riker maintains, is a question whose answer may shed light on the types of literature that have been selected for game-theoretic scrutiny. I pursue this question in later chapters with new applications, focusing on the emotions of frustration and anger in chapters 7 and 10.

1.5 The Rationality of Tragedy

The early use of game theory in literary exegesis includes Anatol Rapoport's interpretations of Shakespeare's *Othello* and Puccini's *Tosca* as nonzero-sum games (Rapoport 1960, 1962). In a two-person normal-form version of *Othello*, Othello may believe or not believe that Desdemona has been faithful, and Desdemona may deny or confess (falsely) her guilt; the tragedy occurs when Desdemona denies that she has given herself to Cassio, but Othello, with seeds of doubt planted by Iago, does not believe her.[9]

Rapoport also considers an extensive-form version of *Othello*, involving the four principals and "chance"; this game has fifty-five distinct

---

9. Neither does Hamlet believe that his uncle, Claudius, innocently acceded to the throne of his father after marrying his mother, Gertrude (Brams 1994b). *Hamlet* is another Shakespearean tragedy that I analyze as a game of incomplete information in section 9.2.

outcomes. The enormity of Desdemona's 16,384 strategies in the game tree (to be discussed in chapter 2) leads Rapoport to remark that "perhaps enough has been said about the practical difficulties of applying game theory in human affairs" (Rapoport 1960, 240). But he argues that "game theory stimulates us to think *about* conflict in a novel way" (Ibid., 242; italics in original) and also shows how interdependent decision situations can be "precisely characterized and rigorously analyzed" (Rapoport 1990).

After analyzing *Othello*, Rapoport turned to *Tosca* (Rapoport 1962), which he portrayed as a 2 × 2 Prisoners' Dilemma. Whereas jealousy fuels the plot in *Othello*, in *Tosca* it is Tosca and Scarpia's mutual betrayal that leads to its tragic end.

In another Shakespearean play, *Much Ado about Nothing*, Chwe (2009) compares the game Beatrice and Benedick play in in their comedic relationship with a game that has exactly the same structure in Richard Wright's dark autobiographical novel, *Black Boy* (Wright 1945). But the outcomes, love in *Much Ado* and hate in *Black Boy*, could not be more different, which can be explained, Chwe argues, because the game—Stag Hunt (sometimes called the Assurance Game or Coordination Game and described in note 9 of chapter 5)—has two Nash equilibria (to be discussed in chapter 2). At the better equilibrium, the players choose a risky strategy, which happened in *Much Ado*, whereas at the worse equilibrium, which happened in *Black Boy*, there is no risk. Chwe also analyzes trickster folk tales, which involve surprisingly sophisticated calculations that game theory helps to elucidate.[10]

In Teodorescu-Brinzcu's (1977) analysis of *Othello*, she assumes that Othello and Iago are involved in a zero-sum game, which, especially from Othello's perspective (who is sympathetic to Iago until the end), seems to me a misinterpretation. Second, she assigns payoffs so that Iago has a dominant strategy, and Othello a best response, but then argues that this "wise [minimax] solution" was not chosen because "it lacks dramatic consistency as it is very commonplace." Instead, "the psychological reality requires that in this clash of passions the Moor's jealousy and Iago's hatred should overcome any lucid calculations and drive them

---

10. In an earlier work, Chwe (2001) analyzed game-theoretic calculations that underlie rituals, especially those that depend on coordination and common knowledge, in both factual and fictional situations.

both to destruction"; indeed, they "die devoured by their own passion" (Teodorescu-Brinzcu 1977, 373).

Coupled with Desdemona's murder, this tragedy suggests to me that there were no winners, making the game decidedly nonzero-sum. Thus, I think the interpretation of this tragedy as zero-sum is untenable.

Teodorescu-Brinzcu's (1977) contention that great drama may require that the characters reach beyond themselves (irrationally?) to seize the moment—sealing their fate and, quite often, their destruction—deserves further comment. This view seems to be a tenet of Marcus's (1977) so-called Romanian school of mathematical linguistics and poetics, because it is also reflected in Lalu's (1977) game-theoretic analysis of Shakespeare's *Richard III*.[11]

Lalu (1977) analyzes this play as an extensive-form nonzero-sum game and concludes that

what the playwright considers as the optimal strategies are in fact optimal for the tension and the rhythm of the performance, seldom for the "actual life" of the character. A cautious hero would be uninteresting. Paradoxically, the optimal strategy of the character is, more often than not, that of "the mad risk." Therefore, the main characters may seldom be considered as perfectly rational players; as far as we view the play in terms of "a slice of life," the characters make mistakes. The optimal strategies for their destinies of actual human beings will seldom be followed; on the contrary, the characters will act following those strategies which the author (perhaps the only rational player) thinks optimal according to an aesthetic criterion. (Lalu 1977, 343)

Lalu (1977, 343) then asks what the point of applying game theory is and answers that she is interested in exploring *deviations* from rationality that are "optimal within the frame of the whole play, regarded as a work of art."

In my opinion, there is considerable arbitrariness in Lalu's assignment of specific numerical values to outcomes and specific probabilities to

---

11. On the other hand, Steriadi-Bogdan (1977), also a disciple of this school, argues in a game-theoretic analysis of Agatha Christie's play *The Mousetrap* that the characters made rational choices. But *The Mousetrap* is a detective story, or whodunit, which is not generally considered to be a great tragedy, whereas "in studying Shakespeare's *Othello*, namely Iago's strategy, you have to observe that Iago does not look for what in the Mathematical Game Theory is called the *best* strategy, but rather for the worst strategy" (Marcus 1990; italics in original). I remain unconvinced that Iago chose, say, a dominated strategy—at least in the beginning, when his plan seemed to be working quite nicely—but I agree that combining "strategic and psychological aspects . . . is a rather delicate task" (Ibid.).

chance events in *Richard III*. These assignments vitiate her claim that Richard chose his worst strategy, though I would not dispute her claim that Shakespeare sought "the ruin of the character [Richard] . . . for the sake of the tension of the performance" (Lalu 1977, 349).

The issue is whether this tension was achieved by making Richard's choices irrational. I think it was not, and an alternative and more defensible game-theoretic analysis—not to be developed here—would demonstrate that Richard was eminently rational. Briefly, the argument underlying this alternative interpretation is that Richard, brilliant and diabolical, knew that he could act boldly with a high likelihood of success; in fact, he rapidly dispatches several of his opponents at the beginning of the play. Although lacking the contemplative character of a Richard II or Hamlet, who seem to weigh options more carefully, as Lalu points out, Richard III, nevertheless, seems no less rational (and tragic) a hero.

I agree with Lalu that Richard III is not prudent, but prudence, which Lalu equates with the minimax principle and estimating the odds in lotteries, is not synonymous with rationality. And neither is a hero's "tragic fall" synonymous with irrationality. In fact, contrary to Lalu, I believe the tragic fall is made more, not less, poignant when characters are driven by an inexorable rationality toward some terrible end.

Interestingly, the hero (or anti-hero) of Joseph Heller's *Catch-22* (1961), John Yossarian, escapes tragedy, even though *catch-22* has come to signify a frustrating situation from which there is no escape. Dixit and Nalebuff (2008, 45) describe the situation in which Yossarian finds himself embroiled in a Prisoners' Dilemma. Brams and Jones (1999) argue that Yossarian played a different game, which I analyze in chapter 10. There I argue that Yossarian faced a catch-22, which can be modeled as a "generic game" that subsumes several specific games. One of these games models Yossarian's dilemma, whereas another models the difficult choices of players in medieval witch trials.

1.6 Coordination Problems, Signaling, and Commitment

Unlike *Othello* and *Tosca*, in which the characters displayed a stunning lack of trust in each other—for good reason in *Tosca* but less so in *Othello*—the theorists who have analyzed O. Henry's short story "The

Gift of the Magi" see conflict arising for almost the opposite reasons. The husband, who sells his watch to buy his wife combs, and the wife, who sells her hair to buy her husband a watch fob, are blinded by their love and perhaps too trusting.

Their blindness leads to a failure to coordinate their gift giving, and great sadness in the end (at least for the reader—more on the game between the author and the reader later) when the consequences of each trying to surprise the other are discovered. Rapoport (1960, 171) speaks of the couple's "misplaced altruism"; Vorob'ev (1968, 370–372) views the game as a battle of the sexes (the usual story illustrating this classic game is given in Luce and Raiffa (1957, 90–94); and Rasmusen (1989, 40) argues that the couple's failure to communicate may, ironically, have been rational, because communication would have ruined the surprise. Indeed, their sacrifices affirmed their great love for each other, despite their misfortune.

Eric Rasmusen (1990) points out that the couple, in effect, chose a mixed-strategy equilibrium;[12] the pure-strategy equilibria would be the outcome in which either the husband or the wife gives a gift but the other does not. Although game theory tells us that the mixed-strategy equilibrium is inefficient, and may be disastrous when the players choose noncomplementary mixed strategies (as occurred in the story), it does not tell us how such a dismal state of affairs may arise. By contrast, the story suggests that

the act of communication would lower utility by eliminating the fun of being surprised. So the example says something about how to apply the theory. The theory also says something about the example: that even if the two people suspected that the ridiculous outcome might occur, they might do it anyway. And it also makes you think about what might have been one of O. Henry's points, that it is the thought that counts in gift giving. (Rasmusen 1990)

Indeed, O. Henry endorses this point of view at the end of the story: "O all who give and receive gifts, such as they are wisest. . . . They are the Magi."

---

12. Williams (1954/1966, 201–203) discussed such an equilibrium as the solution to a "marriage game" in Shakespeare's *The Merchant of Venice*. But this game, which is between Portia's father, Shylock, and her suitors, is zero-sum, because Shylock wants to frustrate, not coordinate with, Portia's suitors. The father in Giuseppe Verdi's opera *Rigoletto* has a similar goal, but this turns into a tragedy when he mistakenly kills his daughter.

Rasmusen (1990) draws a larger lesson from the story:

In general, examples are good for suggesting wrinkles that might not otherwise occur to the theorist. The easiest way to break out of a paradigm is to have the real world suggest a problem with it, since often the scholars are too used to thinking in one particular way. It is perhaps harder to be surprised by theories than by data.

I concur with these views but do not know of any direct evidence whereby a game-theoretic analysis of fiction has generated significant new theory. However, a large literature on so-called signaling games that has developed in recent years is germane to the strategic exegesis of plots. Avinash Dixit (1990) gives an interesting example:

If you read past all the four-letter words and the graphic violence, the whole theme of *Cogan's Trade* by George V. Higgins [1985] is reputation. For reasons too complicated to explain in brief, the bosses of organized crime in Boston have lost their reputation for protecting the activities they sponsored. How to regain it? This is a signaling game, and as usual there is excessive investment in signaling, in this case quite literally overkill. And the theory of this is almost fully and correctly explained by the enforcer (Cogan) in a conversation with The Man's counsellor.

By contrast, in Shakespeare's *King Lear* there is no enforcer—or any other mechanism—to guarantee that Lear's three daughters will keep their promises to their father, which he learns to his chagrin in the end (Dixit and Nalebuff 2008, 203, 434).[13]

Schelling (1960, 140; 1966, 11, 37) offers examples of the subtle and not-so-subtle signaling of threats in Shakespeare's *Henry V* and *Measure for Measure* and Joseph Conrad's *The Secret Agent*.[14] Citing different passages from *Henry V*, Dixit and Nalebuff (1991, 160–162) show how

---

13. Lear's willingness to succumb to flattery, abetted by the information problem he faced in learning of the true intentions of his daughters, is analyzed in Chami 1996.

14. Why these literary choices? Schelling (1991) reports:

My use of Henry V in *Arms and Influence* came from just seeing the play in London in 1965; I certainly didn't go to the play looking for illustrative material. I have no recollection of *Measure for Measure*, but I must have seen it in New Haven on the stage because I cannot imagine that I ever would have read it. . . . I do specifically remember how I was led to Conrad's *The Secret Agent*. I heard it from Daniel Ellsberg and when I wanted to use it I called him up and asked whether he was planning to use it in print in the near future and he said no and I asked whether he would release it and he said yes and I read the book and found no other useful examples but did use that one.

Henry inspired his troops, and thereby made his commitment credible, before the battle of Agincourt. His "steel my soldiers' hearts" exhortation echoes Lady Macbeth's plea to the "spirits," as she plans the murder of King Duncan in *Macbeth*, to "Make thick my blood/Stop up access and passage to remorse/That no compunctious visitings of nature shake my fell spirit" (see Brams 1997a, which is also discussed in section 7.5 of this book). Going one step further, in Homer's *Odyssey*, Odysseus (or Ulysses, as he was known in Roman myths) has himself bound to his ship's mast to ensure that he will not give in to the temptation of the sirens (Elster 1979, 36).[15]

Elster (1999, 2009) and Fisher (2002) consider how rationality and emotions mix in other literary works, but they develop no game-theoretic models of this mélange. Neither does Livingston (2001) in his study of rationality in literature.[16]

By contrast, Harmgart, Huck, and Müller (2008, 2009) and Huck (2008) use central ideas from game theory—mixed strategies, counterfactuals, and agreement theorems about beliefs—to render explicable some puzzling choices of the characters in two Wagner operas, *Tannhäuser* and *Lohengrin*. There is not space to describe these, but suffice it to say that the authors use both the music and the words of each opera to offer subtle, detailed interpretations that are persuasive without being overly technical.

1.7 The Devil and God

In Goethe's *Faust*, Faust gambles not just his wealth or reputation but also his life in making a compact with the devil. By selling his soul to Mephisto in exchange for knowledge and power for twenty-four years (in other versions of the Faust legend, sex or youth is the lure), Faust appears to commit himself irrevocably to eternal damnation when the

---

15. Mehlmann (2000, 132–142) develops an elaborate signaling game to model different choices of Ulysses. He offers other examples from literature (as well as movies), one of which I briefly discuss in section 1.7.

16. But other literary scholars have proposed simple ordinal games to model the choices of characters in several French literary works by Pierre Corneille, Guy de Maupassant, and Alain Robbe-Grillet (de Ley 1988) and the work of Polish writer Stanislaw Lem (Swirski 1996, 2007). I do not include these writings in the list in table 1.1 so as not to extend this list unduly.

"supreme moment" arrives. Fortunately for Faust, his final repentance saves his immortal soul from Mephisto, though not all versions of this legend have such a felicitous ending.

Mehlmann (2000, 72–78) uses differential game theory to analyze Goethe's great drama, making certain assumptions about the linkage between the players' beliefs about the timing of the supreme moment and also about how the players' payoffs are affected by each other's activities (repentance by Faust, temptation by Mephisto). He demonstrates consequences of these assumptions for the equilibrium path, arguing that Faust's "will to strive" (i.e., to repent), as the supreme moment approaches, explains his salvation.

Alexander Mehlmann (1990) cites other purported explanations (literary, legal) for Faust's salvation but claims that his mathematical model has "all the ingredients needed." Although I am not convinced that he has captured the essence of the drama in the parameters and functions he assumes, his application illustrates how advanced tools of game theory can be employed in literary exegesis.

Mehlmann (1990) reports that he has "always been interested in unusual applications of mathematics" and believes that "mathematics should play the role of an art rather than that of a science." Searching for a dynamic conflict situation to which he could apply differential game theory, "by chance . . . *Faust* came into my mind." He says that this application makes contributions both to the mathematical theory and to the modeling of player beliefs.

My motivation for applying game theory to the Hebrew Bible came from teaching a humanities seminar at New York University for freshmen and sophomores, which required that primary sources be used. I hoped to show, through a careful reading of certain narratives in the Hebrew Bible, how elementary game theory could lend coherence to the strategic interpretation of these stories. I also hoped that the analysis of several individual stories would allow me to draw general conclusions about the games that the biblical characters (God included) played. The seminar, which included orthodox Jews, devout Catholics, fundamentalist Protestants, and others turned out to be very stimulating and led to *Biblical Games* (Brams 1980/2003), which I draw examples from in chapters 2 and 5 (section 5.5). Dixit and Nalebuff (2008) also cite several passages from the Bible, including the New Testament, in discussing the "art" of strategy.

In *Biblical Games*, I show that biblical characters are, by and large, rational in the twenty or so stories of conflict and intrigue that I analyze. God is a "superlative strategist," but having granted free will to His human subjects (which justifies a game-theoretic treatment), He is besieged by problems that their freedom engenders. These cause Him great anguish, leading to very human-like displays of anger, frustration, and jealousy.[17]

God's wrath is especially great when his chosen people, the Israelites, cross Him (see section 5.5). It is sometimes expressed in petty, sometimes vindictive, behavior, but He is also merciful, always stopping short of wiping the slate clean, at least for His chosen people.

I believe that the Bible, as well as other religious works regarded as sacred, can be viewed at two levels. One level is as a literary work, with the stories it tells being susceptible to the same kind of game-theoretic analysis that helps to make the strategic aspects of secular stories perspicuous. The other level takes account of religious questions, such as the rationality of belief in a superior being or the problem of evil, which I have addressed in another work (Brams 1983/2007) and draw examples from in chapter 3.

The profound and profane may not be so different, at least in terms of the kinds of game-theoretic models needed to explicate their strategic structures. For example, if a superior being is immortal, it must be concerned with its reputation, which in fact obsesses the biblical God, especially in the Torah (the first five books of the Hebrew Bible). Thus, it makes sense to consider a concern with reputation as a correlate of immortality, to which the substantial literature on reputation in repeated games is pertinent.

1.8 Reputation and Intrapsychic Games

In Verdi's opera, *Rigoletto*, an assassin, Sparafucile, reports that Rigoletto "pays me and he buys my loyalty." It is Rigoletto's "strong reputation," Dixit and Nalebuff (2008, 210) argue, that prevents Sparafucile from killing him (though it does not prevent tragedy from

---

17. The anger and frustration of human characters are modeled in Brams 1997a and Brams and Jones 1999, which will be discussed in chapters 7 and 10.

befalling Rigoletto's daughter, Gilda). But what if one loses one's reputation? In Shakespeare's *Othello*, Cassio experienced all too well the
calamity that ensues: "Reputation, reputation, reputation! O, I have lost
my reputation! I have lost the immortal part of myself, and what
remains is bestial."

Reputations are based on beliefs, and the modeling of such beliefs is a
central feature of O'Neill's (1991) application of game theory to *Sir
Gawain and the Green Knight*, a Middle English poem of the late four-
teenth century that was only rediscovered in the nineteenth century. This
poem describes the sudden appearance of a Green Knight of immense
size, who challenges the hero, Sir Gawain, to behead him in exchange for
a return blow.[18] After accepting the dare, which results in the beheading
but not the death of the Green Knight, the poem recounts Gawain's
search for the Green Knight, including tests of chivalry he must endure,
before the Green Knight is allowed his turn to behead Sir Gawain a year
and a day later. Feigning a beheading, the Green Knight inflicts a minor
wound on Sir Gawain, presumably to symbolize Gawain's imperfection.

Now considered a great literary work that is rivaled only by Chaucer's
poetry of the same period, *Sir Gawain* "engages modern readers by
addressing modern problems," in particular "the predicament of how to
follow one's ideals when the world maneuvers them into opposition to
each other" (O'Neill 1990). Although the story might seem fantastic, the
Green Knight is not described in just supernatural terms but is given a
distinct human dimension, suggesting him to be vulnerable emotionally
if not physically.

O'Neill (1991) analyzes two games, the first having to do with Gawain's
reputation, which the Green Knight throws into doubt by his bold challenge to Arthur and the Round Table (Gawain persuades Arthur to let
him stand in for him). O'Neill (Ibid.), postulating different beliefs that
the players might have in different versions of a game of incomplete
information, analyzes why the Green Knight throws down the gauntlet,
and why Gawain accepts.

In one version, for example, he argues that Gawain seeks to enhance
his reputation by placing a high value on his reputation, defined recur-

18. O'Neill 1991 also analyzes *The Feast of Bricriu*, an Old Irish medieval tale that describes
another beheading, but its analysis is similar to that of *Sir Gawain*, so I do not discuss
it here.

sively. In other words, Gawain wants to be seen as someone to be reckoned with generally, independent of the specific challenge he faces. The Green Knight makes a similar calculation in uttering his dare, and the players compete in a contest to bolster their *relative* reputations.

The second game O'Neill (1991) analyzes is that between Gawain's two natures—one chivalrous and the other self-preserving—that echoes the conflict between the id and the superego in Freud's theory. (The third component in Freud's theory, the ego, might come into play if there were a mediator or arbitrator involved.) In effect, Gawain must play against himself, not knowing whether the Green Knight is (1) chivalrous and vulnerable or (2) malevolent and invulnerable, which would make the game fair or unfair, respectively. If (1), then Gawain owes the Green Knight fair play, which will be reciprocated; if (2), then Gawain is absolved of his duty to rise to the challenge and should instead avoid being killed.

There is psychic harmony in this game if Gawain's two natures agree on the character of the Green Knight, but each of the natures prefers a different interpretation: The chivalrous nature prefers (1), and the self-preserving nature prefers (2). If the two natures disagree, there is tension, which is worse for both players (i.e., Gawain's two natures) than harmony. The resulting game, in which the two natures are locked in battle, is the classic battle of the sexes, which has two Nash equilibria in pure strategies and one in mixed strategies.

The lack of an obvious solution, O'Neill (1991) argues, renders the outcome equivocal, which "makes for a good literary plot." Unlike the Romanian school, however, O'Neill (Ibid.) does not contend that a character must act irrationally in order to dramatize the conflict. Instead, the players' harrowing choices, due largely to a coordination problem caused by the lack of information on how to regard the Green Knight, sustain our keen interest in the story.[19]

Which, if either, persona of Gawain has its preferred outcome chosen (the chivalrous nature prefers a chivalrous Green Knight, the self-preserving nature a malevolent Green Knight) depends on how the intrapsychic battle between Sir Gawain's two natures is resolved. The

---

19. A reader, in my view, is much more likely to identify with a rational protagonist than an irrational one, especially one, like the Green Knight, who seems so unbelievable from the start.

actual resolution in favor of chivalry validates Sir Gawain's acceptance of the dare, but through most of the narrative the rationality of this course of action is anything but apparent.

Barry O'Neill's motivation for analyzing a literary work is very different from Mehlmann's:

I wasn't looking for a place to apply game theory. Instead I was reading the work . . . and then it occurred to me that it was an interesting problem to formulate the hero's situation as a game. . . . Some of the hero's problems were the same as problems in my life at the time . . ., and this led me to think very hard about the poem. I read it and pondered on it. I would walk around thinking about it. It was not just for entertainment. (O'Neill 1990)

Like other theorists, O'Neill (1990) believes that game theory can clarify a literary work. Nonetheless, he points out that some "past applications of game theory . . . did not take the literary work seriously in its details" or take account of "good ideas scattered through the informal literature."

1.9   Wherein Lies the Future?

Besides taking the textual details of a literary work seriously, O'Neill (1990) claims that "it is also necessary to relate our work to the vocabulary already in use" if game theory is to make a contribution to literary analysis. (He is less sanguine that the game-theoretic analysis of literature will lead to mathematical advances.) More practically, O'Neill (Ibid.) is concerned that neither literary nor mathematics journals are generally open to a linkage of these very different interests.

It is difficult to say how much the lack of publishing outlets has retarded interdisciplinary work. My own belief is that linkages between mathematics and literature are not viewed as worth exploring by young scholars in either field if they are interested in advancing their careers. Aggravating this problem is that there is no interdisciplinary training for people who might be interested in the combination, with the possible exception of the Romanian school mentioned in section 1.5.

A related problem is that several of the applications I have discussed are no more than off-the-cuff illustrations. While most of the authors are mathematically sophisticated, they have made little effort to find nontrivial applications of game theory. Of course, they cannot be faulted if a probing literary analysis was not their objective, but still one might hope for a more serious concern with the literary work. O'Neill (1990) speculates that Vorob'ev, a respected Russian mathematician who offered cursory analyses of several fictional works (see table 1.1) but did not report his own views, "perhaps regarded his study of game theory and literature as an interesting diversion, reading for the masses."

By contrast, in cases where the literary work was primary, the game-theoretic analysis was sometimes flawed (true of some of the Romanian authors). The opposite problem plagues Mehlmann (2000), where the mathematical structure is impressive but is not persuasively related to the narrative.

Howard (1971) and O'Neill (1991) use nontrivial game theory to construct plausible strategic interpretations of the play and poem, respectively, each analyzes. Interestingly enough, both authors, as noted earlier, indicated that they did not set out to "apply" game theory, but the literary works themselves riveted their attention.

Other tools of mathematical analysis have been applied to literature, but they generally give short shrift to plot (some citations are given in O'Neill 1991). Game theory makes plot front and center; when there is no strong plot or story line, as is the case in much contemporary fiction, then the theory has little to offer. I share Howard's (1990) view that "plot is essential for the kind of great art which really changes people," so I am not worried that game theory will suffer from lack of literary material to which to apply its methods, some contemporary fiction notwithstanding.

Howard (1990), who reported that he analyzed "every incident and conversation as a set of interlinked games" in Anthony Trollope's *The Warden* and then transposed the novel into a modern setting (Howard's reworked version was not published), indicates that game theory may have other roles to play, such as

to help writers construct plots. In film-making, where many people have to cooperate, it would be exceedingly useful to work with a clear game-theoretically analyzed plot—just as musicians find it useful to have a score.

He added that this kind of analysis can also help game theory, because game theorists benefit from the great store of intuitive wisdom about human behaviour contained in the world's fiction. They should continually be testing their theories against this. If it doesn't make sense to Shakespeare, perhaps it doesn't make sense!

Game theory, in my view, should be able to do more than suggest that there is a problem in a relationship. The fact that Scarpia and Tosca are enmeshed in a Prisoners' Dilemma, or the husband and wife in "The Gift of the Magi" have a coordination problem à la the battle-of-the sexes game, is not particularly enlightening. Why are these stories compelling and not just humdrum illustrations of these games?

O'Neill (1990) suggests that the tragic or surprising aspects of these stories require that we look more deeply into the information available to the players, and how it was used, in order to understand their human dramas. Indeed, the lack of information may itself be a central strategic feature of a story, as I showed in the players' choices of mixed strategies in *Light in August*.[20]

The game played between the author and the reader, as the reader progressively acquires more information (not necessarily accurate, such as the false clues in a mystery), is one that does not seem to have been analyzed for any literary work.[21] An appropriate framework for such an analysis might be the theory of psychological games (Geanakoplos, Pearce, and Stacchetti 1989) or "information-dependent games" (Gilboa and Schmeidler 1988), in which the players' payoffs depend on whether certain postulated beliefs are fulfilled.

Thus, a reader may be either thrilled or disappointed not only by the way a story evolves but also whether tension builds or he or she is surprised by the ending. If a horrific ending turns out only to have been a

20. Holler and Klose-Ullmann (2008) also suggest the use of mixed strategies in Friedrich von Schiller's play trilogy, *Wallenstein* (1800); they are not interpreted as "probabilities or chance" but as "a level of expected action." In my opinion, this interpretation is a sensible one that game theorists might well incorporate into their models, notwithstanding the authors' disclaimer that "the intention of this article is to convince theatergoers and people who work in the theatrical arts that it is worthwhile to study some game theory. . . . It is not this article's purpose to teach game theorists."

21. However, this subject is the main theme of a horror novel, *Misery* (1987), by Stephen King, which was made into a movie in 1990. In the novel, a reader takes revenge on an author for killing off her favorite character in the last of a series of novels, forcing the author to burn the manuscript of his next novel and resurrect this character in a new novel.

dream, a reader may feel either manipulated or relieved—depending on the reader's prior expectations—by the author's choice.[22]

Situated, as they are, in different worlds, game theory and literature have their own coordination problem, with game theorists and humanists not often benefiting from each others' insights. What makes a literary creation succeed is not just its overall structure but also its details, including the emotional lives of its characters. Game theorists need to ponder these and adapt their theory accordingly, just as literary scholars need to appreciate that game theory has its own richness that goes beyond mathematical symbols and abstract forms.

---

22. We sometimes use the term *cop-out* when we feel betrayed by the author. To avoid this feeling, authors might try to take account of the expectations of their readers in constructing plots and portraying characters. Thus, mystery writers might aim to surprise their readers, whereas other writers might prefer no surprises in order to stress the unrelieved boredom of the human condition (as in Samuel Beckett's play *Waiting for Godot*). Still others may search for an appropriate resolution to some conflict. If game theory were used to help authors in this manner, it would radically change the theory's purpose: Instead of using it to show that characters in a text act rationally, one would start with the characters' (or the author's) motives and write the text to show the rational working out of these motives, reversing the order in which game theory is applied from before to after the text is written.

2   The Bible: Sacrifice and Unrequited Love

2.1   Introduction

The Bible is a sacred document to millions of people.[1] It expresses supernatural elements of faith that do not admit of any natural explanations.
At the same time, however, some of the great narratives in the Bible do
not seem implausible reconstructions of historical events. Moreover, biblical characters often exhibit ordinary human failings in their behavior
toward one another.

Is it possible to reconcile natural and supernatural elements in the
Bible? This would not seem an easy task, because God, in some ineffable
manifestation, makes His presence felt in practically all biblical stories.
A naturalistic interpretation of the Bible immediately confronts His
commanding presence and uniqueness.

In any biblical analysis or interpretation, then, God must be given His
proper due. He *is* the central character in the Bible. Accordingly, I
propose to treat Him as such, but my treatment assumes more than His
omnipresence. I also assume that God is motivated to do certain things—
that He has goals He would like to achieve.

I do not assume that God is omnipotent. To be sure, He can perform
miracles and even endow others with great powers. But the Bible is
clear on one thing: Human beings *do* have free will and can exercise
it, even if it invokes God's wrath. Consequently, God, powerful as He
is, is sometimes thwarted in His desires. For example, after the creation,

1. This chapter is adapted from Brams 1979, 1980/2003, and 1994b with permission and
treats only stories in the Hebrew Bible (Old Testament); for an interesting application to
the New Testament, see Hassner 1993.

Adam and Eve disobey God, though they are punished for their misbehavior.

Since God does not always get His way, He can properly be viewed as a participant, or *player*, in a game. A *game* is an interdependent decision situation, whose outcome depends on the choices of *all* players.

Like human players, God chooses among different courses of action to try to achieve certain goals. By the same token, human characters, knowing of God's presence, make choices to further their own ends in light of possible consequences they perceive might occur. In sum, players in biblical games, including God, act *rationally*: Given their preferences and their knowledge of other players' preferences, they make strategy choices that they think will lead to preferred outcomes.

In this chapter, I show this in two very different stories from the Hebrew Bible. In section 2.2, I describe Abraham's attempted sacrifice of his son, Isaac, as related in the book of Genesis, in which Abraham played a game with God. Different interpretations of this game suggest there is a trade-off between faith and rationality: The more sophisticated the rationality calculation of Abraham, the less need for him to have blind faith in God in order to achieve his goals.

Thus, as the faith of a character wavers, his rationality may sustain him. Indeed, a rational interpretation of Abraham's action seems no less plausible than a faith interpretation. One might even argue that a more mundane rational explanation, precisely because it does not assume superhuman righteousness in the face of adversity, is more believable.

This is not to say, however, that faith is irrational. On the contrary, being faithful means having preferences such that one's rational strategy is independent of the strategy of another player—that is, one's own values completely determine how one acts.

In section 2.3, I ask whether Abraham might have achieved a better outcome if he had made a choice—contrary to fact—that he apparently rejected.[2] In the game I propose, I do not, as earlier, simply write down

---

2. Counterfactual analysis has probably been mostly applied to international politics and military affairs. See, for example, Tetlock and Belkin 1996 and Cowley 2000, 2003, 2004. Two contributions to the Tetlock and Belkin volume make explicit use of game theory: Bueno de Mesquita 1996 and Weingast 1996.

the preferences of the players. Instead, I derive them from primary and secondary goals that I attribute to the players.

I also highlight the role that threats played in the story and discuss how they may be made credible. For this purpose, I introduce some nonstandard game theory, based on the theory of moves (TOM), which is developed more fully in Brams 1994b.

I use TOM to analyze a more secular conflict between Samson and Delilah, in which God's name is invoked at the beginning but in which He plays no further role. After describing their conflict in section 2.4, in section 2.5 I elaborate TOM's rules of play relating to possible moves that the players can make. Specifically, I illustrate the use of "backward induction" by the players for the purpose of looking ahead and determining "nonmyopic equilibria."

This analysis shows that Samson's seemingly foolish behavior is grounded in rational calculations that TOM helps to clarify. Admittedly, Samson took risks, but they were not unwarranted by the incomplete information he had about Delilah and her motives. I show how the starting point, and therefore the history of play, matters when applying TOM, which explicates the dynamics of play and may predict different outcomes from standard game theory.

In section 2.6, I point out that not all moves, according to TOM, may be feasible, so the analyst must take into account the situation being modeled and constraints on moves. The infeasibility of certain moves affects the possible choices of characters in the Samson and Delilah story, as do emotions—in particular, Samson's expressed love for Delilah. By contrast, Abraham seems emotionless as he prepares to sacrifice Isaac, which has disturbed moral philosophers and others. I suggest in the counterfactual analysis of this story that more morally courageous action by Abraham is also consistent with his acting rationally.

2.2 Abraham's Sacrifice

With characteristic economy of language, chapter 22 of Genesis begins, "Some time afterward, God put Abraham to the test."[3] Then, in just eighteen verses, one of the greatest and most poignant stories from the

---

3. All quotations in this section are from *The Torah: The Five Books of Moses* (1967).

Bible is told. The significance of this story, and its interlocking themes of faith and sacrifice, have been subjected to prodigious analysis and interpretation, some of which I briefly discuss in section 2.4.

In the story, God commands Abraham:

Take your son, your favored one, Isaac, whom you love and go to the land Moriah, and offer him there as a burnt offering on one of the heights which I will point out to you. (Gen. 22:2)

Faithful servant of God that he is, Abraham sets out on his ass with Isaac, accompanied by two of his men with firewood for the sacrifice.

On the third day of the journey, Abraham sees the place for the sacrifice and leaves his ass and two men behind. He gives Isaac the firewood to carry, and he himself carries the firestone and the knife. When Isaac asks, "Here are the firestone and the wood; but where is the sheep for the burnt offering?" (Gen. 22:7), Abraham answers, "God will see to the sheep for His burnt offering, my son" (Gen. 22:8).

Abraham builds an altar and lays out the wood, after which he binds Isaac and lays him on the altar on top of the wood. As he picks up his knife to kill his son,

An angel of the LORD called to him from heaven: "Abraham! Abraham!" And he answered, "Here I am." And he said, "Do not raise your hand against the boy, or do anything to him. For now I know that you fear God, since you have not withheld your son, your favored one, from me." When Abraham looked up, his eye fell upon a ram, caught in the thicket by its horns. So Abraham went and took the ram and offered it up as a burnt offering in place of his son. (Gen. 22:11–13)

Abraham is then rewarded for his faithfulness—or, at least, his obedience to authority—when the angel calls from heaven a second time:

By Myself I swear, the LORD declares: because you have done this and have not withheld your son, your favored one, I will bestow My blessing upon you and make your descendants as numerous as the stars of heaven and the sands on the seashore; and your descendants shall seize the gates of their foes. All the nations on earth shall bless themselves by your descendants, because you have obeyed my command. (Gen. 22:16–18)

If this game is viewed as one played between Abraham and God, Abraham has two strategy choices:

1. Offer Isaac: O.

2. Don't offer Isaac: $\overline{O}$.

God, in turn, has two strategy choices:

1. Renege (if Abraham offers)/relent (if not): R.

2. Don't renege/relent: $\overline{R}$.

God's first choice is a cooperative response implying—whatever Abraham does—that He intended just to test him. On the other hand, God's second choice would indicate that He was deadly serious about His command to sacrifice Isaac. The consequences of these strategy choices for both players are summarized in the 2×2 outcome matrix shown in figure 2.1. For example, if Abraham does not attempt to sacrifice Isaac, and God is unmerciful, Isaac's fate (as well as Abraham's) is uncertain.

		God			
		Renege (if Isaac offered)/relent (if not): R		Don't renege/relent: $\overline{R}$	
Abraham	Offer Isaac: O	Abraham faithful,	i. (4,4)	Abraham faithful,	i. (3,3)
		God merciful,	ii. (4,4)	God adamant,	ii. (2,3)
		Isaac saved	iii. (4,4)	Isaac sacrificed	iii. (1,3)
	Don't offer Isaac: $\overline{O}$	Abraham resistant,	i. (2,1)	Abraham resistant,	i. (1,2)
		God merciful,	ii. (3,1)	God adamant,	ii. (1,2)
		Isaac saved	iii. (3,1)	Isaac's fate uncertain	iii. (2,2)

Key:

(x,y) = (payoff to Abraham, payoff to God)

4 = best; 3 = next-best; 2 = next-worst; 1 = worst

i. Abraham faithful regardless: prefers O over $\overline{O}$

ii. Abraham wavers somewhat: prefers God's choice be R instead of $\overline{R}$

iii. Abraham wavers seriously: Isaac's life paramount—same as (ii), except if God chooses $\overline{R}$, would prefer $\overline{O}$

Figure 2.1
Outcome matrix of Abraham's sacrifice

I next rank the outcomes of each player, but I will not attempt to attach specific values, or cardinal utilities, to them. The ranks for each player range from best to worst according to the following scale:

4 = best; 3 = next-best; 2 = next-worst; 1 = worst.

Hence, the higher the number, the better the outcome, which I will refer to as the *payoff* to a player.[4]

The first number, x, of each pair of payoffs, (x, y), indicates the payoff to the row player (Abraham), the second number, y, the payoff to the column player (God). Thus, for example, the payoff $(2, 3)$ indicates the next-worst payoff to Abraham and the next-best payoff to God.

A game in which each player knows the other player's preferences as well as his or her own is called a game of *complete information*. When players not only possess this information but also know that they know it, and so on ad infinitum, they are said to have *common knowledge*. Henceforth, games presented in this book will be assumed to be games of complete information and common knowledge unless otherwise indicated.

Starting with God, I assume that He prefers in all cases that

• Abraham show his faith by offering Isaac (O), so OR and O$\overline{\text{R}}$ in the first row of the figure 2.1 outcome matrix are His two most-preferred outcomes (3 and 4).[5]

Given that Abraham chooses O, I assume that God prefers

• to put Abraham to the test—as the Bible says He intends—and not allow Isaac actually to be sacrificed ($\overline{\text{R}}$), so for God OR = 4 and O$\overline{\text{R}}$ = 3.

If Abraham does not offer Isaac ($\overline{\text{O}}$), however, I assume that God prefers

• not to relent ($\overline{\text{R}}$), so $\overline{\text{O}}\,\overline{\text{R}}$ = 2 and $\overline{\text{O}}$R = 1.

---

4. This is somewhat an abuse of terminology, because payoffs in standard usage are cardinal utilities, not ranks.

5. As will be seen shortly, this implies that O "dominates" $\overline{\text{O}}$.

Given these assumptions about God's preferences, one can now analyze what consequences they have for the rational play of the game when Abraham is (i) faithful regardless, (ii) wavers somewhat, or (iii) wavers seriously. What each of these assumptions implies about Abraham's preferences is shown in the key to figure 2.1.

First, however, I note that the players did not make their choices simultaneously, as assumed in the 2 × 2 matrix in figure 2.1. Instead, the proper representation of the game is as a *sequence* of moves, in which Abraham—following God's command to prepare Isaac for sacrifice— can choose to offer Isaac or not. Although I could start play of the game with God's initial command, it seems evident that God was motivated to test Abraham's faith, whereas the motivations underlying Abraham's and God's subsequent actions are less evident, making them more worthy of being modeled.

The *game tree* in figure 2.2 shows the sequence of moves. Abraham's choices are at the top of the tree, where the branches indicate that he can offer or not offer Isaac for sacrifice. Once Abraham has made his

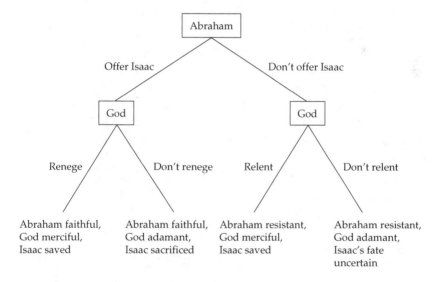

Figure 2.2
Game tree of Abraham's sacrifice

choice and God knows it, God chooses between reneging if Abraham offers and relenting if he does not.[6]

Because God's move occurs after Abraham's, in full knowledge of Abraham's strategy choice (O or $\overline{O}$), the game in matrix form needs to be represented as a 2 × 4 game (Abraham has two strategies, God has four), as shown in figure 2.3. After Abraham chooses between O and $\overline{O}$, God has four possible subsequent choices that are contingent on Abraham's initial choice:

1. R/R *Be merciful regardless*: Renege if Isaac offers, relent if not.

2. $\overline{R}/\overline{R}$ *Be adamant regardless*: Don't renege if Isaac offered, don't relent if not.

3. R/$\overline{R}$ *Tit-for-tat*: Renege if Isaac offered, don't relent if not.

4. $\overline{R}$/R *Tat-for-tit*: Don't renege if Isaac offered, relent if not.

Complete plans of what a player will do in all contingencies are called *strategies*. These are shown for each possible set of preferences of Abraham—that he is (i) faithful regardless, (ii) wavers somewhat, or (iii) wavers seriously. Operationally, these assumptions have the following interpretations:

i. *Faithful regardless*   Whatever God chooses subsequently, Abraham prefers to offer Isaac (O). Of course, Abraham would prefer that God renege on His demand that Isaac be sacrificed (R), so OR = 4 and O$\overline{R}$ = 3, which makes God's and Abraham's first two preferences identical. If Abraham does not offer Isaac ($\overline{O}$), he would prefer to do so when God relents (R) and Isaac is thereby saved, so $\overline{O}$R = 2 and $\overline{O}\overline{R}$ = 1 for Abraham.

ii. *Wavers somewhat*   Whatever Abraham chooses, he prefers that God subsequently renege/relent (R). Since Abraham would prefer to show his faith by offering Isaac (O), OR = 4 and O$\overline{R}$ = 3. If God is adamant ($\overline{R}$), however, Abraham would prefer to offer Isaac (O) as a show of his faith, so O$\overline{R}$ = 2 and $\overline{O}\overline{R}$ = 1 for Abraham.

6. Once payoffs at the endpoints of this tree are specified, "backward induction" can be used to determine the rational choices of the players, which coincide with those I derive in the 2 × 4 matrix in figure 2.3. (In section 2.5, I use backward induction to derive "non-myopic equilibria" using game trees turned on their sides.) Here the use of payoff matrices facilitates better than game trees comparisons among the possible games that Abraham and God played.

i. Abraham faithful regardless: prefers O over Ō

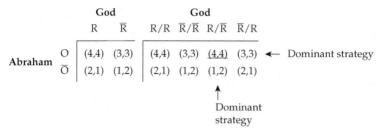

		God	God				
		R	R̄	R/R	R̄/R̄	R̄/R	R̄/R
Abraham	O	(4,4)	(3,3)	(4,4)	(3,3)	(4,4)	(3,3)	← Dominant strategy
	Ō	(2,1)	(1,2)	(2,1)	(1,2)	(1,2)	(2,1)

↑
Dominant
strategy

ii. Abraham wavers somewhat: prefers God's choice be R instead of R̄

		God	God				
		R	R̄	R/R	R̄/R̄	R̄/R	R̄/R
Abraham	O	(4,4)	(2,3)	(4,4)	(2,3)	(4,4)	(2,3)	⎱ Undominated strategies
	Ō	(3,1)	(1,2)	(3,1)	(1,2)	(1,2)	(3,1)	⎰

↑
Dominant
strategy

iii. Abraham wavers seriously: Isaac's life paramount—same as (ii), except if
God chooses R̄, would prefer Ō

		God	God				
		R	R̄	R/R	R̄/R̄	R̄/R	R̄/R
Abraham	O	(4,4)	(1,3)	(4,4)	(1,3)	(4,4)	(1,3)	⎱ Undominated strategies
	Ō	(3,1)	(2,2)	(3,1)	(2,2)	(2,2)	(3,1)	⎰

↑
Dominant
strategy

Key: (x,y) = (payoff to Abraham, payoff to God)

4 = best; 3 = next-best; 2 = next-worst; 1 = worst

Nash equilibrium associated with God's dominant strategy underscored

Figure 2.3
Payoff matrices of Abraham's sacrifice

iii. *Wavers seriously*   Same as (ii), except now, given God is adamant ($\overline{R}$), Abraham would prefer not to offer Isaac ($\overline{O}$)—perhaps hoping that this will save his son's life, even if he himself is punished—so $\overline{O}\,\overline{R}$ = 2 and $O\overline{R}$ = 1. This assumption says, in effect, that Isaac's life is paramount—Abraham's worst outcome occurs when Isaac is offered and God does not arrest his sacrifice.

What are the game-theoretic implications of these different preference assumptions I have posited for God? Notice, first, that in all three 2×4 payoff matrices in figure 2.3, God's tit-for-tat strategy of $R/\overline{R}$ is *weakly dominant*: For each of Abraham's strategies, it is at least as good, and sometimes better, than any of His other three strategies (God's strategy would be *strongly dominant* if it were always better).

To see this, observe that when God chooses tit-for-tat, He receives 4 if Abraham selects O and 2 if Abraham selects $\overline{O}$, in each of the three 2×4 games in figure 2.3. Whichever one of the other three strategies God selects in these games, God cannot do worse and sometimes does better by choosing tit-for-tat. For example, if God chooses R/R in each of the three games, He would get 4 if Abraham selects O but would get only 1 (instead of 2) if Abraham selects $\overline{O}$. Thus, tit-for-tat gives to God at least as good a payoff, and sometimes a better one, than that associated with any of His other three strategies, regardless of the strategy Abraham selects.

In game (i) Abraham has a strongly dominant strategy—to offer Isaac. It gives him a higher payoff than not offering Isaac, whatever strategy God chooses. (For simplicity, in the subsequent analysis, I will refer to both weakly and strongly dominant strategies as *dominant*.) The intersection of Abraham's dominant strategy, O, and God's dominant strategy, $R/\overline{R}$, yields the best outcome, (4,4), for both players. Of course, this was the outcome that was actually chosen in the game.

The mutually best outcomes in games (ii) and (iii) are also (4,4), but a somewhat wavering or a seriously wavering Abraham in these games no longer has such a straightforward choice. Rather, because Abraham does not have a dominant strategy in these games, he must anticipate the strategy that God will choose in order to determine his own best choice.

What strategy, then, will God, as a rational player, choose? Since God's tit-for-tat strategy of R/R̄ is dominant in games (ii) and (iii) as well as game (i), I assume He will choose it. Anticipating God's choice of tit-for-tat, Abraham in both cases obtains a higher payoff (4) by selecting O rather than Ō, which would yield him payoffs of only 1 and 2, respectively, in games (ii) and (iii). In a game of complete information, I assume that a rational player who does not have a dominant strategy—but, instead, *undominated strategies*—anticipates the choice of a player who does, and he or she selects the best response to this dominant strategy.

If rational, then, Abraham will choose O. The choice of O by Abraham, and R/R̄ by God, results in both players' obtaining their mutually best outcome of (4,4). This outcome, associated with the dominant strategy of God and the best response to it by Abraham, leads to a *Nash equilibrium*, or an outcome from which neither player would depart unilaterally because he or she would do worse doing so.[7]

Now, however, the process by which Nash equilibria are arrived at in games (ii) and (iii) is different. Specifically, a wavering Abraham in these games must first anticipate God's rational (dominant) strategy choice before he can decide what is best for himself. In game (i), by contrast, Abraham has no need to make such a calculation since he himself has a dominant strategy—a best choice not conditional on what God might subsequently choose—and hence can act rationally without knowing anything about God's preferences and the choices they might entail.

The conclusion I draw from this analysis of Abraham's sacrifice is that faith in God may ease the often difficult choices biblical characters face.[8] Faith, at least in Abraham's case, meant that he did not have to consider

---

7. A Nash equilibrium is actually the strategy pair that defines this outcome, not the outcome itself. Henceforth, however, I will identify Nash equilibria by the outcomes they yield. This will cause no confusion in 2 × 2 strict ordinal games, because a strategy pair is uniquely defined by each of its four outcomes. In 2 × 4 games, however, where there is some duplication of outcomes, I will be more specific as to which outcome or outcomes are Nash equilibria associated with dominant strategies. Thus in figure 2.3, the two (4,4) outcomes in each of the three 2 × 4 games are Nash equilibria, but only the (4,4) outcome associated with God's tit-for-tat strategy in the third column of each game is the product of God's dominant strategy.

8. A possible exception is Job, who faltered after terrible things befell him but whose faith ultimately sustained him.

God's possible reactions to his own best course of action, which was to obey God in game (i).[9]

To obey God blindly is, in fact, to act *as if* one has a dominant strategy that requires no detailed preference information about the other player, much less an anticipation of what strategy he or she might choose. On the other hand, when a character's faith in God is not blind, he or she needs to make more sophisticated calculations to ascertain how to act rationally. Although his or her strategy choice may be the same in either case, the logical process needed to arrive at it in the second case will be more demanding in terms of both the preference information required and the sophistication needed to process this information.

To argue that Abraham indeed acted rationally, it is important to ascertain that he knew, or had some inkling of, God's preferences in the three games I have postulated he might have played. To be sure, in the case of game (i) for Abraham, it does not matter whether Abraham

---

9. Alternatively, Abraham's faith might have been fueled by his *fear* of God as much as his faith, but the Bible provides insufficient information to say whether Abraham's possible blind faith was induced by fear. The element of fear is expressed in the lyrics of Bob Dylan's song, "Highway 61 Revisited":

Oh God said to Abraham, "Kill me a son"
Abe says, "Man, you must be puttin' me on"
God say, "You can do what you want, Abe, but
The next time you see me comin' you better run,"
Well, Abe says, "Where do you want this killin' done?"

("Highway 61 Revisited." Written by Bob Dylan. Copyright © 1965 by Warner Bros. Inc.; renewed 1993 by Special Rider Music. All rights reserved. International copyright secured. Reprinted by permission.)

By comparison, here is how Woody Allen (2007, 138) injects black humor into the dialogue between Abraham and God:

At the last minute the Lord stayed Abraham's hand and said, "How could thou doest such a thing?"
And Abraham said, "But thou said—"
"Never mind what I said," the Lord spake. "Doth though listen to every crazy idea that comes thy way?"
And Abraham grew ashamed. "Er—not really . . . no."
"I jokingly suggest that thou sacrifice Isaac and thou immediately runs out to do it."
And Abraham fell to his knees, "See, I never know when you're kidding."
And the Lord thundered, "No sense of humor. I can't believe it."

knows God's preferences, for he has a dominant strategy that is better whatever strategy God subsequently chooses.

But it does matter that Abraham know God's preferences in the case of games (ii) and (iii). However, for a somewhat or seriously wavering Abraham, it is sufficient that he believe God's attitude toward his behavior be either forgiving regardless (R/R) or tit-for-tat (R/$\overline{R}$), for both these attitudes imply Abraham should offer Isaac (O).

There was good reason for Abraham to harbor such beliefs. On several previous occasions, God had been magnanimous with Abraham, telling him, among other things,

I will make of you a great nation,
And I will bless you;
I will make your name great;
And you shall be a blessing. (Gen. 12:2)

I will make your offspring as the dust of the earth, so that if one can count the dust of the earth, then your offspring too can be counted. (Gen. 13:16)

"Look toward heaven and count the stars, if you are able to count them." And He added: "So shall your offspring be." (Gen. 15:5)

I make you the father of a multitude of nations. I will make you exceedingly fertile, and make nations of you; and kings shall come forth from you. I will maintain My covenant between Me and you, and your offspring to come, as an everlasting covenant through the ages, to be God to you and to your offspring to come. (Gen. 17:5–7)

Speaking of Abraham's wife, Sarai (later called Sarah), who had been barren for many years, God said to Abraham:

I will bless her; indeed, I will give you a son by her. I will bless her so that she shall give rise to nations; rulers of people shall issue from her. (Gen. 17:16)

That son, of course, was Isaac, whom Sarah bore at the age of ninety (Abraham was then one hundred). God further said:

I will maintain My covenant with him as an everlasting covenant for his offspring to come. (Gen. 17:19)

Given all these assurances, is it conceivable that Abraham could have believed that God meant him to sacrifice Isaac, the progenitor-to-be of multitudinous offspring?

My answer is that it is conceivable, given the steadfastly righteous man that Abraham appears to be. But it is also conceivable that Abraham suspected that he was only being tested and made the calculation that, in that event, it was rational for him to offer Isaac.

That Abraham was not above this kind of thinking is illustrated by a story from his earlier life in which he passed off Sarah as his sister. Because of Sarah's great beauty, Abraham feared that if it were known that he was her husband, he would be killed by the Egyptians so that the Pharaoh at the time could take Sarah as his wife.[10] In fact, Pharaoh did take Sarah as his wife under this misrepresentation, but when the truth came out, Pharaoh angrily ordered the dissembling couple out of Egypt.

I offer this background information to make the point that while it is hard to say exactly what game Abraham was playing, it is certainly not impossible to imagine that he knew something about God's preferences and hence was aware that he was indeed a player in a game. The three games I have posited all offer, in my view, plausible game-theoretic explanations for Abraham's sacrificial offering of Isaac to God. One is based on the blind faith of an unswerving Abraham; the other two on the more sophisticated calculations of a concerned father. Since all games dictate the same rational choice for Abraham (O), they do not really test the "blindness" of Abraham's faith.

Thus, although God's harrowing test of Abraham succeeds in establishing that Abraham would obey His command—however ghastly—Abraham may well have done so for reasons other than faith. Hence, God's test does not assuredly dispel doubts about Abraham's faith, given Abraham knows God's preferences and is rational.

2.3   What If Abraham Had Refused to Sacrifice Isaac?

In section 2.2, I showed that it was rational for Abraham to offer to sacrifice his son Isaac, whether Abraham was faithful regardless, wavered somewhat, or wavered seriously. These varying levels of faith were operationalized by the different preferences that I postulated for Abraham while holding God's preferences fixed.

---

10. For an alternative motive that emphasizes Abraham's desire to protect his wife rather than himself, see *Anchor Bible: Genesis* (1964, xl–lxi). Whatever Abraham's precise motive may have been, he appears not to have been above calculation that involved deceit.

In each situation, the game-theoretic analysis demonstrated that the rational outcome was a mutually best (4,4) for Abraham and God. However, if Abraham either wavers somewhat or wavers seriously, he does not have a dominant strategy of offering Isaac. Instead, he must anticipate what God's choice will be in order to determine whether offering or not offering Isaac is his optimal strategy.

Fortunately for Abraham, even if he wavers seriously, it is still rational for him to offer Isaac, anticipating that God's best response will be to renege on his command to sacrifice Isaac. By contrast, later a warrior named Jephthah is not so fortunate after making the following fateful vow (for details, see Brams 1980/2003, chap. 3):

> If you deliver the Ammonites into my hand, then whatever comes out of the door of my house to meet me on my safe return from the Ammonites shall be the LORD's and shall be offered by me as a burnt offering. (Judg. 11:30–31)

When, to his utter dismay, Jephthah is greeted by his daughter, there is no reprieve. God is in a more vindictive mood and holds him to his sacred vow. Grimly, Jephthah sacrifices his beloved daughter.

What makes matters "easier" for Abraham than for Jephthah is that the three games I assume Abraham might have played all contain a (4,4) outcome. True, various commentators, including Kierkegaard (1954), have argued that Abraham's decision was anything but easy—in fact, monumentally difficult. How could any father offer to sacrifice his beloved child?

Several modern commentators consider Abraham's decision, despite its favorable consequences, odious. Some believe that Abraham should have pleaded for Isaac's life, as he did for saving the inhabitants of Sodom and Gomorrah. Others consider Abraham's attempt to sacrifice Isaac a morally reprehensible act.[11]

Before condemning Abraham, however, let us suppose that his preferences were somewhat different from those I postulated earlier. In particular, suppose Abraham cared greatly for his son and preferred not to offer him. In this case, might Abraham have displayed the kind of moral fiber that the aforementioned commentators think he lacked?

To frame this question in terms of two levels of goals, suppose that Abraham considered not offering Isaac for sacrifice because his (i) primary and (ii) secondary goals were as follows:

---

11. An excellent summary of these views can be found in Dershowitz 2000.

Abraham (i) preferred that God renege on his command; (ii) preferred not to offer Isaac.

As for God, suppose that His goals were similar but not identical to Abraham's:

God (i) preferred to renege on his command; (ii) preferred that Abraham offer Isaac.

I will justify these goals in some detail later.

The primary and secondary goals of each player, taken together, completely specify the players' orderings of outcomes from best to worst. The primary goal distinguishes between the two best (4 and 3) and the two worst (2 and 1) outcomes of a player, whereas the secondary goal distinguishes between 4 and 3, on the one hand, and 2 and 1 on the other.[12]

Thus in the 2×2 payoff matrix shown in figure 2.4 (left side), (i) establishes that Abraham preferred outcomes in the first column (4 and 3), associated with God's strategy of renege/relent (R), to outcomes in the second column (2 and 1), associated with His don't

		God		God				
		R	$\overline{R}$		R/R	$\overline{R}/R$	$R/\overline{R}$	$\overline{R}/R$
Abraham	O	(3,4)	(1,2)		(3,4)^G	(1,2)	(3,4)	(1,2)
	$\overline{O}$	(4,3)	(2,1)		(4,3)	(2,1)	(2,1)	(4,3)

Undominated strategies

↑
Dominant
strategy

Key: (x,y) = (payoff to Abraham, payoff to God)

    4 = best; 3 = next-best; 2 = next-worst; 1 = worst

    Nash equilibrium associated with God's dominant strategy underscored

    G = threat power outcome God can induce

Figure 2.4
Payoff matrix of Caring Game (game 33)

---

12. This is an example of a *lexicographic decision rule*, whereby outcomes are first ordered on the basis of a most important criterion, then a next most important criterion, and so on (Fishburn 1974a).

renege/relent ($\overline{R}$) strategy. Between the two states in each column, (ii) establishes that Abraham preferred not to offer Isaac (hence, 4 and 2 are associated with $\overline{O}$) than to offer him (3 and 1 are associated with O).

Likewise for God, (i) says that He preferred the outcomes associated with R to those associated with $\overline{R}$. Unlike Abraham, however, God preferred that Abraham offer Isaac, so 4 and 2 are associated with O and 3 and 1 are associated with $\overline{O}$. In the 2 × 4 expansion of the 2 × 2 matrix—reflecting the fact that Abraham must act before God responds—God has a dominant strategy of R/R, and Abraham's best response to it is $\overline{O}$. (Notice that $\overline{O}$ is not a dominant strategy for Abraham; he must anticipate God's choice of R/R to make his own rational choice of $\overline{O}$.)

Because Abraham chose O, the 2 × 4 game in figure 2.4, which I call the Caring Game (game 33),[13] does not provide an explanation of Abraham's action. Although it may justify Abraham's counterfactual action of not offering Isaac because he is caring, how can it be reconciled with the outcome in the Bible?

The reconciliation, in my opinion, comes after Isaac asks Abraham, "But where is the sheep for the burnt offering?" (Gen. 22:7). Abraham's answer, "God will see to the sheep for His burnt offering, my son" (Gen. 22:8), strongly indicates that Abraham knew Isaac would not be sacrificed and, moreover, did not want to alarm Isaac or the servants. As additional evidence, Abraham had told his servants, before leaving them and the ass behind, that "we will return to you" (Gen. 22:5). As I showed in section 2.2, this apparent foreknowledge of Abraham—even if he were somewhat wavering or seriously wavering—robbed him of any reason to defy God's edict or plead for Isaac's life.

But now consider the goals I have postulated for Abraham in the Caring Game. As was true of a somewhat and seriously wavering Abraham whose behavior I analyzed in section 2.2, Abraham's primary goal in the Caring Game translates into his attributing high value to preserving Isaac's life. However, because I now suppose that Abraham prefers not to offer Isaac, the question becomes whether he can do so with impunity.

---

13. "Game 33" refers to the number of the 2 × 2 version of this game given in the appendix. Henceforth, I identify games in the text by their numbers in the appendix.

The answer would appear to be "yes," because God has a dominant strategy of R/R in the Caring Game, which He did not have in the figure 2.3 games ($R/\overline{R}$ was his dominant strategy in all three 2×4 games). But because Abraham did in fact choose O, should not the Caring Game be rejected as a model of what happened?

I think not, because the Almighty can *threaten* to choose $\overline{R}/\overline{R}$, prior to Abraham's choice, if Abraham does not choose O. Observe that $\overline{R}/\overline{R}$ contains Abraham's two worst outcomes (1 and 2). (They also are God's two worst outcomes, which is a matter I will return to shortly.) If Abraham believes that God's threat of choosing $\overline{R}/\overline{R}$ is real, then Abraham should choose O, because his next-best (3,4) outcome is preferable to his next-worst (2,1) outcome, especially if Abraham is risk-averse.

True, God never uttered a threat about what would happen to Isaac if Abraham defied his command to offer him as a burnt offering. But this threat was implicit in the language of the command, in which God stressed the sacrifice would be of your "favored one, whom you love" (Gen. 22:2). By revealing that He knew that Abraham prized Isaac above all else, God was almost daring Abraham to defy him—and suffer the consequences if he did. Fearing the worst, Abraham chose what the aforementioned commentators consider a less-than-honorable avenue of escape.[14]

But if we suppose the Caring Game is an accurate rendition of the players' preferences, then Abraham *could* have afforded to ignore God's implicit threat, or at least pleaded for Isaac's life. By refusing to offer Isaac initially ($\overline{O}$), Abraham would have set up a situation in which God must choose between His next-best (4,3) outcome and His worst (2,1) outcome.

In effect, having the first move puts Abraham in the position of being able to force a choice on God that, if He chooses rationally, leads to Abraham's best outcome, (4,3). Thereby God's implicit threat is undermined, rendering it more a bluff than a serious threat, *unless* God desires to set a terrible example for those who defy him—and suffer Himself for

14. The question of honor, and the use of dares to test a person's fearlessness when his or her honor is impugned, is imaginatively discussed in O'Neill 1999, chap. 7.

doing so by foreclosing the "great nation" (Gen. 12:2) that He had promised Abraham He would found and bless (section 2.2).[15]

Was God's threat irrational, then? I have argued elsewhere that the
nature of a threat is that it is costly for both the threatener and the
threatened party if it is carried out (Brams 1994b, chap. 5). (If this were
not the case, there would be no need to threaten—taking immediate
action against a transgressor would be rational.) Threats are made to
deter *future* transgressions; they are irrational to carry out if there is no
future. That is why God's implicit threat to kill Isaac, and thereby terminate the future of the great nation He had promised Abraham He would
establish and make prosper, is problematic.

The fact that God chose to test Abraham under these circumstances
raises the following question: Would He have done so if he thought
Abraham would fail the test? Perhaps not. But God endowed people
with free will, presumably understanding that this might cause Him grief
later (Brams 1980/2003, chap. 2). When it does, God sometimes finds it
rational to swallow His pride and not exact the full retribution he had
threatened (for example, against Adam and Eve, Cain, and the Israelites
after their idolatry at Mount Sinai, which I analyze in section 5.5).

Because there is a mutually best (4,4) outcome in all of the figure 2.3
games, it is no great feat for the players to achieve it. In the Caring Game,
by comparison, there is no such outcome but instead two competing
outcomes—(4,3) favoring Abraham, and (3,4) favoring God. Both of
these outcomes are *efficient*, or *Pareto-optimal*, because there is no other
outcome better for *both* players; by comparison, this is not true of either
(1,2) or (2,1).

Game theory predicts (4,3), because it is a Nash equilibrium, in which
God has a dominant strategy of R/R but Abraham does not. Anticipating
God's choice of His dominant strategy, Abraham's best response is not
to offer ($\overline{O}$), so neither player has an incentive to depart from (4,3).

By contrast, from (3,4) Abraham would benefit by switching from
O to $\overline{O}$, which yields (4,3). Although God cannot improve on His next-
best outcome of 3 at (4,3) by switching from R/R to any other strategy,

---

15. Miles (1995, 60) views the test as a combination of "bluff and ruse." He questions to
what extent God had the upper hand if Abraham understood what the test was intended
to do.

the fact that Abraham can do better at (3,4) prevents it from being a Nash equilibrium.

Nonetheless, the *deterrent threat power* of God enables Him to disrupt (4,3) in this game.[16] Underlying threat power is the ability of one player to threaten a *Pareto-inferior* outcome—called a *breakdown* outcome—that is worse for both players than a Pareto-optimal outcome, which cannot be improved upon for both players. Not only can a player with threat power threaten such a breakdown outcome, but this player also can hold out longer at it than can the player without such power.

To illustrate in the Caring Game, God's threat would be to choose R/$\overline{R}$; if Abraham chooses $\overline{O}$, both players would suffer at (2,1), compared to (3,4) if Abraham chooses O.[17] Hence, if God has threat power, this threat will deter Abraham from choosing $\overline{O}$, because God can better endure staying at the (Pareto-inferior) breakdown outcome of (2,1) than Abraham can.

Although God regularly clamped down on recalcitrants in order to deter future challenges, He sometimes backed off, as He did with Abraham. I believe there are two reasons why He would have done so in Abraham's case had Abraham refused to offer Isaac:

---

16. *Threat power* is formally defined in Brams and Hessel 1984 and Brams 1994b, chap. 5, where it is applied to a variety of situations. In section 7.2, I offer a more systematic development, with illustrations, of this concept. In the Caring Game, Abraham has a "compellent" threat and God has a "deterrent" threat. But God's deterrent threat is not credible, because Abraham chooses first. This game, incidentally, is called a "king-of-the-mountain game" in Brams and Jones 1999; such games are analyzed in section 10.6. Threat power, moving power, and order power are all concepts defined and analyzed in the theory of moves (TOM) in Brams 1994b, which will be further developed in later chapters. In this chapter, I concentrate on defining *nonmyopic equilibrium* in section 2.5—the main stability concept of TOM—and illustrating its application to the story of Samson and Delilah. TOM, incidentally, is not without its critics; see, for example, the exchange between Stone (2001) and Brams (2001), which includes additional citations to the TOM literature. Other critics include Woerdman (2000) and Hoffman (2001); the work of some scholars who have modified, extended, or applied TOM will be mentioned later.

17. They would also suffer if, not implausibly, the 3 and 2 payoffs for God were interchanged in the 2 × 2 game, so (4,3) would be (4,2) and (1,2) would be (1,3). In the resulting 2 × 4 game, God has the same dominant strategy and threat opportunity as in the Caring Game; the difference is that for God, saving Isaac's life if Abraham offers him for sacrifice (3) is ranked above sacrificing Isaac if he is offered (2). While God is less forgiving in this variation of the Caring Game, it would still be in His interest to renege if Abraham offers Isaac, because (4,2) is better for God than (2,1).

1. As already noted, Isaac's sacrifice would have brought an end to the chosen people, whom God had promised would multiply and prosper. This would have been a huge disappointment to God, throwing away everything He had done since the Creation.

2. It would have been foolish of God to allow the sacrifice of Isaac simply because Abraham failed a test that may have better reflected Abraham's strategic acumen than his true faith.

To be sure, God, aware of Abraham's calculating nature, presumably knew that His test of Abraham's faith was flawed. Nevertheless, God still probably derived satisfaction from Abraham's passing the test, even if it was bogus. After all, it proved that Abraham was astute enough to anticipate God's preferences; going through the motions of sacrificing Isaac was better for God than defiance. And it would also impress on others that Abraham was no wimp and could, if necessary, do the unthinkable.

But now I postulate a *caring* Abraham who, contrary to what happened, would prefer not to offer Isaac if God is likely to renege. For if Isaac is saved, having a son traumatized by the belief that his father was ready to sacrifice him would hardly lead to a warm and loving relationship between father and son. And if Isaac were killed, Abraham would probably be wracked by the guilt that he might have saved his son by acting differently.

In my opinion, Abraham probably could have gotten away with refusing to sacrifice Isaac. For one thing, God's threat was never explicit, so there would not have been an enormous need for face-saving on God's part. For another, God did prove willing to listen to Abraham's appeals on behalf of Sodom and Gomorrah and offer them reprieves, even though, in the end, these cities did not have enough righteous inhabitants to be worth saving.

I believe God would have been more open to an appeal on behalf of an innocent child than the wicked inhabitants of Sodom and Gomorrah, even if Abraham's refusal to offer Isaac was not what God most wanted. From a moral standpoint, Abraham's refusal would have shown him to have had the courage to stand up for something of paramount importance to himself, just as Moses, while infuriated by the behavior of the Israelites for building the golden calf (Brams 1980/2003, chap. 5, and section 5.5 of this book), still stood up for their survival. But I conclude reluctantly that Abraham was no Moses, about whom it was said, "Never again did there arise a prophet like Moses" (Deut. 34:10).

The Caring Game, and the preferences on which it is built, suggest that Abraham's refusal would *not* have been catastrophic either for him or for God. Contrary to what happened in one of the most wrenching situations to face a character in the Hebrew Bible, I believe the counterfactual can be entertained. If Abraham were indeed the caring father— which is a big if—he (rationally) could have ignored God's implicit threat, or at least pleaded for Isaac's life, which doubtless would have solidified his reputation as not only a patriarch of the Jews but also a morally upright one.

2.4   Samson and Delilah

Before recounting the story of Samson and Delilah from the book of Judges, it is useful to offer some background.[18] After abetting the flight of the Israelites from Egypt and delivering them into the promised land of Canaan, God became extremely upset by their cantankerous ways and punished them severely:

The Israelites again did what was offensive to the LORD, and the LORD delivered them into the hands of the Philistines for forty years. (Judg. 13:1)

But a new dawn appeared at the birth of Samson, which was attended to by God and Whose angel predicted: "He shall be the first to deliver Israel from the Philistines" (Judg. 13:5).

After Samson grew up, he quickly manifested carnal desires that were quite ecumenical:

Once Samson went down to Timnah; and while in Timnah, he noticed a girl among the Philistine women. On his return, he told his father and mother, "I noticed one of the Philistine women in Timnah; please get her for me as a wife." His father and mother said to him, "Is there no one among the daughters of your own kinsmen and among all our people that you must go and take a wife from the uncircumcised Philistines?" (Judg. 14:1–3)

---

18. All translations in this section are from *The Prophets—Nevi'im* (1978).

Samson, however, was not to be deterred by such remonstrations, though the Bible explains that God was surreptitiously manipulating events:

His father and mother did not realize that this was the LORD's doing: He was seeking a pretext against the Philistines, for the Philistines were ruling over Israel at that time. (Judg. 14:3–4)

The woman whom Samson sought indeed pleased Samson, and he took her as his wife. At a feast, Samson posed a riddle that stumped everybody, and the celebrants appealed to Samson's wife for help:

Coax your husband to provide us with the answer to the riddle; else we shall put you and your father's household to the fire; have you invited us here in order to impoverish us? (Judg. 14:15)

Samson's wife was distraught and accused her husband of not loving her, even hating her. At first Samson refused to tell his wife the answer to the riddle, but because she "continued to harass him with her tears, . . . on the seventh day he told her, because she nagged him so" (Judg. 14:17).

Angered by the whole business, Samson "left in a rage for his father's house" (Judg. 14:19). Samson's wife, extremely upset, then "married one of those who had been his [Samson's] wedding companions" (Judg. 14:20).

Samson then had second thoughts about abandoning his wife. When told by his wife's father that it was too late to reconsider, Samson flew into a rage and declared: "Now the Philistines can have no claim against me for the harm I shall do them" (Judg. 15:3).

After devastating their fields and vineyards, Samson fought a couple of vicious battles with them. Included among the victims in these cruel encounters were Samson's ex-wife and father-in-law, who were burned to death by the Philistines.

Samson came out of these battles with a reputation as a ferocious warrior of inhuman strength. This served him well as judge (leader) of Israel for twenty years. Samson also cemented his reputation as a man of the flesh by his encounters with prostitutes and other dalliances that he had.

This background on Samson's early life helps to make perspicuous his reckless, or at least intemperate, behavior in his last and fatal tryst with a woman named Delilah.[19] She was another Philistine with whom Samson fell in love.

Samson's love for Delilah was not requited. Rather, Delilah was more receptive to serving as bait for Samson for appropriate recompense. The lords of the Philistines made her a proposition:

Coax him and find out what makes him so strong, and how we can overpower him, tie him up, and make him helpless; and we'll each give you eleven hundred shekels of silver. (Judg. 16:5)

After assenting, Delilah asked Samson: "Tell me, what makes you so strong? And how could you be tied up and be made helpless?" (Judg. 16:6). Samson replied: "If I were to be tied with seven fresh tendons, that had not been dried, I should become as weak as an ordinary man" (Judg. 16:7).

After Delilah bound Samson as he had instructed her, she hid men in the inner room and cried, "Samson, the Philistines are upon you!" (Judg. 16:9). Samson's lie quickly became apparent:

Whereat he pulled the tendons apart, as a strand of tow [flax] comes apart at the touch of fire. So the secret of his strength remained unknown. Then Delilah said to Samson, "Oh, you deceived me; you lied to me! Do tell me how you could be tied up." (Judg. 16:9–10)

Twice more Samson gave Delilah erroneous information about the source of his strength, and she became progressively more frustrated by his deception. In exasperation, Delilah exclaimed:

"How can you say you love me, when you don't confide in me? This makes three times that you've deceived me and haven't told me what makes you so strong." Finally, after she had nagged him and pressed him constantly, he was wearied to death and he confided everything to her. (Judg. 16:15–17)

The secret was Samson's long hair. When he told his secret to Delilah, she had his hair shaved off while he slept. The jig was then up when he was awakened:

---

19. A theory of how past experiences may influence a person's future decisions is offered in Gilboa and Schmeidler 2001.

For he did not know that the LORD had departed him. The Philistines seized him and gouged out his eyes. They brought him down to Gaza and shackled him in bronze fetters, and he became a mill slave in the prison. After his hair was cut off, it began to grow back. (Judg. 16:20–22)

Thus, a slow time bomb is set ticking. Ineluctably, the climax approaches when Samson is summoned and made an object of derision and sport by the Philistines in a great celebration:

They put him between the pillars. And Samson said to the boy who was leading him by the hand, "Let go of me and let me feel the pillars that the temple rests upon, that I may lean on them." Now the temple was full of men and women; all the lords of the Philistines were there, and there were some three thousand men and women on the roof watching Samson dance. Then Samson called to the LORD, "O Lord GOD! Please remember me, and give me strength just this once, O God, to take revenge of the Philistines if only for one of my two eyes." (Judg. 16:25–28)

Samson, his emasculated strength now restored, avenged his captors in an unprecedented biblical reprisal that sealed both his doom and the Philistines':

He embraced the two middle pillars that the temple rested upon, one with his right arm and one with his left, and leaned against them; Samson cried, "Let me die with the Philistines!" and he pulled with all his might. The temple came crashing down on the lords and on all the people in it. Those who were slain by him as he died outnumbered those who had been slain by him when he lived. (Judg. 1:29–30)

There is irony, of course, in this reversal of roles, whereby the victim becomes the vanquisher. I do not suggest, however, that Samson, intrepid warrior that he was, planned for his own mutilation and ridicule only to provide himself with the later opportunity to retaliate massively against the Philistines. Perhaps this was in God's design, as foretold by the angel at Samson's birth. The more explicit reference to God's "seeking a pretext against the Philistines" (Judg. 14:4), when Samson married, reinforces this view.

To me, however, these auguries smack of insertions probably made for didactic purposes. They are not central to the narrative, which proceeds well enough without these lessons being drawn.

The didactic references present another problem: God's apparent meddling contradicts the free will humans are presumed to have. It is a tenet of game theory that players make their own independent choices, based on the information they possess about the particular game being played.

Also puzzling is why, if God is playing some kind of undercover game, He should want so much to help the Israelites after the Bible reports that He delivered them into the hands of the Philistines. In short, the signals given by references to God's purpose and control over events are confusing.

By comparison, I think Samson's behavior as both a truculent warrior and an insatiable lover is consistent and credible. On occasion, perhaps, Samson's strength strains credibility, as when he reportedly slays a thousand men with the jawbone of an ass. Other incidents in his life, such as tearing a lion to pieces, also are stupendous feats, but they are really no more than the normal hyperbole one finds in the Bible. Unquestionably, miraculous achievements, whether God-inspired or not, add drama to the stories, but a game-theoretic interpretation should not stand or fall on whether they can be explained in everyday terms.

If Samson's immense strength, or its source, seems beyond human capabilities, his passion for women is not so difficult to comprehend. As the story of his adult life makes clear, Samson lusted after several women, and Delilah was not the first to whose blandishments he fell prey. When he earlier caved in to his wife after she badgered him for several days about the riddle, the pattern was set: He would not withhold information if the right woman was around to wheedle it out of him. While Samson could fight the Philistines like a fiend, he could readily be disarmed by women after whom he hankered.

The payoff matrix of the game I posit that Samson played with Delilah is shown in figure 2.5 (game 56). Samson's desire having been kindled, Delilah could trade on it either by nagging Samson for the secret of his strength (N) or not nagging him ($\overline{N}$) but hoping it would come out anyway. Samson, in turn, could either tell (T) the secret of his strength or not tell it ($\overline{T}$).[20]

---

20. Although Samson can move from $\overline{T}$ to T, he cannot reasonably move from T to $\overline{T}$, retracting his secret once it is out. I later call this an "infeasible" move.

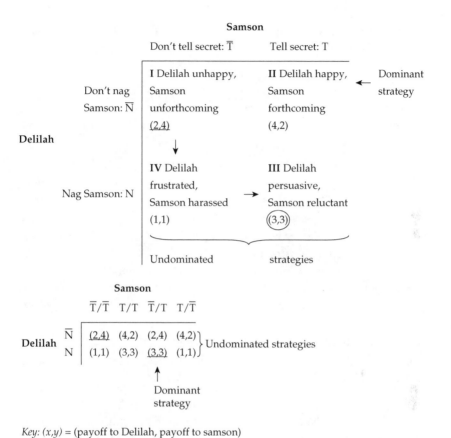

Key: (x,y) = (payoff to Delilah, payoff to samson)

4 = best; 3 = next-best; 2 = next-worst; 1 = worst

Nash equilibria underscored

Nonmyopic equilibrium (NME) from (2,4) in 2 × 2 game circled

Arrows indicate progression of states to NME from initial state (2,4)

Figure 2.5
Outcomes and payoffs of Samson and Delilah Game (game 56)

Consider the consequences of each pair of strategy choices, starting from the upper left-hand state and moving in a clockwise direction:

I. $\overline{\text{N}}\overline{\text{T}}$: Delilah unhappy, Samson unforthcoming—(2,4) The next-worst outcome for Delilah, because Samson withholds his secret, though she is not frustrated in an unsuccessful attempt to obtain it; the best outcome for Samson, because he keeps his secret and is not harassed.

II. $\overline{\text{N}}$T: Delilah happy, Samson forthcoming—(4,2) The best outcome for Delilah, because she learns Samson's secret without making a pest of herself; the next-worst outcome for Samson, because he gives away his secret without good reason.

III. NT: Delilah persuasive, Samson reluctant—(3,3) The next-best outcome for both players, because though Delilah would prefer not to nag (if Samson tells), and Samson would prefer not to succumb (if Delilah does not nag), Delilah gets her way when Samson tells; and Samson, under duress, has a respectable reason to tell his secret (i.e., Delilah's nagging).

IV. N$\overline{\text{T}}$: Delilah frustrated, Samson harassed—(1,1) The worst outcome for both players, because Samson does not get peace of mind, and Delilah is frustrated in her effort to learn Samson's secret.

Later I will consider a plausible reordering of Delilah's preferences.

The game starts at (2,4), when Delilah chooses $\overline{\text{N}}$ and Samson chooses $\overline{\text{T}}$ during their period of acquaintance. Delilah's strategy is dominant, and Samson's strategy is a best response to her strategy, giving the Nash equilibrium of (2,4) in the 2×2 game that is shown in figure 2.5.

When this game is expanded to a 2×4 game—wherein Delilah moves first—then Samson's choice of tit-for-tat ($\overline{\text{T}}$/T) is dominant. Moreover, Delilah no longer has a dominant strategy: Her best strategy depends on Samson's; anticipating that he will choose his dominant strategy, it is rational for Delilah to select N, leading to (3,3), the outcome of the game.

This outcome is a Nash equilibrium, but not the only one; one of the (2,4) outcomes in the 2×4 game, which is underscored, is also a Nash equilibrium. Which one will be chosen, and when?

Standard game theory does not illuminate the *dynamics* of the players' switching their strategies—first Delilah, by moving from $\overline{N}$ to N in the 2×2 game, putting the players at outcome (1,1); and then Samson, by responding with T, leading to (3,3). To shed light on the rationality of these moves and countermoves, I next describe and illustrate the application of the theory of moves to 2×2 games like that between Samson and Delilah (Brams 1994b).

2.5 Theory of Moves (TOM)

The starting point of TOM is a payoff matrix, or *game configuration*, in which the order of play is not specified. In fact, the players are assumed not even to choose strategies but instead to move and countermove from outcomes, or *states*, by looking ahead and using "backward induction" to determine the rationality of both their moves and those of another player (or players).

Because standard game theory assumes that players choose strategies simultaneously in games in normal or strategic form,[21] it does not raise questions about the rationality of moving or departing from outcomes—at least beyond an immediate departure, à la Nash. In fact, however, most real-life games do not start with simultaneous strategy choices but instead commence at outcomes, which represent the status quo. The question then becomes whether a player, by departing from an outcome, can do better not just in an immediate or myopic sense but, rather, in an extended or nonmyopic sense.

In the case of 2×2 games, TOM postulates four *rules of play*, which describe the possible choices of the players at different stages:

21. Strategies may allow for sequential choices, but game theory models, in general, do not make endogenous who moves first, as TOM does, but instead specify a fixed order of play (i.e., players make either simultaneous or sequential choices). There are some exceptions, however, including Hamilton and Slutsky 1993; Rosenthal 1991; Amir 1995; and van Damme and Hurkens 1996. Typically, these models allow a player in the preplay phase of a game to choose when he or she will move in the play of the game. Yet the choice of when to move applies only to a player's initial strategy choice, whereas the nonmyopic calculations to be described here assume that players, starting at states, make moves and countermoves that depend on thinking several steps ahead. I do not attempt a full technical exposition here, which can be found, with examples, in Brams 1994b.

1. Play starts at an outcome, called the *initial state,* which is at the intersection of the row and column of a 2×2 payoff matrix.

2. Either player can unilaterally switch his or her strategy, and thereby change the initial state into a new state, in the same row or column as the initial state.[22] The player who switches, who may be either row (R) or column (C), is called player 1 (P1).

3. Player 2 (P2) can respond by unilaterally switching his or her strategy, thereby moving the game to a new state.

4. The alternating responses continue until the player (Pl or P2) whose turn it is to move next chooses not to switch his or her strategy. When this happens, the game terminates in a *final state,* which is the *outcome* of the game.

Note that the sequence of moves and countermoves is strictly alternating: First, say, R moves, then C moves, and so on, until one player stops, at which point the state reached is final and, therefore, the outcome of the game.[23]

The use of the word *state* is meant to convey the temporary nature of an outcome, before players decide to stop switching strategies. I assume that no payoffs accrue to players from being in a state unless it is the final state and, therefore, becomes the outcome (which could be the initial state if the players choose not to move from it).

Rule l differs radically from the corresponding rule of play in standard game theory, in which players simultaneously choose strategies in a matrix game, which determines its outcome. Instead of starting with strategy choices, I assume that players are already in some state at the

22. I do not use *strategy* in the usual sense to mean a complete plan of responses by the players to all possible contingencies allowed by rules 2–4, because this would make the normal form, represented by a payoff matrix, unduly complicated to analyze. Rather, *strategies* refer to the choices made by players that define an initial state, and *moves and countermoves* refer to the players' subsequent strategy switches from an initial state to a final state in an extensive-form game represented by a game tree, as allowed by rules 2–4. For another approach to combining the normal and extensive forms, see Mailath, Samuelson, and Swinkels 1993, 1994.

23. An emendation in the rules of TOM that allows for backtracking would be appropriate in games of incomplete information, wherein players may make mistakes that they later wish to rectify. Implications of allowing backtracking on "nonmyopic equilibria," which are discussed in section 2.5, are analyzed in Willson 1998.

start of play and receive payoffs from this state if they stay. Based on these payoffs, they decide, individually, whether or not to change this state in order to try to do better.[24]

To be sure, some decisions are made collectively by players, in which case it would be reasonable to say that they choose strategies from scratch, either simultaneously or by coordinating their choices. But if, say, two countries are coordinating their choices, as when they agree to sign a treaty, the most important strategic question is what individualistic calculations led them to this point. The formality of jointly signing the treaty is the culmination of their negotiations, which does not reveal the move-countermove process that preceded it. This is precisely what TOM is designed to uncover.

In summary, play of a game starts in a state, at which players accrue payoffs only if they remain in that state so that it becomes the outcome of the game. If they do not remain, they still know what payoffs they would have accrued had they stayed; hence, they can make a rational calculation of the advantages of staying versus moving. They move precisely because they calculate that they can do better by switching states, anticipating a better outcome when the move-countermove process finally comes to rest.

Rules 1–4 say nothing about what causes a game to end, but only when: Termination occurs when a "player whose turn it is to move next chooses not to switch its strategy" (rule 4). But when is it rational not to continue moving, or not to move in the first place from the initial state?

To answer this question, I posit a rule of *rational termination* (first proposed in Brams 1983, 106–107), which has been called "inertia" by Kilgour and Zagare (1987, 94). It prohibits a player from moving from an initial state unless doing so leads to a better (not just the same) final state:

24. Alternatively, players may be thought of as choosing strategies initially, after which they perform a thought experiment of where moves will carry them once a state is selected. The concept of an "anticipation game," developed in section 5.4, advances this idea, which might be considered dynamic thinking about the static play of a matrix game. Generally, however, I assume that *moves* describe actions, not just thoughts, though I readily admit the possibility of a thought interpretation.

5. A player will not move from an initial state if this move

(i) leads to a less preferred final state (i.e., outcome); or

(ii) returns play to the initial state (i.e., makes the initial state the outcome).

I discuss shortly how rational players, starting from some initial state, determine by backward induction what the outcome will be.

Condition (i) of rule 5, which precludes moves that result in an inferior state, needs no defense. But condition (ii), which precludes moves to the same state because of cycling back to the initial state, is worth some elaboration. It says that if it is rational for play of the game to cycle back to the initial state after P1 moves, P1 will not move in the first place. After all, what is the point of initiating the move-countermove process if play simply returns to "square one," given that the players receive no payoffs along the way (i.e., before an outcome is reached)?

Not only is there no gain from cycling but also, in fact, there may be a loss because of so-called transaction costs—including the psychic energy spent—that players suffer by virtue of making moves that, ultimately, do not change the situation.[25] Therefore, it seems sensible to assume that P1 will not trigger a move-countermove process if it only returns the players to the initial state, making it the outcome.

I call rule 5 a *rationality rule,* because it provides the basis for players to determine whether they can do better by moving from a state or remaining in it. Still another rationality rule is needed to ensure that both players take into account each other's calculations before deciding to move from the initial state. I call this rule the *two-sidedness rule*:

6. Given that players have complete information about each other's preferences and act according to the rules of TOM, each takes into account the consequences of the other player's rational choices, as well as his or her own, in deciding whether to move from the initial state or subsequently, based on backward induction. If it is rational for one player to move and the other player not to move from the initial state, then the player who moves takes *precedence*: His or her move overrides

25. However, other rules of play allow for cycling, as I will illustrate in section 3.4 and develop more systematically in section 10.2.

the player who stays, so the outcome is that induced by the player who moves.

Because players have complete information, they can look ahead and anticipate the consequences of their moves. I next show how, using backward induction, Samson and Delilah can do this.

I suppose that Delilah, because she is unhappy in initial state (2,4), calculates the rational consequences of moving from it—what counter-move, on the part of Samson, her move from this state would trigger, what counter-countermove she would make, and so on. I assume that the players base their calculations on *backward induction* (to be illustrated). Starting from (2,4) and cycling back to this state, I then show where R (Delilah) and C (Samson) will terminate play.

If R moves first, the counterclockwise progression from (2,4) back to (2,4)—with the player (R or C) who makes the next move shown below each state in the alternating sequence—is as follows (see figure 2.5):[26]

	State 1	State 2	State 3	State 4	State 1
	R	C	R	C	
R starts:	(2,4) →	(1,1) →	(3,3) →|	(4,2) →	(2,4)
Survivor:	(3,3)	(3,3)	(3,3)	(2,4)	

The *survivor* is determined by working backward, after a putative cycle has been completed. Assume that the players' alternating moves have taken them counterclockwise from (2,4) to (1,1) to (3,3) to (4,2), at which point C must decide whether to stop at (4,2) or complete the cycle and return to (2,4). Clearly, C prefers (2,4) to (4,2), so (2,4) is listed as the survivor below (4,2): Because C *would* move the process back to (2,4) should it reach (4,2), the players know that if the move-countermove process reaches this state, the outcome will be (2,4).

Knowing this, would R at the prior state, (3,3), move to (4,2)? Because R prefers (3,3) to the survivor at (4,2)—namely, (2,4)—the answer is no.

---

26. Effectively, this is a game tree showing a sequence of alternating choices of the players, except that instead of going from top to bottom, as in figure 2.2, the choices of the players go sideways, from left to right. More conventional game trees that illustrate TOM calculations are given in Taylor and Pacelli 2008. Because I did not include payoffs in figure 2.2, the survivor states described next could not be determined in the figure 2.2 game.

Hence, (3,3) becomes the survivor when R must choose between stopping at (3,3) and moving to (4,2)—which, as I have just shown, would become (2,4) once (4,2) is reached.

At the prior state, (1,1), C would prefer moving to (3,3) than stopping at (1,1), so (3,3) again is the survivor if the process reaches (1,1). Similarly, at the initial state, (2,4), because R prefers the previous survivor, (3,3), to (2,4), (3,3) is the survivor at this state as well. I underscore (3,3) at the point that it becomes the survivor state.

The fact that (3,3) is the survivor at initial state (2,4) means that it is rational for R initially to move to (1,1), and C subsequently to move to (3,3), where the process will stop, making (3,3) the rational choice if R has the opportunity to move first from initial state (2,4). That is, after working *backward* from C's choice of completing the cycle or not at (4,2), the players can reverse the process and, looking *forward,* determine that it is rational for R to move from (2,4) to (1,1), and C to move from (1,1) to (3,3), at which point R will stop the move-countermove process at (3,3).

Notice that R does better at (3,3) than at (2,4), where it could have terminated play at the outset, and C does better at (3,3) than at (1,1), where it could have terminated play, given that R is the first to move. I indicate that (3,3) is the consequence of backward induction by underscoring this state in the progression; it is the state at which *stoppage* of the process occurs. In addition, I indicate that it is not rational for R to move on from (3,3) by the vertical line blocking the arrow emanating from (3,3), which I refer to as *blockage:* A player will always stop at a blocked state, wherever it is in the progression. Stoppage occurs when blockage occurs for the *first* time from some initial state, as I illustrate next.

If C moves first from (2,4), backward induction shows that (2,4) is the last survivor, so (2,4) is underscored when C starts. Consequently, C would *not* move from the initial state, where there is blockage (and stoppage), which is hardly surprising since C receives its best payoff in this state:[27]

---

27. But it is rational in several 2×2 games for a player to depart from its best state (4), because in these games a player may do worse if its opponent departs first (Brams 1994b, chap. 3). An example is given in section 8.2.

	State 1		State 2		State 3		State 4		State 1
	C		R		C		R		
C starts:	<u>(2,4)</u>	→|	(4,2)	→|	(3,3)	→	(1,1)	→	(2,4)
Survivor:	(2,4)		(4,2)		(2,4)		(2,4)		

As when R has the first move, (2,4) is the first survivor, working backward from the end of the progression, and it is also preferred by C at (3,3). But then, because R at (4,2) prefers this state to (2,4), (2,4) is temporarily displaced by (4,2) as the survivor. However, (2,4) returns as the last survivor, because C at (2,4) prefers it to (4,2), so I underscore (2,4).

Although the first blockage and, therefore, stoppage occurs at (2,4), blockage would occur subsequently at (4,2) if, for any reason, stoppage does not terminate moves at the start. In other words, if C moved initially, R would then be blocked. Hence, blockage occurs at two states when C starts the move-countermove process, whereas it occurs only once when R has the first move.

The fact that the rational choice depends on which player has the first move—(3,3) is rational if R starts, (2,4) if C starts—leads to a conflict over what outcome will be selected when the process starts at (2,4). However, because it is not rational for C to move from the initial state, R's move takes precedence, according to rule 6, and overrides C's decision to stay. Consequently, when the initial state is (2,4), the result will be (3,3), with movement first through the mutually worst state of (1,1) to get to this outcome.

The outcome into which a state goes is called the *nonmyopic equilibrium* (NME) (Brams and Wittman 1981). NMEs may be viewed as the consequence of the players' looking ahead and making rational calculations of where the move-countermove process will transport them, based on the rules of TOM, from each of the four possible initial states.

To summarize, TOM leads to a unique prediction of (3,3) if play starts in state (2,4), which is the actual outcome of the story (other initial states lead to other outcomes in this game). Doubtless, Samson did not anticipate having his eyes gouged out, and being derided as a fool before the Philistines, when he responded to Delilah's chronic nagging by revealing his secret. On the other hand, because he was later able to wreak destruction on thousands of Philistines while simultaneously ending his own humiliation, it does not seem unfair to characterize the dénouement of this story as next best for Samson. Perhaps Samson foresaw that revealing his secret to Delilah could create problems, but he almost surely never anticipated that this choice would result in vilification, mutilation, and ultimately death. If so, he might well have put up with Delilah's nagging.

Although he surrendered his secret to the treacherous Delilah, Samson apparently never won her love, which seems to be the thing he most wanted. In fact, Delilah's decisive argument in wheedling the truth from Samson was that because he did not confide in her, he did not love her. What better way was there for Samson to scotch this contention, and prove his love, than to comply with her request, even if it meant courting not just Delilah but disaster itself?

As for Delilah's preferences, I think it hard to quarrel with the assumption that her two best states were associated with Samson's choice of T. I am less sure, however, about her preferences for her two worst states. It seems to me, contrary to the representation in figure 2.5, that Delilah might have preferred to nag Samson than not had he in the end repudiated her. For even though she would have failed to elicit Samson's secret, Delilah would perhaps have felt less badly, after having tried, than if she had made no effort at all.

If this is the case, then 2 and 1 for Delilah would be interchanged in the payoff matrix of figure 2.5, and the game configuration would be different. But like the figure 2.5 game, the NME when play starts at (1,4) leads again to (3,3), so this reordering of Delilah's preferences would not affect the rational outcome, according to TOM: Thinking nonmyopically, Delilah would still switch to N, and Samson in turn would switch to T.

So far I have implicitly assumed that players, by switching strategies, can make moves that effect different states in a game; in the end, these moves terminate at some NME. After Samson fell in love with Delilah, for example, she switched from being a seductress to being a nag, and Samson in turn switched—admittedly, reluctantly—from being mum about the secret of his strength to letting it out.

Delilah got her silver, but Samson suffered greatly for succumbing to his desire for Delilah. Nevertheless, Samson seemed to believe, when he made his decision to reveal his secret, that it would lead to a preferred state. For one thing, he detested being nagged by Delilah, as by his wife earlier. For another, he had great difficulty resisting women who exploited the love (lust?) he had for them. While Samson's response to Delilah, fueled as it was by sexual attraction, might seem overwhelmingly emotional, preferences rooted in emotions may be perfectly rational from a game-theoretic point of view.

2.6 Emotions, Feasible Moves, and Morality

Emotions, as much as more "objective" factors, define a player's preferences.[28] Whatever the basis of a player's preferences, however, they are neither rational nor irrational. Only the *choices* (of strategies and moves) that a player makes, founded on these preferences, can be evaluated in terms of their rationality, based on the rules of play and the rationality rules.

It would seem in the case of Samson that sexual attraction made it harder for him to evaluate his position "objectively." Not only did the sexual bond prove hard to break, but Samson suffered greatly for succumbing to his carnal desire, especially because his love was unrequited.[29]

While the sexual bond may complicate certain relationships, it need not make players irrational. They still seek to act in their self-interest, but they are working within constraints that sex adds to the mélange of emotions, which I explore further in chapters 7 and 10.

---

28. Howard et al. (1993) and Howard (1994, 1996) develop a "theory of drama," rooted in part in game theory, which makes emotions the means by which players escape the so-called paradoxes of rationality (Howard 1971). This ingenious twist turns game theory on its head, as it were: Rational players find it expedient to react emotionally—even "irrationally"—to the paradoxes with threats, promises, and the like; in the end, they alter their preferences to achieve a dramatic resolution of their conflict and a new self-realization of their situation. See also Frank 1988 and Hirshleifer 1987, 2000 on the strategic role that emotions play in conflict.

29. Another example of unrequited love from the Bible is that between Vashti and her husband, King Ahasuerus. After being spurned by Vashti, Ahasuerus searches for a new wife; she turns out to be a Jew, Esther, who succeeds in saving the other Jews in the Persian kingdom from the wicked Haman (Brams 1980/2003, chap. 8). Significantly, it is the women in both this story and that of Samson and Delilah who initiate the conflict and succeed, at least initially, in getting their way.

If rational choices need not be objective, they may be *infeasible* because, practically speaking, a player cannot make them due to "environmental constraints" (Brams 1994b, 40–42; Zagare 1984, 4). For example, suppose that the 2×2 game between Samson and Delilah in figure 2.5 does not start at (2,4) but instead commences at (3,3). Then TOM predicts that the game will move from (3,3) to (1,1), and thence to (2,4), where moves will cease.

But Samson's initial move from T to $\overline{\text{T}}$ makes no sense: Once his secret is out, he can hardly retract it, especially in light of the fact that Delilah tested every explanation, true or false, that he gave for his colossal strength. So this move must be ruled out, but not because it is irrational— it induces Delilah subsequently to move from (1,1) to (2,4), which certainly is feasible (she can stop nagging) and best for Samson. Rather, it is incoherent: It contradicts what a reasonable interpretation of strategies in this game would permit.

Whereas it is permissible for Samson to move from $\overline{\text{T}}$ to T, a reverse switch is hard to entertain in the context of the story, though not necessarily in other interpretations of the figure 2.5 game. I conclude that in using TOM to model a strategic situation, the analyst must be sensitive to what strategy changes are infeasible so as not to violate the interpretation of the game being modeled. In the case of Samson and Delilah, TOM gives insight into the *dynamics* of player moves that are not so apparent in the 2×4 game.

To return to the sacrifice of Isaac, it would seem that Abraham must have been deeply troubled by God's command to sacrifice his only son. However, the Bible reports nothing in Abraham's demeanor or actions to indicate this, perhaps because Abraham anticipated that God would relent—as, in fact, He did—by preventing the sacrifice.

To test the notion that Abraham had a viable alternative choice, I explored the consequences of Abraham's refusing God's command in the Caring Game, presuming that Abraham's actual choice was not devoid of anguish. If so, might Abraham have made a different rational choice? Because, as I argued, Abraham would not have been severely punished for his defiance and would, additionally, have benefited from refusing to carry out a morally repugnant act, the counterfactual analysis suggests that an emotionally fraught Abraham would have acted differently and would probably have "gotten away" with it.

Ethics and strategy intersect in a story like Abraham's: They suggest that a morally righteous choice may be rationally justified. In a sense, Abraham had it both ways by *not* revealing his emotional turmoil— if, indeed, he experienced it—while obtaining the outcome he wanted (the salvation of Isaac and the approval of God). The one thing he failed to earn was the approbation of moral philosophers for seeming to countenance human sacrifice, but this did not seem to disturb him at the time.

3 Theology: Is It Rational to Believe in God?

3.1 Introduction

Theology studies the relationship between human beings and God.[1] Game theory seems well suited for analyzing this relationship, though some may question the seemingly impious view that God plays games with us.[2] But the game-like view is inherent in those Western religions that presume God can be conceived of in personal terms and, more specifically, is in a one-to-one relationship with each of us.

The idea of a personal God, especially one who is a game player, is alien to most eastern religions. I confess that the present analysis has a Western religious bias, perhaps epitomized by the view of Martin Buber (1958, 135):

The description of God as a Person is indispensable for everyone who like myself means by "God" not a principle . . . not an idea . . . but who rather means by "God," as I do, him who—whatever else he may be—enters into a direct relation with us.

Despite this focus on a personal God, however, I begin by considering the possibility that God may more accurately be conceived of as a "state of nature"—not a player in a game as such—with nature being neutral or indifferent. This contrasts with the view that I offered in sections 2.2

---

1. This chapter is adapted from Brams 1983/2007, chap. 2, with permission.

2. This will be true for those who see God as a lofty and majestic figure, someone of overpowering grandeur and infinite wisdom and strength. But this image is challenged by the picture drawn in the Hebrew Bible, in which God is variously angry, jealous, petulant, or arbitrary (Brams 1980/2003).

and 2.3, in which God, as a player, presents Abraham with choices and has His own preferences as well.

In this chapter I do not, at the outset, presuppose even the existence of God. Instead, I ask in section 3.2 a theological question concerning the relationship between a person (P) and a Superior Being (SB): Is it rational for P to believe in SB's existence? While SB may be thought of as God, I assume SB may be some other religious figure (e.g., Jesus Christ), or a secular force with supernatural powers.

The rationality of believing in God in the Judeo-Christian tradition is a venerable question that has been the subject of an enormous body of literature, both classical and modern. The most famous rational argument for believing in God is that of Blaise Pascal, whose wager to justify such belief I analyze in section 3.2 and then reframe as the Search Decision, which incorporates the possibility that a search by P may be indeterminate.

Pascal's approach is decision-theoretic—he does not assume we play games with God, in which God actively chooses strategies. Instead, he supposes that each person makes a calculation about whether or not believing in God in an uncertain world is justified (Landsberg 1971; Rescher 1985; Chimenti 1990; Jordan 2006).

This kind of choice is a decision in a *one-person game*, or a game against nature, wherein "nature" is God or some other SB. Unlike a player in a two-person game, God, if He or She exists, is assumed to be neither benevolent nor malevolent, though I do suggest in section 3.2 that the Search Decision becomes more like a game if God or SB can influence the choice of a state of nature.

I do not analyze the so-called proofs of God's existence (or nonexistence) in this chapter. In an excellent synthesis of the literature, beginning with Descartes, on the existence of God, Hans Küng (1980) argues that all such proofs are flawed, and I share his view. In place of proof, Küng argues for a "rationally justified" faith, which of course does not have the force of a logical proof but, as the subtitle of his book suggests, is "an answer for today." This answer, according to Küng, is rooted in developing a fundamental "trust in reality"; Pascal's wager may be seen as a reason, perhaps cynical, to develop this trust.

In section 3.3, I introduce the Concern Decision, wherein P chooses whether or not to be concerned with SB, which depends on whether or not SB is aware and cares about P. I show that, as in the Search Decision, P does not have a dominant strategy—his or her best choice depends on the state of nature, though SB may influence P's choice if it can signal whether or not it cares (henceforth, I use the impersonal "it" in referring to SB).

The question of whether this answer is satisfactory as a religious response I leave to theologians and philosophers of religion. Instead, I focus here on a related, if more subjective, question: Is it rational to *believe* in SB's (or God's) existence—and, thereby, search for evidence or even be concerned? I stress that the rationality of theistic belief is separate from its truth—a belief need not be true or even verifiable to be rational if, for example, it satisfies certain psychological or emotional needs of a person. Here, however, I tie the rationality of belief to the "evidence" at hand.

For this purpose, I construct in section 3.4 a genuine two-person Revelation Game, in which P and SB make choices that lead to four possible outcomes. In this game, I assume that SB is not indifferent but instead makes strategy choices—whether to reveal itself or not. Revelation provides evidence for P to believe, but it is something that SB would prefer not to provide, because it does not test P's faith (i.e., his or her belief in SB *without* evidence).

Like the Caring Game between Abraham and God that I analyzed in section 2.3, the Revelation Game is founded on primary and secondary goals that I postulate for SB and P. I then analyze the rational choices of the players, and the stability of different outcomes, from different game-theoretic and move-theoretic perspectives. If the reader disagrees with my attributions of preferences, I invite him or her to propose different goals and to redo the analysis, based on his or her revisions. In this manner, the robustness of the conclusions I derive from my assumptions about player goals and their ordering can be tested.

I stress that it is the theoretical approach, and the game-theoretic methodology for implementing it, that is key. If other plausible goals lead to different conclusions about rational play and stable outcomes, they are fair game (no pun intended).

It is worth noting that the question of God's existence is almost never raised in the Bible. When it is, as in Moses's confrontation with Pharaoh in the Book of Exodus (Brams 1980/2003, chap. 5), it is the tangible evidence of God's miraculous powers that settles the issue for Pharaoh, at least temporarily.

For many today, however, the evidence is not so compelling. In this chapter, I attempt to show why, concluding in section 3.5 by comparing the ability of decision theory and the ability of game theory to answer this question.

3.2   Pascal's Wager and the Search Decision

In his *Pensées*, published posthumously in the late seventeenth century, Pascal (1670/1950) assumes a person is in a betting situation and must stake his destiny on some view of the world. Starting from the agnostic assumption stated in no. 223 of *Pensées* that "if there is a God . . . we are incapable of knowing what He is, or whether He is," and "reason can settle nothing here . . . a game [!] is on," Pascal proceeds to invoke reason to say that a prudent person, in his cosmic ignorance, should bet his life on God's existence (for Pascal, this meant in the Roman Catholic faith). If one believes, then the two possible states of nature that may occur have the following consequences:

1. God exists: One enjoys an eternity of bliss (infinite reward).

2. God does not exist: One's belief is unjustified ("loss of nought"), or, at worst, one is chagrined for being fooled (finite penalty).

Because outcome 1 promises an infinite reward, whereas outcome 2 leads at worst to a finite penalty, the choice seems clear to Pascal: One should believe in God's existence.

This argument, made in no. 223 of *Pensées*, implies that belief in God is justified by the infinite reward, but it needs elaboration. A person, P, is choosing between belief and nonbelief, as shown by the rows of the outcome and payoff matrix in figure 3.1.

In this situation, it is proper to compare the "expected payoffs" that each of these alternative courses of actions yields and choose the higher one. Pascal is not explicit about this, but the calculation of expected payoff for nonbelief that I next describe is suggested by his discussion of the "fear of hell" in no. 227 of *Pensées*.

Pascal's argument, as already stated, holds even if it is not true, as Pascal assumed, that "the chances of gain [if God exists] and loss [if God

State of nature

	God exists	God doesn't exist
Believe in God	Belief justified: infinite reward	Belief unjustified: finite penalty
Don't believe in God	Nonbelief unjustified: infinite penalty	Nonbelief justified: finite reward

P

Figure 3.1
Outcome and payoff matrix of Pascal's wager

does not exist] are equal." For however small (though positive) the chance of state 1 is, when multiplied by an infinite gain, the resulting *expected payoff* (sum of utilities of outcomes times their probabilities of occurrence) for believing in God's existence is infinite. Because an infinite payoff has no obvious meaning, one might think of this payoff as some stupendous, but finite, reward.

By comparison, if one bet that state 2 (God does not exist) was true, but it turned out to be false, one would suffer an eternity of torment (infinite penalty)—or a huge loss from not believing. (Henceforth, stupendous rewards and huge penalties might be substituted for infinite gains and infinite losses to make this discussion more concrete—and mathematically acceptable since, technically, one would evaluate a player's expected utility as the reward or penalty approaches, in the limit, positive or negative infinity.)

To summarize, believing in God's existence yields an infinite positive expected payoff (infinite reward minus finite penalty is infinitely rewarding, whatever the probabilities), whereas not believing yields an infinite negative expected payoff (infinite penalty minus finite reward is infinitely penalizing). Because this calculation can be made before the outcome is known (if it ever is!), it suggests that P's key to happiness—and perhaps heaven—is being prepared for the possibility that God exists by believing in Him.

Even if one should not attain eternal bliss, at least it can be said that one made an honest effort to achieve nirvana. Furthermore, Pascal avers that the very act of believing in this calculated fashion sets up the conditions for developing genuine faith and becoming a true believer, so there is nothing insincere or dishonest about starting off by making the expected payoff calculation, though one's faith is ultimately sustained "by taking holy water, by hearing mass, etc."—the accoutrements of religion.

One weakness, I believe, in Pascal's wager argument is that he never postulated a third possibility (or still others): SB's existence is indeterminate, because information that would settle this question is unattainable. I next add this as a state of nature, or a situation that might arise in the world.

Now the three states of nature, which I assume P perceives, are the following:

1. SB's existence is verifiable.

2. SB's nonexistence is verifiable.

3. SB's existence or nonexistence is indeterminate (insufficient information).

True, state 3 may in fact hide one of the other two states (e.g., because the search did not go on long enough), but P may simply be incapable of verifying SB's existence or nonexistence. If the latter is the case, state 3 and the other two states are mutually exclusive in P's eyes: Observing or experiencing state 3 precludes observing or experiencing states 1 and 2, just as the latter two states preclude each other and state 3.

It is perhaps strange that Pascal did not postulate state 3 in his wager, because he said that God, being "infinitely incomprehensible," forecloses the possibility that His existence can ever be determined. Pascal's wager, in other words, presumes a bet whose outcome will never be known—at least in one's present life—so one must be wagering about one's rewards or penalties in an afterlife.

To put it somewhat differently, Pascal seems to have thought we will experience only indeterminacy in our present lives. Nevertheless, he postulates the possibility of the other two states, presumably because he thinks we will learn of God's existence or not in the hereafter. I am not so sure this is the case and, therefore, prefer to retain state 3 in the calculations we make while still alive.

The three postulated states of nature in the Search Decision are shown in figure 3.2. Combined with P's two strategies of searching (S) and not

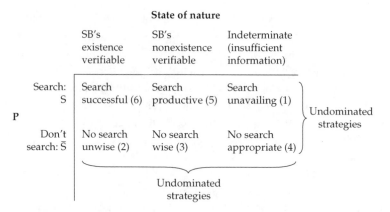

Key: 6 = best; . . . 1 = worst for P

Figure 3.2
Outcome and payoff matrix of Search Decision

searching ($\bar{S}$) for SB, there are six possible outcomes. I interpret S to mean that P tries to learn about SB's existence or nonexistence, whereas $\bar{S}$ means P makes no effort to solve the great mystery, if you will, about SB's existence.

P's ranking of payoffs associated with the six possible outcomes are also shown in figure 3.2, with 6 being the highest and 1 the lowest. I assume that P would most like the search to verify SB's existence (6) and least like it to fail (1). In between, P would prefer to search even if the search only succeeds in verifying SB's nonexistence (5), or not search if SB's existence is indeterminate (4).

Worse than the latter outcomes is when searching would have uncovered valuable information—in particular, information that would verify SB's nonexistence (3) or existence (2). Conceivably, P might rank this last outcome worst—switching 2 and 1 in figure 3.2—because it would be more damaging to ignore available information on SB's existence than search and find nothing. This alternative ranking of P's two worst outcomes, however, does not affect the argument I make in the next paragraph.

Whatever utilities one attaches to the outcomes consistent with the ranks in figure 3.2, P does not have a *dominant*, or unconditionally best, strategy: S is better than $\bar{S}$ if SB's existence or nonexistence is verifiable (states of nature 1 and 2); but $\bar{S}$ is better than S if the situation is indeterminate (state of nature 3). This complicates P's decision, because his or her rational choice depends on what state obtains.

To be sure, if state 1 occurs, P realizes an infinite reward (eternal bliss) from choosing S and an infinite penalty (eternal torment) from choosing $\bar{S}$. Clearly, these infinite values swamp the positive or negative values of other outcomes, making P's choice clear: He or she should choose S and, if state of nature 1 occurs, believe. But if these high and low values are not infinite, the expected payoff for choosing S will not necessarily exceed that for choosing $\bar{S}$, especially if the probability of state 3 is very high. Without having this information about states of nature, however, P will remain in a quandary, able only to ponder the imponderable.

For the sake of argument, assume that the states of nature do *not* occur by chance, each with some nonzero probability, but that SB can choose which one will arise, or can induce P to think that one has occurred.[3] That is, SB can choose a state, like a strategy in a game, that would indicate that its existence is verifiable (state 1), its nonexistence is verifiable (state 2), or its existence cannot be determined (state 3). As an illustration, SB might indicate state 1 by signs of revelation, or state 3 by giving no signs. (How SB would indicate its nonexistence is verifiable in state 2 is not so clear.)

What state will SB choose? Like P, SB has no dominant strategy in this decision-transformed-into-a-game if SB's ordering of the six outcomes is exactly the same as P's. But in such a game of total agreement, a mutually best (6,6) outcome would almost surely induce both players to choose their strategies associated with it.

As I will argue in the Revelation Game in section 3.4, SB has good reason *not* to make its existence apparent, though SB might want to signal that state 1, and maybe state 2, should not be ruled out in order to push P in the direction of searching. This may induce P to be obedient, too, though to what end is not evident.

---

3. In decision theory, this is a violation of what Binmore (2009, 5, 31) calls "Aesop's principle" (based on one of Aesop's fables), whereby the states of nature are assumed independent of a player's choices. In the Hebrew Bible, God frequently violates this principle, inducing states that He thinks will influence a character's choices. In section 3.4, I explicitly model these interdependent choices between SB and P in a full-fledged game.

To most agnostics, the signals, if they hear or see any, are ambiguous. This probably predisposes them to think indeterminate state 3 is most probable, and hence their search should not continue, unless they associate very high utility with being successful in their search (in improbable states 1 and 2).

I will not speculate further on P's choices in this situation—or on SB's choices if in fact it has them in a game wherein it can choose the states of nature. I note, however, that P's apparent certitude in favor of belief in Pascal's wager may be dashed in the Search Decision, because P does not have a dominant strategy. Moreover, an expected-payoff calculation that favors S or $\bar{S}$ cannot be made without information on the probabilities of the states. If, following Pascal's recommendation, P chooses to believe anyway and so commences a search, he or she will be disappointed if state 3 turns up (and perhaps state 2 as well, because P started out with the wrong a priori belief).

The lack of a clear-cut choice in the Search Decision is likely to be unsatisfactory to those who seek definite answers, not further qualifications. These qualifications, however, cannot easily be dismissed in any rational assessment, though one might contend that belief in SB (or God) is not, or cannot be, a rational choice. William James (1902/1967, 723), for example, maintained that our beliefs ought to be determined by our "passional nature" when their truth cannot "be decided on intellectual grounds."

But "passions," like preferences and goals, are neither rational nor irrational—it is the choices based on them that are. Although passions tend to be more identified with emotions than logic, to be "driven" by one's passions is in fact tantamount to trying to satisfy one's preferences and achieve one's goals (see chapter 7, especially, for examples).

Even if one cannot articulate a logic to one's passions, is it not rational to try to satisfy them? I explore this question by analyzing a different decision in the next section.

3.3 The Concern Decision

In the Concern Decision shown in figure 3.3, P's choices are to be concerned or not with SB; the states of nature for SB are that it is aware, and so cares about, what P chooses, or is not aware and does not care.

State of nature

	SB aware/cares whether P is concerned	SB not aware/does not care whether P is concerned	
Be concerned: C	Concern justified (4)	Concern unjustified (2)	⎫ Undominated
P			
Be unconcerned: $\overline{C}$	Unconcern unjustified (1)	Unconcern justified (3)	⎬ strategies ⎭

Key: 4 = best; 3 = next-best; 2 = next-worst; 1 = worst

Figure 3.3
Outcome and payoff matrix of Concern Decision

I assume that SB's awareness implies that it cares, and its unawareness implies that it does not care, so awareness and caring by SB are inextricably linked. Unlike the Search Decision, the Concern Decision imputes feelings of awareness and caring to SB, and by extension concern by P about the consequences of his or her choices. I ask: Is P's concern or unconcern justified or not?

Whether P's choice to be concerned (C) or not ($\overline{C}$) is viewed as a logical decision or an emotional choice, the rational calculus is the same. Of course, passions may dictate a different assignment of utilities to outcomes than "mere" preferences, but this has no bearing on P's making a rational choice that mirrors his or her passions or preferences.

If SB does not care, I assume that P is better off choosing $\overline{C}$ and not expending any effort (even if P is empathetic, because SB in this case is not worthy of empathy). I make no assumption about SB's preferences, only that it may or may not be aware and care.

P most prefers C when SB cares (4, concern justified); next-best for P is $\overline{C}$ when SB does not care (3, unconcern justified). These outcomes rank higher than P's choosing C and SB's not caring (2, concern unjustified) and P's choosing $\overline{C}$ even though SB cares (1, unconcern unjustified). The latter outcome is P's worst, because he or she abandons an SB who cares; in Pascal's wager, this would lead to unmitigated agony for P.

Even though P's choice here—to be concerned or not about SB—is not exactly the way Pascal presented alternatives in his wager, Pascal,

I imagine, would advise as follows: Be concerned, for there is an infinite reward associated with rank 4, and an infinite penalty with rank 1, whereas the payoffs associated with ranks 2 and 3 are finite and so do not matter in an expected-payoff calculation. More precisely, whatever the probabilities associated with each state of nature are, as long as they are positive there is an infinite gain associated with being concerned, and an infinite loss with not being concerned.

If one does assume infinite rewards and penalties, however, but considers only P's ranking of the four possible outcomes, P would be in a dilemma. Without a dominant strategy, his or her best choice depends on what state of nature arises.[4]

Most theists, I presume, would assert that God is aware/cares, whereas most atheists would say that the question is meaningless, because God does not exist. Thus, because of their different "passional natures"—believers with a passion for a caring God, nonbelievers with a passion against believing in any God—neither would have a problem about which choice to make in the Concern Decision. For agnostics, in contrast, being concerned or unconcerned are undominated strategies, based on P's assumed ranking of the four outcomes.

If this was indeed Pascal's ranking, he could, as I suggested earlier, resolve the dilemma by assigning infinite positive utility to rank 4, infinite negative utility to rank 1; practically speaking, however, what do these colossal rewards and penalties signify? They might be considered a gauge of P's very strong passions, but are they meaningful if P thinks that the probability of the first state (SB aware/cares) is negligible? If, instead, SB is much more likely to be unaware or indifferent, perhaps these attributions of infinite value should be ignored in favor of choosing between the middle rankings in the second state (SB not aware/does not care). In this case, P's decision would favor $\overline{C}$ (because $3 > 2$).

One possible way around the dilemma created by undominated strategies would be to alter P's ranks, switching, say, 4 and 2 or 4 and 1. In the former case, C would be a dominant strategy; in the latter case, $\overline{C}$ would be a dominant strategy.

---

4. This question is also posed by another conundrum, Newcomb's problem, which I show is intimately tied to the game of Prisoners' Dilemma (Brams 1975, 1983/2007); see also Lewis 1985 and Hurly 1994. Two-person and n-person versions of Prisoners' Dilemma are analyzed in chapter 5.

However, I find it difficult to justify these new assignments, which say that P's best outcome is to be concerned when SB does not care, or to be unconcerned when SB does, reversing the preferences it seems to me reasonable to impute to P. These switches smack of playing with numbers to sidestep a genuine dilemma; in my opinion, they are quite absurd.

What may be more defensible is to switch 3 and 4, arguing that justified unconcern, which might save P much time and effort, is better than justified concern. After all, each expression—of concern or unconcern—is consistent with the "facts" (i.e., the state of nature). Similarly, switching 1 and 2, based on a similar argument that to be concerned is more demanding than being unconcerned (even unjustifiably), also seems defensible.

Unfortunately for P, neither the 3–4 nor the 1–2 switch, or even both together, would endow him or her with a dominant strategy. The dilemma would remain: P's preferred choice, at least based on these rankings, would depend on the state of nature that arises.

This dilemma also underlies the Search Decision. To see this, simplify this decision by removing the first state of nature (SB's existence verifiable) or the second state (SB's nonexistence verifiable) in figure 3.1. Because P's two best outcomes lie along the main diagonal (from upper left to lower right) of the resulting payoff matrix, and his or her worst outcomes along the off-diagonal (from lower left to upper right), P does not possess a dominant strategy. Moreover, no switching of either the diagonal or the off-diagonal ranks changes this lack of dominance.

To return to the Concern Decision, one's passions, such as those Pascal assumed for heaven and against hell, may offer relief by decisively throwing the choice one way or the other. But the rankings by themselves that I have assumed do not, because the strategies in both the Search and Concern Decisions are undominated.

For the agnostic who has the assumed preferences, the absence of a best choice, independent of what state of nature arises, poses a problem. It complicates the easy calculus of Pascal's wager, leading more to indecision, and possibly anxiety, than Pascal's presumed resolution in favor of believing—by searching in the Search Decision and being concerned in the Concern Decision.

3.4   The Revelation Game

Using a 2×2 game to model the relationship between P and SB drastically simplifies a deep and profound religious experience for many people. My aim, however, is not to describe this experience but to abstract from it, using the game to analyze a central theological question: Can belief in SB be conceptualized as a rational choice when SB is not a state of nature but has its own goals?

The answer depends, in part, on whether it is proper to view SB as a game player, capable, like P, of making independent choices. Or is SB too ethereal or metaphysical an entity to characterize in these terms? If God, as Buber put it, is in a "direct relation" with us (see section 3.1), it is not a great leap of faith, in my view, to model His relationship to us by a game.[5]

The game I use to explore the rationality of belief in some SB is the Revelation Game (game 48), in which SB has two strategies: reveal itself (R), which establishes its existence, and don't reveal itself ($\overline{R}$), which does not establish its existence. Similarly, P has two strategies: believe in SB's existence (B), and don't believe in SB's existence ($\overline{B}$).

Instead of writing down and trying to justify the preferences of the players at each outcome, I begin by specifying the (i) primary and (ii) secondary goals of each player, as I did for Abraham and God in section 2.3:

SB (i) wants P to believe in its existence; (ii) prefers not to reveal itself.

P (i) wants belief (or nonbelief) in SB's existence confirmed by evidence (or lack thereof); (ii) prefers to believe in SB's existence.

Goal (ii) of P implies that he or she is happier being a believer than a nonbeliever, given goal (i) is satisfied.

Recall that the primary and secondary goals of each player, taken together, completely specify a player's ordering of outcomes in a 2×2 game. The primary goal distinguishes between the two best (4 and 3) and

5. As Cohen (1991, 24) points out, however, in the non-Western world "the concept of a personal, unmediated relationship between human being and deity is quite incomprehensible."

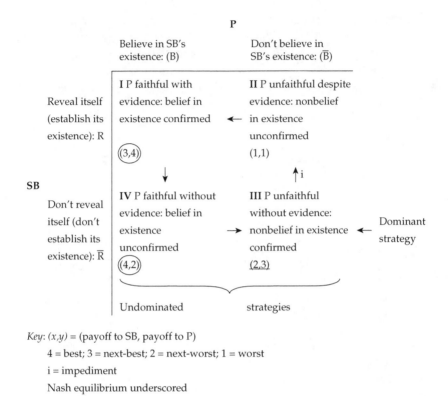

Figure 3.4
Outcome and payoff matrix of Revelation Game (game 48)

the two worst (2 and 1) outcomes of a player, whereas the secondary goal distinguishes between 4 and 3, on the one hand, and 2 and 1 on the other.

Thus for SB, (i) establishes that it prefers outcomes in the first column (4 and 3) of the figure 3.4 outcome and payoff matrix (associated with P's strategy of B) to outcomes in the second column (2 and 1, associated with P's strategy of $\overline{\text{B}}$). Between the two outcomes in each of the columns, (ii) establishes that SB prefers not to reveal itself (hence, 4 and 2 are associated with $\overline{\text{R}}$) over revealing itself (so 3 and 1 are associated with R).

Likewise for P, (i) says that P prefers to have his or her belief or non-belief confirmed by evidence (so the main-diagonal outcomes are 4 and 3) to being unconfirmed (so the off-diagonal outcomes are 2 and 1). Between the pairs of main-diagonal and off-diagonal outcomes, (ii) says that P prefers to believe (so 4 and 2 are associated with B) rather than not to believe (so 3 and 1 are associated with $\overline{B}$).

In the contemporary world, evidence from one's observations, experiences, and reflections accumulates, which predisposes one to believe or not believe in the existence of God or some other supernatural being or force—or leaves the issue open, as I suggested might be the case by postulating indeterminacy as a state of nature in the Search Decision in section 3.2. How beliefs are formed about a deity is less well understood.[6]

Of course, religions predispose one toward particular views, which religious works may reinforce. I next offer some brief remarks on the Hebrew Bible, which may lend plausibility to the goals of P and SB that I have assumed.

Evidence that the biblical God wanted His supremacy acknowledged by both Israelites and non-Israelites is plentiful in the Hebrew Bible. Moreover, the biblical narratives make plain that He pursued this goal with a vengeance not only by severely punishing those who did not adhere to His commands and precepts but also by bestowing rewards on the faithful who demonstrated their unswerving belief through good deeds and sacrifices.

Yet beyond providing indirect evidence of His presence through displays of His might and miraculous powers, the biblical God has an overarching reason for not revealing Himself directly: It would undermine any true test of a person's faith, which I assume to be belief in God not necessarily corroborated by direct evidence. Only to Moses did God confirm His existence directly—"face-to-face" (Exod. 33:11; Num. 12:6–8; Deut. 34:10)—but that Moses actually saw God firsthand is contradicted by the statement God made to Moses: "But," He said, "you cannot see My face, for man may not see Me and live" (Exod. 33:20).

---

6. For a developmental analysis of faith, see Fowler 1981. Different kinds of theological evidence, and the different kinds of rationality that they give rise to, are discussed in Swinburne 1981, chaps. 2 and 3.

Because a person cannot be truly tested if God's existence has already been confirmed by some unequivocal revelatory experience, I assume that God most desires from His subjects an expression of belief that relies only on faith (i.e., belief without direct evidence). Indeed, it is not unfair, in my opinion, to read the Bible as the almost obsessive testing of human beings by God to distinguish the faithful from those whose commitment to Him is lacking in zeal or persistence (remember that Job's faith faltered, but he never abandoned God).

This all-too-brief justification of SB's goals by way of the biblical God's statements and actions will not be persuasive to those who regard the Bible as an unreliable source at best, pure fantasy at worst.[7] It is *not*, however, a nonbeliever—or, for that matter, a believer—whom I postulate as P in the Revelation Game. Instead, I assume that P is somebody who takes the Bible (or other monotheistic religious works) seriously. Although these works may describe experiences that are outside P's ken or beyond the secular world, I suppose that P has yet to make up his or her mind about the existence of an "ultimate reality" embodied in some SB.

While P entertains the possibility of SB's existence, and in fact would prefer confirmatory to nonconfirmatory evidence in the Revelation Game (according to his or her secondary goal), *evidence is P's major concern* (i.e., primary goal). Moreover, P realizes that whether or not SB provides it will depend on what SB's rational choice in the game is.

To highlight the quandary that the Revelation Game poses for both players, observe that SB has a dominant strategy of $\overline{R}$: This strategy is better for SB whether P selects B [because SB prefers (4,2) to (3,4)] or $\overline{B}$ [because SB prefers (2,3) to (1,1)]. Given SB's dominant strategy of $\overline{R}$, P, who does not have a dominant strategy but prefers (2,3) to (4,2) in the second row of the payoff matrix, will choose $\overline{B}$ as a best response. These strategies lead to the selection of (2,3), which is the unique Nash-equilibrium outcome in the Revelation Game and is Pareto-inferior to (3,4).

Even though (3,4) is better for both players than (2,3), (3,4) is not a Nash equilibrium, because SB has an incentive, once at (3,4), to depart

7. For more evidence on God's goals beyond the cursory biblical citations provided here, see Brams 1980/2003.

to (4,2). Neither is (4,2) an equilibrium, because once there P would prefer to move to (2,3). And, of course, both players would prefer to move from (1,1). Thus, if the players have complete information about each other's preferences and choose their strategies independently of each other, game theory predicts the choice of (2,3) that, paradoxically, is worse for both players than (3,4).[8]

According to the theory of moves (TOM) that I introduced in section 2.5, the Revelation Game is "cyclic" in a counterclockwise direction, as shown by the arrows in figure 3.4 (Brams 1994b, chap. 4). From every state except the Nash equilibrium, (2,3), it is rational for the player with the next move in the cycle to move to a different state to improve its payoff. In the case of (2,3), the fact that the row player would prefer not to move in the direction of the arrow to (1,1) creates what I call an *impediment* (indicated by "i" in figure 3.4), but it does not preclude the Revelation Game from being cyclic.

A 2 × 2 game is *cyclic*—in either a clockwise or counterclockwise direction (it cannot be cyclic in both directions, as shown in Brams 1994b, 90–91)—if the player with the next move in the cycle never receives its best payoff (4). Thus, from (2,3), the row player moves to a less-preferred state, (1,1), but its move is not from a best state but from its next-worst (2), rendering the Revelation Game cyclic in a counterclockwise direction.[9]

Because there is one impediment to the players' moves shown in figure 3.4, the Revelation Game is *moderately cyclic*. A game is *strongly cyclic* if it has no impediments, and it is *weakly cyclic* if it has two impediments (a 2 × 2 game cannot have more than two impediments, one for each player; see Brams 1994b, 94). The fact that the Revelation Game is

---

8. This is also the paradox in game theory's most famous game, Prisoners' Dilemma (see chapter 5). The Revelation Game differs from Prisoners' Dilemma in being asymmetrical—the players do not have the same strategic choices—with only one player (SB) having a dominant strategy and the other player (P) having a best response to it. Note that if SB were able to commit itself to R, or actually choose it initially, then P's best response would be to choose B in the resulting 2 × 4 game, yielding the Pareto-superior outcome, (3,4). But then SB would be abandoning the possibility of testing P's faith. I think it more likely that the players are caught up in a cyclic game (to be described next in the text) and so analyze the consequences of one player's having *moving power* in such a game.

9. This game is not cyclic in a clockwise direction, because a move by SB from (4,2) to (3,4), or a move by P from (3,4) to (1,1), requires that the mover move from its best state to an inferior one.

moderately cyclic suggests that there will be some "friction" in the counterclockwise movement of the players around the matrix.

Before applying TOM—and, specifically, the concept of "moving power"—to the Revelation Game, let me clarify SB's choice of $\overline{R}$, which I interpreted earlier as "don't establish its existence" (see figure 3.4). From P's perspective, $\overline{R}$ may occur for two distinct reasons: (1) SB does not in fact exist as a player, or (2) SB exists but does not choose to reveal itself. Not only can P not distinguish between these two reasons for nonrevelation, but also even if SB exists, P knows that SB has a dominant strategy of $\overline{R}$ and would, therefore, presumbably choose it in the Revelation Game.

For this reason, I do not assume that P would ever think there is con-clusive evidence of *nonexistence*, so I do not give P this option in the Revelation Game. Instead, P can choose *not to believe* in SB's existence and—though this is not shown in the matrix—not to believe in SB's nonexistence, either, which is to say that P is agnostic. That is, P suspends judgment, which I interpret as a kind of commitment to remain noncommital.[10]

In a sense, a thoughtful agnostic plays the Revelation Game all his or her life, never certain about SB's strategy choice, or even that SB exists. In choosing $\overline{B}$, I interpret P to be saying that he or she does not believe either in SB's existence or nonexistence *yet*—in other words, P wants to keep his or her options open.

Should P become either a believer or a nonbeliever, then he or she no longer would be torn by the self-doubt reflected by P's choices in the Revelation Game. The evidence, so to speak, would be in. But I assume that P is neither an avowed theist nor an avowed atheist but a person with a scientific bent, who desires confirmation of either belief or non-belief. Preferring the former to the latter as a secondary goal, P is defi-nitely not an inveterate skeptic.

What SB might desire, however, is harder to discern. Certainly the God of the Hebrew Bible very much sought, especially from His chosen

10. Not everyone believes such openness is desirable, at least in the case of God. For example, Hanson (1971, 303–311) thinks that the proper position of the agnostic on the question of God's existence should be one of reasonable doubt. For Hanson, moreover, the evidence is tipped decisively against God's existence. Hanson's view is echoed in a host of recent books, including Dawkins 2006, Dennett 2006, and Hitchens 2007.

people, the Israelites, untrammeled faith and demonstrations of it. Although He never revealed Himself in any physical form, except possibly to Moses before he died, He continually demonstrated His powers in other ways, especially by punishing those He considered transgressors.

SB has *moving power* if it can continue moving when P will, eventually, be forced to stop.[11] That is, SB has the endurance or stamina to continue the counterclockwise cycling, whereas P does not and must, at some point, "call it quits."

With moving power, SB can induce P to stop at either (4,2) or (1,1), where P has the next move. P would prefer (4,2), which gives SB its best payoff: P's belief without evidence satisfies both of SB's goals. But P obtains only his or her next-worst payoff in this state, satisfying only his or her secondary goal of believing in SB's existence, but not his or her primary goal of having evidence to support this belief.

Endowing SB with moving power raises a feasibility question (see section 2.6). Whenever P oscillates between belief and nonbelief, I assume that SB can switch back and forth between revelation and non-revelation. But once SB has established its existence, can it be denied? I suggest that this is possible, but only if one views the Revelation Game as a game played out over a long period of time.

To illustrate this point, consider the situation recounted in chapter 19 of Exodus. After God "called Moses to the top of the mountain" (Exod. 19:20) to give him the Ten Commandments, there was "thunder and lightning, and a dense cloud ... and a very loud blast of the horn" (Exod. 19:16). This display provided strong evidence of God's existence to the Israelites, but for readers of the Bible today, it is perhaps not so compelling.

However, the Israelites became wary and restive after Moses's absence on Mount Sinai for forty days and nights. With the complicity of Aaron, Moses's brother, they revolted and built themselves a golden calf. God's earlier displays of might and prowess had lost their immediacy and therefore their force.

---

11. Moving power is more formally developed and analyzed in section 10.3; here I illustrate its application to the Revelation Game. Kilgour and Zagare (1987) introduce a related notion, "holding power," which they apply to the 1948 Berlin crisis between the Western powers and the Soviet Union.

This insurrection enraged Moses and God. Moses destroyed the Ten Commandments and, with God's assistance, provoked the slaughter by the Levites (a tribe of Israelites) of three thousand other Israelites for their idolatry. In section 5.5, I show how Moses was able to rally the Levites to his side in a kind of referendum on his leadership.

Jumping ahead to the present, the basis of belief for agnostics would seem even more fragile. Those who seek a revelatory experience from reading the Bible may find it, but many do not. For them, God remains hidden or beyond belief unless they can apprehend Him in other ways.

This is where the problem of revelation arises. Without a personal revelatory experience, or the reinforcement of one's belief in God that may come from reading a religious work or going to religious services, belief in God's existence may be difficult to sustain with unswerving commitment.

Revelation, also, may be a matter of degree. If God appears with sound and fury, as He did at Mount Sinai, He may disappear like the morning fog as memories of Him slowly fade. Thereby seeds of doubt are planted. But a renewal of faith may also occur if a person experiences some sort of spiritual awakening.

A wavering between belief and nonbelief, created by SB's moving between revelation and nonrevelation, shows that P's belief in SB *may have a rational basis for being unstable.* Sometimes the evidence manifests itself, sometimes not, in the Revelation Game. What is significant in this cyclic game is that SB's exercise of moving power is consistent with SB's sporadic appearance and disappearance—and with P's responding to revelation by belief, to nonrevelation by nonbelief (up to a point).

In the Bible, God seems to want to remain inscrutable, as the following colloquy suggests:

Moses said to God, "When I come to the Israelites and say to them 'The God of your fathers has sent me to you,' and they ask me, 'What is His name?' what shall I say to them?" And God said to Moses, "Ehyeh-Asher-Ehyet" ["I Am That I Am"]. He continued, "Thus shall you say to the Israelites, 'Ehyey [I Am] sent me to you.'" (Exod. 3:13–14)

As enigmatic as this reply was, however, God was also quick to trumpet His deeds and demonstrate His powers, as when He said in His and

Moses's confrontation with Pharaoh that He would "multiply My signs and marvels in the land of Egypt" (Exod. 7:4).

Visiting ten plagues upon the Egyptians, God induced Pharaoh to release the Israelites from their bondage. When the Egyptians pursued the Israelites to the Red Sea, which had parted for them, God locked the chariot wheels of the Egyptians as they crossed the parted sea, causing them all to drown when the sea swept together again.

Relying on faith alone, when reason dictates that it may be insufficient to sustain belief, produces an obvious tension in P. Over a lifetime, P may move back and forth between belief and nonbelief as seeming evidence appears and disappears. For example, the indescribable tragedy of the Holocaust destroyed the faith of many believers, especially Jews, in a benevolent God; for some it will never be restored.

But for others it has been restored. Furthermore, many former non-believers have conversion experiences—sometimes induced by mystical episodes—and, as a result, pledge their lives to some deity. For still others, there is a more gradual drift either toward or away from religion and belief in an SB.

More broadly, there are periods of religious revival and decline, which extend over generations and even centuries, that may reflect a collective consciousness about the presence or absence of an SB—or maybe both. As Kolakowski (1982, 140) remarked, "The world manifests God and conceals Him at the same time."

It is, of course, impossible to say whether an SB, behind the scenes, is ingeniously plotting its moves in response to the moves, in one direction or another, of individuals or society. For many today, this is an Age of Reason, which has had different names in the past (e.g., Age of Enlightenment), wherein people seek out a rational explanation. But there is also evidence of a religious reawakening (e.g., as occurred during the Crusades), which often follows periods of secular dominance. This ebb and flow is inherent in the instability of moves in the Revelation Game, even if an SB, possessed of moving power, has its way on occasion and is able temporarily to implement (4,2).

Perhaps the principal difficulty for SB in making this outcome stick is that people's memories erode after a prolonged period of nonrevelation. Consequently, the foundations that support belief may crumble. Non-belief sets up the need for some new revelatory experiences, sometimes embodied in a latter-day messiah, followed by a rise and then another collapse of faith.

If P, perhaps implausibly, is treated as the player who possesses moving power, then it can induce (3,4) by forcing SB to choose between (3,4) and (2,3), given that SB must stop at one of those states when it has the next move. Because SB prefers (3,4), it will stop at this state, which is P's best state and the outcome it can induce with moving power.

If the idea of "forcing" SB to reveal itself at this outcome—and, on this basis, for P to believe—sounds absurd, it is useful to recall that the biblical God exerted Himself mightily on occasion to demonstrate His awesome powers to new generations. By the same token, God left the stage at times in order to test a new generation's faith, usually being forced to return in order to foster belief again.

The effects of moving power, whether possessed by SB or P, seem best interpreted in the Revelation Game as occurring over extended periods of time. Memories fade, inducing SB to move from nonrevelation to revelation when the next generation does not understand or appreciate SB's earlier presence. Even when SB moves in the opposite direction, going from revelation to nonrevelation, its actions may not appear inconsistent if P, effectively, is a different player. Thereby the earlier concern I raised about infeasible moves is dissipated in an extended game in which the identity of P changes.

The Revelation Game has two nonmyopic equilibria (NMEs) (see section 2.5):

- (4,2) when play starts from this state.
- (3,4) when play starts from any other state.

Because this game does not have an obvious starting point, I think it better to view it as a cyclic game in which the player who possesses moving power can determine which of these two outcomes will be chosen, at least temporarily.

In the Revelation Game, either player, if it possesses moving power, can induce its best outcome. But this outcome may not be final but more likely a temporary "passing through," because the other player can respond, at least for a while, by switching strategies. Ultimately, the player without moving power will be forced to desist. If it is P, who believes for a time without evidence, then he or she will be replaced by another P who feels less pious in the face of an ineffable SB.

Feasibility may militate against too-quick switches on the part of the players, but fundamentally the Revelation Game is a game for the ages. Fluidity—rather than the stability of NMEs—is its most striking feature.

3.5 Decisions versus Games

In this chapter, I have analyzed vexing theological questions that inhere in two different kinds of choice situations:

• *decisions*, in which states of nature arise, according to some chance device, that characterize SB's presence or interests, but in which P alone makes choices without ever being certain in what state he or she is choosing;

• *games*, in which SB is an active player with preferences, like P, and makes choices in order to try to obtain a preferred outcome.

In the case of decisions, however, I did allow for the possibility that SB might be able to induce certain states of nature in order to advance its goals, making P's decision more gamelike.

In both decisions and games, players are assumed to make rational choices, which means choosing a dominant strategy if one has one; anticipating the other player's choice of such a strategy if one does not have one; or making a choice that maximizes one's expected payoff. The latter choice takes into account the player's utilities for outcomes and the probabilities that different states of nature occur.

In the Search Decision and Concern Decision, P's choice of searching for, or being concerned about, SB depends on the verifiability of SB's existence or nonexistence, or on SB's awareness and caring for P. Pascal's neat solution to this intellectual puzzle was to suppose payoffs for P that postulated a halcyon heaven or a horrible hell. Thereby Pascal was able to justify belief in God—or at least appearing to believe—as infinitely rewarding, even if this belief turned out to be false.

Pascal's payoff assumptions may strike agnostics as loading the dice to prop up a result that Pascal sought to find rational arguments to support. By contrast, a rational choice in the Search Decision and the Concern Decision is not so evident, because P does not have a dominant (or dominated) strategy in either. Instead, his or her strategies are undominated, whereby P's best choice depends on the state of nature.

Our "passional nature," in James's felicitous phrase, may help resolve this difficulty if it implies utilities—and perhaps probabilities—that swing the balance toward the choice of one strategy. While goals are neither rational nor irrational, the utilities we assign to achieving them, when multiplied by their probabilities of occurrence, yield expected utilities that, except for ties, render one strategy more beneficial than others.

Turning to the Revelation Game, I showed that for plausible assumptions about SB's and P's preferences, SB has a dominant strategy of nonrevelation, which induces P not to believe in its existence, yielding the Nash equilibrium of (2,3). Unfortunately for the players, this outcome is Pareto-inferior to (3,4), wherein SB reveals itself and P believes, which is the nonmyopic equilibrium (NME) that P can induce with moving power. If SB has moving power, it can induce the other NME, (4,2), wherein SB does not reveal itself yet P believes.

Which of the two NMEs occurs depends on the initial state, according to the theory of moves (TOM) described in section 2.5. Precisely because the initial state is not apparent, I analyzed the effects of moving power in this game. This concept, also based on TOM, seems appropriate when one player, presumably SB, is more powerful—in the sense of being able to continue cycling longer—than the other (P).

While SB can induce its most-preferred state, (4,2), with this power, it seems not beyond the pale that P—whose identity changes over time and who may not readily recall the past—can induce his or her most-preferred state, (3,4). This suggests why, as the players cycle counterclockwise around the Revelation Game, we go through periods of religious revival and decline.

Neither Pascal's wager nor the Search and Concern Decisions offers insight into why such cycling occurs. On the other hand, a game-theoretic perspective, based on TOM, does. It also clarifies why the answer that Pascal's wager gives for believing in God may not always be persuasive.

4 Philosophy: Paradoxes of Fair Division

4.1 Introduction

A paradox occurs when two plausible lines of reasoning lead to a contradiction.[1] A main concern of philosophy is to resolve paradoxes, especially those that raise fundamental questions, such as what constitutes a just society. A contradiction arises if we define a just society to be one that respects individual rights and maximizes social welfare, but these properties cannot be satisfied simultaneously.

Game theory provides an important tool for addressing such questions. A game in *characteristic-function form* is one in which each subset of players can ensure itself of a specified portion of some valued good like money.[2] In such a game, game theory asks what coalitions will form and be stable, and how much each player will receive in this coalition structure, based on strategic considerations and different criteria of

1. This chapter is adapted from Brams, Edelman, and Fishburn 2001 with permission.

2. This branch of game theory is referred to as *cooperative game theory*, wherein agreements are assumed to be enforceable. Because most of the analysis in this chapter is ordinal, which assumes that players can only rank or order items, I do not specify a characteristic function, which assumes that each subset of players can guarantee some cardinal value for itself. Although I use a modified Borda count to measure the value of items each player receives, this value does not describe what coalitions of players are likely to form and be stable. Nevertheless, the analysis in this chapter is in the spirit of cooperative game theory, prescribing what allocations of items are likely to satisfy the players, based on properties of fairness. Admittedly, its thrust is very different from the noncooperative strategic analysis in the rest of the book (with the exception of section 6.4, which applies the Banzhaf index of power to the Roosevelt Supreme Court), but this underscores the breadth of game-theoretic reasoning. For noncooperative models that incorporate fairness into the utility functions of players, based in part on beliefs about others players' actions and beliefs, see Rabin 1993 and Fehr and Gächter 2000.

fairness. In this chapter, I propose various criteria and analyze trade-offs among them.

My focus on paradoxes of fair division has a precedent in voting theory, which was greatly stimulated by the *Condorcet paradox*. It was discovered by the Marquis de Condorcet (1785), who showed that there may be no alternative that is preferred by a majority to every other alternative, resulting in so-called cyclical majorities. Its modern extension and generalization is Arrow's theorem (Arrow 1951/1963), which says, roughly speaking, that a certain set of reasonable conditions for aggregating individuals' preferences into a social choice are inconsistent—they cannot be satisfied simultaneously and so lead to a contradiction.

In the last sixty years, hundreds of books and thousands of articles have been written about both social-choice paradoxes and theorems, as well as their ramifications for voting and democracy. Nurmi 1999 provides a good survey and classification of voting paradoxes, and he also offers advice on "how to deal with them."[3]

There is also an enormous literature on fairness, justice, and equality, and numerous suggestions on how to rectify the absence of these properties or to attenuate their erosion. But paradoxes do not frame the study of fairness in the same way that they have inspired social-choice theory.

To be sure, the notion that justice and order may be incompatible, or that maximin justice à la John Rawls (1971)—two different versions of which will be described later—undercuts the motivation of individuals to strive to do their best, underscores the possible trade-offs in making societies more just or egalitarian. More specifically, an egalitarian society may require restrictions on free choice to ward off anarchy; but rewarding the worst-off members of a society may deaden competition among the most able when their added value is siphoned off to others.

Obstacles like these, which stand in the way of creating a just society, are hardly surprising. They are not paradoxes in the strong sense of constituting a logical contradiction between equally valid principles.

---

3. For other studies of voting paradoxes, see Fishburn 1974b, Fishburn and Brams 1983, and Saari 2008. Collections of paradoxes include Rescher 2001 and Clark 2002.

Here I use paradox in a weaker sense—as a conflict among fairness conditions that one might expect to be compatible. Insofar as this conflict is surprising, it is "nonobvious," which is the adjective I applied to a collection of paradoxes in politics (Brams 1976).

The fair-division paradoxes I present here all concern how to divide up a set of *indivisible* items among two or more players. For some paradoxes, I assume that the players can do no more than rank the items from best to worst, whereas for others they can, in addition, indicate preferences over subsets, or packages, of items. While this framework is generally an ordinalist one—in which players can rank or order alternatives but do not attach cardinal utilities to them—I do introduce one cardinalization of ranks, based on the Borda count used in voting, to facilitate certain comparisons, particularly those involving allocations with different numbers of items.

4.2   Criteria and Classification

The main criteria I invoke are *efficiency*, or *Pareto-optimality* (there is no other division better for everybody, or better for some players and not worse for the others) and *envy-freeness* (each player likes his or her allocation at least as much as those that each of the other players receives and so does not envy anybody else). But because efficiency, by itself, is not a criterion of fairness (an efficient allocation could be one in which one player gets everything and the others nothing), I also consider other criteria of fairness besides envy-freeness, including two different measures of how a worst-off player fares (maximin and Borda maximin).

I contrast these two maximin notions with a utilitarian notion of overall welfare (Borda total score). Ruled out, besides the splitting of items, is the possibility of randomizing among different allocations, which is another way that has been proposed for "smoothing out" inequalities caused by the indivisibility of items.[4]

---

4. Fair-division procedures that allow for the splitting of (divisible) goods or the sharing of (indivisible) goods—possibly based on a randomization process that determines time shares—are discussed in, among other books on fair division, Broome 1991; Young 1994; Roemer 1996; Brams and Taylor 1996, 1999; Robertson and Webb 1998; Moulin 2003; and Brams 2008. For an overview of the literature, see Brams 2006.

The paradoxes demonstrate the opportunities as well as the limitations of fair division. Thus, for example, while the only division of items in which one player never envies the allocation of another may be nonexistent or inefficient, there is always an efficient and envy-free division for two players—even when they rank all items the same—as long as they do not rank all subsets of items the same. I also show that fair division may entail an unequal division of the items, in which some players receive more items than others.

The eight paradoxes I analyze are classified into three categories:

1. The conflict between efficiency and envy-freeness (paradoxes 1 and 2);

2. The failure of a unique efficient and envy-free division to satisfy other criteria (paradoxes 3 and 4);

3. The desirability, on occasion, of dividing items unequally (paradoxes 5, 6, 7, 8).

While the paradoxes highlight difficulties in creating "fair shares" for everybody, they by no means render the task impossible. Rather, they show how dependent fair division is on the fairness criteria one deems important as well as the trade-offs one considers acceptable. Put another way, achieving fairness requires some consensus on the ground rules (i.e., criteria) and some delicacy in applying them (to facilitate trade-offs when the criteria conflict).

I mention three technical points before proceeding to specific examples. First, I assume that players cannot compensate each other with side payments—the division is only of the indivisible items. Second, all players have positive values for every item. Third, a player prefers one set S of items to a different set T if (i) S has as many items as T and (ii) for every item t in T and not in S, there is a distinct item s in S and not in T that the player prefers to t. For example, if a player ranks items 1 through 4 in order of decreasing preference 1 2 3 4, I assume that he or she prefers

• the set {1,2} to {2,3}, because {1} is preferred to {3}; and

• the set {1,3} to {2,4}, because {1} is preferred to {2} and {3} is preferred to {4}, whereas the comparison between sets {1,4} and {2,3} could favor either one.

4.3   Efficiency and Envy-Freeness: They May Be Incompatible

Paradox 1   *A unique envy-free division may be inefficient.*

Suppose there is a set of three players, {A, B, C}, whose members must divide a set of six indivisible items, {1, 2, 3, 4, 5, 6}. Assume the players strictly rank the items from best to worst as follows:

Example 4.1

A: 1 2 3 4 5 6

B: 4 3 2 1 5 6

C: 5 1 2 6 3 4

The unique envy-free allocation to (A, B, C) is ({1,3}, {2,4}, {5,6}), or for simplicity (13, 24, 56), whereby A and B get their best and third-best items, and C gets its best and fourth-best items. (For convenience, I will henceforth use the pronoun "it" to refer to players A, B, and C.) Clearly, A prefers its allocation to that of B (which are A's second-best and fourth-best items) and that of C (which are A's two worst items). Likewise, B and C prefer their allocations to those of the other two players. Consequently, the division (13, 24, 56) is envy-free: All players prefer their allocations to those of the other two players, so no player is envious of any other.

Compare this division with (12, 34, 56), whereby A and B receive their two best items, and C receives, as before, its best and fourth-best items. This division *Pareto-dominates* (13, 24, 56) because two of the three players (A and B) prefer the former allocation, whereas both allocations give player C the same two items (56).

Division (12, 34, 56) is Pareto-optimal, or efficient, because no player can do better with some other division without some other player or players doing worse, or at least not better. This is apparent from the fact that the only way A or B, which get their two best items, can do better is to receive an additional item from one of the two other players—assuming all items have some positive value for the players—but this will necessarily hurt the player who then receives fewer than its present two items. Whereas C can do better without receiving a third item if it receives item 1 or 2 in place of item 6, this substitution would necessarily hurt A, which will do worse if it receives item 6 for item 1 or item 2.

The problem with efficient allocation (12, 34, 56) is that it is not *assuredly* envy-free. In particular, C will envy A's allocation of 12 (second-best and third-best items for C) if it prefers these two items to its present allocation of 56 (best and fourth-best items for C). In the absence of information about C's preferences for subsets of items, therefore, we cannot say that efficient allocation (12, 34, 56) is envy-free.

An *assuredly envy-free* division—henceforth, envy-free for short—is one whereby no matter how the players value subsets of items consistent with their rankings, no player prefers any other player's allocation to its own. If a division is not envy-free, it is *envy-possible* if a player's allocation *may* make it envious of another player, depending on how it values subsets of items, as illustrated by division (12, 34, 56). It is *envy-ensuring* if it causes envy, independent of how the players value subsets of items.

In effect, a division that is envy-possible has the potential to cause envy. By comparison, an envy-ensuring division always causes envy, and an envy-free division never causes envy.

But the real bite of paradox 1 stems from the fact that not only is the inefficient division (13, 24, 56) envy-free, but it also is uniquely so—there is no other division, including an efficient one, that guarantees envy-freeness. To show this in example 4.1, note first that an envy-free division must give each player its best item; if not, then a player might prefer a division, like envy-free division (13, 24, 56) or efficient division (12, 34, 56), that does give each player its best item, rendering the division that does not envy-possible or envy-ensuring. Second, even if each player receives its best item, this allocation cannot be the only item it receives, because then the player might envy any player that receives two or more items, *whatever* these items are.

By this reasoning, then, the only possible envy-free divisions in example 4.1 are those in which each player receives two items, including its top choice. It is easy to check that no efficient division is envy-free.[5] Similarly, one can check that no inefficient division, except (13, 24, 56), which gives each player two items—including its best—is envy-free, making this division uniquely envy-free.

---

5. I previously showed that division (12, 34, 56) is not envy-free. As another example, consider efficient division (16, 34, 25). Whereas neither B nor C envies each other or A, A might envy either B's 34 or C's 25 allocations, making this division envy-possible.

Paradox 2   *There may be no envy-free division, even when all players have different preference rankings.*

While it is bad enough when the only envy-free division is inefficient (paradox 1), it seems even worse when there is no envy-free division. This is trivial to show when players rank items the same. For example, if two players both prefer item 1 to item 2, then the player that gets item 2 will envy the player that gets item 1.

In the following example, each of three players has a different ranking of three items:

Example 4.2

A: 1 2 3

B: 1 3 2

C: 2 1 3

There are three divisions of (A, B, C) that are efficient—(1, 3, 2), (2, 1, 3), and (3, 1, 2)—in which at least one player gets its best item. It is evident that none is envy-free, because the player that gets item 1 in each (A or B) will be envied by at least one of the other two players. For instance, in the case of the division (2, 1, 3), both A and C will envy B.

Can an inefficient division be envy-free, as was the case in example 4.1? It is not hard to see that this situation cannot occur in example 4.2 for the reason already noted: The player that gets item 1 will be envied. But in the case of an inefficient division, "trading up to efficiency" reduces the *amount* of envy. For example, consider inefficient division (2, 3, 1), in which each player receives its second-best choice. Because A envies C, B envies C, and C envies A, a trade of items 1 and 2 between A and C is possible. It yields efficient division (1, 3, 2), in which only B envies A.

Besides (2, 3, 1), the other two inefficient divisions—(1, 2, 3) and (3, 2, 1)—also allow for trading up to efficiency. In the first, a trade of items 2 and 3 between B and C yields efficient division (1, 3, 2); in the second, a trade of items 1 and 2 between B and C yields efficient division (3, 1, 2). Three-way trades are also possible. For instance, starting from inefficient division (3, 2, 1), a three-way trade, whereby A sends item 3 to B, B sends item 2 to C, and C sends item 1 to A, yields efficient division (1, 3, 2).

Trading up to efficiency is also possible in example 4.1: By exchanging items 2 and 3, A and B can turn inefficient division (13, 24, 56) into efficient division (12, 34, 56). As in example 4.2, however, no efficient division is envy-free in example 4.1. The difference between examples 4.1 and 4.2 is that example 4.2 does not admit even an inefficient envy-free division.

4.4   Unique Efficient and Envy-Free Divisions: Their Incompatibility with Other Criteria

Paradox 3   *A unique efficient and envy-free division may lose in voting to an efficient and envy-possible division.*

So far I have shown that efficiency and envy-freeness may part company either by there being no envy-free division that is also efficient (example 4.1), or no envy-free division at all (example 4.2). But when these properties coincide, and there is both an efficient and an envy-free division, it may not be the choice of a majority of players, as illustrated by the following example:

Example 4.3

A: 1 2 3 4 5 6

B: 5 6 2 1 4 3

C: 3 6 5 4 1 2

There are three efficient divisions in which (A, B, C) each get two items: (12, 56, 34); (12, 45, 36); and (14, 25, 36). However, only the third division, (14, 25, 36), is envy-free. Whereas C might envy B's 56 allocation in the first division, and B might envy A's 12 allocation in the second division, no player envies another player's allocation in (14, 25, 36).

But observe that both A and B prefer the first division, (12, 56, 34), to the envy-free third division, (14, 25, 36), because they get their top two items in the first division; only C gets its top two items in (14, 25, 36). Hence, the first division would defeat the envy-free third division, (14, 25, 36), by a simple majority.

The situation is not so clear-cut when we compare the second division, (12, 45, 36), with the envy-free (14, 25, 36). In fact, there would be a tie vote: C would be indifferent, because it gets its top two items, 36, in each division; A would prefer the second division (top two items versus best and fourth-best items); and B would prefer the envy-free division, (14, 25, 36) (best and third-best items versus best and fifth-best items).

Thus, if there were a vote, the unique envy-free division, (14, 25, 36), would lose to the envy-possible division, (12, 56, 34), and it would tie with the other envy-possible division, (12, 45, 36). Now assume there is approval voting (Brams and Fishburn 1983/2007), whereby voters can vote for as many alternatives as they like, each alternative approved of receives one vote, and the alternative with the most votes wins. If A, B, and C voted only for the divisions that give each player its two best items, then the envy-free division, (14, 25, 36), would get 1 vote, compared to 2 votes each for both of the envy-possible divisions, (12, 56, 34) and (12, 45, 36). In sum, players will choose an envy-possible over the unique envy-free division, (14, 25, 36), in either pairwise comparisons or under approval voting when they approve of exactly those allocations that give them their two best items.

Paradox 4   *Neither the Rawlsian maximin criterion nor the Borda total-score criterion may choose a unique efficient and envy-free division.*

Besides using voting to select an efficient division, consider the following Rawlsian maximin criterion to distinguish among efficient divisions: Choose the division that maximizes the minimum rank of items that players receive, making a worst-off player as well off as possible. To illustrate in example 4.3, envy-possible division (12, 45, 36) gives a fifth-best item to B, whereas each of the two other efficient divisions gives a player, at worst, a fourth-best item. Between the latter two divisions, the envy-possible division, (12, 56, 34), is arguably better than the envy-free division, (14, 25, 36), because it gives the other two players—those that do not get a fourth-best item—their two best items, whereas envy-free division (14, 25, 36) does not give B its two best items.[6]

Now apply a *modified Borda count* to example 4.3, which awards 6 points for obtaining a best item, 5 points for obtaining a second-best

---

6. This might be considered a second-order application of the maximin criterion: If, for two divisions, players rank the worst item any player receives the same, consider the player that receives a next-worst item in each, and choose the division in which this item is ranked higher. This is an example of a *lexicographic decision rule* (Fishburn 1974a), as discussed in chapter 2, note 12.

item, . . . , 1 point for obtaining a worst item.[7] This gives the nod to the envy-possible division, (12, 56, 34), which gives a total of 31 points to the three players, compared not only with the envy-free division, (14, 25, 36), but also with the other envy-possible division, (12, 45, 36), which both give 30 points.

Call these scores the *Borda total scores*, which I use as a measure of the *overall* utility or welfare of the players (unlike maximin, which gives priority to making worst items as highly ranked as possible). Example 4.3 shows that an envy-possible division may beat the unique envy-free division, based on both the maximin criterion and the Borda total-score criterion. In section 4.5, I apply the modified Borda count to individual players, asking what division maximizes the minimum Borda score that any player receives.

4.5   The Desirability of Unequal Divisions (Sometimes)

Paradox 5   *An unequal division of items may be preferred by all players to an equal division.*

In section 4.4 I showed that neither (i) pairwise comparison voting or approval voting (paradox 3), nor (ii) the maximin criterion or the Borda total-score criterion (paradox 4), always selects a unique efficient and envy-free division. In the following example, there is also a unique efficient and envy-free division—in which all players receive the same number of items (henceforth called an *equal division*)—but there may be grounds for choosing an efficient but unequal envy-possible division:

Example 4.4

A: 1 2 3 4

B: 2 3 4 1

It is not difficult to show that (13, 24) is the only efficient and envy-free division. Two other equal divisions, (12, 34) and (14, 23), while better for one player and worse for the other, are envy-possible.

---

7. The standard scoring rules for the Borda count when there are six items gives 5 points to a best item, 4 points to a second-best item, . . . , 0 points to a worst item. I depart slightly from this standard scoring rule to ensure that each player obtains some positive value for all items, including its worst choice, as assumed earlier. When I refer to Borda scores subsequently, I will mean scores based on the modified Borda count.

The aforementioned three equal divisions all give Borda total scores of 12 points to their players. If we eliminate the envy-possible division, (14, 23), on the grounds that it fails the maximin criterion by giving A its worst item (item 4), then the comparison reduces to that between envy-free division (13, 24) and envy-possible division (12, 34).

Curiously, *both* A and B prefer the unequal envy-possible division, (134, 2), to the equal envy-possible division, (12, 34), if A prefers 34 to 2, and B prefers 2 to 34. Thus, unequal divisions might actually be better for all players than equal divisions (i.e., Pareto-dominate them).

Ruling out equal division (12, 34) in such a situation, compare unequal division (134, 2) with equal division (13, 24), which is envy-free. Clearly, (134, 2) is better than (13, 24) for A, but it is worse for B.

This leaves open the question of which of these two divisions, involving an equal and an unequal division of the items, comes closer to giving the two players their "fair shares." As the next paradox shows, an unequal division may actually be more egalitarian—as measured by Borda scores for individual players—than an equal division.

Paradox 6 *An unequal division of items may (i) maximize the minimum Borda scores of players (Borda maximin) and (ii) maximize the sum of Borda scores (Borda maxsum).*

In paradox 5, I showed that an unequal but envy-possible division of items may compare favorably with an equal and envy-free division. To make this kind of comparison more precise, consider the following example:

Example 4.5

A: 1 2 3 4 5 6 7 8 9

B: 3 1 2 4 5 6 7 8 9

C: 4 1 2 3 6 5 7 8 9

On the one hand, there are exactly two unequal divisions, (12, 357, 4689) and (12, 3589, 467), that maximize the minimum Borda scores of players, which are [17, 17, 17] for both divisions.[8] On the other hand,

---

8. Henceforth I will indicate the Borda scores of players [in brackets] to distinguish them from item allocations (in parentheses).

there are two equal divisions, (129, 357, 468) and (129, 358, 467), that maximize the minimum Borda scores of players, which are [18, 17, 16] for the first division and [18, 16, 17] for the second division. The Borda total scores in each case are 51, which, it can be shown, is the maximal sum, or *Borda maxsum*, among all possible divisions (equal or unequal).

Notice that the worst-off player in the two unequal divisions garners 17 points (so does the best-off player, because the Borda scores of all players are the same), whereas the worst-off player in the two equal divisions receives fewer points (16). By the maximin criterion, but now based on Borda scores, the unequal divisions are more egalitarian. We call this the *Borda maximin* criterion, which is especially useful in comparing equal and unequal divisions.[9]

None of the four equal or unequal divisions is envy-free—all are envy-possible or envy-ensuring. Likewise, all four divisions are *efficient-possible* in the sense that there may be a more efficient division, but this is not guaranteed.

Take, for example, the unequal division (12, 357, 4689). B or C might prefer A's 12 allocation, just as A might prefer B's or C's allocation, so a trade could make two, or even all three, players better off. Unlike our previous examples, in which divisions called "efficient" were all "efficient-ensuring" (i.e., there were no trades that could improve the lot of all traders, however players valued subsets of items), this is not the case in example 4.5.

The Borda maximin criterion seems a reasonable one to distinguish among all efficient-possible and envy-possible divisions. In example 4.5, unequal divisions not only do best according to this criterion, but they also are Borda maxsum, making them both fair and utility-maximizing (according to the Borda cardinalization of utility—more later on its limitations, illustrated in example 4.7).

---

9. To see why, consider the two unequal divisions in example 4.4 in which no player receives a fourth-best item: (1, 234) and (123, 4). To call these divisions maximin—like equal division (13, 24), in which no player receives a fourth-best item as well—seems highly questionable, because the player receiving its top three items in these two divisions can hardly be considered worse off (because it receives a third-best item) than the player receiving only its top item. Indeed, the Borda scores of the players in the two unequal divisions, [4, 9] and [9, 2], reveal how inegalitarian these divisions are, particularly when compared to equal division (13, 24) with Borda scores of [6, 6].

Paradox 7 *An unequal division of items may be Borda maxsum but not Borda maximin.*

There was no conflict between Borda maxsum and Borda maximin in example 4.5—two unequal divisions satisfied both these properties. But as the next example illustrates, this need not be the case.

Example 4.6

A: 1 2 3

B: 1 3 2

There are two unequal maxsum divisions, (12, 3) and (2, 13), whose Borda scores are, respectively, [5, 2] and [2, 5]. Each gives a Borda total score of 7, and a minimum Borda score of 2 for a player.

By contrast, there are two Borda maximin divisions, (1, 23) and (23, 1), both of which give Borda scores of [3, 3]. While they give the players a lower Borda total score (6) than the Borda maxsum divisions, they give the players a higher minimum score of 3.

Presumably, the egalitarian would choose one of the two Borda maximin divisions, whereas the utilitarian would choose one of the two Borda maxsum divisions. Because there are an odd number of items to divide in example 4.6, all the divisions between A and B are necessarily unequal.

Borda maximin divisions and Borda maxsum divisions can be either equal or unequal. Thus, two of the Borda maxsum divisons in example 4.5 are equal and two are unequal. In the case of Borda maximin divisions, (13, 24) in example 4.4 is an equal division, whereas the two Borda maximin divisions in example 4.6 are unequal. It also turns out that Borda maxsum and Borda maximin scores can be arbitarily far apart (Brams, Edelman, and Fishburn 2003).

When Borda maximin and Borda total scores choose different divisions, Borda maximin, in my view, generally gives the fairer division by guaranteeing that the Borda score of the worst-off player is as great as possible.[10] As I show in the final paradox, however, a Borda

---

10. To be sure, assuming that the differences in ranks are all equal, as Borda scoring does, is a simplification. If cardinal utilities could be elicited that reflect the players' intensities of preference, then these utilities—instead of the rank scores—could be used to equalize, insofar as possible, players' satisfaction with a division of the items. For fair-division bidding schemes that incorporate cardinal information, see Brams and Taylor 1999; Brams and Kilgour 2001; and Brams 2008, chaps. 12 and 14.

maximin division may be quite implausible, depending on how players value subsets; or it may not be envy-free when, at the same time, there exists an envy-free division that is neither maximin nor Borda maximin.

Paradox 8 *If there are envy-free divisions, none may be maximin or Borda maximin.*

In the following example, there are two players but an odd number of items, so no equal division of the items is possible:

Example 4.7

A: 1 2 3 4 5

B: 1 2 3 4 5

Because the players rank the items exactly the same, all divisions are efficient, making the choice of a fairest one difficult.

Only six divisions, however, are what Brams and Fishburn (2000) call *undominated splits*:

$(1, 2345)$; $(12, 345)$; $(13, 245)$; $(14, 235)$; $(15, 234)$; $(145, 23)$.

These divisions are those in which, in the absence of information about preferences over subsets, either of the two allocations in each might be preferred by a player, making each undominated. All these divisions, therefore, are *envy-possible*.

The Borda maximin divisions are the third and fourth, $(13, 245)$ and $(14, 235)$, which give Borda scores of, respectively, $[8, 7]$ and $[7, 8]$ to the players. But neither division is envy-free when, say, *both* players prefer allocation 13 to 245 in the third, and allocation 14 to 235 in the fourth—that is, both prefer the "same side" of each division. These preferences imply that both prefer allocation 12 to 345 in the second division, $(12, 345)$, and allocation 145 to 23 in the sixth division, $(145, 23)$, precluding these divisions, as well, from being envy-free.

Thus, the preferences of A and B assumed earlier would eliminate four of the undominated splits from being envy-free, allowing the two remaining divisions (first and fifth) to be so. For example, A might prefer allocation 1 in the first division and allocation 15 in the fifth, whereas B might prefer the complements: allocations 2345 in the first, and allocation 234 in the fifth.

In none of our previous examples with envy-free divisions was such a division not Borda maximin. But as I have just illustrated, there may be several envy-free divisions, none of which is Borda maximin. This divergence points to the limitation of Borda maximin as a criterion for choosing divisions, because Borda scoring may not reflect the intensity of player preferences, which can be better gleaned from player preferences over subsets.[11]

However, one does not need to know player preferences over subsets to show that an envy-free division may not be Borda maximin.

Example 4.8

A: 1 2 3 4 5 6 7 8 9

B: 5 8 1 2 6 7 3 4 9

C: 3 4 9 1 2 5 6 7 8

It is not difficult to show that division (127, 568, 349) is envy-free, but it gives a seventh-best item to A. By contrast, division (126, 587, 349) gives sixth-best items to A and B and the same 349 allocation to C.

Because no other divisions (equal or unequal) give players lowest-ranked items that are as high as sixth-best, division (126, 578, 349) is maximin. However, it is not envy-free: B may envy A, because it may prefer allocation 126 to 578, making this division envy-possible.

The Borda scores of the envy-free division are [20, 22, 24], whereas those of the maximin division are [21, 21, 24], so the maximin division is also Borda maximin. Both the envy-free and maximin/Borda maximin divisions have total Borda scores of 66, which is also the Borda maxsum in example 4.8.

This example illustrates what I consider the most striking paradox. Specifically, without any special assumptions about the preferences of the players for subsets of items, it shows the clash between envy-freeness and both maximin and Borda maximin. Furthermore, because there are no unequal divisions in example 4.8 that satisfy any of the fairness criteria—or, for that matter, the Borda maxsum criterion—

---

11. These are taken into account in Brams, Kilgour, and Klamler 2009, whose authors show that there is always an envy-free division of indivisible items between two players, except when the subsets they regard as "ordinally minimal" are all the same.

it highlights the difficulty of choosing a fairest allocation, even in the equal-division case: Should one help the worst-off or avoid envy when one cannot do both?

This question is more fully explored in Brams and King (2005), in which it is shown not only that maximin and Borda maximin divisions may not be envy-free but also that *all* such divisions may actually ensure envy. To illustrate this conflict, consider the following example:

Example 4.9

A: 1 2 3 4 5 6

B: 1 2 3 4 5 6

C: 1 5 4 6 2 3

There are four Borda maximin divisions—(14, 23, 56), (23, 14, 56), (13, 24, 56), (24, 13, 56), each giving a minimum Borda score of 8 to a player—which are also maximin divisions (a worst-off player receives a fourth-best item). In addition, there are two maximin divisions that are not Borda maximin divisions—(12, 34, 56), (34, 12, 56)—that also give a worst-off player a fourth-best item.

All six divisions ensure envy: In each, one player prefers another player's two items to its own. This example demonstrates that maximin and Borda maximin divisions, rather than just precluding envy-freeness, may *guarantee* envy (i.e., be envy-ensuring rather than just envy-possible, as in example 4.8). Furthermore, unlike example 4.2, in which the unique efficient maximin and Borda maximin division, (1, 3, 2), is also envy-ensuring, the present example involves each player receiving two items, which one might think would be sufficient to allow a maximin or Borda maximin division to be envy-possible, if not envy-free. This, however, is not the case, underscoring the seriousness of the conflict among the fairness criteria.

4.6   Summary and Conclusions

Cooperative game theory focuses on the fair division of value to players, based on what coalitions will form to support this division. How to divide indivisible items is the central question I raise in this chapter, in which I assume that there are two or more players who rank them from best to worst. They may, as well, be able to indicate preferences over subsets, or packages, of items.

The main criteria used to assess the fairness of a division are efficiency (Pareto-optimality) and envy-freeness. I also suggested other criteria, including a Rawlsian criterion that the worst-off player be made as well off as possible and a scoring procedure, based on the Borda count, that helps in defining allocations that are valued as equally as possible.

I described, and classified into three categories, eight paradoxes that involve unexpected conflicts among the criteria. The paradoxes pinpoint difficulties in dividing up indivisible items so that each player feels satisfied, in some sense, with its allocation. The first two paradoxes show that efficient and envy-free divisions may be incompatible, because the only envy-free division may be inefficient, or there may be no envy-free division at all.

Both of these paradoxes require at least three players (Edelman and Fishburn 2001). When there are only two players, even when they rank items exactly the same, it turns out that efficient and envy-free divisions can always be found, except when the players have the same preferences over all subsets of items (Brams and Fishburn 2000; Brams, Kilgour, and Klamler 2009).

But the existence of even a unique efficient and envy-free division may not be chosen by the players for other reasons. In particular, such a division will not necessarily be selected when players vote for the division or divisions that they prefer. Also, a unique efficient and envy-free division will not necessarily be the division that maximizes the minimum rank of items that players receive, so the Rawlsian maximin criterion of making the worst-off player as well off as possible may not single it out.

As a way of valuing allocations in order to find the divisions that are most egalitarian, especially in comparing equal and unequal divisions, Borda scoring, based on player rankings of the items, was used. I showed that a Borda maximin division may not be a Borda maxsum division, indicating the possible conflict between egalitarian and utilitarian divisions.

This difference may show up when there are as few as two players dividing up three items, making it impossible to divide the items equally between the players. But even when this is possible, unequal divisions of items may be the only ones that satisfy the Borda maximin criterion. While indicating a preference for this criterion over the Borda maxsum criterion when the two clash, I illustrated how Borda maximin divisions may fail badly in finding envy-free divisions. Indeed, there may be no overlap between Borda maximin and envy-free divisions.

My purpose is not just to indicate the pitfalls of fair division by exhibiting paradoxes that can occur. There are also opportunities, but these depend on the judicious application of selection criteria when not all criteria can be satisfied simultaneously.

A number of recent papers have analyzed constructive procedures, or algorithms, for finding the most plausible candidates for fair division of a set of indivisible items.[12] This direction seems promising, because it is potentially applicable to ameliorating, if not solving, practical problems of fair division—from the splitting of marital property in a divorce, the allocation of cabinet ministries to political parties in a parliamentary system, and the determination of who gets what in an international dispute. While some conflicts are ineradicable, as the paradoxes demonstrate, the trade-offs that best resolve these conflicts are by no means evident and, therefore, worthy of careful study.[13]

---

12. Several different algorithms, applicable to a variety of real-life situations, are discussed in Brams 2008, part 2; see also Brams and Straffin 1979; Herreiner and Puppe 2002; Brams and Kaplan 2004; and Brams, Kilgour, and Klamler 2009.

13. A firm, Fair Outcomes, Inc. (http://FairOutcomes.com), offers several fair-division algorithms on the Internet.

5 Political Philosophy: How Democracy Resolves Conflict in Difficult Games

5.1 Introduction

The dual problems of fostering cooperation in societies and choosing leaders to govern them, while briefly mentioned in the Hebrew Bible when Saul becomes the first Israelite king (Brams 1980/2003, chap. 7), are more systematically analyzed by the classical Greek philosophers, Plato and Aristotle.[1] Two thousand years later English political philosopher Thomas Hobbes (1588–1679) maintained that the only escape from anarchy was the imposition of rule by a "leviathan," a strong central authority to whom citizens would cede their natural rights through a social contract. More recent political philosophers have suggested more benign means for forging consensus in a civil society, including voting, and have proposed a variety of constitutional structures for making public choices.

Today, fair and periodic elections are considered a cornerstone of democracy. While there is an ongoing debate about how best to conduct elections (Brams 2008, part 1), I consider in this chapter the seemingly simple situation in which voters choose between just two alternatives, and the alternative with the most votes wins. But, as I will show, there are complications even in this case.

Voting in a democracy will be said to *resolve conflict* if the electorate believes that (1) the voting process is fair and (2) the outcome chosen is acceptable. There may not be a consensus among the voters that the alternative chosen is the best, but as long as some agreed-upon minimum

---

1. This chapter is adapted from Brams and Kilgour 2009 with permission.

number of voters (e.g., a majority) support an alternative, this outcome will be implemented.

I focus in this chapter on choices that are costly to implement. For example, if voters in a referendum decide to finance a public project, the cost of this project will be reflected in higher taxes they must pay.

Suppose that the project is renovation of a public park, which can benefit everybody—but more so those who use the park frequently than those who do not. In this case, some would argue that those who use the park frequently should pay more for its renovation, such as through the Central Park Conservancy in New York City, which solicits voluntary contributions.

But this voluntary approach leads to a *public-goods* or *free-rider problem*. This occurs when a player can benefit from the contributions of others to a *public good*, which is a good that cannot be withheld from anybody (e.g., clean air), but who has no incentive to contribute to its provision.

I model this problem as a two-person Prisoners' Dilemma (2-person PD) in section 5.2 and then as an *n*-person PD in section 5.3. I show how voting resolves conflict in the PDs in each case and illustrate the *n*-person resolution with an example in section 5.4.

This resolution stabilizes the cooperative outcome in a PD by transforming it into a game in which voters are presented with a choice between a cooperative outcome and a Pareto-inferior noncooperative outcome. In the transformed games, it is always rational for voters to vote for the cooperative outcome, because cooperation is a weakly dominant strategy, independent of the decision rule and the number of voters who choose it.

In section 5.5, I turn to the Hebrew Bible to demonstrate how Moses, after the idolatry of the Israelites at Mount Sinai, effectively conducted a referendum on his leadership, albeit without a formal vote. After receiving the total support of his own tribe, the Levites, he engineered the elimination of dissidents, which appeased God.

In section 5.6, I identify the ten difficult 2×2 ordinal games, in addition to PD, in which voting induces cooperation. I conclude in section 5.7 by pointing out that voting is not a panacea, particularly in developing countries, which often lack a rule-of-law tradition, or countries in which the enforcement of laws is lax or nonexistent.

5.2 Resolution by Voting in a 2-Person PD

To render the analysis as transparent as possible, I begin with a 2-person PD, wherein one player is a wealthy individual who can make a large contribution to the renovation of the park. Suppose his or her contribution is expected to equal the contributions made by the rest of the public, whom I treat as a single player. In the ranking of payoffs to the players in figure 5.1, assume that the wealthy individual and the rest of the public both prefer outcomes in the following order: partial renovation without contributing (4) to full renovation with contributing (3) to no renovation without contributing (2) to partial renovation with contributing (1).

Each player's strategy of don't contribute strongly dominates its strategy of contribute, because it is better whichever strategy the other player chooses. Each player, therefore, has an incentive to be a *free rider*, obtaining the benefit of the public good without contributing to its provision.

But the choice by both players of don't contribute leads to the next-worst outcome of (2,2), which is the unique Nash equilibrium—neither player would have an incentive to depart from it unilaterally lest it do worse (by obtaining 1). The dilemma is that (2,2) is worse for both players than the cooperative outcome of (3,3), wherein both players

		Rest of public	
		Contribute	Don't contribute
Wealthy individual	Contribute (C)	I Full renovation (3,3)	II Partial renovation (1,4)
	Don't contribute (D)	IV Partial renovation (4,1)	III No renovation (2,2)

Key: (x, y) = payoff ranking to (wealthy individual, rest of public)

4 = best; 3 = next-best; 2 = next-worst; 1 = worst

Nash equilibrium underscored

Figure 5.1
Outcome and payoff matrix in 2-person PD (game 32)

Rest of public

		Vote to finance	Vote not to finance
	Vote to finance	I Full renovation <u>(3,3)</u>	II No renovation (2,2)
Wealthy individual			
	Vote not to finance	IV No renovation (2,2)	III No renovation (2,2)

Key: (x, y) = payoff ranking to (wealthy individual, rest of public)

4 = best; 3 =next-best; 2 = next-worst; 1 = worst

Nash equilibrium underscored

Figure 5.2
Outcome and payoff matrix of transformed 2-person PD

contribute. But the latter outcome is not a Nash equilibrium—each player would have an incentive unilaterally to depart from its strategy associated with it (to obtain 4)—rendering it unstable.

To be sure, (3,3) may be stabilized under certain conditions—for example, in tournament play (Axelrod 1984), in strategies that evolve over time (Skyrms 1996; Nowak 2006), or when players are farsighted, as discussed in section 2.5.[2] However, this is not the argument I make for its choice in the voting game I describe next.

Assume that the players in the figure 5.1 PD can first vote on whether or not to contribute to financing the renovation of the park. If a majority (i.e., both players) must vote to finance the park in order that it be renovated, then their choices and the resulting outcomes are shown in figure 5.2.

Notice that the option that the park be partially renovated does not appear in the payoff matrix. Instead, the outcomes are starker: The park

2. Farsightedness offers a very different resolution of PD than either tournament play or evolution. Pinker (2007, 71) distinguishes the former from the latter by arguing that "natural selection [in evolution] is like a design engineer in the sense that parts of animals become engineered to accomplish certain things, but it is not like a design engineer in that it doesn't have long-term foresight." Presumably, only humans possess this foresight and can anticipate that if they move from (3,3), it will not necessarily induce their best outcome of (4,1) or (1,4) but, instead, may trigger a countermove by the player receiving 1 to (2,2). Because this outcome is worse for both players than (3,3), (3,3) is a nonmyopic equilibrium (NME) in PD if the players start at this outcome and think ahead.

is either fully renovated or not renovated, which renders the cooperative outcome of full renovation the unique Pareto-optimal Nash equilibrium; moreover, it is supported by weakly dominant strategies of the players.[3] This transformation may be viewed as a mapping of two of the four outcomes in the PD (full renovation and no renovation) into the new game, with voting determining the outcomes (i.e., partial renovation) that these two outcomes replace.

5.3   Resolution by Voting in an n-Person PD

To extend this resolution of a 2-person PD to an n-person public-goods game, assume there are $n \geq 2$ players and two strategies, Cooperate (C) and Defect (D), that each player can choose. If k players cooperate, the payoff to each cooperator is the amount $c(k)$, where $k = 1, 2, \ldots, n$, and the payoff to each defector is the amount $d(k)$, where $k = 0, 1, \ldots, n-1$.[4] An n-person game that satisfies the three properties given below mimics the characteristics of the 2-person PD:

Properties of n-Person PD

1. The payoffs $c(k)$ and $d(k)$ are increasing in k. That is, when more players cooperate, all benefit—whether they chose C or D—because more of the public good is provided.

2. For each $k = 1, 2, \ldots, n$, $c(k) < d(k-1)$. That is, comparing the situations in which there are (i) k cooperators and (ii) $k-1$ cooperators after the defection of a cooperator, each of the defectors in the latter situation receives a greater payoff than each of the cooperators in the former situation, given that the strategies of all other players are fixed.

3. $c(n) > d(0)$. That is, when all players choose D, the resulting outcome is Pareto-inferior, or worse for all players, than the outcome in which all cooperate.

---

3. Unlike each player's noncooperative strategy in PD, each player's cooperative strategy associated with (3,3) in the transformed game is not strictly better, whichever strategy the other player chooses: If the other player votes not to finance, either voting to finance or voting not to finance leads to the same outcome of (2,2). Because of this "tie," voting to finance is not *always* better than voting not to finance, making this strategy weakly dominant.

4. Because $c(k)$ and $d(k)$ are indexed differently, I can compare $c(k)$ and $d(k-1)$ over all k, as I do in property 2.

Property 2 implies that, for each player, C is a strongly dominated strategy. To see this, fix a player and suppose that $k - 1$ other players choose C and the remaining $n - k$ choose D. Then the focal player will receive $c(k)$ for choosing C and $d(k–1)$ for choosing D. Because this conclusion holds for every value of k, D strongly dominates C for every player.

It follows that the unique Nash equilibrium in the n-person PD is for all players to choose D and receive $d(0)$. Because this strategy is supported by strongly dominant strategies, the resulting all-D Nash equilibrium is especially stable. But by property 3, the nonequilibrium outcome of all-C, at which all players receive $c(n)$, is strictly preferred by all players to $d(0)$. Thus, this n-person PD has a unique strongly dominant strategy of D for each player, but when all players choose it, a strictly Pareto-inferior outcome results.

The resulting n-person PD has all the problems of the 2-person PD and more. When there are only two players, they may well stabilize the cooperative outcome by implementing an enforcement mechanism, such as regular inspections in an arms-control agreement, that transforms the PD into a more benevolent game, with the cooperative outcome as the unique Nash equilibrium.

But if there are many players,[5] this becomes far less feasible—short of transforming the game into a voting game, as I show next. Whereas the voting game described in section 5.2 required that only two players agree to contribute to renovation of the park, assume now that a decision rule is chosen that determines whether a public good is provided. More specifically, suppose that with the introduction of voting by the players, the n-person PD is played according to the following rules:

Rules of Transformed n-Person PD

1. A decision rule r, satisfying $0 < r \le n$, is fixed and announced to all players.

---

5. In the preceding example, I treated the "rest of the public" as a single player, but if the game is among many similar players, then it is properly modeled as an n-person PD. To ameliorate the problem of defections in such a game, wealthy individuals often commit to match the donations of small contributors, thereby enhancing the incentive of these individuals to contribute by guaranteeing that their donations will be increased by some factor.

2. The players vote, independently and simultaneously, for either C or D.

3. If the number of players that vote for C is $m < r$, then the all-D outcome is implemented, so all players receive $d(0)$. But if $m \geq r$, then the all-C outcome is implemented, so all players receive $c(n)$.

It is easy to check that a player's choice of C or D only affects its payoff when exactly $r - 1$ other players choose C. In this case, the player receives $c(n)$ for choosing C and $d(0)$ for choosing D; by property 3, the player prefers $c(n)$.

Because voting for C sometimes results in a better outcome and never results in a worse outcome, it is a weakly dominant strategy, just as it is in the transformed 2-person PD. Thus, the all-C outcome, supported by the players' weakly dominant strategies of voting for C, is the unique Pareto-optimal Nash equilibrium in the transformed n-person PD.[6]

5.4 Example of an n-Person PD

Suppose there are $n = 10$ players, and the payoff functions to the cooperators and the defectors are $c(k) = 10k - 50$ and $d(k) = 10k$. It is easy to show that the three properties of an n-person PD are satisfied:

1. The payoffs to the players are increasing in k.

2. $c(k) = 10k - 50 < d(k - 1) = 10(1 - k)$, which simplifies to $-50 < -10$, and so is satisfied.

3. $c(n) = 100-50 > d(0) = 0$, which simplifies to $50 > 0$, and so is satisfied.

Let $k = 1, 2, \ldots, 10$. The payoff for being the kth cooperator, $c(k)$—as opposed to defecting and there being one less cooperator, $d(k - 1)$—are shown for representative values of k in figure 5.3.

Notice that $k = 5$ cooperators make the value of cooperation, $c(5) = 0$, equal to the value of defection by everybody, $d(0) = 0$, in the n-person PD. Thus, 5 cooperators is the breakeven number at which

6. Hardin (1971) shows that all-C is a *Condorcet alternative* when pitted against any other strategy combination—that is, a majority of voters would prefer it, except in the case of a tie—but he does not provide a procedure that would implement all-C.

Number of other cooperators

	$k = 1$	$k = 2$	$k = 5$	$k = 9$	$k = 10$
Cooperation: $c(k)$	−40	−30	0	40	50
Noncooperation: $d(k-1)$	0	10	40	80	90

Figure 5.3
Payoff of cooperation and noncooperation when k others cooperate

funding the project has the same value for the cooperators as not funding it.

Whereas all-D at $d(0)$ is the Nash equilibrium in the n-person PD, all-C at $c(10)$, which gives a payoff of 50 to each player, is not an equilibrium. The latter outcome is unstable because if one player defects from all-C, he or she receives a payoff of $d(9) = 90$. In fact, as shown in section 5.3, every player has a strongly dominant strategy of defecting in the n-person PD, however many cooperators there are.

Now assume simple-majority rule is used in the transformed n-person PD (i.e., $r = 6$), so if there are 5 or fewer cooperators, no project is funded. But if there are 6 or more cooperators, everyone, including the defectors, gets a payoff of 50. Depicting the game as a 10-dimensional array in which each of the 10 players can choose between C and D, then C weakly dominates D for each player, whatever the value of r is, but the contingency in which C makes a difference (by raising a player's payoff from 0 to 50) changes when r changes.

Although the value of r does not affect the weak dominance of C, it would be strange indeed if r were not at least a simple majority (6 in the example), because less than a majority of cooperators could implement a project, perhaps against the wishes of a majority. (In the extreme case, it would be a single player—a dictator, in effect—who would call the shots.) Accordingly, I propose that r be at least a simple majority in the transformed n-person PD.

In fact, a simple majority may be preferable to a qualified majority, because a simple majority is more robust against defectors. Thus in the example, selecting $r = 6$ means that even if up to 4 players choose D (for whatever reasons), the majority would still triumph, whereas this would not be the case for a greater r. In particular, if $r = 10$ (unanimity), one defector can undermine the choice of C by the other 9 players.

Finally, I introduce a note of caution on the link between voting and democracy. While free and fair elections are a key to democracy, the solution I propose to the free-rider problem is also applicable to oligarchies, wherein only few members of an elite (e.g., the ten players in the previous example) vote. Insofar as elites are elected to councils or legislatures, however—as occurs in a representative democracy—it seems fair to say that voting by these voting bodies resolves the free-rider problem in a way akin to voting by all the citizens in the electorate.

5.5 A Biblical Tale

A story from the Hebrew Bible, alluded to in section 3.4, illustrates how a group, aided by a charismatic leader, can resolve an n-person PD when individuals alone cannot not do so.[7] The story begins after Moses descends from Mount Sinai and discovers that the Israelites, who had grown restive during his absence of forty days and nights, had, with the complicity of Moses's brother, Aaron, built and worshipped a golden calf.

Observing the revelry of the Israelites at the base of the mountain, Moses is enraged and destroys the Ten Commandments. But he must also deal with another problem—the extreme anger of God, who is infuriated by the idolatry of the Israelites and threatens to destroy them:

---

7. This section is adapted from Brams 1980/2003, 94–98, but the interpretation of Moses's resolution of an n-person PD via a kind of referendum is based on Brams and Kilgour 2009. Passages from the Bible are drawn from *The Torah: The Five Books of Moses* (1967). Schelling (1978, chap. 7) gives several contemporary examples of n-person PDs, such as whether a hockey player should wear a helmet, which was not mandated by the National Hockey League (NHL) until the 1990s. Prior to 1990, most players refused to wear helmets because it put them at a strategic disadvantage, limiting their peripheral vision, though they were at a substantially greater risk of serious head injury. The dilemma was resolved not by a secret vote of the players, which arguably would have led to the requirement of helmets in the 1970s, but by a public outcry caused by head injuries, which put pressure on the NHL. Even so, players who entered the league before the helmet requirement were exempted; the last player to refuse to wear a helmet retired in 1997.

"I see this as a stiffnecked people. Now, let Me be, that My anger may blaze forth against them and I may destroy them, and make of you a great nation." But Moses implored the LORD his God, saying, "Let not Your anger, O Lord, blaze forth against Your people, who You delivered from the land of Egypt with great power and a mighty hand. Let not the Egyptians say, 'It was with evil intent that He delivered them, only to kill them off in the mountains and annihilate them from the face of the earth.'" (Exod. 32:9–12)

Moses offers a cogent reason why the Israelites should be spared, asking God to

turn from Your blazing anger, and renounce the plan to punish Your people. Remember Your servants, Abraham, Isaac, and Jacob, how You swore to them by Your Self and said to them: I will make your offspring as numerous as the stars of heaven, and I will give to your offspring this whole land of which I spoke, to possess forever." And the LORD renounced the punishment He had planned to bring upon His people. (Exod. 32:14–15)

Thus God, realizing the enormous investment he has made in His chosen people, does not brush aside His handiwork out of pique.

Although God relents, Moses must still convince Him that His decision to save His chosen but "stiffnecked" people, who had "acted basely" (Exod. 32:7), is not a foolish one. After wringing a confession out of Aaron for his part in the idolatrous affair, Moses looks with horror on the Israelites, who are "out of control" (Exod. 32:25).

Moses averts catastrophe by seizing the initiative: "Whoever is for the LORD, come here" (Exod. 32:26). Moses's gamble pays off, at least for one tribe:

And all the Levites rallied to him. He said to them, "Thus says the LORD, the God of Israel: Each of you put sword on thigh, go back and forth from gate to gate throughout the camp, and slay brother, neighbor, and kin." The Levites did as Moses had bidden, and some three thousand of the people fell that day. And Moses said, "Dedicate yourselves to the LORD this day—for each of you has been against son and brother, that He may bestow blessing upon you today." (Exod. 32:26–29)

I interpret Moses's summons to "come here" as less a command than a desperate plea for a sizeable number—if not a majority—of the Israelites to rally to the side of the LORD and renounce their sinful behavior. In effect, Moses, acting as a political entrepreneur, asks the Israelites to vote in a referendum on his leadership.

If only a few Israelites had heeded Moses's plea and supported him, their numbers would not have been sufficient to persuade God that they were willing to turn from their idolatrous ways and worship Him as their rightful God, "who brought you [the Israelites] out of the land of Egypt!" (Exod. 22:8). But Moses not only wants a vote of confidence but also seeks the annihilation of all dissidents.

This serves his and God's purpose by wiping out the last vestiges of idolatry among the Israelites. That the faithful are spared reinforces God's message since the time of Adam and Eve: He is stern in punishing sinners, but He is also merciful in protecting those who redeem themselves.

Effectively, Moses's solution to the n-person PD—whereby D represents worship by the Israelites of the golden calf and C represents their return to the God of Israel—is to exclude the outcome in which some Israelites choose D and some choose C, by eliminating those who choose D. True, it is nowhere specified that if r Israelites choose C, C will be implemented. To prevent defections from this outcome, Moses deemed it necessary that those who chose D be decimated. This is a gruesome way to achieve consensus, but it is hardly unknown in recent times.

The solution worked, at least for a while. (The Israelites would become restive again.) However, I strongly recommend voting, without the sacrifice, as a more civilized way to resolve n-person PDs.

5.6   Other Difficult Games

The hypothetical example discussed in section 5.4 illustrates a public-goods or common-pool game (Ostrom, Gardner, and Walker 1994), in which there is a free-rider problem unless a mechanism like voting is introduced to transform the game into one that encourages cooperation. In the biblical example in section 5.5, no Israelite *alone* has an incentive to support Moses—knowing that his or her faith in God will not appease Moses or save the Israelites from the wrath of God—but if Moses can turn the game into a referendum on his leadership and rally a sufficient number to his cause to show their collective commitment, then he can snuff out idolatry, especially if those who refuse are eliminated. Note that this kind of commitment is public, whereas voting about the provision of public goods will generally be private.[8]

PD is only one of the fifty-seven distinct 2 × 2 ordinal *games of conflict,* in which there is no mutually best (4,4) outcome.[9] How many of these games can be transformed into more cooperative games through voting?

Define a *cooperative outcome* in a 2 × 2 ordinal game to be one in which each of the two players obtains either its best (4) or its next-best (3) outcome. Call the players' strategies associated with this outcome *cooperative strategies.* Call the other strategies *noncooperative strategies,* and the outcome associated with these the *noncooperative outcome.* A 2 × 2 ordinal game is *difficult* if it satisfies the following three conditions:

1. There is only one cooperative outcome.

---

8. The privacy of a voting booth is important, because voters might be under social pressure to vote differently if their votes were known. To be sure, this social pressure might be critical to the passage of certain kinds of legislation, such as that backed by a political party that can punish defectors who are revealed during a roll-call vote. Perhaps the support that Moses, who was a Levite, received from his fellow Levites was reinforced by the public nature of those rallying to his side. By contrast, the ringleaders on a ship who pledge in writing to participate in a mutiny are immediately identifiable, and subject to severe punishment, if they are discovered before the mutiny—and, worse, were the first to sign the pledge. The institutional solution that mutineers devised to prevent the discovery of the ringleaders was to write their names in a circle ("round robin"): Leeson 2010; see also Leeson 2009 and Crain 2009.

9. If games with (4,4) outcomes are included, there are twenty-one additional games, making for a total of seventy-eight distinct 2 × 2 ordinal games (Rapoport and Guyer 1966; Rapoport, Guyer, and Gordon 1976); see Robinson and Goforth 2005 for a further elaboration of these games and their properties. I exclude the games with (4,4) outcomes because these outcomes are the unique Pareto-optimal Nash equilibria in them, rendering (4,4) the likely outcome that players would choose without the need for voting. The one exception is a game variously referred to as Stag Hunt, Assurance, or Coordination (Skyrms 2004):

| (4,4) | (1,3) |
| (3,1) | (2,2) |

If either player in this game chooses its second strategy, it assures itself of a minimum of 2, whereas choosing its first strategy may lead to 1. Thus, a player's second strategy is, in a sense, less risky; its choice by both players yields (2,2), which is a second Nash equilibrium, albeit Pareto-inferior to (4,4).

Class 1 (four games)

					Prisoners' Dilemma			
1 (27)		**2 (28)**		**3 (32)**		**4 (48)**	
(3,4)	(1,2)	**(3,4)**	(1,3)	**(3,3)**	(1,4)	**(3,4)**	(1,1)
(4,1)	(2,3)	(4,1)	(2,2)	(4,1)	(2,2)	(4,2)	(2,3)

Class 2 (four games)

						Chicken	
5 (22)		**6 (35)**		**7 (50)**		**8 (57)**	
(3,3)	(2,4)	**(4,3)**	(2,4)	**(4,3)**	(2,4)	**(3,3)**	(2,4)
(4,1)	(1,2)	(3,1)	(1,2)	(3,2)	(1,1)	(4,2)	(1,1)

Class 3 (four games)

9 (29)		**10 (31)**		**11 (46)**	
(4,3)	(1,4)	**(4,3)**	(1,4)	**(3,4)**	(2,1)
(3,2)	(2,1)	(2,2)	(3,1)	(4,2)	(1,3)

Key: (x, y) = payoff ranking to (row, column)

4 = best; 3 = next-best; 2 = next-worst; 1 = worst

Nash equilibria underscored

Cooperative outcomes in boldface

Figure 5.4
Eleven difficult games

2. The cooperative outcome is not a Nash equilibrium, so at least one player has an incentive to defect from it.

3. The noncooperative outcome is Pareto-inferior to the cooperative outcome, so both players would prefer the cooperative outcome to it.

Obviously, a 2-person PD meets these conditions, but so do the ten other games shown in figure 5.4.[10] The eleven games, which constitute 19

10. Schelling 1978, chap. 7, offers a different classification of PD and non-PD games, using lines and curves on a graph. Still other classifications of the seventy-eight 2 × 2 ordinal games, which include the fifty-seven games of conflict and twenty-one games with a mutually best (4,4) outcome, are given in Rapoport and Guyer 1966, Rapoport, Guyer, and Gordon 1976, and Brams 1977; a topology of such games, and a new classification in a "periodic table," are developed in Robinson and Goforth 2005.

percent of all the 2×2 conflict games, can be broken down into three classes:

1. The Nash equilibria in four games, including PD, are the Pareto-inferior noncooperative outcomes. Either one or both (in the case of PD) players has a strongly dominant strategy associated with this equilibrium, and neither player has a dominant strategy associated with the cooperative outcome.

2. The Nash equilibia in three games, including Chicken (see section 9.5 for an application of this game), destabilize the cooperative outcome by inducing the player(s) receiving a payoff of 3 at the cooperative outcome to defect from it.

3. Three games have no Nash equilibria, with one player having an incentive to defect from each outcome, including the cooperative outcome.

Note that only PD and Chicken are *symmetric games*, in which the payoff ranks along the main diagonal are the same for each player and the payoff ranks along the off-diagonal are mirror images of each other.

Clearly, the cooperative outcome in all eleven games has a shaky status, because it is not a Nash equilibrium. But when these games are transformed into voting games in the manner we illustrated for PD, the cooperative outcomes take on a new status: Each becomes the unique Nash equilibrium, stabilized by the weakly dominant strategies that support it.

Unlike PD, I will not try to illustrate these games with examples. But it is worth noting that whether all players receive the same payoff of 3 at the cooperative outcome, or one set of players receives 3 and the other set receives 4 so their benefits differ (think of frequent and infrequent users of a public park), neither set has an incentive to defect from this outcome in the transformed voting game.

If this outcome does not receive at least r votes, its failure cannot be attributed to a public-goods or free-rider problem. Rather, it fails because more voters view the provision of the public good as detrimental—that is, they see the cooperative outcome as Pareto-inferior, not Pareto-superior, to the noncooperative outcome. Put another way, it is a public bad, presumably because of its cost, unworthy of the voters' support.

5.7 Summary and Conclusions

Democracy resolves conflict in difficult games like PD and Chicken by stabilizing their cooperative outcomes. It does so by transforming them into games in which voters are presented with a dichotomous choice between a cooperative outcome and a Pareto-inferior noncooperative outcome. In the transformed game, it is always rational for voters to vote for the cooperative outcome, because C is a weakly dominant strategy independent of the decision rule r and the number of voters who choose C.

Why, then, is the cooperative outcome not always selected, given that voters have no incentive to be free riders in the transformed game? The answer is that the public good may not be viewed by enough voters to be worth the cost of providing it. This explanation for the failure of cooperation—that a majority see the public good as, in fact, a public bad—is very different from the claim that free riders undercut the provision of public goods in a democracy. They do so only if enough voters view them as public bads.

What is "enough"? I suggested that simple-majority rule is more robust than qualified majority rule, because it is not so vulnerable to defectors who may, perhaps out of ignorance, fail to recognize what a majority see as a genuine public benefit.

Even charismatic leaders like Moses, whose brilliant defense of the Israelites—despite their serious lapses—persuaded God that some deserved a reprieve, cannot act alone. He succeeded by persuading the Levites, in a kind of referendum, to renounce their idolatry and, less defensibly, slaughter those who did not go along.

In a standard 2-person PD, it would be odd indeed to ask the players to vote on whether to select C and, if both do, implement the cooperative outcome. The difficulty of doing so—say, in an arms race—is that there may be no mechanism to enforce cooperation, even when both sides agree to it.

But when a government can credibly commit to providing a public good that a majority support (e.g., through taxes), the solution that democracy provides is compelling. However, in situations in which crime or corruption is rampant, or social capital or trust are lacking, voters will need assurances that procedures have been put in place that ensure that a cooperative outcome that a majority supports will actually be implemented. Thus, while the appeal of democracy is considerable in difficult games, questions about how, practically, to resolve conflicts and implement cooperative outcomes must also be answered.[11]

11. Beginning in the 1960s, the United States and the Soviet Union were able to reach limited arms-control agreements, because both sides could detect violations of these agreements with a sufficiently high probability (e.g., via satellite reconnaissance) and take appropriate countermeasures if a violation were detected. By and large, this deterred both superpowers from violating these agreements.

6   Law: Supreme Court Challenges and Jury Selection

6.1   Introduction

The three traditional branches of government in the United States—
the Presidency, the Congress, and the Supreme Court—have never
been entirely at ease with each other. The most persistent and rancor-
ous conflicts have been between the president and Congress, especially
when one or both of its two houses (the House of Representatives and
the Senate) are controlled by a different party from that of the
president.

The U.S. Constitution allows the president to veto bills passed by
Congress, but Congress can override a presidential veto by two-thirds
majority votes in both its houses. Consequences of these rules for the
distribution of power among the president, the House, and the Senate
are analyzed in Brams, Affuso, and Kilgour 1989. In this federal system,
the Supreme Court is also a significant player, because it can, by a simple-
majority vote, declare laws passed by Congress and signed by the president unconstitutional.

In this chapter, I begin by analyzing two games that were played
between the president and the Supreme Court, whose members the
president nominates and whose nominations must be ratified by the
Senate. More specifically, in section 6.2, I describe a game played between
President Richard M. Nixon and two of his appointees to the Supreme
Court, who clashed over the release of White House tape recordings
made during the Watergate crisis of 1974. In section 6.3, I show that
by threatening not to release the tapes describing an attempted cover-up
of a burglary that he had instigated, Nixon precipitated his own
downfall.

Nixon's threat was not the first time a president had challenged the Supreme Court's authority to interpret the laws and determine their constitutionality. However, his threat is the only one ever to lead to the resignation of a president. Earlier, President Franklin D. Roosevelt had vehemently disagreed with some of the rulings of the Supreme Court on the constitutionality of his New Deal legislation. In section 6.4, I describe how he attempted to "pack" the Court by appointing additional justices who would favor New Deal legislation, but his strategy backfired and he was forced to retreat.

Although both Nixon's and Roosevelt's challenges ultimately failed, the games these presidents played with the Supreme Court are quite different. In fact, I use different game theory models—noncooperative in the case of the Nixon, cooperative in the case of the Roosevelt—to explain these failures.

In both cases, I focus not on the Court as a single player but on specific members of the Court and the choices they made. In the case of the Roosevelt Court, I illustrate how the voting power of different ideological blocs on the Court can be measured.

In section 6.5, I develop a model in which the prosecution and defense, before the commencement of a trial, attempt to select a jury that they believe will be as favorable to their side as possible, based on a two-person constant-sum game (so that what is best for the prosecution is worst for the defense, and vice versa). Because the calculations are complex, however, I give only examples illustrating a player's optimal choices.

The analysis provides insight into the kinds of strategic calculations attorneys make in selecting a jury, which I illustrate with a well-known case in the 1970s. But the analysis also pinpoints a procedure that would make such calculations irrelevant and, I argue, would lead to more impartial juries. In section 6.6, I summarize the results and offer some thoughts on treating law as a subject in the humanities.

6.2 The White House Tapes Case

When Richard Nixon resigned his presidency on August 9, 1974, the most immediate cause was a decision in *United States v. Nixon*, handed down on July 24 by the Supreme Court, ordering him to release certain

White House tapes.[1] These were recordings of conversations relating to a break-in at the Watergate housing complex in Washington, DC, which had been planned in the White House, and the subsequent attempt to cover up this crime after it was discovered.

The Court unanimously ruled that Nixon must cease his efforts to withhold the tapes from Special Prosecutor Leon Jaworski in the so-called Watergate cover-up case. That same day the president, through his attorney, James St. Clair, announced his compliance with the ruling—he would release the White House tapes that the special prosecutor had sought.

Fifteen days later, the Nixon presidency ended in ruins, a direct result of the Court's action. This case is of special interest, because optimal strategies in the game played over the release of the tapes, as I reconstruct it, led to a paradoxical consequence—an outcome worse for both sides than a more "cooperative" outcome in the game—that seems to challenge the rationality of the players' choices.

The history of the White House tapes decision began on March 1, 1974, when a grand jury indicted seven former White House and campaign aides for attempting to cover up the Watergate burglary (*United States v. Mitchell et al.*). On April 16, the special prosecutor petitioned Judge John Sirica in the federal district court of the District of Columbia to subpoena tapes and documents of sixty-four presidential conversations Nixon had with advisors John Dean, Robert Haldeman, John Erlichman, and Charles Colson; Judge Sirica issued this subpoena on April 18.

The prosecutors moved quickly to prevent delay. On the day that an appeal by St. Clair was filed in the Court of Appeals, Leon Jaworski, using a seldom invoked procedure, went to the Supreme Court and sought a writ of *certiorari before judgment* that would leapfrog the appeals process. Citing the imminent cover-up trial date, Jaworski also noted the necessity to settle expeditiously an issue that was paralyzing the government. He requested the Court not only to issue the writ but also, because of the "imperative public importance" of the case, to stay in session into the summer (Lukas 1976, 495).

1. This and the next section are adapted from Brams and Muzzio 1977a, 1977b with permission; see also Muzzio 1982, chap. 3, and Brams 1985, chap. 7.

That way the case could be decided in sufficient time for the tapes to be used as evidence at the cover-up trial, should Judge Sirica's ruling be upheld. The Supreme Court agreed on May 31 and heard oral arguments on July 8.

When the Supreme Court justices went into conference on July 9, each of the eight justices who were to consider the case had basically two choices—decide for or decide against the president.[2] It appears from the record that six of the justices reached an early consensus against the president on all three of the major issues: (1) whether the Court had jurisdiction in the case—legal standing to sue—since Jaworski was an employee of the executive branch; (2) whether executive privilege was absolute; and (3) whether Jaworski had demonstrated a sufficient need for the subpoenaed materials.

Justices Warren E. Burger and Harry A. Blackmun, while concurring with the majority on limiting executive privilege, believed that the special prosecutor lacked standing to sue the president. For this reason, it appears, they voted originally against granting the case certiorari (Totenberg 1975).

Justices Burger and Blackmun are conceived of as one player. This is because it was almost axiomatic that Blackmun voted with Burger: In the first five terms (1970–1974) that Burger and Blackmun served together on the Court, they agreed on 602 of the 721 cases they both heard (83.5 percent), which was the highest agreement level of any pair of justices who served over these five terms.[3] They were referred to as the "Minnesota Twins" by the Supreme Court staff.

As deliberations proceeded, Burger and Blackmun had a choice of two strategies:

1. To decide for the president (F), forming a minority to create a 6–2 "weak" decision; or

---

2. Associate Justice William Rehnquist (who later became the chief justice) withdrew from the case, evidently because of his previous service in the Justice Department under Attorney General John Mitchell, though he never publicly stated a reason for disqualifying himself.

3. Data on case agreement can be found in the November issues of the *Harvard Law Review* (1971–1975). On the concurrence of Burger and Blackmun, see the *New York Times*, July 1, 1974, 10; and Totenberg 1975.

2. To decide against the president (A), joining the other six justices to create a unanimous decision.

President Nixon's possible response to an adverse Supreme Court ruling was long a matter of doubt—and one Burger and Blackmun could not afford to ignore. On July 16, 1973, White House Deputy Press Secretary Gerald Warren stated that President Nixon would abide by a "definitive decision of the highest court." Nixon, at a news conference on August 22, 1973, endorsed the Warren formulation, but neither he nor White House spokesmen would expand on the original statement (*New York Times*, July 22, 1974, 18; *Time*, July 22, 1974, 15–17). These statements were made in reference to the president's refusal to obey a subpoena from the first special prosecutor, Archibald Cox, for nine White House tapes.

That case never reached the Supreme Court. The Court of Appeals ruled against the president, who, after a delay of eleven days, agreed to submit the tapes, but not before he had dismissed Cox. The question of what "definitive" meant then became moot.

The issue arose again on May 24, 1974, when Cox's successor, Jaworski, filed his appeal with the Supreme Court. On July 9 St. Clair made it clear that the president was keeping open the "option" of defying the Court. The question of compliance, St. Clair stated, "has not yet been decided" (*New York Times*, July 10, 1974, 1).

Since the expectation at the time was that the Court would rule against the president (*Newsweek*, July 22, 1974, 18; *Time*, July 22, 1974, 15–17), President Nixon had two strategies:

1. Comply (C) with an adverse Court ruling; or

2. Defy (D) an adverse Court ruling.

Several factors help to explain President Nixon's refusal to make an unambiguous commitment concerning his response to a Court decision. If he stated that he would not comply, his statement might be used as a ground for impeachment. If he stated that he would comply, the House Judiciary Committee might argue that the president would either have to comply with its subpoenas, too, or be impeached (*New York Times*, July 10, 1974, 1).

More important, though, the president's refusal to assure his compliance with an adverse decision was designed to threaten the Court and lead the justices to render either a favorable decision or, at worst, an adverse, but closely divided, split decision that Nixon could claim was insufficiently "definitive" for a matter of this magnitude. Evans and Novak (1974, A29) noted at the time, "The refusal of St. Clair to say Nixon would obey an adverse decision has disturbed the judicial branch from the high court on down."

If the president's intent was to threaten the Court, the threat backfired. Why? To explain why Justices Burger and Blackmun departed from their apparent personal preferences and eventually sided with the Court majority, I next describe the game they and Nixon played.

The possible strategies of the two players (F and A for Burger and Blackmun; C and D for Nixon), and the probable outcomes and their rankings by the players, are shown in figure 6.1, starting from the upper left-hand cell and proceeding clockwise.

I. FC: Burger and Blackmun pleased, Nixon satisfied—(4,3) A constitutional crisis is averted and the majority-rule principle (to be described) is preserved; Nixon is not impeached for noncompliance.

		Nixon	
		Comply with Court (C)	Defy Court (D)
Burger and Blackmun	Decide for president (F)	I Burger and Blackmun pleased, Nixon satisfied (4,3)	II Burger and Blackmun dismayed, Nixon happy (1,4)
	Decide against president (A)	IV Burger and Blackmun satisied, Nixon unhappy (3,2)	III Burger and Blackmun unhappy, Nixon defeated (2,1)

Key: (x,y) = (payoff to Burger and Blackmun, payoff to Nixon)

4 = best; 3 = next-best; 2 = next-worst; 1 = worst

Figure 6.1
Payoff matrix of White House Tapes Game (game 27)

II. FD: Burger and Blackmun dismayed, Nixon happy—(1,4) A constitutional crisis ensues because of Nixon's defiance; Nixon is impeached by the House, but his conviction by the Senate is uncertain.

III. AD: Burger and Blackmun unhappy, Nixon defeated—(2,1) There is a constitutional crisis, but it is resolved by the impeachment and certain conviction of Nixon.

IV. AC: Burger and Blackmun satisfied, Nixon unhappy—(3,2) A constitutional crisis is averted, but the majority-rule principle is weakened; Nixon is not impeached for noncompliance but is forced to resign.

To justify these outcomes and their rankings, first consider the consequences associated with Nixon's defiance of an adverse Supreme Court ruling (AD). Unquestionably, if the president defied the Court, his defiance would represent a direct assault on the Supreme Court's constitutional place as the "principal source and final authority of constitutional interpretation" (Stephenson 1975, 292) and thereby threaten the very structure of the American political system.

Indeed, it seems highly probable that Nixon would have plunged the country into its deepest constitutional crisis since the Civil War. No previous president had ever explicitly defied an order of the Supreme Court, though such action had apparently been contemplated (Scigliano 1971, chap. 2).

At the time of the decision in *United States v. Nixon*, it appeared that the result of presidential defiance would be impeachment by the House on the ground of withholding evidence from the special prosecutor or violation of the principle of separation of powers. While the outcome of a trial in the Senate was less certain, a unanimous adverse decision (A) by the Court that included three conservative Nixon appointees (Burger, Blackmun, and Lewis F. Powell, Jr.) would preempt changes that the president was the victim of what presidential counselor Dean Burch called a "partisan lynch mob" (Lukas 1976, 510).[4] Pointedly, on the day of the decision, St. Clair warned the president that he would surely be

4. I do not include Powell as a Court player, because he originally favored granting certiorari; also, he "demonstrated the highest level of independence within the Nixon Bloc" and was described as "one of the least predictable of the eight and most flexible of the Nixon appointees" (*New York Times*, July 1, 1974, 10; *Time*, July 22, 1974, 16).

impeached and swiftly convicted if he were to defy the unanimous ruling of the Court (Ibid., 519).

Yet, Jaworski believed, "if the vote against [the president] was close he would go on television and tell the people that the presidency should not be impaired by a divided Court" (Jaworski 1976, 164). A "weak" decision from which at least some of the more conservative Nixon appointees dissented would also allow the president to continue his "one-third plus one" strategy in the Senate (FD) to avoid conviction and removal from office (by a two-thirds or greater majority).

Consider next the consequences associated with Nixon's compliance with an adverse Supreme Court decision (AC). Clearly, compliance would avert a constitutional crisis, and Nixon would thereby avoid immediate impeachment in the House for not complying with the Court. However, compliance posed problems for the president: He had reason to believe that the subpoenaed material, if released, would prove damaging and might even lead to his eventual impeachment by the House. In fact, upon hearing of the Court's decision, Nixon, who was at his San Clemente, California, home, telephoned White House Special Counsel Fred Buzhardt in Washington, saying, "There may be some problems with the June 23 tape" (*Washington Post*, September 9, 1974, A1).

Although the revelation of this tape ultimately forced his resignation, Nixon apparently did not fully realize at the time the incriminating nature of the recorded conversations. Woodward and Bernstein (1976, 176), on the one hand, report that Buzhardt felt that the tape was "devastating." Nixon, on the other hand, felt that Buzhardt was "overreacting," that it was "not that bad." Even as late as August 5, in his statement accompanying the public release of the tape transcripts, Nixon reflected his evaluation of the tape's impact: "I recognize that this additional material I am now furnishing may further damage my case . . . I am firmly convinced that the record, in its entirety, does not justify the extreme step of impeachment and removal from office" (*New York Times* staff 1974, 324).

Compliance—or, more accurately, the announcement of compliance— would allow the president to fall back on his long-used strategy of delay, though it would not necessarily remove the threat of impeachment and ultimate conviction, especially if the Court was unanimous in its judgment. For Justices Burger and Blackmun, who had voted originally against granting the case review, supporting and enlarging the majority (A), possibly against their convictions, to counter a presumed threat to the Court's authority might weaken the majority-rule principle that *any* majority is sufficient for a decision to have the force of law. But voting their convictions (F) would be hazardous should the president use a divided decision as a pretext to defy the Court.[5]

These conflicting considerations can be combined to yield the ranking of outcomes that I posited earlier. I start with President Nixon, who preferred the *risk* of conviction and removal to its virtual certainty. Thus, the president would prefer to defy a weak decision (outcome II in figure 6.1) than to defy a unanimous decision (outcome III), which I indicate by II ≻ III. For the same reason, Nixon would prefer to comply with any adverse decision (I or IV) than to defy a unanimous decision (III)—his worst outcome—so I, IV ≻ III.

Defying a weak decision (II) is considered preferable to complying with any adverse decision (I or IV), for such defiance would preclude the release of potentially devastating evidence and at the same time present Nixon with the possibility of avoiding conviction and removal for noncompliance; hence, II ≻ I, IV. Between the two compliance outcomes (I and IV), I assume that the president preferred to comply with a weak decision (I) than a unanimous decision (IV), so I ≻ IV.

A weak decision with some justices dissenting would leave the issue confused and subject to interpretation; it would also leave room to maneuver for partial compliance.[6] Putting the partial preference rankings together, the president's ranking of the four outcomes is II ≻ I ≻ IV ≻ III.

I next turn to the rankings of Burger and Blackmun. Although I suggested earlier that Burger and Blackmun would prefer to decide for the president on at least one of the strictly legal questions (standing to sue by the special prosecutor), there is no doubt the that the justices believed

5. This view is corroborated by H. R. Haldeman: "If the Supreme Court had handed down a [nonunanimous] majority decision, Nixon would have defied the Court and refused its order to turn over the tapes" (Haldeman and DiMona 1978, 310).

6. It can reasonably be argued that the president preferred to comply with a unanimous decision (IV) than a "nondefinitive" ruling that he had been threatening to ignore (I), so IV ≻ I. The reversal of the ranking of the two compliance outcomes leads to essentially the same results that I will subsequently describe, except that the Nash equilibrium becomes (3,3) rather than (3,2).

that compliance by the president with any adverse Court ruling (I or IV) would be preferable to defiance (II or III); hence, their partial ranking is I, IV $\succ$ II, III. Indeed, in the Court's opinion, which Burger wrote but which actually was drafted by the other justices (Schwartz 1996, 147; Woodward and Armstrong 1979, 340–341), the chief justice quoted Chief Justice John Marshall in *Marbury v. Madison* (1803): "It is emphatically the province and duty of the Judicial Department to say what the law is."[7]

It is plausible to assume that if the president complied, the justices would prefer to decide for him (I) rather than against him (IV); hence I $\succ$ IV. After all, the notion that the Court must be unanimous or close to it to make a decision credible, and thereby induce compliance, is an undesirable restriction of the Court's authority and might establish an unhealthy precedent.

Finally, I assume that the justices preferred that the president defy a unanimous decision (III) than a weak decision (II)—to which his chances of eventual success would be higher—so III $\succ$ II. Putting the partial preference rankings together, the justices' ranking of the four outcomes is I $\succ$ IV $\succ$ III $\succ$ II.

6.3 Analysis of the White House Tapes Game

Because the players in the White House tapes game did not make simultaneous choices in ignorance of each other, the payoff matrix in figure 6.1 is not an accurate representation of this game according to standard game theory (in note 8 I briefly comment on the application of TOM to this game). As in the Abraham-God game in section 2.2, however, the 2 × 2 game offers a convenient way to describe player preferences, even if it was not the game played.

In fact, Burger and Blackmun—and the rest of the Court—acted first. Only then did Nixon have to make a strategy choice, as shown in the 2 × 4 payoff matrix in figure 6.2, wherein Burger and Blackmun have two strategies whereas Nixon has four. This is because each of Nixon's two original strategies, comply (C) and defy (D), are contingent

---

7. *Marbury* is analyzed as a two-person game between President Thomas Jefferson and Chief Justice John Marshall in Clinton 1994.

Nixon

	Comply regardless: C if F, C if A	Defy regardless: D if F, D if A	Tit-for-tat: C if F, D if A	Tat-for-tit: D if F, C if A
Burger and Blackmun Decide for president (F)	(4,3)	(1,4)	(4,3)	(1,4)
Decide against president (A)	(3,2)	(2,1)	(2,1)	(3,2)

Dominant strategy

Key: *(x,y)* = (payoff to Burger and Blackmun, payoff to Nixon)

4 = best; 3 = next-best; 2 = next-worst; 1 = worst

Nash equilibrium underscored

Figure 6.2
Revised payoff matrix of White House Tapes Game

on what Burger and Blackmun decide: for (F) or against (A) the president.

In the figure 6.2 game, tat-for-tit is a weakly dominant strategy for Nixon. While Burger and Blackmun do not have a dominant strategy, they can anticipate Nixon's choice in a game of complete information. To maximize their payoff in the fourth column associated with Nixon's weakly dominant strategy, Burger and Blackmun would choose A, because they prefer (3,2) to (1,4).

As already indicated, the Supreme Court did decide unanimously against President Nixon. Nixon was reportedly shocked by the Court's ruling, feeling himself "sold out" by his three appointees, Chief Justice Burger and Associate Justices Blackmun and Powell. Charles Colson claimed that the president counted on all three justices. Others say he was certain only of Burger and Blackmun.

When he learned of the decision, Nixon used foul ("expletive-deleted") language to describe Burger. The president could not believe that the

Court's ruling had been unanimous. "Significantly, the President's greatest fury seems to have been directed not at the decision itself but at the three Justices who 'deserted' him" (Lukas 1976, 519).

In any event, the decision was unanimous, with no dissenting or concurring opinions. "It was the Court's seamless unity which made defiance so difficult" (Ibid.). Eight hours after the decision was handed down, the president, through St. Clair, announced his compliance with the decision "in all respects."

The game-theoretic analysis explains well, in terms of the foregoing reconstruction of the players' strategies and preferences for outcomes, why they acted as they did: (3,2) is the unique Nash equilibrium in the figure 6.2 matrix. Notice, however, that both players could have done better if they had chosen strategies associated with either of the two (4,3) outcomes in the 2 × 4 game.

Both of these Pareto-superior outcomes involve the choice by Burger and Blackmun of deciding for the president, and the choice by Nixon of compliance. The president can implement this Pareto-superior outcome by choosing either comply regardless or tit-for-tat.

Unfortunately for the players, however, neither of the outcomes that yield (4,3) is in equilibrium: Nixon in each case has an incentive to depart unilaterally from his strategies associated with (4,3) in order to bring about his best outcome, (1,4). Not only are the (4,3) outcomes not in equilibrium, but also Nixon's strategies associated with these outcomes are weakly dominated by his strategy of tat-for-tit.

For these reasons, therefore, it is hard to see how both players could have done better, even though the opportunity existed. Only if Burger and Blackmun had believed that their dissent would not trigger presidential defiance could they have voted their convictions with greater equanimity. The public record, however, shows that Burger and Blackmun never received any such assurance.

Quite the contrary: Nixon and his spokesmen, as indicated earlier, continually held out the possibility of defying a Supreme Court decision that was not "definitive." Thus, Burger and Blackmun had no choice—despite their disagreement with some arguments of the special prosecutor—but to decide against the president. Thereby the Supreme Court decision was rendered unanimous and both players in the White House tapes game lost out, in a sense, on greater payoffs that, at least in principle, were attainable.

The public probably gained from this outcome, however. If one identifies the public with the special prosecutor, then the game that the special prosecutor set up, though he himself was not a player, yielded the public, at (3,2), probably its best possible outcome of the four that were possible. This is certainly a reasonable inference from Jaworski's remarks immediately after the Court decision: "I feel right good over what happened. We can move ahead now. . . . I'm especially pleased it was a unanimous decision. It doesn't leave any doubt in anyone's mind" (*New York Times*, July 25, 1974, 22).

It is worth pointing out that a variety of bizarre motives (need to fail, death wish) and personality traits (self-destructive) have been attributed to Richard Nixon. The analysis here, however, suggests that his stance in the White House tapes case, which pushed his confrontation with the special prosecutor and then the Supreme Court beyond the point of no return, was not at all strange. Rather, Nixon was caught up in an intractable game—partly of his own making—that, perhaps with greater prescience, he could have avoided.[8]

After the Court rendered its verdict, Nixon gave an eminently sensible reason for resigning: "I no longer have a strong enough political base [to complete the term of office]" (*New York Times* staff 1974, vii). This rationale is as good as his reason for obeying the Supreme Court's

8. So how might the Pareto-superior (4,3) outcome have been induced? According to TOM (section 2.5), (4,3) is the unique nonmyopic equilibrium (NME) in the 2 × 2 game in figure 6.1, so wherever play starts, farsighted players would ultimately choose it. In addition, the exercise of moving power (section 3.4)—whichever player possesses it—reinforces the choice of (4,3). Finally, the exercise of threat power (to be discussed in section 7.2) by either player also leads to its choice. Perhaps the best TOM-based explanation of why (4,3) was *not* chosen is that Burger and Blackmun were not capable of threatening Nixon with the possibility of a unanimous decision before they had to decide, which complements the explanation given in the text—Burger and Blackmun's choice in the 2 × 4 game in figure 6.2 precedes Nixon's choice, so they cannot signal Nixon of their intent before acting. In retrospect, Nixon was foolish to threaten the Court with the possibility of defiance; anticipating this choice in the figure 6.1 game, Burger and Blackmun rationally responded by voting against the president, because they preferred (2,1) to (1,4). To be sure, had Nixon been more reassuring that he would comply with *any* Supreme Court decision, including a divided one, then he would have been in deep trouble if Burger and Blackmun had chosen F and made the decision 6–2. For then he would have had to backtrack on his promise to comply, which almost surely would have led to his impeachment and conviction. In short, Nixon was in a no-win situation, whatever he said about the Supreme Court's impending decision. A TOM analysis of the strategic interaction over several decades between the Israeli Supreme Court—a more powerful court than the U.S. Supreme Court—and the Knesset (the Israeli parliament) is given in Meydani and Mizrahi 2010.

edict—that he could not do better by defiance. Complex and enigmatic as Nixon was, he was, at root, a rational player.

6.4   The Roosevelt Court and the New Deal

Franklin D. Roosevelt was inaugurated as president on March 4, 1933.[9] Less than a year earlier, on March 14, 1932, Benjamin Cardozo had been sworn in as associate justice of the Supreme Court, which rounded out the group of justices that would preside over Roosevelt's first term as president.

Cardozo quickly allied with the Court's two liberal associate justices, Louis Brandeis and Harlan Stone. Together, this trio formed a bloc that would be almost completely unshakable for the next six years on a Supreme Court led by Chief Justice Charles Evans Hughes, a former governor of New York (1907–1910), associate justice of the Supreme Court (1910–1916), Republican presidential candidate (1916), and secretary of state (1921–1925).

On the opposite end of the Court's ideological spectrum was a conservative bloc of four associate justices, who were known as the Four Horsemen for their unmerciful attacks on President Roosevelt's New Deal legislation. This quartet comprised Willis Van Devanter, George Sutherland, Pierce Butler, and the infamously sour James McReynolds, the most implacable opponent of the New Deal and also a notorious anti-Semite (Shesol 2010, 102).

In the center of the spectrum, playing moderators between the two often-warring factions, was Hughes and the incomprehensibly unpredictable Associate Justice Owen Roberts. In effect, the Court had four independent players, the Trio, the Horsemen, Hughes, and Roberts.

As Roosevelt's New Deal legislation came before the Court, these players had to decide on the constitutionality of the progressive laws that had been passed by Roosevelt's Democratic Party-controlled Congress. In the rows of figure 6.3, I show all possible winning coalitions on the Supreme Court, with at least five members, who can rule on the constitutionality of these laws and so determine their fate.

---

9. I am grateful to Edward W. Larroca for giving me permission to adapt material from his student paper for this section.

	Player			
	Trio	Hughes	Roberts	Horsemen
Winning coalition				
Trio, Hughes, Roberts	×	×	×	
Trio, Horsemen	×			×
Trio, Hughes, Horsemen				×
Trio, Roberts, Horsemen				×
Trio, Hughes, Roberts, Horsemen				
Horsemen, Hughes		×		×
Horsemen, Roberts			×	×
Horsemen, Hughes, Roberts				×
Number of critical defections of player	2	2	2	6
Banzhaf power of player	1/6	1/6	1/6	1/2

Figure 6.3
Critical defections and Banzhaf power of players

In each row of figure 6.3, the ×s indicate the players who are *critical* in each coalition: By defecting from a winning coalition, each would cause it to be losing. For example, in the first row, if any one of the Trio, Hughes, or Roberts defected, the five-person winning coalition would be reduced to losing status. By contrast, in the fifth row, no defection of any player from the grand coalition of all the players would cause it to be losing.

Counting up the ×s in each column, and dividing by the total number of ×s of all the players (twelve), gives the percent of voting power of each player. This measure of relative power is called the *Banzhaf index* (Banzhaf 1965). It has been applied to many voting bodies with differently weighted players.[10]

10. For an overview of the Banzhaf and related power indices, their properties, and their applications, see Felsenthal and Machover 1998.

Figure 6.3 shows that the Horsemen, whose votes are critical in six of the eight winning coalitions, have 1/2 the voting power. Compared with the Trio—with only one less vote—the Horsemen have three times as much voting power (1/2 versus 1/6). In fact, the Trio has exactly the same voting power as each of the single moderates, Hughes and Roberts.

Does this index provide an accurate reflection of the distribution of power on the Court? The answer is no, because it supposes that all conceivable winning coalitions of the four players are equally likely, which was decidedly not the case.

In fact, the Trio *never* coalesced with the Horsemen, with or without the moderates, in cases that involved New Deal legislation. In the fifteen such cases that the Court heard between 1934 and 1937, none was decided by any of the coalitions that are crossed out in figure 6.4.

	Player			
	Trio	Hughes	Roberts	Horsemen
Winning coalition				
Trio, Hughes, Roberts	×	×	×	
~~Trio, Horsemen~~	×			×
~~Trio, Hughes, Horsemen~~				×
~~Trio, Roberts, Horsemen~~				×
~~Trio, Hughes, Roberts, Horsemen~~				
Horsemen, Hughes		×		×
Horsemen, Roberts			×	×
Horsemen, Hughes, Roberts				×
Number of critical defections of player	1	2	2	3
Banzhaf power of player	1/8	1/4	1/4	3/8

Figure 6.4
Critical defections and Banzhaf power of players with restriction

With these ×s eliminated, the distribution of voting power changes radically. While the Horsemen drop from 1/2 to 3/8 and the Trio from 1/6 to 1/8, Hughes and Roberts each go from 1/6 to 1/4, increasing their voting power by 50 percent. Astonishingly, each of the moderates is now twice as powerful as the Trio, even though the Trio has three times as many votes. Additionally, the sum of the Banzhaf powers of the two moderates (1/2) is greater than the Banzhaf power of the four Horsemen (3/8), which is also the power of moderates acting as a bloc.[11]

The power of the moderates derives from their being *swing* justices, each able to make the Horsemen winning and, together, being able to make the Trio winning. In fact, the Banzhaf attribution of power to the moderates, given the restriction on coalitions that can form, echoes well what happened on the Court. When the moderates became the decisive players, President Roosevelt bitterly complained at his weekly press conferences that the economic stability of the nation rode on the whims of Hughes and Roberts (McKenna 2002, 217).

From early 1934 until Roosevelt announced his Judiciary Reorganization Bill in 1937, the Court rendered ten divided cases, relating to the New Deal legislation, by margins of 5–4, 6–3, and 7–2. Roberts voted with the majority in every one—in fact, eight were decided by his vote—siding with the Trio five times and the Horsemen five times. He often articulated sweeping legal precedents in his opinions, sometimes voting against decisions that he had supported only months earlier.

Chief Justice Hughes was hardly more consistent. He voted with the Trio in all of the New Deal cases in 1934 and 1935, but then he ended up voting with the Horsemen in half of the nonunanimous cases of 1936 and the Trio in the other half.

By mid-1936, Roosevelt was infuriated at the see-sawing decisions of the Court. After winning a resounding victory for a second term on November 3, 1936—receiving 61 percent of the popular vote and more electoral votes than had ever been won in a presidential election—he decided to try to gain more decisive control over the erratic decisions of the Court.

---

11. Later in this section I show that if the moderates form their own bloc, their power is equal to that of the Trio and Horsemen combined, again assuming the latter two players cannot be members of the same winning coalition.

Emboldened by his election triumph, he announced his plan to "pack" the Supreme Court on February 5, 1937, soon after he was inaugurated. The Judiciary Reorganization Bill of 1937 (a.k.a "JRB" or "the court-packing plan") would allow the president to appoint a new Supreme Court justice, up to a maximum of six, whenever a current justice over the age of 70 had not retired.

For Roosevelt, this would mean the appointment of six new justices, increasing the size of the Court from nine to fifteen justices. A public outcry against Roosevelt's plan ensued, however, causing the defeat of JRB by 70–20 in a Senate vote on July 22, 1937. But the *threat* to pack the Court had, arguably, already compelled it "to assume a more liberal outlook" (Shesol 2010, 502).

In calculating Banzhaf voting power, so far I have assumed that Hughes and Roberts act independently. Would they do better if they formed a two-person moderate bloc (Duo) that always voted together— assuming they can vote either with the Trio or the Horsemen, but the Trio and Horsemen can never vote with each other?[12]

Now there are only two winning coalitions that are possible: (Duo, Horsemen) and (Duo, Trio). Because the Duo is critical in two and the Horsemen and Trio in one each, the Banzhaf power of Duo is 1/2 and of Horsemen and Trio 1/4 each. Paradoxically, this gives the smallest player power equal to the two larger players *combined*. Does this attribution reflect what actually happened?

It is instructive to look at both the goals and voting records of Hughes and Roberts. Hughes's primary goal was to maintain the integrity of the Supreme Court. He thought that the authority of the Supreme Court rested on its ability to act cohesively, and he hated handing down 5–4 decisions (Solomon 2009, 49). Voting based on his personal ideology was only a secondary consideration.

---

12. Schubert 1958 also treated Hughes and Roberts (whom he called "Hughberts") as a single player but used a different power index (that of Shapley and Shubik 1954) and made somewhat different assumptions about coalitional alignments that were feasible. He showed that each of the three blocs had approximately equal power, determined empirically, unlike the finding discussed next in the text that the Duo has the same power as Trio and Horsemen combined. For a review of this and other early applications of game theory to the Supreme Court, see Brenner 1980.

It is more difficult to ascertain Roberts's preferences. He liked to present himself as a man of the law and frequently based his vote on legal technicalities. At the same time, he claimed that he approached each case based on its merits and the facts. He said he did not vote along ideological lines, which is a claim that for a time seemed supported by his unpredictable voting record.

Roberts enjoyed spending his time away from Supreme Court work wandering the Capitol grounds, "chatting with the messengers and tourists" (Solomon 2009, 63). He refused to eat his lunch in the Senate cafeteria, dining instead in public places. He fancied himself a man of the people and their advocate on the Court.

After Roosevelt's landslide victory in 1936, Roberts believed that the people had spoken forcefully. Three months after the election, and a mere eight months after ruling a New York state minimum-wage law to be unconstitutional, Roberts reversed himself and voted to uphold a near identical Washington state minimum-wage law in *West Coast Hotel Co. v. Parrish* (1937), casting his vote before the court-packing plan was even announced (McKenna 2002, 418). In effect, Roberts realigned his jurisprudence with the opinion of the citizenry, at least as he interpreted it (Shesol 2010, 405–408, 412–415).

Between March and May of 1937, ten New Deal cases came before the Court, and the Court upheld the legislation's constitutionality in every one. Both Hughes and Roberts voted with the Trio in each, eight of which were decided by a 5–4 vote. In effect, the Trio turned into a New Deal Quintet. Thereby the divided Court swung decisively in favor of the liberals, mirroring the voting power that the Banzhaf index attributes to the moderate Duo when coalitions are restricted in the manner described.

The analysis of this section illustrates another application of cooperative game theory, which was introduced in chapter 4. As in the analysis of the fair division, the question is how to divide something of value (indivisible goods in the case of the fair-division application, voting power in the case of players of different weight). Unlike the earlier analysis, however, this chapter demonstrates how a theoretical model elucidates an empirical case instead of asking what theoretical properties are compatible and normatively desirable.

6.5   Jury Selection

There is probably no right more basic in the western legal tradition than that of trial by jury.[13] It is a right guaranteed by the U.S. Constitution in both civil and criminal cases, although the Constitution leaves undefined the procedure by which a jury is to be selected. Nevertheless, the right of the defense and prosecution to challenge prospective jurors—called *venirepersons* (*venire* is Latin for "to come"), who are summoned to jury duty—has a long history in criminal law, going back at least to Roman tribunals (Abraham 1975, 116).

In the United States, challenges exercised in the selection of a jury are of two types, *for cause* and *peremptory*. In the case of the former, the challenger must advance a bona fide reason why a venireperson is unacceptable, and therefore should be disqualified from service by the court, because of bias, prejudice, or other involvement in the substantive or procedural aspects of the litigation that could affect his or her judgment in reaching a verdict. Because there are no limits on the number of challenges for cause, this type of challenge raises no strategic questions of timing.

In *Swain v. Alabama* (1965), the Supreme Court considered whether peremptory challenges by the prosecution could be used to exclude all blacks from a jury. Upholding peremptories as an absolute and unchallengeable right, the Court said, in a 6–3 decision written by Associate Justice Byron White, that "the function of the [peremptory] challenge is not only to eliminate extremes of partiality on both sides, but to assure the parties the that jurors selected before whom they try the case will decide on the evidence placed before them, and not otherwise."

One implication of this statement is that an impartial jury is one in which the "extremes of partiality" have been eliminated on both sides insofar as possible. Given this interpretation, define the *partiality* of a venireperson as his or her probability of voting for conviction in a criminal trial before hearing the evidence. That is, before the trial commences

---

13. This section is adapted from Brams and Davis 1976, 1978 with permission; a very similar model of jury selection was developed independently by Roth, Kadane, and DeGroot 1977. Related models of sequential selection are analyzed and compared in Alpern, Gal, and Solan 2010 and citations therein.

and evidence is presented, assume that each venireperson can be assigned a probability of voting for conviction. Then define, consistent with the Supreme Court ruling, an *impartial jury* to be one in which those venirepersons with the highest and lowest probabilities are peremptorily challenged by defense and prosecution—assuming excusals for cause have already been rendered—leaving a jury whose members have probabilities in some middle range.

For most jury-selection procedures presently in use, there is no way that the defense and prosecution can exercise their peremptories so as to ensure that one venireperson, selected as a juror, has a less extreme probability than another one not selected to serve. This is because under all procedures except the "struck jury system," peremptories are exercised by each side over time. As the selection process proceeds, one cannot know for sure who the most extreme venirepersons will be and challenge only them.

Jury selection is very different under the *struck jury system*, wherein peremptory challenges are exercised just once after the examination of a panel of venirepersons equal in size to the sum of the number of jurors to hear the case plus the number of peremptory challenges each side is allowed. In fact, only under this system can one assuredly eliminate all venirepersons—up to the limit of one's peremptories—whom one views to be least favorably disposed to one's side. Since one does not have to worry that one will let pass a more extreme venireperson—or challenge a less extreme venireperson—who appears later in the sequence, the most extreme venirpersons can be removed in one fell swoop. If neither side challenges the same venireperson, a jury of requisite size will be chosen.

But what if challenges are sequential, and the prosecution or defense attorneys must decide, immediately after the questioning of a venireperson in the so-called voir dire—literally, "to speak the truth"—whether or not to challenge him or her?[14] This decision cannot be made lightly, because attorneys have a limited number of peremptory challenges to exercise.

More specifically, federal law provides for twenty challenges when the punishment may be death, ten for other felonies, and three for

---

14. While I will speak of "prosecution" in the subsequent discussion, one can substitute "plaintiff" for the side that initiates the case if the trial is civil.

misdemeanors. Statutes in most states provide for a similar distribution, depending on the seriousness of the alleged crime, with no state providing for less than two or more than thirty peremptory challenges. In civil trials, the number of peremptories allotted to each side is generally less than in criminal trials (McCart 1965, 33).

In the *jury-selection game*, each venireperson comes up one at a time for consideration after the voir dire. I assume that both sides agree on his or her probability of voting for conviction, which may vary between a low of 0 and a high of 1. At least for the most extreme venirepersons with very low or very high probabilities, it is reasonable to assume that a venireperson the defense considers most favorable (low probability of convicting) the prosecution will view as most favorable (high probability of convicting), and vice versa.

This view of the game receives support from a report by social scientists working for the defense in the "political" trial of the Harrisburg Seven in 1972 (Schulman et al. 1973). The jury-selection procedure used in this trial was that of panel challenges, whereby a panel of venirepersons was first chosen before peremptory challenges were exercised to reduce it to a jury of twelve members; hence, the one-at-a time assumption is inapplicable. Nonetheless, it is noteworthy that the prosecution applied all six of its peremptory challenges to the eight members of the forty-six-member panel that the defense rated 1 (best) on a five-point scale, thereby eliminating all except two of the defense's choices. If challenges had been exercised randomly by the prosecution against the forty-six-member panel, the chance that it would apply all its peremptories to the defense's eight best choices is less than one chance in 300,000 (Brams and Davis 1978, 976).

A second assumption of the jury-selection game is that both sides know how the probabilities of voting for conviction are distributed in the population from which venirepersons are chosen. They know, for example, whether most venirepersons have low probabilities, high probabilities, or are evenly distributed across the spectrum.

Indeed, in the Harrisburg Seven trial, the defense made a major effort before the start of the trial to survey the community from which the jurors would be drawn and learn something about its attitudes relevant to the defense's case, as well as their correlation with certain demographic factors like age, education, and occupation. This enabled the defense to compare venirepersons against the statistical profile of a favorable juror.

Michael J. Saks (1976, 15), a skeptic of such selection procedures for weeding out unfavorable jurors, argues that "trial evidence is and always has been a far more important determinant of the verdict than who sits on the jury." However, he admits that "if the evidence is close, then scientific jury selection could make the difference," adding that

when the same information is available to a human decisionmaker and a mathematical model, almost without exception the mathematical model makes more reliable predictions. After sixty studies comparing clinical versus statistical prediction, the human beat the computer only once. (Ibid.)

A third assumption of the game is that the venirepersons selected as jurors will independently reach a verdict according to their probabilities of voting for conviction. This assumption, of course, ignores the twin effects of evidence presented in the trial and jurors' influencing each other in their deliberations in the jury room. These effects notwithstanding, the model does give insight into the selection of a jury *before* the start of a trial, which is important if its composition is likely to influence the outcome.

Insofar as this is true, the selection of an "impartial jury" thus becomes an exercise in rejecting the most partial jurors—as scientifically as possible—rather than a high-minded attempt to define and choose fair and impartial jurors. Jurors are selected because they are viewed as favorable to one's case, not because they are considered paragons of fairness.

The forgoing assumptions of the jury-selection game allow one to calculate recursively the threshold probabilities of conviction above which the defense should challenge and below which the prosecution should challenge a venireperson at each point in the selection of a jury. To illustrate how the results of this calculation can be applied, assume that the probabilities of voting for conviction in the population of venirepersons from which jurors are chosen are uniformly distributed: Venirepersons who come up for examination are equally likely to have low, moderate, or high probabilities of voting for conviction.

Assume also that the defense and prosecution each have ten peremptories, and a jury of twelve members is to be chosen that must reach a unanimous decision. At the beginning of the game, when no jurors have yet been chosen, the model prescribes that the defense should challenge a venireperson if he or she has an a priori probability of voting for conviction greater than 0.742, and the prosecution should challenge a venireperson if he or she has an a priori probability of less than 0.407.

Thus, the defense should choose a more "conservative" strategy by challenging venirepersons closer to its extreme of 1 (over the smaller range of 0.742 to 1.000) than the prosecution should by challenging venirepersons farther from its extreme of 0 (over the larger of range of 0 to 0.407). Intuitively, the defense can afford to be more conservative in eliminating venirepersons, because it needs only one vote to prevent conviction of the defendant.

What are the optimal strategies of both players near the end of such a game? Assume eleven jurors have already been chosen, and each side has just one peremptory challenge remaining. Then the defense should now challenge a venireperson with a probability greater than 0.625, and the prosecution should challenge a venireperson with a probability less than 0.375. Thus, the defense should now move farther from its extreme of 1 than previously, and the prosecution should move closer to its extreme of 0, so that now both sides challenge an equal distance from their extremes of 1 and 0.

Similar examples of optimal strategies can be calculated for any stage in the jury-selection game. The two sides need not have equal numbers of peremptories remaining—nor start with equal numbers—nor does the jury have to comprise twelve members. Neither does one need to assume that the probabilities of venirepersons are uniformly distributed; they could, for example, be concentrated in the middle near 0.5, according to a bell-shaped curve, or be skewed negatively (more concentrated on the right toward the prosecution) or positively (more concentrated on the left toward the defense).

The strategies that I have illustrated are optimal in the sense that they minimize for the defense, and maximize for the prosecution, the expected probability of conviction in a two-person constant-sum game between prosecution and defense. Given the assumptions of the model, if either side deviates from these optimal strategies, it will be hurt if the other side plays optimally, rendering these strategies a Nash equilibrium.

The model can be modified to take account of challenges to panels of members. If, for example a panel of twelve venirepersons is first examined before each side can peremptorily challenge any of its members, and those challenged are replaced—and so on, until a jury of twelve unchallenged members is chosen—optimal strategies can be derived, but they are more complicated than those described earlier. Specifically, they are mixed rather than pure strategies, which is to say that both sides must make random choices to hide from the other side exactly whom they challenge at each stage in the game (though this information would become known at the next stage).

It is not necessary to model all extant peremptory-challenge procedures that occur in stages, and derive optimal challenge strategies for each, to prove that they cannot ensure an impartial jury. As I indicated earlier, any procedure that requires that challenges be made sequentially, rather than all at once, allows for the possible selection of more extreme venirepersons than those who are challenged and thereby removed.

One can illustrate this point with the earlier example. Suppose that a venireperson with a probability less than 0.375 comes up near the end of the game, when eleven jurors have already been chosen and each side has one peremptory remaining, so the model prescribes that he or she be rejected by the prosecution. Now since the prosecution has no peremptories remaining after challenging this venireperson, it must accept the next venireperson to come up (if the defense does), even if he or she has a probability of 0 of voting for conviction. Clearly, choosing optimal strategies in the game does not guarantee that the "extremes of partiality," in Justice White's words, will always be eliminated.

The reason for constructing the jury-selection model is that it enables one to establish a challenge threshold as optimal, even in the face of uncertainty. Not knowing who will come up next, but only the distribution from which he or she will be chosen, it tells the prosecution in the foregoing example that it will do worse, on average, by choosing a challenge threshold other than 0.375. It is this threshold, and only this threshold, that maximizes the jury's expected probability of voting for conviction at the particular stage in the game described. But even adopting optimal strategies, the defense and prosecution may not succeed in obtaining impartial juries—as judged by the "extremes of partiality" criterion—

because what is best on average may not be best, ex post facto, in a particular case.

Because trial lawyers must play averages in an uncertain world, the optimal challenge threshold given by the model may be useful, given that its assumptions reasonably approximate actual jury-selection procedures. But the strategic calculations raise a more fundamental question than that of what strategy is best. Because what is best depends on the rules, the question of whether different rules might better enable both sides to eliminate the extremes, and thereby obtain a more impartial jury, is also important to consider.

As I showed earlier, there is no way to guarantee the elimination of these extremes unless peremptories are exercised against all venirepersons at once under a struck jury system. Arguably, this system should replace all other procedures currently governing the exercise of peremptory challenges in trials today. This reform would shift the question of *when and whom* to challenge at each stage to, more simply, *whom* to challenge in a single stage.

Such a reform seems amply justified by the constitutional guarantee of an "impartial jury" explicitly provided for by the Sixth Amendment "in all criminal prosecutions." Even in civil cases covered by the Seventh Amendment, in which the word *impartial* is not used, the language ("the right of trial by jury shall be preserved . . . according to the rules of the common law") conveys, at least implicitly, the spirit of impartiality.

I conclude that all peremptory-challenge procedures except the struck jury system are well supported by both the Constitution and the Supreme Court's interpretation of what constitutes an impartial jury. In fact, the cause of equal justice under the law is best served by a procedure that renders strategic calculations irrelevant and hence affords no advantage to the better strategist. There is no constitutional justification, or other legal basis of which I am aware, for retaining jury-selection procedures that encourage strategic calculations and choices that, even if optimal, may distort the selection of an impartial jury.

6.6 Summary and Conclusions

This chapter has progressively gone back in time. I began with a 1974 presidential challenge to the authority of the Supreme Court that did not, in the end, materialize. I then moved back to a 1937 presidential challenge that also failed. I concluded by exploring how an impartial jury, a notion that is embodied in the U.S. Constitution that was ratified in 1789, could be achieved.

The conflicts between Presidents Nixon and Roosevelt and their Supreme Courts have the drama of a novel; the protagonists make calculations, sometimes flawed, which game theory helps to explicate. Game theory also helps to illuminate the calculations that prosecution and defense make in the selection of an impartial jury and identifies the procedure that would best lead to this ideal.

Richard Nixon, by implicitly threatening not to abide by a decision of the Supreme Court if it were not definitive, was thwarted in his attempt to save his presidency. His threat caused two of his Supreme Court appointees, who thought Nixon had grounds to withhold the tapes, to coalesce with the majority—who were disposed to order the release of the tapes—in order to put up a united front that Nixon would not be able to defy. After the tapes incriminated Nixon in a scheme to cover up a crime, he was forced to resign, though he was later pardoned by President Gerald R. Ford, his vice president who succeeded to the presidency.

Franklin Roosevelt was similarly thwarted by a Supreme Court that was not always willing to uphold his New Deal legislation. In this conflict, the game theory analysis shows how the two members of the Court who could decide which way the Court swung had their power greatly enhanced.

Insofar as these justices acted as a bloc, they had as much power as the other seven justices combined (three liberals, four conservatives), which vividly illustrates how the voting power of blocs, at least as measured by the Banzhaf index, may have little relationship to the numbers of votes controlled by the blocs. As the analysis showed, the ability of players to change outcomes is also a function of where these blocs are situated on the ideological spectrum and, therefore, with which other blocs they will coalesce to form a majority.

The selection of juries has long seemed more an art than a science. Beginning with political trials of dissidents in the 1970s, however, jury selection became more scientific. A game theory model shows, given that both sides can judge the favorableness of prospective jurors, how one can determine thresholds that indicate when these venirepersons should be accepted or challenged.

These calculations are not surefire, however, if one must make them sequentially. Consequently, I argued for a struck jury system, in which such calculations are rendered irrelevant because the peremptory challenges are exercised all at once.

To conclude this chapter, it is worth asking whether law can properly be classified as a humanities discipline. After all, one finds only a scattering of law-related courses taught in humanities fields like history or philosophy. Like medicine, law is first and foremost a profession, taught in law schools.

The inclusion of law in this book is justified, in my view, by the fact that the players in law-related games make fundamentally human choices. Emotions, especially anger, which I analyze more formally in later chapters, are front and center in the Nixon and Roosevelt games. And while I show that jury selection can be mathematized to a degree, the input to the game theory model requires human judgments about the leanings of prospective jurors, which cannot so easily be mathematized.

In short, law is built on the strategic choices made by people in real-life situations; they are not intrinsically different from the cast of characters who populate novels and plays, which Posner (1998) explicates with many examples from the literary canon. Like their fictional counterparts, real characters, when constrained by laws, play games. They just do so more in the shadow of the law than their fictional counterparts.[15]

---

15. Law serves as background to the situations described in Kaminski 2004, whose author demonstrates, using game theory, how criminals incarcerated in Polish prisons strategize.

7 Plays: Modeling Frustration and Anger

7.1 Introduction

Emotions, such as anger, jealousy, or love, are spontaneous feelings that practically all of us experience at one time or another.[1] Although there may be good reasons for us to be angry, jealous, or fall in love, these feelings, especially when they overtake us suddenly, seem not to be the product of rational calculation. Rather, they overpower us, so to speak, which seems the antithesis of the careful means-ends analysis that we normally associate with rational choice. Indeed, Gelernter (1994, 29) argues that "you cannot choose your emotions. Emotions choose themselves," suggesting that emotions have no rational basis.[2] (I rule out emotions that are feigned, which some have called instrumental emotions because they are consciously chosen as an instrument to achieve a particular end.)

In a spate of books and articles, however, scholars from several disciplines have argued that expressing emotions is compatible with acting

---

1. This chapter is adapted from Brams 1997a with permission.

2. Gelernter (1994, 27–28) defines an emotion to be "a mental state with physical correlates; it is a *felt* state of mind, where 'felt' means that signals reach the brain that are interpreted as bodily sensations," creating an "affect link" to thought. Recent research, however, challenges "bodily states as the central feature of emotions" (Parrott and Harré 1996, 14), arguing instead that emotions have strong cultural and social, as well as biological, roots. In the later formal analysis, I show how emotions enable a person to move to an inferior state, if only temporarily, in order to effect a better final state, thereby rendering them rational "expressions of judgement" (Ibid., 1). At a macro level, Ackerlof and Shiller (2009) argue that psychological forces ("animal spirits") influence the behavior of the economy as a whole, but here I focus on the role that emotions play at the individual level.

rationally.[3] Our goals, according to some of these analysts, are not always the narrow ones postulated by economic theory but broader, if somewhat inchoate and ineffable, ends (e.g., about living meaningful lives). Moreover, we are often passionate in our pursuit of these ends, which may undermine the achievement of more commonplace goals, such as ensuring our personal safety or economic security.

How can we explain these passions, and the sudden welling up of emotions that, by one definition, "occur when we perceive positive or negative significant changes in our personal situation" (Ben-Ze'ev 2000, 13)? In this chapter I focus on the negative emotion of *frustration*, which arises from being "prevent[ed] from accomplishing a purpose or fulfilling a desire" (*American Heritage Dictionary* 1980). Although frustration may arise from impersonal forces (e.g., the weather) and not the actions of others, it is often aggravated by a "freely acting agent" (Frijda 1986, 198) who blocks one's preferred choices.

It is these interpersonal situations of frustration that I analyze here. I hypothesize that *people become frustrated when they are in an unsatisfying situation and feel unable to escape it because of the control of others.* This lack of control is especially bothersome when those who could help a person improve his or her situation express no interest in doing so.

Put another way, when a person cannot help himself or herself but must depend on the actions of others who choose not to be helpful, this person will tend to react emotionally, becoming aroused. Feeling hemmed in, without room to maneuver, he or she explodes in *anger*—the most common behavioral response to frustration—to try to escape. Typically, a person's escape involves redressing some perceived but, in his or her eyes, undeserved harm or offense.

One might reasonably argue that anger is the emotion being described, not the frustration that gives rise to it and may be unobservable (though it is likely to have physiological indicators). However, because I will be

3. Economists and game theorists include Hirshleifer 1987, 1994, 2000; Frank 1988; Gilboa and Schmeidler 1988; Geanakoplos, Pearce, and Stacchetti 1989; Huang and Wu 1992; Rabin 1993; Howard et al. 1993; and Howard 1994. Philosophers include de Sousa 1987; Solomon 1993; Ben-Ze'ev 2000; and Ledwig 2006. Other analysts who have discussed the tie-in of emotions to rational choice include a political scientist (Elster 1991, 1994, 1999, 2007, 2009), sociologists and other social scientists (*Emotions and Rational Choice*, 1993), a neurologist (Damasio 1994, 1999), and literary theorists (Livingston 2001; Fisher 2002).

analyzing interpersonal situations that cause frustration, I find it convenient to use "frustration" as a shorthand for "frustration and the anger it evokes."

Psychological theories of frustration and other emotions say little, if anything, about a situation's *structural features* that incite people to become emotional. By contrast, game theory provides powerful tools for identifying situations in which people experience a lack of control—and those in which they can regain it.[4] Expressing an emotion like anger in such a situation is rational if there is good reason to believe it might provide relief, if not rectify, the trying circumstances one experiences.

As in earlier chapters, I analyze ordinal games in which there are two players, each of whom has two strategies. But unlike earlier chapters, I begin by defining 2×2 "generic games," which are games based on partial orderings of the players' preferences. These games comprise several specific games, wherein the players have complete or strict orderings.

In one generic game, I analyze the frustration of a player, whereas in the other I analyze what I call the self-frustration of a player. To illustrate these emotions, I use specific games within each category to model the choices of characters in two plays.

Although there are seventy-eight distinct 2×2 ordinal games (for listings, see Rapoport and Guyer 1966, 1972; Brams 1976; Robinson and Goforth 2005), twenty-one are games in which there is a mutually best outcome, which are unlikely to create frustration for the players. Of the remaining fifty-seven games, which I call *conflict games*, I distinguish two classes, the first of which subsumes twelve frustration games and the second of which subsumes six self-frustration games. Altogether, there are seventeen different games (one game is common to both classes), which is 30 percent of all conflict games.

In the generic Frustration Game, a player's lack of control takes the form of an "advantaged" player's having a dominant strategy that inflicts

---

4. Here I am concerned with emotions that arise in interpersonal situations rather than "existential" (Lazarus and Lazarus 1994, 41–66), "self-conscious" (Lewis 1995), or "moral" (Wollheim 1999, 148–224) emotions, such as anxiety, guilt, remorse, or shame. These emotions, which concern the way we see ourselves, are often independent of the actions of others in a game (though not in *Macbeth*, as discussed in section 7.5). Anger, by contrast, is usually directed at someone.

the two worst outcomes on the frustrated player. In the generic Self-Frustration Game, it is the self-frustrated player who has the dominant strategy; the advantaged player does not, but this player's best response to the self-frustrated player's dominant strategy induces the self-frustrated player's next-worst outcome.

I next consider whether, by applying the theory of moves (TOM) (introduced in sections 2.4 and 6.3), there is any escape from the inferior states that the frustrated and self-frustrated players experience at the outset. It turns out that if the frustrated player has threat power (briefly described in section 2.4), then he or she can induce a better outcome with a deterrent threat in four of the twelve frustration games.

The situation is better for the self-frustrated player in the six self-frustration games. While threat power is effective in these games, the self-frustrated player can always induce a preferred outcome for himself or herself, and sometimes for the other player as well, without resorting to the exercise of such power. This preferred outcome is a nonmyopic equilibrium (NME), which, as described in section 2.5, requires that the players think ahead about the consequences of their moves and countermoves.

The two plays that I use to illustrate the role that emotions play in specific frustration and self-frustration games each has strong political overtones. *Lysistrata,* Aristophanes's most popular play, describes how women in ancient Greece, bitterly frustrated when their men go off to war—leaving them lonely and with little support for their children—are moved to use abstinence from sex as a weapon to induce the men to stop fighting. In *Macbeth*, Shakespeare describes how Lady Macbeth, seething at Macbeth's initial hesitation to seek his prophesied royal destiny, flies into a rage and belittles Macbeth's manhood, which incites him to murder King Duncan.

In both games, the frustrated and self-frustrated players, dissatisfied at the start, actually move to still worse states when they explode in anger. Their rage bursts forth *along the path to an NME*; once there, matters stabilize, and the frustrated player is appeased if not triumphant. More generally, I identify conditions in the generic Frustration and Self-Frustration Games when it is rational for the frustrated and self-frustrated players to express "vehement emotions" (Fisher 2002), including anger.

I emphasize the *dynamic process* by which a stable outcome is achieved, rather than the outcome itself, because once a game has stabilized at an NME, emotions subside. Although emotions may be feigned, I take them to be genuine in the analysis that follows. This is plausible in games in which players have little recourse but to escalate a conflict suddenly in order to try to escape their frustration and seek relief.

7.2   The Frustration Game

The generic Frustration Game, which is shown at the top of figure 7.1, is a 2×2 game in which the row player, Advantaged (A), has two strategies, s_1 and s_2, and the column player, Frustrated (F), also has two strategies, t_1 and t_2. The ordinal payoffs to the players at the resulting four possible outcomes are given by ordered pairs (x_{ij}, y_{ij}), where x_{ij} is the payoff to A and y_{ij} the payoff to F, when A chooses strategy s_i and F chooses strategy t_j $(i, j = 1$ or $2)$.

"Advantaged" does not mean that A has any special prerogatives or privileges. As I will show, A (assumed to be male) always does at least as well and generally better than F (assumed to be female)—in terms of the players' comparative rankings of payoffs—in part because A has a dominant strategy. Associated with his dominant strategy is a Nash equilibrium, which in a 2×2 ordinal game with such a strategy is unique (Hamilton and Slutsky 1993, 50, Lemma 1).

F, who may or may not have a dominant strategy, is "frustrated": Her two worst outcomes are associated with A's dominant strategy, which A would presumably choose.[5] By contrast, with one exception A never suffers his two worst outcomes when F chooses a dominant strategy (if she has one), rendering A's position distinctly advantageous.

More formally, the Frustration Game satisfies the following three conditions:

1. *Dominance for A*   Without loss of generality, assume that s_1 is A's dominant strategy, so

---

5. I will discuss shortly under what circumstances A would *not* choose his dominant strategy, enabling F to escape her lack of control in this game.

Generic game

Frustrated (F)

	t_1	t_2
s_1	(x_{11}, y_{11})	(x_{12}, y_{12})
	2	1
s_2	(x_{21}, y_{21})	(x_{22}, y_{22})

Advantaged (A)

←

Dominant strategy
$(x_{11} > x_{21}$ and $x_{12} > x_{22})$
containing two worst
outcomes of F (1 and 2)

Twelve specific games subsumed by generic game

Class I (eight games): no relief for F from Nash equilibrium of (x_{11}, y_{11})

5	6	10	11
(4,2) (3,1)	(4,2) (3,1)	(3,2) (4,1)	(3,2) (4,1)
(2,4) (1,3)	(1,4) (2,3)	(2,4) (1,3)	(1,4) (2,3)
↑	↑	↑	↑

18	19	25	26
(4,2) (3,1)	(4,2) (3,1)	(3,2) (4,1)	(3,2) (4,1)
(2,3) (1,4)	(1,3) (2,4)	(2,3) (1,4)	(1,3) (2,4)

Class II (four games): relief for F through the exercise of deterrent threat power

22	28	32	35
(4,2) (2,1)	(2,2) (4,1)	(2,2) (4,1)	(4,2) (2,1)
$(3,3)^t$ (1,4)	(1,3) $(3,4)^{t*}$	(1,4) $(3,3)^{t*}$	$(3,4)^t$ (1,3)
	↑	↑	

Key: (x,y) = (payoff to A, payoff to F)

4= best; 3 = next-best; 2 = next-worst; 1 = worst

Nash equilibrium underscored

t/t^* = deterrent threat outcome of F/both players

↑ = dominant strategy for F

Figure 7.1
Frustration Game

$$x_{11} > x_{21}; \quad x_{12} > x_{22}. \tag{7.1}$$

That is, whichever strategy F chooses (t_1 or t_2), A prefers his payoffs associated with s_1 to those associated with s_2, making s_1 his unconditionally better strategy.

2. *Nash equilibrium* Without loss of generality, assume that (x_{11}, y_{11}) is the unique Nash equilibrium that is associated with A's dominant strategy of s_1, so

$$y_{11} > y_{12}. \tag{7.2}$$

That is, F prefers her payoff at (x_{11}, y_{11}) to that which she would receive at (x_{12}, y_{12}) if she switched from t_1 to t_2. Similarly, A prefers (x_{11}, y_{11}) to (x_{21}, y_{21})—and so would not switch from s_1 to s_2—because of the dominance of s_1, assumed in inequalities 7.1.

3. *Lack of control* To state this condition, assume, as in the games in previous chapters, that 4 is the best payoff to a player, 3 the next best, 2 the next worst, and 1 the worst. F's lack of control, and consequent frustration, stem from her two worst outcomes (1 and 2) being associated with A's dominant strategy of s_1. From inequality 7.2 it follows that

$$y_{11} = 2; \quad y_{12} = 1.$$

Depending on whether $y_{21} = 3$ and $y_{22} = 4$, or $y_{21} = 4$ and $y_{22} = 3$, F may have two different complete orderings of her payoffs.

On the other hand, the dominance of s_1 for A, as given by inequalities 7.1 that define a partial ordering of his payoffs, admits six different complete orderings:

$$x_{11} > x_{21} > x_{12} > x_{22}; \quad x_{12} > x_{22} > x_{11} > x_{21};$$
$$x_{11} > x_{12} > x_{22} > x_{21}; \quad x_{12} > x_{11} > x_{21} > x_{22};$$
$$x_{11} > x_{12} > x_{21} > x_{22}; \quad x_{12} > x_{11} > x_{22} > x_{21}.$$

The two payoff orderings of F, and the six payoff orderings of A, define a total of twelve specific games, which are shown in figure 7.1.

These games, which are instances of the *generic* Frustration Game, all satisfy the aforementioned conditions 7.1–7.3. I summarize properties of these games with three propositions, the last of which distinguishes between two classes of these games:

Proposition 7.1   *In six of the twelve specific games subsumed by the generic Frustration Game, F has a dominant strategy (indicated by vertical arrows for games 5, 6, 10, 11, 32, and 35 in figure 7.1), but only in game 32 (Prisoners' Dilemma) does F's choice of this strategy lead to A's two worst outcomes (i.e., 1 and 2).*

Thus, the apparent frustration that F experiences when A chooses his dominant strategy cannot be duplicated by F when she chooses her dominant strategy (if she has one), except in game 32 (Prisoners' Dilemma).

Proposition 7.2   *In the twelve specific games subsumed by the generic Frustration Game, A's ranking of his payoff at the Nash equilibrium is better than F's ranking in ten games and the same as F's in two games (games 28 and 32).*

Of the ten games in which A's ranking is better, six are games in which A obtains his best payoff (4) and four are games in which he obtains his next-best payoff (3). In the two games in which the players tie, they both obtain their next-worst payoffs (2).

So far the picture looks pretty grim for F: She always obtains only her next-worst payoff (2) at the unique Nash equilibrium in the twelve games, whereas A does better than F—at least in terms of comparative rankings—in ten (83 percent) of the games. Because A obtains a higher-ranked payoff in these games, F might not only be frustrated but also envious of A.[6]

Fortunately for F, there is a way out of her plight in four of the twelve games if she possesses "threat power" of the "deterrent" kind (Brams and Hessel 1984; Brams 1994b, chap. 5).[7]

Proposition 7.3   *The exercise of deterrent threat power by F in the class II games in figure 5.1 induces an outcome [i.e., (3,3) or (3,4)] for F at*

6. Note, however, that a player may derive greater utility from an ordinal payoff of, say, 2 (if it is close to that player's 3 or 4) than a player who receives an ordinal payoff of 3 (if it is far from that player's 4). This renders interpersonal comparisons of player rankings dubious, which is why game theorists tend to eschew them.

7. In section 2.3, I informally defined these concepts in a counterfactual game in which it was rational for Abraham not to offer Isaac—unless God had deterrent threat power and communicated His threat to Abraham. Here my development of deterrent threat power is more general and systematic, making it applicable to all 2×2 games.

least as good as and sometimes better than that which A obtains at this outcome (again, in terms of comparative rankings).

In a 2 × 2 ordinal game, a necessary condition for a player to have a *deterrent threat* is that he or she can threaten the choice of a strategy that leads to the other player's two worst outcomes. For example, in game 22 in figure 7.1, F can threaten the choice of t_2, which inflicts upon A a payoff of either 1 or 2; if F carries out her threat, A will presumably choose s_1, which yields (2,1), rather than choose s_2, which yields (1,4). I call the former outcome the *breakdown outcome*, because there is another outcome, associated with F's other strategy (t_1), that is better for both players than the breakdown outcome (i.e., Pareto-superior to it). This outcome, (3,3), is the *threat outcome*, which F can induce if she has "threat power."

Threat power is the ability of the threatener (F in this case) to withstand the Pareto-inferior breakdown outcome [(2,1) in game 22]—if she is forced to carry out her threat—in order to induce the other player (A) to accept a Pareto-superior threat outcome. The credibility of F's threat depends on her being willing and able to carry out her threat.

A threat, of course, must be communicated to the threatened player, either before the players choose their strategies or at a state that the threatener considers unsatisfactory. In game 22, for example, assume that the players are at (4,2). Then F's *threat* would be to switch from t_1 to t_2 if A refuses to move from s_1. This would cause the game to move from (4,2) to the Pareto-inferior breakdown outcome of (2,1)—at which, presumably, the emotional temperature of the conflict would rise—from which F, if she has threat power, can induce the threat outcome (3,3).

How is this possible? Note that both (4,2) and (3,3), associated with F's strategy of t_1, are Pareto-superior to the breakdown state of (2,1) and so are outcomes that both players would prefer to (2,1). However, because F has threat power and prefers (3,3) to (4,2), she can induce (3,3) and thereby prevent the choice of the Nash equilibrium, (4,2).

A similar analysis of game 35 shows (3,4) to be the threat outcome that F can induce with a deterrent threat to choose t_1, with (2,1) again the breakdown outcome. Likewise, in games 28 and 32, F can threaten to choose t_1, leading to the breakdown outcome of (2,2) (also a Nash equilibrium) if her threat is carried out. To avoid these Pareto-inferior outcomes, it is in *both* players' interest that F be able to induce, with threat power, (3,4) in games 28 and 35, and (3,3) in games 22 and 32, rather than suffer the breakdown outcomes.

If A has threat power, he can also induce (3,4) or (3,3), respectively, in games 28 and 32 by threatening, with the choice of s_1, F's two worst outcomes. Clearly, each player's exercise of threat power in games 28 and 32 would have a salutary effect, leading to an outcome preferred by both players. By contrast, in games 22 and 35 there is a conflict of interest between the players, with A's preferring to induce (4,2), which he can do with a "compellent threat" if he has threat power, and F's preferring to induce (3,3) or (3,4) with a deterrent threat.

A *compellent threat* is one that involves not just the threat of choosing but also the actual choice of a strategy. In making this choice, the threatener compels the threatened player to choose between a Pareto-inferior breakdown outcome and a Pareto-superior threat outcome. For example, in game 22, by choosing s_1 and refusing to move from it, A can force F to choose between (4,2) and (2,1); if A has threat power, F will choose t_1, which in this game simply reinforces the choice of the Nash equilibrium.

In both this game and game 35, threat power is *effective*: The player who possesses it does better than if the other player possessed it. By comparison, in games 28 and 32, threat power is *irrelevant*, because the outcome induced is the same whichever player possesses it. (However, it is not irrelevant in the sense that one player's possession of it enables both players to escape the Pareto-inferior Nash equilibrium in these games.)[8]

The possession of threat power by F enables her to relieve her frustration in all the class II games, making these games, in a sense, *controllable* (recall that it is a *lack* of control that leads to frustration). By comparison, F's lack of control in the class I games may turn her frustration into

8. The distinction between *compellence* and *deterrence* was first made, informally, in Schelling 1966. Brams and Hessel (1984) formalized this distinction in terms of threat power; Aumann and Kurz (1977) incorporated the power to hurt others into a different game-theoretic model. For a detailed formal analysis, with examples, of this somewhat informal discussion, see Brams 1994b, chap. 5). Game-theoretic models of deterrence that are especially applicable to international relations are analyzed in Zagare and Kilgour 2000.

despair, or a feeling of helplessness. Of course, A, too, will be frustrated by the choice of (2,2) in games 28 and 32; but he, also, can help the players escape this Pareto-inferior outcome if he is able to exercise threat power. Like F's deterrent threat to choose t_1, A's threat to choose s_1—and inflict on F one of her two worst outcomes—can lead the players to choose their strategies associated with the Pareto-superior (3,4) outcome in game 28 and (3,3) in game 32.

The frustration of players caught in real Prisoners' Dilemmas (game 32) is well known. What is less appreciated is that a deterrent threat on the part of one or both players in this game, as well as in game 28, offers the players an escape from (2,2), but it must be *credible*: The threatener must be able and willing to carry out the threat. A display of emotions can reinforce the commitment to do so (Hirshleifer 1987; Frank 1988).

To be sure, a threat will not be credible unless a game is likely to be repeated, because a threat that leads to a breakdown outcome is, by definition, irrational to carry out in any single play. But if the game is a continuing one, it may be rational to suffer this outcome in early play in order to build up one's reputation for "toughness" in the future.[9] With one's reputation established, the need to carry out threats will be obviated, or at least reduced, rendering the earlier suffering at breakdown outcomes worthwhile.

7.3 *Lysistrata*: Overcoming Frustration with a Credible Threat

Aristophanes's comic yet biting antiwar play, *Lysistrata* (411 BCE), was written in one of Athens's darkest hours, after the total destruction of her expeditionary force in Sicily, the threat of invasion from Sparta and Syracuse, and the defections of some of her allies. It is a "dream about peace" by a playwright who believed "any peace must be satisfactory to both sides, . . . and the women of both sides have to cooperate in bringing it about" (Aristophanes 411 BCE/1973, 177–178).

While *Lysistrata* is part of the Old Comedy of Athens, the dream of Aristophanes is not pure fantasy. For one thing, the calculations of its

---

9. This argument is made in the literature on repeated games, but its assumption of repeated play of a single game, without alteration, is highly unrealistic (Brams 1994b, 23). However, moves *within* a game (to different states), as allowed by TOM, seem plausible.

characters are unremittingly strategic, as in real life. For another, powerful emotions, especially frustration, fuel the central action of the play, giving *Lysistrata* some of the intellectual weight of the Greek tragedies of Aeschylus, Euripides, and Sophocles, who predated Aristophanes.

The play begins when the protagonist, Lysistrata, encounters her neighbor, Calonice, who recognizes that Lysistrata is "bothered" (Aristophanes 411 BCE/ 1973, 180; henceforth, all quotations from Sommerstein's translation will be given only by page numbers). In fact, Lysistrata admits to being "furious," having "called a meeting [of women] to discuss a very important matter [while] our husbands . . . are all still fast asleep" (180). She has hatched a plan, after "many sleepless nights," to "save Greece" (180) from a never-ending battle between Athens and Sparta, which had made the lives of women of both city-states lonesome and desolate, and their male children prospective soldiers who might be killed like their husbands.

But Calonice mocks her:

The women!—what could they ever do that was any use? Sitting at home putting flowers in their hair, putting on cosmetics and saffron gowns and Cimberian see-through shifts, with slippers on our feet? (181)

Yet these are exactly the weapons that Lysistrata intends for the women to use in order to get the men to "no longer lift up their spears against one another . . . nor take up their shields . . . or their swords" (182).

Lysistrata is frustrated, however, because "the ones I was most counting on" haven't shown up at the meeting (182). Eventually they drift in, and Lysistrata lashes out at their collective plight, with more than a touch of acerbic wit:

The fathers of your children—don't you miss them when they're away at the war? I know not one of you has a husband at home. . . . There isn't anyone even to have an affair with—not a sausage! (184)

When, after hesitating, Lysistrata blurts out her plan—that "we must give up—sex" to stop the carnage of war—the stage directions indicate there are "strong murmers of disapproval, shaking of heads, etc. Several of the company begin to walk off" (184). Indeed, there is a chorus of "I won't do it" from several women, including Calonice, who says she will "walk through the fire, or anything—but give up sex, never! Lysistrata, darling, there's just nothing like it" (185).

Next there is a discussion of how women, by threatening abstinence, can use their feminine wiles and charm to induce the men to give up fighting. The women, however, worry that the men might divorce them or, worse, "drag us into the bedroom by force." But Lysistrata points out that, even in this case, the women can be

as damned unresponsive as possible. There's no pleasure in it if they have to use force and give pain. They'll give up trying soon enough. And no man is ever happy if he can't please his woman. (186)

After still more cajoling from Lysistrata, the women take an oath to refrain from sex "with my boyfriend or husband . . . wearing my best make-up and my most seductive dresses to inflame my husband's ardour" (188).

The women then retire to the Acropolis and bar the gates to the men, vowing not to open the gates "except on our terms" (189). In the confrontation that follows, the men are heard to say such things as, "Euripides was right! 'There is no beast so shameless as a woman!'" (195); and "Back to your weaving, woman, or you'll have a headache for a month" (201). But their derision is to no avail.

Lysistrata remonstrates to the men that the women will "unravel this war, if you'll let us. Send ambassadors first to Sparta" (204), she says, to negotiate a peace. She adds poignancy to her argument by describing the particular difficulty women face, which men do not, when the men go off to war:

Even if we've got husbands, we're war widows just the same. And never mind us—think of the unmarried ones, getting on in years and with never a hope— that's what really pains me. . . . A man comes home—he may be old and grey—but he can get himself a young wife in no time. But a woman's not in bloom for long, and if she doesn't succeed quickly, there's no one who will marry her. (205).

The second act of *Lysistrata* occurs five days later, and Lysistrata herself is wavering: She wanders "restless to and fro" from her "sex-starvation" (210). Moreover, some women are reneging on their vows. But Lysistrata resolves to continue and prevails over most women, even persuading a woman named Myrrhine, who sees her own unwashed and unfed baby, to rebut the pleas of her husband for companionship by saying, caustically, to him: "I pity him [the baby] all right. His father hasn't looked after him very well" (217).

Ambassadors from Sparta, whose women have followed the Athenian lead and abstained from sex, meet the Athenian negotiators. The men on both sides are distraught, but they take places on either side of Lysistrata, who makes a triumphant entrance ("no need to summon her") "magnificently arrayed" (226).

Lysistrata begins her soliloquy with the brilliantly disarming statement: "I am a woman, but I am not brainless" (227). Laying guilt on both Athens and Sparta, she helps them reconcile their differences, evoking from one impatient negotiator exactly the connection she wanted to make: "Peace! Peace! Bed! Bed!" (229). The play ends with rejoicing and dancing at a banquet: The women have won.

How did they do it? To begin with, "winning" is not really an accurate characterization of the outcome, because the men and women have strong common interests, as depicted in the game in figure 7.2 (game 35 in figure 7.1, with payoffs rearranged).[10] The women, led by Lysistrata, can either refrain (R) from sex or not refrain ($\overline{R}$), and the men can continue to fight (F) or not fight ($\overline{F}$), giving rise to the four outcomes.

Starting in the upper left-hand cell of the matrix, and moving clockwise, I rank the four outcomes from best (4) to worst (1) for (women, men) as follows:

I. RF: Frustration—(1,2)   The women suffer greatly (1), because their strategy of abstention fails to stop the fighting and, in addition, they are deprived of sex, which makes the men unhappy (2), too.

II. R$\overline{F}$: Partial success for women—(3,1)   Abstention results in an end to fighting, which is good for the women (3)—but not as good as if they had continued sex—whereas the men are extremely upset (1) because they stop fighting, but sex is still withheld.

III. $\overline{R}$F: Success for men—(2,4)   The women are unhappy (2), even though they have sex, because the fighting continues, whereas the men not only enjoy sex but are also able to fight without repercussions (4).

IV. $\overline{R}\overline{F}$: Resolution—(4,3)   The women succeed completely (4), resuming the sex after the fighting ends, and the men benefit from sex but must desist from fighting (3).

10. This game, like the game used to model *Macbeth* in section 7.4, is illustrative. Other situations of frustration might be modeled by one of the eleven other specific games subsumed by the generic Frustration Game in figure 7.1.

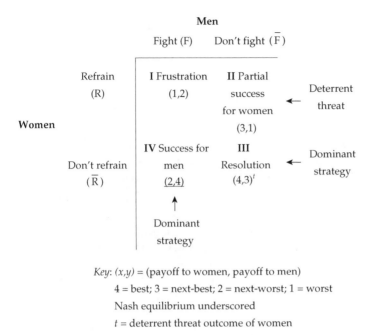

Men

Fight (F)   Don't fight ($\overline{\text{F}}$)

	Fight (F)	Don't fight ($\overline{\text{F}}$)	
Refrain (R)	I Frustration (1,2)	II Partial success for women (3,1)	Deterrent threat ←
Don't refrain ($\overline{\text{R}}$)	IV Success for men (2,4)	III Resolution (4,3)^t	Dominant strategy ←

Dominant strategy ↑

Key: (x,y) = (payoff to women, payoff to men)
4 = best; 3 = next-best; 2 = next-worst; 1 = worst
Nash equilibrium underscored
t = deterrent threat outcome of women

Figure 7.2
Frustration Game of Lysistrata (game 35)

While the benefits of fighting for the men may not be readily apparent today, the perspective I offer is that of the characters in the play.

The reason that game 35 in figure 7.2 looks different from the game in figure 7.1 is that I have interchanged the row and column players, and their strategies, in figure 7.2. Structurally, however, these games are the same, with the women having a dominant strategy of $\overline{\text{R}}$ and the men having a dominant strategy of F, which yields (2,4) in the figure 7.2 game.

Frustrated at this outcome, and being only able by themselves to move to the breakdown (and Pareto-inferior) outcome, (1,2), the women rebel. They not only threaten the men with R but also carry out this threat, which leaves the men the choice of their two worst outcomes. Between (1,2) and (3,1), the men would choose (1,2), except that the threat outcome, (4,3), that the women offer entices them. With apparently few regrets, the men stop fighting, and the women resume sex.

What is most relevant, from the viewpoint of implementing her desired outcome, is the emotional head of steam Lysistrata worked up to get the men to capitulate. First, she realized that her threat had to be carried out to be real. Using an artful combination of logic and zeal, she rallied the women, and later the men, to her side. Furthermore, she expressed her heartfelt anger with clarity and force, as I noted earlier, and often with ribaldry, sometimes referring explicitly to male and female sex organs.[11]

What invests this comedy with a razor edge is the serious nature of the choices the characters face. Both the men and the women are torn by conflicting feelings and do not make their choices frivolously, justifying a game-theoretic view of their situation. At the same time, the characters do not place themselves purely on an intellectual plane, which gives the women's threats, especially, credibility. Indeed, the characters are variously infused with feelings of sadness, despair, frustration, anger, and betrayal (e.g., when some women desert Lysistrata). In the end, though, even the men seem pleased by the reconciliation between Athens and Sparta that Lysistrata orchestrates.

7.4   The Self-Frustration Game

It is one thing for F to experience a lack of control when it is A's dominant strategy that leads to her (F's) two worst outcomes. But what if it is F, not A, who has the dominant strategy. Then F is likely to be frustrated if A's best response is to choose the one of his undominated strategies that leads to F's two worst outcomes.

Now F's grief at A's choice seems as much attributable to her as to A: It is F's preferences—and dominant strategy—that induce A to frustrate her, rather than A's preferences and his dominant strategy. (Recall that in the Frustration Game, it is A who always has a dominant strategy.) If F is at least partially to blame for her grief in this situation, is escape from frustrating herself any easier than escape from being frustrated by A?

In order to answer this question, I define a new generic game, which I call the Self-Frustration Game (see figure 7.3). In this game, the row

---

11. Suffering setbacks in the beginning, Lysistrata followed the adage of "one step backwards, two steps forward"; she seems to have been sustained by a healthy self-confidence and farsighted thinking—her belief that her persistence would pay off in the end. And of course it did.

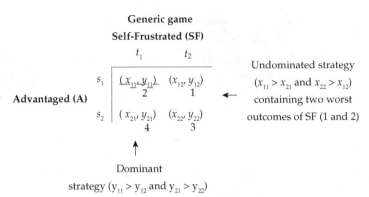

Generic game
Self-Frustrated (SF)

	t_1	t_2
s_1	$\underline{(x_{11}, y_{11})}$ 2	(x_{12}, y_{12}) 1
s_2	(x_{21}, y_{21}) 4	(x_{22}, y_{22}) 3

Advantaged (A)

← Undominated strategy
$(x_{11} > x_{21}$ and $x_{22} > x_{12})$
containing two worst
outcomes of SF (1 and 2)

↑
Dominant
strategy $(y_{11} > y_{12}$ and $y_{21} > y_{22})$

Six specific games subsumed by generic game

Class I (three games): (x_{22}, y_{22}) Pareto-superior to Nash equilibrium of (x_{11}, y_{11})

27		28		48	
(3,2)	(2,1)	(2,2)	(3,1)	(3,2)	(1,1)
[4,3]	[4,3]	[4,3]	[4,3]	[4,3]	[4,3]
(1,4)	$(4,3)^{Ad}_{SFc}$	(1,4)	$(4,3)^{Ad}_{SFc}$	$(2,4)^{Ad}_{SFc}$	$(4,3)^{SFc}$
[4,3]	[4,3]	[4,3]	[4,3]	[2,4]	[4,3]

Class II (three games): (x_{22}, y_{22}) not Pareto-superior to Nash equilibrium of (x_{11}, y_{11})

49		50		56	
$(4,2)^{Ac}$	(2,1)	$(4,2)^{Ac}$	(1,1)	$(4,2)^{Ac}$	(1,1)
[3,3]	[4,2]/[3,3]	[3,4]	[3,4]/[4,2]	[3,3]	[3,3]/[4,2]
(1,4)	$(3,3)^{SFc}$	$(3,4)^{SFd}$	(2,3)	$(2,4)$	$(3,3)^{SFc}$
[4,2]	[4,2]	[3,4]	[4,2]/[3,4]	[2,4]	[4,2]

Key: (x,y) = (payoff to A, payoff to F)
    $[x,y]$ = [payoff to A, payoff to F] in anticipation game (AG)
    4 = best; 3 = next-best; 2 = next-worst; 1 = worst
    A and *SF's* compellent (*c*) or deterrent (*d*) threat outcomes indicated
    Nash equilibria underscored (except in anticipation games 27 and 28)
    Nonmyopic equilibria (NMEs) in original game circled

Figure 7.3
Self-Frustration Game

player, Advantaged (A), is, as before, male; the column player, whom I call Self-Frustrated (SF), is female.

The Self-Frustration Game satisfies the following four conditions:

1. *Dominance for SF*   Without loss of generality, assume that t_1 is SF's dominant strategy, so

$$y_{11} > y_{12}; \quad y_{21} > y_{22}. \tag{7.3}$$

That is, whatever strategy A chooses (s_1 or s_2), SF prefers her payoffs associated with t_1 to those associated with t_2, making t_1 SF's unconditionally better strategy.

2. *Nash equilibrium*   Without loss of generality, assume that (x_{11}, y_{11}) is the unique Nash equilibrium that is associated with SF's dominant strategy, t_1, so

$$x_{11} > x_{21}. \tag{7.4}$$

That is, A prefers his payoff at (x_{11}, y_{11}) to that which he would receive at (x_{21}, y_{21}) if he switched from s_1 to s_2. Similarly, F prefers (x_{11}, y_{11}) to (x_{12}, y_{12})—and so would not switch from t_1 to t_2—because of the dominance of t_1, assumed in inequalities 7.3.

3. *Undominatedness for A*   Given inequality 7.4, to prevent s_1 from being dominant requires that

$$x_{22} > x_{12}. \tag{7.5}$$

4. *Lack of control*   SF's two worst outcomes (1 and 2) are associated with A's strategy of s_1. From the first inequality of 7.3, it follows that

$$y_{11} = 2; \quad y_{12} = 1.$$

To ensure the dominance of t_1, the second inequality of 7.3 requires that

$$y_{21} = 4; \quad y_{22} = 3,$$

which gives a complete ordering of payoffs for SF of

$$y_{21} > y_{22} > y_{11} > y_{12}.$$

In contrast, the fact that (x_{11}, y_{11}) is a Nash equilibrium but A does not have a dominant strategy associated with it—as given by inequalities 7.4

and 7.5—defines a partial ordering of payoffs for A that admits six different complete orderings:

$x_{11} > x_{21} > x_{22} > x_{12}$; $x_{22} > x_{11} > x_{12} > x_{21}$;
$x_{11} > x_{22} > x_{12} > x_{21}$; $x_{22} > x_{11} > x_{21} > x_{12}$;
$x_{11} > x_{22} > x_{21} > x_{12}$; $x_{22} > x_{12} > x_{11} > x_{21}$.

The one ordering of SF, and the six orderings of A, define a total of six different ordinal games subsumed by the generic Self-Frustration Game, which are divided into two classes in figure 7.3.[12] I summarize properties of these games with three propositions, the last of which distinguishes between two classes of these games:

Proposition 7.4 *In the six specific games subsumed by the generic Self-Frustration Game, A's ranking of his payoff at the Nash equilibrium is better than SF's ranking in five games and the same as SF's in one game (game 28).*

Of the five games in which A's ranking is better, three are games in which A obtains his best payoff (4), and two are games in which he obtains his next-best payoff (3). In game 28, which is also a Frustration Game (when the players are interchanged), both players obtain only their next-worst payoffs (2).

Like F in the generic Frustration Game, SF in the generic Self-Frustration Game always obtains her next-worst payoff (2) at the unique Nash equilibrium in the six games, whereas A does better than SF—at least in terms of comparative rankings—in five (83 percent) of the six games. But unlike F, SF can escape her frustration in all six specific self-frustration games, provided she has threat power (which, it will be recalled, offered an escape in only four of the twelve specific frustration games):

Proposition 7.5 *The exercise of either compellent or deterrent threat power by SF always results in a better outcome [either (3,3) or (3,4)] for her than that which she obtains at the Nash equilibrium. In the class I games, this outcome is, in fact, better for both players; it can also be induced by A's exercise of deterrent threat power.*

12. Ignore for now the bracketed outcomes, shown below the outcomes in parentheses in figure 7.3.

But what if the players do not have threat power? And what if the exercise of threat power leads to different outcomes—as it does in the three class II games—depending on which player (if either) possesses it? As I next show, TOM offers SF, in particular, the opportunity to break out of the Nash equilibrium in both the class I and class II self-frustration games—without relying on threat power—given that the players are nonmyopic in the sense described in section 2.5.

Recall from section 2.5 that the outcome into which a state goes is the nonmyopic equilibrium (NME) from that state, which is (3,3) in game 56 when the initial state is (4,2). To take another example, backward induction from each state in game 27 in figure 7.3 shows that each state will go into (4,3). Thus in game 27, wherever play starts, the players can anticipate that they will end up at (4,3), making it the unique NME in game 27. This is also true of (4,3) in game 28, but not in game 48, another class I game. Starting at (2,4) in game 48, the players will not depart from this state, making (2,4) as well as (4,3) an NME in this game.

The four bracketed states of each game in figure 7.3 define what I call the *anticipation game (AG)*, with each state in this matrix an NME. Insofar as players choose strategies as if they were playing a game based on this matrix, one can determine which NMEs are Nash equilibria in the AG and, therefore, are likely to be chosen.[13]

Observe that all class II games in figure 5.3 contain at least two NMEs. But some of these NMEs are *indeterminate*, because there is a conflict over who will move first. In game 50, if (1,1) is the initial state, [3,4]/[4,2] in figure 7.3 indicates that when R moves first from (1,1), then (3,4) will be outcome, whereas when C moves first, (4,2) will be the outcome.[14]

---

13. Because the NMEs in games 27 and 28 are the same, the strategies of the players in their AGs are indistinguishable, making all four states Nash equilibria. Only in game 49 is the Nash equilibrium in the AG, [4,2], also the Nash equilibrium, (4,2), in the original game.

14. Actually, the result of backward induction by R from (1,1) in game 50 is (2,3) rather than (3,4). But, as I argue in Brams 1994b, 114n20, the players would have a common interest in implementing the Pareto-superior (3,4) to implementing (2,3) when there is clockwise movement from (1,1). However, the implementation of (3,4) would require a binding commitment on the part of R not to move on from (3,4) to (4,2), which is not assumed possible in noncooperative game theory. The conclusion I reach (with an interchange of players and their payoffs) is the following: "I do not see an airtight case being made for either (2,3) or (3,4) as *the* NME from (1,1) when R moves first, which nicely illustrates the nuances that TOM surfaces that the rules of standard game theory keep well submerged." Incidentally, game 50 is the only game of the seventy-eight 2 × 2 ordinal games in which this kind of ambiguity about NMEs arises.

Because R prefers (4,2) whereas C prefers (3,4), each player will try to hold out longer in order to induce the other player to move first. Who wins in this struggle will depend on which player has *order power*—that is, who can determine the order of moves, starting at (1,1) (Brams 1994b, chap. 5).

In general, every 2 × 2 game contains at least one NME, because from each initial state there is an outcome (perhaps indeterminate) of the move-countermove process. If this outcome is both determinate and the same from every initial state, then it is the only NME; otherwise, there is more than one NME.

In game 56 in figure 7.3, there are three different NMEs, which is the maximum number that can occur in a 2 × 2 strict ordinal game; the minimum, as already noted, is one. All except two of the seventy-eight 2 × 2 games (game 56 and Chicken, which is not shown in figure 7.3 but is in the appendix as game 57) have either one or two NMEs.

To summarize, where players start in the original games in figure 7.3 may not be where they end up according to TOM.[15] Thus, a game may mask a good deal of instability when the players can move and counter-move from states.

7.5 *Macbeth*: From Self-Frustration to Murder

A central feature of Shakespeare's great tragedy, *Macbeth* (Shakespeare 1606/1994), is the conflict between Lady Macbeth and her husband Macbeth over murdering King Duncan. Duncan's demise would facilitate their ascent to the throne as king and queen of Scotland, but there are risks.

Lady Macbeth's ambition is fed by a letter she receives from Macbeth prophesying his greatness, based on his meeting with three "Weird Sisters" (who are considered to be witches). After mentioning in his letter that the Sisters saluted him with "Hail King that shalt be," he writes his wife—"my greatest partner of greatness"—of "what greatness is promised thee" (I:v:10–12).[16]

---

15. Even the choice of a Nash equilibrium associated with a dominant strategy in the AGs offers no assurance that players will stay at this state. Indeed, except for one of the two states associated with the (3,4) Nash equilibria in the AG of game 50, the players will move from *every* such state to some different NME in the six AGs in figure 7.3.

16. This ordered triple indicates (act:scene:verse), as given in Shakespeare 1606/1994.

But Lady Macbeth worries—with good reason, it turns out—that her husband's "nature . . . is too full o'th' milk of human kindness/To catch the nearest way" (I:iv:15–17). Consequently, she wishes

That I may pour my spirits in thine ear,
And chastise with the valour of my tongue
All that impedes thee from the golden round. (I:iv:25–27)

The advice she gives to Macbeth that will advance him to the "golden round" (i.e., crown) is prefigured by her own earlier musings.

Upon receiving news that King Duncan will be visiting Macbeth at his castle that very evening, Lady Macbeth thinks about his "fatal entrance . . . under my battlements" (I:v:38–39). She immediately steels herself psychologically for his murder:

Come, you spirits
That tend on mortal thoughts, unsex me here,
And fill me from the crown to the toe, top-full
Of direst cruelty. Make thick my blood,
Stop up the access and passage to remorse,
That no compunctious visitings of nature
Shake my fell purpose. (I:v:40–45)

As if intending to murder Duncan herself, she says:

Come, thick night,
And pall thee in the dunnest smoke of Hell,
That my keen knife see not the wound it makes. (I:v:49–51).

But, in fact, it is not Lady Macbeth—now shed of the womanliness in herself that she despises—who wants to carry out the dastardly deed. Instead, she earnestly hopes that her husband, though he looks "like th'innocent flower," will prove to be "the serpent under't" (I:v:63–64). Macbeth, however, has grave doubts, especially that the regicide will "return/To plague th'inventor" (I:vii:9–10), and that King Duncan's "virtues/Will plead like angels" (I:vii:18–19) if he is assassinated.

While Macbeth confesses to "vaulting ambition, which o'erleaps itself/ And falls on th'other" (I:vii:27–28), assassinating King Duncan to satisfy this ambition is another matter. Indeed, Lady Macbeth is furious when he tells her, while feasting with Duncan at their castle, that "we will proceed no further in this business/He hath honoured me of late" (I:vii:31–32). She immediately accuses her husband of cowardice, even unmanliness, saying that *she* would, as a mother, have "dashed the brains out [of her baby], had I so sworn/As you have done to this [sworn to murder King Duncan]" (I:vii:57–58).

Still wavering, Macbeth asks, what "if we should fail?" (I:vii:59). Lady Macbeth brushes him off:

We fail?
But screw your courage to the sticking place,
And we'll not fail. (I:vii:60–62)

Lady Macbeth then indicates how, when Duncan sleeps, the assassination will be carried out. Macbeth finally agrees, but he is haunted by fear—an emotion that even Lady Macbeth's ferocity cannot dispel—of this "terrible feat" (I:vii:80).[17]

The game played between Lady Macbeth and Macbeth involves her choosing to incite him to murder (I) or not incite him ($\bar{\text{I}}$), and Macbeth's killing Duncan (K) or not killing him ($\bar{\text{K}}$). Starting in the upper left-hand cell of the matrix in figure 7.4, and moving clockwise, I rank the states from best (4) to worst (1) for (Lady Macbeth, Macbeth) as follows:

I. IK: Murder motivated—(3,3)   Lady Macbeth is pleased that Macbeth carries out the murder—even if she must strenuously prod him to do so (3)—and Macbeth is pleased to satisfy her desire, demonstrate his manliness, and ascend to the throne (3).

II. I$\bar{\text{K}}$: Extreme frustration—(1,1)   To the great chagrin of both Lady Macbeth (1) and Macbeth (1), her pleas are ignored and his courage is thrown into question.

III. $\bar{\text{I}}$K: Murder unmotivated—(4,2)   Lady Macbeth is most pleased if Macbeth murders King Duncan without her having to shame him (4), but Macbeth is plagued by guilt and self-doubt when not incited by her (2).

IV. $\bar{\text{I}}\bar{\text{K}}$: Status quo—(2,4)   Lady Macbeth is angry at Macbeth and disgusted with herself when neither she nor Macbeth acts to change the

---

17. But the murder, Taylor (1996, 64) argues, rids Macbeth of another emotion—the shame he felt in dishonoring his king and house guest—because, once the murder is carried out, Macbeth's feelings of cowardice and inadequacy are replaced by pride in successfully pursuing his overriding ambition to be king. Lady Macbeth's plunge into madness later in the play eventually undoes the couple, but that unanticipated outcome does not bear on the rationality of their current moves.

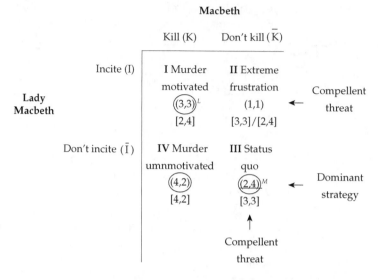

Key: (x,y) = (payoff to Lady Macbeth, payoff to Macbeth)

[x,y] = [payoff to Lady Macbeth, payoff to Macbeth] in anticipation game (AG)

4 = best; 3 = next-best; 2 = next-worst; 1 = worst

Compellent threat outcomes of Lady Macbeth (L) and Macbeth (M) indicated

Nash equilibria underscored (except in anticipation games 27 and 28)

Nonmyopic equilibria (NMEs) in original game circled

Figure 7.4
Self-Frustration Game of Macbeth (game 56)

status quo (2), whereas Macbeth is happy to be honored by King Duncan and not to have to act treacherously against him, especially as his host (4).

Structurally, this is game 56 in figure 7.3, except that the row and column players, and their strategies, are interchanged in its figure 7.4 representation.

Play commences at the status quo of (2,4), which is upsetting to Lady Macbeth once she has read the letter from her husband: She realizes that the throne is within their grasp, but her husband may fail her in the clutch. Because her dominant strategy of Ī is associated with this state, however, standard game theory predicts that she will not move from it;

neither will Macbeth, because it is a Nash equilibrium. But TOM makes a different prediction.

Specifically, Lady Macbeth would calculate the rational consequences of moving from (2,4)—what countermove, on the part of Macbeth, her move from this state would trigger, what counter-countermove she would make, and so on. The reasoning is precisely the same as that given in section 2.5 for the Samson and Delilah game, which is also game 56 wherein Delilah, like Lady Macbeth, sought relief from (2,4).

In the present game, Lady Macbeth escapes, at least temporarily, her self-frustration at the status quo by relentlessly hounding Macbeth to murder King Duncan. But when Macbeth temporizes, Lady Macbeth explodes in anger, bringing the players to (1,1). This state seems to undermine Macbeth's self-esteem and impels him finally to act, bringing the players to (3,3) after the murder is committed.[18]

The couple is able, for a while, to escape suspicion, placing the blame on the servants, who are also murdered, and King Duncan's sons, who flee. When Banquo, who had also heard the prophecy of the Weird Sisters, seems likely to uncover the Macbeths' plot, Macbeth has him killed. In the end, however, the previously indomitable Lady Macbeth comes apart emotionally and commits suicide.[19] Without her formidable presence, Macbeth loses faith and is slain by Macduff, whose entire family he had ordered to be killed.

Remorseless as Lady Macbeth is until the end, she is a volcanic character, brimming with emotion. She uses her frustration to great advantage to push her reluctant and vacillating husband over the brink, so to speak, which, as I showed in section 2.5, Delilah did to Samson through harassment and threats.

---

18. By drugging the servants who were supposed to guard Duncan and making sure the door to his chamber is unlocked, Lady Macbeth is certainly an accessory to murder. But this legalistic interpretation glosses over her preeminent role, which she maintained by an implacable display of cold fury and hot anger. In fact, the NME of (3,3) is reinforced by Lady Macbeth's compellent threat of choosing strategy I and sticking with it, but I prefer the NME explanation for (3,3), because it relies only on the farsighted thinking, not any special powers, of the players.

19. The most famous mad scene in opera (that of Lucia in Gaetano Donizetti's *Lucia di Lammermoor*) also occurs in the wake of a murder by the main female character, but what motivates Lucia to commit murder (unrequited love) is a far cry from what motivated Lady Macbeth.

What happened in the Bible and *Macbeth* also occurs in real-life self-frustration games. Consider, for example, the Japanese attack on Pearl Harbor in 1941, or President Anwar Sadat's 1977 peace initiative and visit to Jerusalem, both provoked by the pent-up frustration of players who sought to escape their trying situations. Their moves in these military and diplomatic games engendered great shock and surprise (Brams 1997b), which is an emotional reaction in its own right triggered by the surpriser's (in this case, Japan's and Egypt's) unanticipated actions.

TOM, by explicating the rationale of such moves, makes them less surprising. It turns out that the six specific games subsumed by the Self-Frustration Game in figure 7.3 are precisely the games subsumed by a so-called generic Surprise Game (Brams 1997b) and a generic Freedom Game (Brams 1999b), in which the player with the dominant strategy (SF in figure 7.3) finds it rational, according to TOM, to switch to her dominated strategy, in turn inducing A to switch his strategy, too.

This move and subsequent countermove from the unique Nash equilibrium (upper left-hand states in the games in figure 7.3) brings both players to the lower right-hand states. From the latter states, the players would return to the Nash equilibrium (if given the chance). Unfortunately for Macbeth and Lady Macbeth, they met their end before this could happen, making these subsequent moves infeasible (see section 2.5 for infeasible moves in the Samson and Delilah game).

7.6 Summary and Conclusions

Frustration is expressed when players who are dissatisfied and lack control are forced to make "desperate" choices—choices that hurt them, at least temporarily, because they involve moves from a Nash equilibrium. But they are not unmotivated choices. When players erupt with anger or rage in moving to their disadvantage, they signal that they want this loss of control to end—in particular, they want the other player to respond in a way that helps both players.

I have suggested that TOM, which offers a rationale for players' making dynamic choices in games, can rationally explain these seemingly irrational choices. In the case of the generic Frustration and Self-Frustration Games, players express frustration when they threaten the opposing player and are forced to carry out the threat.

As I showed in the Frustration Game, Frustrated (F) can break out of the unique Nash equilibrium, at which she suffers her next-worst outcome, with a deterrent threat in four of the twelve specific games. But this threat is effective only if F can endure the breakdown outcome better than Advantaged (A), who has a dominant strategy. The women (F) in *Lysistrata* had such threat power in the form of withholding sex from the men (A), which induced the men to stop fighting, making the women ecstatic and the men at least reasonably happy.

The Self-Frustration Game leaves the player with the dominant strategy, Self-Frustrated (SF), dissatisfied at the unique Nash equilibrium. In this game, I assumed that each player considers the consequences of moving from that state, the other player's countermoving, and so on, which eventually brings both players to an NME. This is the outcome that rational players would be expected to migrate to—and from which, I assume, they derive their payoffs—if it is rational for them to move at all (based on backward induction).

It turns out that in the six specific games subsumed by the Self-Frustration Game, SF can, starting at the Nash equilibrium, induce an NME better for herself, and sometimes for A, than the Nash equilibrium. Threat power of either the compellent or deterrent kind is also effective in these games for one or both players. In *Macbeth*, however, it seems less that Lady Macbeth could threaten Macbeth with anything—except, perhaps, withdrawal of her love—than that she could switch to her dominated strategy to induce Macbeth, in turn, to switch his strategy.

This move and countermove led the couple to plot the murder of King Duncan and successfully execute it. The fact that their monstrous crime later unraveled, however, does not undermine the rationality of their calculations at the time. Indeed, their rationality was undergirded by the Weird Sisters' prophecy of Macbeth's future greatness, though it was Lady Macbeth who was relentless in trying to make it happen.

Beyond using game theory to explain the choices of players, I have emphasized in this chapter how TOM can be used to interpret their emotional responses as they move along the path to an NME. It is *during* these moves that human emotions come to the fore, though payoffs to the players in the long term accrue only when an NME is reached.

I believe other emotions besides frustration can be fruitfully studied using TOM. Thus, for example, an Envy Game might be one in which the good fortune of one player is tied to the bad fortune of the other, suggestive of pure-conflict games, though Elster (1991, 57) argues that this need not be the case.

For the game theorist, unlike the psychologist, the structure of the situation that triggers emotions, rather than the emotions themselves, is of primary interest. No generic game that mirrors such structures, however, will capture all the subtleties of emotional interactions that people have in literary as well as real-life games. But one psychologist has argued that "a necessary first step is to develop a theoretical system that can account successfully for a reasonably large number of 'emotional' phenomena" (Mandler 1994, 243).[20]

A dynamic game-theoretic model offers a promising start on understanding when frustration is likely to explode into anger. Nonetheless, the classification of the different possible paths, the assessment of their payoff consequences, and a psychological interpretation of the emotions these different paths are likely to evoke requires considerably more investigation and analysis, even for 2×2 games.

To further this endeavor, I propose as a working hypothesis that the more players suffer in nonpreferred states along a path to nonmyopic equilibria, the more intense will be their emotions. Insofar as nonmyopic equilibria offer "relief" to the players—in the sense of providing them with a preferred state—this emotion will, in the end, be positive. In a sense, the emotion will have been tamed, and the players will have successfully coped with its expression,

But if one player remains dissatisfied at this equilibrium state, he or she may want to depart, rendering this equilibrium unstable. Thereby one might analyze the *stability* of nonmyopic equilibria—a major refinement of the current concept—showing how it depends on the nature of the path taken to reach it and the emotions evoked along this path.

A subsidiary hypothesis is the following: The more difficult the path to a nonmyopic equilibrium, the more likely this equilibrium will remain stable. "Difficulty" might be measured by the number of Pareto-inferior states that a 2×2 game contains, especially if it is a cyclic game, as

20. Mor (1993) indicates other linkages of the psychology literature to the game-theoretic modeling literature (including that based on TOM), especially in international relations.

described in section 3.4, in which both players have a continuing incentive to move.

According to this hypothesis, a resolution of a crisis in cyclic games (thirty-six of the seventy-eight 2×2 games) that contain two Pareto-inferior states (twenty-two games) is more likely to hold than in cyclic games that contain only one such state (twelve games) or no such state (two games, both of which are games of pure conflict). The underlying reason for this greater stability is that the players in games with more Pareto-inferior states suffer together when an equilibrium is upset.

As a case in point, the stability achieved in the aftermath of the 1962 Cuban missile crisis, at least with respect to a nuclear threat and possible war, may stem not only from the fact that a mutually disastrous nuclear war was averted but also—from an emotions viewpoint—because future superpower leaders have had no desire to repeat such a traumatic experience.[21] In this sense, the high drama of agreements forged in crises may be an antidote to their later breakdown, compared with agreements reached in noncrisis situations in which there is no possibility of mutual disaster.

It is surely no accident that the great tragedies of fiction arise in crises from which there is no escape. The drama of plays is expressed through dialogue and actions in the theater, which our examples show sometimes allow for escape (*Lysistrata*) but other times do not (*Macbeth*).

21. Nikita Khrushchev's sense of loss of control in this crisis is reflected in the following statement he made in a letter written to John F. Kennedy: "If people do not show wisdom, then in the final analysis they will come to clash, like blind moles" (Divine 1971, 47). For more on this crisis, see sections 9.5 and 9.6.

8 History: Magnanimity after Wars

8.1 Introduction

History is the study of the past.[1] Typically, it involves identifying the set of events that give rise to particular outcomes, which may range from elections to social movements to wars.

Some historians, however, take a more social-scientific view. They do not stress the peculiar or unique but instead attempt to analyze the underlying forces that produce outcomes across cultures and time, such as the rise and fall of empires. To do so, they may focus on the accumulation of wealth, the nature of political institutions, the qualities of leadership, and the like in order to try to identify key causal factors associated with the outcomes they seek to explain.[2]

My approach is similar, except I use game theory and the theory of moves (TOM). I begin this chapter by explaining the magnanimity of a victor—or the lack thereof—in its treatment of the defeated side after a war.[3] By defining a generic Magnanimity Game (MG), which subsumes twelve specific games, I suggest a general explanation of not only when a victor will or will not be magnanimous in the aftermath of a war but also when the defeated player will or will not be cooperative.

1. This chapter is adapted from Brams and Mor 1993 and Brams 1994b, 159–163, with permission.

2. While not all historians, the authors of Bates et al. 1998 epitomize this approach in explicating "analytical narratives."

3. Game theory has also been applied to decisive battles, such as that which led to Napoleon's defeat at the Battle of Waterloo (Mongin 2009). Other applications of game theory to military conflicts are discussed in Brams 1975/2004; O'Neill 1994, 2007; and Zagare 2011.

More specifically, I attempt to explain why events unfold the way they do after wars, based on the strategic choices the players face. TOM assumes that these choices engender new choices that the players can anticipate and asks what the players will do, looking ahead. Independent of the time and place of wars—at least of those I briefly survey in the nineteenth and twentieth centuries—I show that the answer depends on the nonmyopic equilibria (NMEs) in the specific MG games they play, which fall into three classes.

The chapter proceeds as follows. In section 8.2 I introduce with an example the "two-sidedness convention," which refines the backward-induction analysis—described in sections 2.5 and 7.4—for identifying NMEs in 2×2 conflict games. In section 8.3 I discuss the views of different analysts on the rationality of a victor treating its erstwhile enemy magnanimously. Not surprisingly, these analysts have taken diametrically opposed positions on this question.

The analysis of MG in section 8.4 demonstrates that both positions may be correct, depending on the specific MG game being played. In fact, the theoretical analysis provides conditions under which each view is valid, which I summarize with three propositions.

In section 8.5, I give several empirical examples from wars over the past two hundred years that illustrate the occurrence of the four different outcomes in MG, each of which may be an NME in one or more of the twelve specific games that the generic game subsumes. In section 8.6, I show how the situation at the outset of the U.S. Civil War can be modeled by one of these games, whose unique NME is for the Union *not* to be magnanimous after its victory. This finding raises a question—namely, if the Confederacy could have anticipated this outcome, why did it provoke war in the first place?

An explanation lies in the Confederacy's attempt to exercise threat power by way of a series of successful attacks on Union forces, beginning at Fort Sumter, located in Charleston, South Carolina, in 1861. Thereby the Confederacy sought decisively to establish the credibility of its challenge to the Union, which it hoped would lead the Union to seek a negotiated settlement. Ultimately this challenge to the Union's supremacy failed, due principally to the persistence of Abraham Lincoln in pursuing the war to its bitter end.

I conclude in section 8.7 by summarizing the analysis and discussing how MG might be used for normative purposes. Besides its use in explaining past outcomes, it can also provide a tool for anticipating future moves and possibly avoiding disastrous outcomes, especially in situations wherein a player, by acting generously, can induce an opponent to be cooperative in return.

8.2 The Two-Sidedness Convention

Assume the initial state for the row player (R) in a 2×2 conflict game is either (4,1) or (4,2). Paradoxically, it may be rational for R to move, even though it obtains its best payoff by staying in this state, assuming that the column player (C) also stays.

The reason is that it may be rational for C to move from (4,1) or (4,2), according to TOM, but this results in an outcome in which *both* players are worse off than if R moved first. Accordingly, R should move first and, by so doing, be "magnanimous"—that is, move to a state where it receives 3 instead of 4, and in which C also improves its lot, compared with the situation in which C moves first.

Game 28 in figure 8.1 illustrates this problem for R. Standard game theory predicts as an outcome the unique Pareto-inferior Nash equilibrium, (2,2), which is the product of R's dominant strategy of s_1 and C's best response—given R's dominant choice—of t_1. TOM, on the other

Column (C)

t_1 t_2

s_1 (2,2)   (4,1)   ← Dominant strategy

Row (R)   [3,4]   [3,4]

s_2

(1,3)   ((3,4))

[3,4]   [3,4]

Key: $(x,y) =$ (payoff to R, payoff to C)

$[x,y] =$ [payoff to R, payoff to C] in anticipation game (AG)

4 = best; 3 = next-best; 2 = next-worst; 1 = worst

Nash equilibrium in original game underscored

Nonmyopic equilibrium (NME) circled

Figure 8.1
Illustration of the two-sidedness convention (TSC) (game 28)

hand, predicts the choice of the unique NME of (3,4), which is Pareto-superior to (2,2), wherever play starts.

To see this, consider what happens when (4,1) is the initial state:

	R		C		R		C		
R starts:	(4,1)	→|	(3,4)	→|	(1,3)	→	(2,2)	→	(4,1)
Survivor:	(4,1)		(3,4)		(2,2)		(2,2)		

	C		R		C		R		
C starts:	(4,1)	→	(2,2)	→|	(1,3)	→|	(3,4)	→	(4,1)
Survivor:	(2,2)		(2,2)		(1,3)		(4,1)		

When R starts, there is blockage (and stoppage) at the outset at (4,1), whereas when C starts, it moves to (2,2), where play stops. These outcomes are underscored. Because C's rational choice of moving to (2,2) takes precedence over R's rational choice of staying at (4,1)—according to rule 6 of TOM (section 2.5)—TOM would appear to predict (2,2) to be the outcome, the same as standard game theory.

But the relevant portion of rule 6 covering this case is actually ambiguous on the matter: If it is rational for one player to move and the other player not to move from the initial state, then the player who moves takes *precedence*: Its move overrides the player who stays, so the outcome will be that induced by the player who moves. Is it rational, however, for C to move and induce (2,2) as the outcome? And is it rational for R to stay, anticipating this outcome?

The answer for both players to these questions is surely no. Although these choices are rational, based on the backward induction of each player alone, this one-sided analysis is flawed in game 28: It does not take into account R's possibility of moving past its *initial* blockage at (4,1) to (3,4). If R does, there is again blockage at (3,4), but now it is in *both* players' interest that the process stop, compared to stopping at (2,2) when C moves first from (4,1).

In fact, C's moving first to (2,2) is inconsistent with a portion of rule 5 (section 2.5):

A player will not move from an initial state if this move (i) leads to a less preferred final state (i.e., outcome).

Clearly, (2,2) is less preferred than (3,4) not only by C but also by R.

But rules 5 and 6 can be reconciled with what I call the *two-sidedness convention (TSC)*: If one player (say, C), by moving, can induce a better state for itself than by staying—but R by moving can induce a state Pareto-superior to C's induced state—then R will move, even if it otherwise would prefer to stay, to effect a better outcome.

Game 28 illustrates this convention. Clearly, R would prefer to stay at (4,1). But recognizing that if C moves the outcome will be (2,2), it is in both R's and C's interest that R move first and induce the Pareto-superior outcome of (3,4).

In section 2.5 I called rule 6 the "two-sidedness rule." While I could make TSC rule 7, I think it better to call it a "convention," because it clarifies the interpretation of the aforementioned portions of rules 5 and 6. That is, it says under what conditions "it is rational for one player to move" (rule 6), but not on the basis of one-sided backward induction alone. Rather, it may be rational to move in order to deter the other player from making a prior move that "leads to a less preferred final state (i.e., outcome)" [part (i) of rule 5].

Implicitly, rule 5 (about moving only if one can improve the outcome) and rule 6 (about the precedence of moving over staying)—together with TSC, which clarifies *when* players will move to effect a better outcome—define an NME. That is, an NME is the product of two-sided rationality calculations, which these rules and TSC spell out, along with the usual rules of play (rules 1–4).

In Brams (1994b, 70–73), I used game 28 to model the conflict between a mugger and a victim, showing that the victim should submit—even though the victim would prefer to resist if he or she can frighten away the mugger—and compared this outcome with data on actual choices by muggers and victims in robberies. The data supported the TOM outcome: Most victims voluntarily give up their money to muggers, going from 4 to 3 to induce state (3,4) in order to avoid state (2,2) of resisting, causing the mugger to use force (for an alternative view of this game, see Hoffman 2001).

To preview the application of TSC to the aftermath of wars, I review in section 8.3 the views of different analysts on whether or not it is rational for the victor in a war to be magnanimous toward the country it defeats. In section 8.4 I then apply TOM to the following question: When is it rational for the victor to be magnanimous? Here the issue is less for a player to give *in* (e.g., to a mugger) and more for it to give *up* some spoils (or other perquisites) of victory in order to induce future cooperation from the vanquished.

8.3 Different Views on the Rationality of Magnanimity after Wars

A dilemma facing every victor in an interstate war is how to treat the vanquished opponent when hostilities end. Should the victor strive for a postwar settlement that addresses at least some of the grievances of the vanquished, or should it implement a new status quo that does not acknowledge these grievances? Magnanimity may quell the desire of the vanquished for revenge, but nonmagnanimity may prevent the vanquished from acquiring the means to mount future challenges.

If, as Clausewitz (1832/1966) argued, wars are fought over the preferred political order, the vanquished's position in this order, after the war, cannot be ignored. Several scholars of international relations have analyzed the vanquished's role in the postwar stability of a system. Based on his analysis of early nineteenth-century Europe, Kissinger (1964) concluded that restoring stability to a postwar system requires magnanimity toward the vanquished opponent by the defenders of the status quo. Oren (1982, 150), focusing on two-state conflicts, also assembled evidence that "prudence in victory" is more stabilizing than punitive behavior by the victor, because the latter strategy produces a desire for revenge on the part of the vanquished.

Aron (1966), by contrast, advanced a "peace by empire" argument, claiming that postwar stability is better served by a total subjugation of the opponent, which robs it of the means, and hence the opportunity, to initiate future conflicts. Maoz (1984), using aggregate data on interstate disputes from the nineteenth and twentieth centuries, tested the contradictory Oren and Aron theses and found empirical support for peace-by-empire. Later Maoz (1990, 256–257) offered a rationale for this policy, showing it to be part of a Nash equilibrium in a specific 2×2 nonstrict ordinal game (i.e., in which one player has tied preferences for some outcomes).

In the remainder of this chapter, I approach the problem of magnanimity from a different perspective—namely, that the victor's dilemma cannot be resolved exclusively in favor of magnanimity or nonmagnanimity. I show the conditions under which prudence-in-victory on the one hand, and peace-by-empire on the other, are rational, given possible counteractions that the defeated party can take.

This perspective assumes that the defeated party is not inert but itself a player in a game. (True, there have been wars in which the defeated party was utterly devastated and, therefore, incapable of making any choices, but these are relatively rare.) The postwar political order is thereby the product of interdependent choices of the victor and the defeated party, with the players' preferences dependent on both (1) the victor's choice of magnanimity or nonmagnanimity and (2) the defeated party's choice of cooperation or noncooperation in a game. To analyze the rationality of these strategic choices, I define a generic Magnanimity Game (MG), which subsumes different strategic situations that may arise in the aftermath of victory.

These situations reflect the different preferences that the victor and the defeated party may have for the four possible outcomes in MG. Thus, rather than positing a specific game between the victor and the defeated party, I allow for two types of victor and six types of defeated, which defines twelve specific games. I then show when magnanimity or non-magnanimity by the victor, and cooperation or noncooperation by the defeated party, are NMEs in each of the games, and I draw some generalizations across the games.

The postwar situation, in the wake of victory, defines the initial state. The NMEs that may arise from this state fall into three classes of games, which together allow for each possible state to be the outcome. Applying MG to several historical cases—mostly the aftermaths of wars in the nineteenth and twentieth centuries—illustrates, empirically, the different possible outcomes in the generic game.

8.4 The Magnanimity Game (MG)

Consider the aftermath of a war or other major international dispute, such as a crisis, in which one player, the victor (V), prevails over another player, the defeated (D). In the postwar or postdispute situation, assume V has a choice of being either magnanimous (M) or not magnanimous ($\overline{M}$) to D, and D has a choice of either cooperating (C) or not cooperating ($\overline{C}$) with V.

		Defeated (D)	
		Cooperate (C)	Don't cooperate ($\overline{\text{C}}$)
Victor (V)	Don't be magnanimous ($\overline{\text{M}}$)	I Status Quo (v_4, d_i)	II Rejected Status Quo (v_s, d_j)
	Be magnanimous (M)	IV Magnanimity (v$_3$, d$_{i+}$)	III Rejected Magnanimity (v_t, d_{j+})

Key: (x,y) = (payoff to V, payoff to D)

$v_4 > v_3 > v_s, v_t$ (s, t = 1 or 2)

$d_{i+} > d_i, d_{j+} > d_j$

Figure 8.2
Generic Magnanimity Game (MG)

In section 8.5 I will discuss the meaning of these choices, and the resulting outcomes, in some historical cases. For now assume that, immediately after the war, the players are at Status Quo in the payoff matrix of figure 8.2. In this state, V is in its best position and D is in an inferior position—that is, there is at least one other state that D would prefer.

To give further structure to this postdispute situation, I make some additional assumptions about how the players rank the various states in figure 8.2. In this representation, the higher the numerical subscripts of v and d, the greater the payoffs. How these payoffs compare with the payoffs having lettered subscripts is indicated below, moving clockwise from the upper left-hand state in figure 8.2:

I. $\overline{\text{M}}$C: Status Quo   Best for V (v_4) and inferior to Magnanimity for D ($d_i < d_{i+}$).

II. $\overline{\text{M}}\overline{\text{C}}$: Rejected Status Quo   Inferior for V (v_s, where s = 1 or 2, i.e., this state is either worst or next-worst) and inferior to Rejected Magnanimity for D ($d_j < d_{j+}$).

III. M$\overline{\text{C}}$: Rejected Magnanimity   Inferior for V (v_t, where t = 1 or 2, i.e., this state is either worst or next-worst) and superior to Rejected Status Quo for D ($d_{j+} > d_j$).

IV. MC: Magnanimity   Next-best for V (v_3) and superior to Status Quo for D ($d_{i+} > d_j$).

These rankings, because they do not give a complete ordering of states from best to worst for each player but only a partial ordering, do not define a specific ordinal game but rather a generic game, like the Frustration and Self-Frustration Games in chapter 7. The resulting Magnanimity Game (MG) subsumes the preference orderings of twelve specific games (to be given shortly). MG generalizes postdispute situations by allowing for all reasonable possibilities of preference orderings by the two players.

Thus, when D chooses $\overline{C}$, I leave unspecified whether V prefers Rejected Magnanimity (v_t) to Rejected Status Quo (v_s). V might prefer the former if its generosity cannot be seriously exploited by an "ungrateful" D and will ultimately redound to V's favor. By contrast, if V's generosity creates an opportunity for D to recoup its losses and fight V again, V might prefer to clamp down by being nonmagnanimous.

In either event—whether V is magnanimous or not—I assume that V is always better off when D cooperates ($v_4 > v_3 > v_s$, v_t, where $s, t = 1$ or 2). Not only is V always better off, but I also assume that Magnanimity (v_3) is next-best to Status Quo (v_4) when D chooses C. Thus, V gives up something to improve D's lot in moving from Status Quo to Magnanimity, but V suffers still more (v_1 or v_2) when D chooses $\overline{C}$.

The partial ordering of payoffs I assume for D is less complete than that assumed for V. Because D prefers its payoffs with "plus" subscripts to comparable payoffs without the plus, D desires that V always be magnanimous. But because I assume no ordering between the i and $i+$ payoffs on the one hand, and the j and $j+$ payoffs on the other, I cannot make any comparisons between D's payoffs associated with C and $\overline{C}$.

These partial orderings of the players in MG do not render any state a Nash equilibrium, much less endow either player with a dominant strategy, in standard game theory. Neither, according to TOM, is any state of MG an NME.

To determine which states *may* be NMEs, I show in figure 8.3 the eleven distinct specific games subsumed by MG. Actually, twelve games are shown in figure 8.3, because game 22 is shown twice (once in class 1 with an "a" after its number, and once in class 3 with a "b" after its number), with players V and D, as well as their strategies, interchanged.

Even though *a* and *b* are the same game configuration (i.e., game 22), their players receive different payoffs in Status Quo (state I in figure

Class 1: Status Quo is NME (four games)

22a	33	34	35
⟨(4,2)⟩ (2,1)	⟨(4,3)⟩ (2,1)	⟨(4,3)⟩ (1,1)	⟨(4,2)⟩ (2,1)
	[4,3] [4,3]	[4,3] [4,3]	[4,2] [4,2]
[3,3] [1,4]	(3,4) (1,2)	(3,4) (2,2)	(3,4) (1,3)
	[3,4] [4,3]	[3,4] [4,3]	[3,4] [4,2]

Class 2: Magnanimity is NME (four games)

Prisoners' Dilemma

28	29	32	50
(4,1) (2,2)	(4,1) (2,1)	(4,1) (2,2)	(4,2) (1,1)
		[3,3] [2,2]	[3,4] [3,4]/[4,2]
⟨(3,4)⟩ [1,3]	⟨(3,4)⟩ (2,3)	⟨(3,3)⟩ (1,4)	⟨(3,4)⟩ (2,3)
		[3,3] [3,3]	[3,4] [4,2]/[3,4]

Class 3: Rejected Status Quo or Rejected Magnanimity is NME (four games)

Total Conflict   **Chicken**

11	18	22b	57
(4,1) ⟨(2,3)⟩	(4,1) (1,3)	(4,1) (1,2)	(4,2) (1,1)
			[3,3]/[2,4] [2,4]/[4,2]
(3,2) (1,4)	(3,2) ⟨(2,4)⟩	(3,3) ⟨(2,4)⟩	⟨(3,3)⟩ ⟨(2,4)⟩
			[3,3] [4,2]/[2,3]

Key: (x,y) = (payoff to V, payoff to D)

   $[x,y]$ = [payoff to V, payoff to D] in anticipation game (AG)

   4 = best; 3 = next-best; 2 = next-worst; 1 = worst

   Nash equilibria in original games and AGs (only those with more than one
      NME shown) underscored

   Nonmyopic equilibria (NMEs), when Status Quo is initial state, circled

Figure 8.3
Twelve specific games subsumed by MG

8.2). Thus in game 22a, D receives a payoff of 2 in this state, whereas D receives a payoff of 1 in game 22b.

This fact makes these games different in the present analysis, in which I assume that *play always starts at Status Quo*, just after the conclusion of a dispute. Each player must then decide whether to depart from (v_4, d_i) or not.[4]

I have circled the outcomes in figure 8.3 that are NMEs from Status Quo. If a game contains more than one NME, they are indicated in brackets below the initial states from which they originate in the anticipation game (AG) (section 7.4). Thus in game 32 (Prisoners' Dilemma), Status Quo of (4,1) goes into (3,3), which is circled, but (2,2) goes into itself, which makes it another NME but not one that is induced from Status Quo.[5]

In figure 8.3, I have divided the twelve specific games subsumed by MG into three classes:

1. *Status Quo is NME (four games)*   It is rational for V not to be magnanimous, because D will not depart from Status Quo.

2. *Magnanimity is NME (four games)*   It is rational for V to be magnanimous, because otherwise D will depart from Status Quo, leading to a worse outcome. These games include Prisoners' Dilemma (game 32).

3. *Rejected Status Quo or Rejected Magnanimity is NME (four games)*   Even being magnanimous does not prevent the choice of $\overline{C}$ by D in these games, which include Chicken (game 57).[6] Rejected Magnanimity is rational in three of these games (18, 22b, and 57), whereas Rejected

---

4. Brams and Mor (1993) give necessary and sufficient conditions for the departure (or nondeparture) of each player from Status Quo to each of the other states. Their analysis is based on somewhat different rules than those given here, but the results are the same as those for TOM, except for game 57 (Chicken), in which their rules identify only (2,4), not (3,3), as the NME from Status Quo.

5. With the exception of Chicken (game 57), all the NMEs induced from Status Quo are Nash equilibria in the AG, but there may be other Nash equilibria in the AG. Indeed, every entry in the AG of a one-NME game is a Nash equilibrium.

6. Because of its indeterminate NME of [3,3]/[2,4] at Status Quo, which includes [3,3], Chicken also falls into class 2; for convenience I list it only in class 3 because of its NME of [2,4]. However, Chicken's NME of (3,3) at Status Quo is different from the other class 2 Magnanimity NMEs. In Chicken, V's move to Magnanimity at (3,3) is rational because D, by moving first, can induce (2,4), which is better for it and worse for V. By contrast, in the other class 2 games, V's move to Magnanimity is rational, because it is the only NME from Status Quo.

Status Quo is rational in the remaining game (11), which is the only *game of total conflict* (what is best for one player is worst for the other, and what is next-best for one player is next-worst for the other) among the twelve specific games subsumed by MG.

Although there is an even 4–4–4 split of the specific games among the three classes, these numbers do not necessarily bear a relation to the empirical relative frequency with which Status Quo, Magnanimity, and Rejected Status Quo or Rejected Magnanimity are actually chosen in real-life games.

I next state three propositions that follow from the analysis of the twelve specific games:

Proposition 8.1 *It is rational for V to be magnanimous in seven games (the NMEs in all class 2 games, and games 18, 22b, and 57 in class 3, are associated with this strategy) and not magnanimous in five games.*

It is worth noting that the NMEs from Status Quo in the twelve games do not always coincide with Nash equilibria. True, the NMEs coincide with Nash equilibria in class 1 and class 3 games [except for (3,3) in Chicken (game 57)], but in all class 2 games, including Prisoners' Dilemma (32), the NME (Magnanimity) is *never* a Nash equilibrium. In fact, Magnanimity is not a Nash equilibrium in any of the twelve specific 2×2 games, which makes this outcome inexplicable as a rational choice, according to standard game theory.

According to TOM, however, V will move from Status Quo to Magnanimity in all class 2 games. In game 32 (Prisoners' Dilemma) and game 28 (discussed in section 8.2), in particular, Magnanimity obviates the choice of the Pareto-inferior Nash equilibrium, (2,2). More generally, one can readily verify

Proposition 8.2 *The NMEs in all twelve games are Pareto-optimal—there is no other outcome better for both players.*

Finally, observe in figure 8.3 that all games with a (4,3) "cooperative" Status Quo are in class 1, whereas no games in class 1 have a total-conflict (4,1) Status Quo, giving

Proposition 8.3 *Status Quo is never an NME when it is D's worst state (1), but it is always an NME when it is D's next-best state (3).*

In other words, the better off D is at Status Quo, the more likely this state is an NME. Status Quo may or may not be an NME when it is (4,2)—it is the NME in two games (22a and 35) but not in two others (50 and 57).

8.5 Applications of MG to Historical Cases

My discussion of historical cases in this section is meant to be illustrative and not a systematic test of the predictions of MG. An empirical test would require ascertaining the specific preferences of players in the aftermaths of particular wars and trying to corroborate that they made strategy choices consistent with TOM.

I will give several examples in which the four different states of MG, all of which may be NMEs, appear to have been selected as outcomes. These examples lend plausibility to MG as an aid in thinking about the conditions that give rise to magnanimity or nonmagnanimity of the victor, and its acceptance or rejection by the defeated.

Status Quo

One war from the nineteenth century and two from the twentieth century illustrate this outcome. After France's defeat in the Franco-Prussian War of 1870–1871, Prussia humiliated France by issuing a proclamation of the new German empire at the Versailles Palace of Louis XIV, which it followed with a victory parade through the streets of Paris. More significant, France was required to pay an indemnity of five billion francs (with German occupation troops remaining until payment was completed in 1873); and the French provinces of Alsace and Lorraine were annexed to Germany.[7]

Although Chancellor Otto von Bismarck successfully opposed some of the more extreme demands his army generals made against France in 1871, it is clear that Germany chose M and France could do little but swallow its defeat. Indeed, contemplating their day of revenge, which was to come at Versailles almost fifty years later (1919), the French coined the rueful phrase, "Never speak of it, always think of it" (Ziegler 1984, 17).

In the aftermath of World War I, not only was Germany defeated unconditionally, but it also was forced to accept the harsh terms

---

7. In its successful war against Austria five years earlier (1866), Prussia, by contrast, treated Austria much more leniently, as I will discuss shortly.

of a settlement imposed by the allies. Likewise, the surrenders of Nazi Germany and Japan at the end of World War II were unconditional; moreover, Germany was divided into four zones that were occupied by the allies. Once again, the allies made no concessions after the war, although the Marshall Plan, beginning in 1947, helped tremendously in the later reconstruction of Europe, including West Germany.[8]

There was no Marshall Plan following World War I. Germany, destitute and plagued by inflation, moved inexorably toward Nazism, especially after 1933. One might contrast the aftermaths of the two world wars by saying that, immediately after both, the allies chose $\overline{M}$ and Germany could do no better than choose C, resulting in Status Quo. But a subsequent shift toward M by the allies after World War II engendered West Germany's continuing choice of C (Magnanimity), whereas the lack of such a shift by the allies after World War I led Germany eventually to choose $\overline{C}$ (Rejected Status Quo).

In summary, the *immediate* aftermath of the Franco-Prussian War and both world wars was Status Quo. By the dawn of World War I in 1914, however, the 1871 Status Quo had probably deteriorated to Rejected Status Quo—to the detriment, ultimately, of France and Germany, both of which suffered horrendous losses in World War I.

Likewise, the Status Quo of 1918 became Rejected Status Quo some twenty years later when the world was on the verge of World War II. By comparison, only ten years after World War II, the outcome had certainly become Magnanimity; West Germany joined NATO in 1955, and Japan became part of the Western Alliance, too. On the other hand, the two main victors of World War II parted ways to become competing superpowers.

Magnanimity

The Magnanimity outcome after World War II became a reality only some years after the war, which raises the question of what time span the model supposes. This is an empirical question to which different answers are possible.

There are certainly examples of the choice of Magnanimity immediately after a war. Consider the behavior of the Prussians after their

8. Of course, the aid provided was in part spurred by U.S.–Soviet rivalry after the war.

victory in the Seven Weeks' War (1866) against the Austrians, which I alluded to earlier (note 7):

After defeating the Austrian army at the decisive battle of Sadowa, the Prussian army did not pursue the Austrian army across the Danube River. It did not hold a victory parade through the streets of Vienna ... [and it] did not annex portions of Austria near its own borders, even though some justification could have been made for incorporation. (Ziegler 1987, 15)

What was the rationale of Bismarck's choice?

This policy of restraint was achieved by some effort on Bismarck's part, against the desires of the king and some of his advisers. Bismarck realized, as the king did not, that the work of German unification was not yet completed, and a humiliated and bitter Austria would be a potential ally for the new obstacle that now stood in Prussia's way: France. (Ziegler 1987, 15)

Prussia thereby headed off Austria's choice of $\overline{C}$ by instead moving to M, unlike its later choice of $\overline{M}$ against France. Indeed, the short duration of the Seven Weeks' War can in part be explained by Bismarck's limited war aim, which was to prevent Austrian influence in Prussian affairs—but not to acquire territory, as Prussia later did against France.

A more recent example of a magnanimous victor is David Ben Gurion after Israel's War of Independence. Although in late 1948 and early 1949 Israeli military capabilities permitted further territorial expansion to the north, east, and south, Ben Gurion "brought the war to an end and drew the lines delineating the new state under the guidance of the precepts of prudent moderation" (Oren 1982, 155). Most noteworthy was his decision to withdraw Israeli troops from the Rafa heights, a key strategic point on the southern front, over the strong objections of his army staff (Sachar 1979, 346).

The 1962 Cuban missile crisis is, arguably, another case ending in Magnanimity. Although the Soviet agreement to withdraw their missiles from Cuba was an outcome that President John F. Kennedy could present as an American victory, his brother, Robert F. Kennedy, wrote that

after it was finished, President Kennedy made no statement attempting to take credit for himself or for the Administration for what had occurred. He instructed all members of the ExCom (Executive Committee of the National Security Council) and government that no interview would be given, no statement made, which would claim any kind of victory. (Kennedy 1969, 126–127)

And in his subsequent public statements on October 28 and November 2 and 28, 1962, President Kennedy refrained from claiming victory and emphasized instead the broad themes of peace in the Caribbean and the reduction of world tensions.[9]

Rejected Status Quo
The 1979 Soviet invasion of Afghanistan illustrates this outcome. After the Soviets captured Kabul, executed the Afghan president, and installed their own puppet ruler, the Afghan rebels continued to resist, waging a long and costly guerrilla war—with considerable help from the United States—that eventually forced the Soviets to withdraw in 1988 and led to the collapse of the Afghan government in 1992.

Similarly, although Israel managed to defeat and eject the Palestine Liberation Organization (PLO) from Lebanon after its 1982 invasion, raids by the PLO continued. In 2006, Israel fought a brief war with Hezbollah in Lebanon, and in 2008–2009 with Hamas in the Gaza strip. In each case, these groups were clearly unwilling to cooperate with Israel.[10]

Rejected Magnanimity
This outcome seems the most difficult to document, because magnanimity, like beauty, is in the eye of the beholder. Thus, if V claims it was magnanimous, D can respond that this was not so, and, hence, by not cooperating it never "rejected" magnanimity. Nonetheless, I present two cases that seem to illustrate the selection of this outcome.

After its invasion of Cyprus on July 20, 1974, Turkey could credibly claim victory on August 16, having gained control of 40 percent of the island. On February 13, 1975, Turkish Cypriot leaders declared a separate state on the northern part of the island. At the same time, they offered Greek Cypriots a confederacy, with power to be shared

---

9. On the other hand, Secretary of State Dean Rusk's statement, "We're eyeball to eyeball, and I think the other fellow just blinked"—spoken at the climactic moment of the crisis and reported several weeks later—does sound suspiciously like a victory claim. *Eyeball to Eyeball* is the title of one book on the crisis (Brugoni 1992).

10. By contrast, Egypt and Israel chose Magnanimity after the 1973 Yom Kippur War, which resulted in a peace agreement at Camp David in 1978, mediated by President Jimmy Carter, which was formalized as a peace treaty in 1979. Likewise, Jordan and Israel signed a peace treaty in 1994.

equally in a single state (though Greek Cypriots outnumbered Turkish Cypriots by four to one). This offer, whose magnanimity might be questioned, was rejected, and a formal settlement of this conflict has yet to be achieved.

A quick settlement was attempted by Saddam Hussein after his invasion of Iran on September 22, 1980. Although his forces encountered only feeble and disorganized resistance initially, Hussein did not capitalize on his advantage. Instead, he "voluntarily halted the advance of his troops within a week after the onset of hostilities, and then announced his willingness to negotiate an agreement" (Karsh 1989, 211). Not only was this offer summarily rejected by Ayatollah Khomeini, but also the war ground on for nearly eight more years.

Because the Iran–Iraq War had just commenced at the time of Hussein's offer, this case is not strictly comparable to earlier cases, in which a decisive military victory had been achieved. Indeed, Hussein's offer and Khomeini's rejection may be closer to the Rejected Status Quo cases of the Soviet invasion of Afghanistan and the Israeli invasion of Lebanon in 1982. Although the initial victories in the latter cases were more consequential, the aftermath of each invasion was continued fighting that blurred the identification of a victor and a defeated party.

8.6 Why Did the Confederacy Initiate the U.S. Civil War?

In this section I apply MG to a civil war, but not to explain why non-magnanimity was chosen in its aftermath. Instead, I ask why war broke out in the first place when one side was perceived to be overwhelmingly more powerful than the other.

The conflict between the Union and the Confederacy in 1861, just before the outbreak of the U.S. Civil War, can be represented by game 22. This game is one of the MG games that I showed as game 22a and game 22b in figure 8.3, depending on where play starts. Wherever play starts, however, the unique NME in game 22 is (4,2), which I interpret as "Confederacy submits" (see figure 8.4, which I will justify shortly).

The Confederacy was indeed decisively defeated in 1865. This outcome is associated with the strategies of the Union not compromising and the

Confederacy

		Compromise (C)	Don't compromise ($\overline{C}$)
	Compromise (C)	**I** Compromise (3,3)$^{\cdot}$ [4,2]	**II** Union submits (1,4) [4,2]
Union			
	Don't compromise ($\overline{C}$)	**IV** Confederacy submits (4,2)$^{\#}$ [4,2]	**III** Civil War (2,1) [4,2]

← Dominant strategy

Key: (x,y) = (payoff to Union, payoff to Confederacy)

$[x,y]$ = [payoff to Union, payoff to Confederacy] in anticipation game (AG)

4 = best; 3 = next-best; 2 = next-worst; 1 = worst

Nash equilibrium in original game underscored

Nonmyopic equilibrium (NME) circled

* = Confederacy's deterrent threat outcome

= Union's deterrent threat outcome

Figure 8.4
Union-Confederacy Game (game 22)

Confederacy compromising, which in this instance meant that the latter was forced to surrender after a long and bloody struggle.

But a puzzle remains: Why did the Confederacy not recognize, insofar as its conflict with the Union can be modeled as game 22 and was perceived as such at the time (more on this shortly), that the Union would not be magnanimous—not just in the aftermath of the war, which I do not analyze here,[11] but also in its prosecution, which was devastating to the Confederacy? One explanation is that there was no clear recognition of the lopsided balance of forces in 1861, which greatly favored the North.

---

11. Suffice it to say that the states in the South that had joined the Confederacy were treated harshly in the so-called Reconstruction period after the war.

However, there is evidence that at least some Confederate leaders understood that the South was in a decidedly inferior position. They chose to escalate the crisis, nevertheless, but not with the expectation of committing political or military suicide. Although they had little hope of winning a civil war—if it came to that—they thought that by demonstrating their unswerving commitment to secede, they could convince the North to back down, once it understood the depth of their commitment and the costs the Union would incur in trying to put down an insurrection by the Confederacy.

Thereby threats, and the Confederacy's attempted exercise of threat power at the outset, played a crucial role in its instigating the Civil War. But this attempt failed because, ultimately, it was the Union that had threat power; it was better equipped to withstand the costs of war and, eventually, to prevail. The consequence was that instead of one or the other side's implementing its threat state, a breakdown state—worse for both sides than either threat state—became the outcome.

Before the outbreak of the war, the overriding issue was the institution of slavery and whether it would be permitted to persist in the United States. Each side could choose between a strategy to compromise and a strategy not to compromise:

1. Union Compromise (C) means permitting the Confederacy to keep its slaves and then negotiating their allowance in certain other territories, whereas $\overline{C}$ means demanding the immediate abolition of slavery.

2. Confederacy Compromise (C) means accepting restrictions on slavery outside the South, whereas $\overline{C}$ means demanding the right to hold slaves in the United States or, more likely, seceding from the Union and maintaining slavery in the South, probably as an independent country.

The preferences of the players for the four possible states, moving clockwise from the upper left-hand state in figure 8.4, are as follows:

1. CC: Compromise—(3,3) A negotiated settlement, whereby slavery would be allowed in the South but restrictions would apply elsewhere, which is next-best for both players.

II. C̄C̄: Union submits—(1,4) Slavery is permitted in the United States—or, alternatively, the Confederacy secedes without a civil war—which is worst for the Union and best for the Confederacy.

III. C̄C̄: Civil war—(2,1) Negotiations fail because neither side backs down and a major war ensues. This is next-worst for the Union, on the expectation that it will prevail in the end—albeit at a high price—and worst for the Confederacy on the expectation that it will be defeated and slavery will, consequently, be abolished.

IV. C̄C: Confederacy submits—(4,2) Slavery is abolished without civil war, which is best for the Union but next-worst for the Confederacy.

As can be seen from figure 8.4, the Confederacy always prefers that the Union choose C (4 and 3) rather than C̄ (2 and 1). Given the Union's choice of C, the Confederacy prefers C̄ (4) to C (3)—that is, having the Union submit (II) rather than compromise (I).

But what if the Union chooses C̄, which is, after all, its dominant strategy? I presume in the ranking that the Confederacy prefers C (2) to C̄ (1)—submission rather than civil war—which is supported by the observation of a contemporary observer:

> The truth was, the southern disunionists did not wish war, and they did not believe it would happen. The state of their finances would not sanction it, to say nothing of the dubious result of a collision with the colossal power of the north, backed by her navy. (Headley 1863, 52–53)

Just as the Confederacy most desired compromise on the part of the Union, the Union had a similar desire that the Confederacy choose C (4 and 3), with an obvious preference for submission by the Confederacy (4) to compromise (3). But unlike the Confederacy, the Union did not prefer C over C̄ if the Confederacy was adamant (chose C̄): "Let there be no compromise on the question of *extending* slavery," Abraham Lincoln wrote to Lyman Trumbull on December 10, 1860 (cited in Staudenraus 1960, 52; italics in original). As another indicator of Union steadfastness on the slavery issue, Congressman Oris S. Ferry of Connecticut advised Gideon Welles on December 11, 1860, that ten years of civil war would be preferable to a division of the union (Stampp 1950, 28).

Given the unique NME, (4,2), in game 22 (Confederacy submits), which is also the Nash equilibrium supported by the Union's dominant strategy of $\overline{C}$, why did the players not choose this state? The answer, I believe, depends on which player could exercise threat power (sections 2.3 and 7.2).

On the one hand, some Confederacy leaders thought that their deterrent threat of choosing $\overline{C}$, which includes the two worst states (1 and 2) of the Union, would induce compromise, yielding (3,3). On the other hand, the Union has a compellent threat of choosing $\overline{C}$ to induce (4,2), which is best for the Union. Clearly, the question of which side prevails in a "threat contest" depends on which side possesses threat power.[12]

Although a lack of information about who possessed such power is surely one explanation of why the threat contest escalated into a civil war, an alternative explanation is also persuasive: The Confederacy, recognizing its weaker position (the white population of the South was less than one-third that of the North), sought to prove that it was at least the equal of the North in other ways. By launching an attack on Fort Sumter in April 1861, and scoring early victories that it hoped would demoralize the North, a prolonged and costly war, it believed, could be avoided:

The surest way to prevent this [war] would be to make the contest appear equal as possible by getting the entire south to act in unison. Then the North would shrink from the appalling evils of a civil war, and grant them their independence. (Headley 1863, 53)

Thus, it seems, the bloodiest war in American history was provoked, at least in part, because the Confederacy thought it could threaten the Union into acquiescence, if not submission, with an early and effective show of force. Although the show of force was impressive, the North,

---

12. While (4,2) is the unique NME in game 22, this explanation of the eventual outcome does not offer a plausible account of why the two sides suffered through four years of harsh war at (2,1) before the Confederacy submitted. By contrast, the miscalculation of the Confederacy to provoke war with the expectation that it could conclude it on favorable terms at its deterrent threat outcome of (3,3) is a plausible reason. That the Confederacy underestimated the tenacity of Lincoln to preserve the Union and use everything in his power to gain the upper hand—in the end forcing the Union's compellent threat outcome of (4,2)—renders more plausible why the game remained so long at (2,1).

under President Lincoln, was not intimidated and fought doggedly on for four years, which eventually led to Sherman's devastating march through the South and the Confederacy's surrender at Appomattox in April 1865.

Perhaps many in the South would have preferred to sue for peace after the tide of battle turned in favor of the North at the Battle of Gettysburg in July 1863. But by then it was too late for the South to withdraw. When the North was finally able to assert its threat power, Lincoln was determined to make it palpably clear that the North could better withstand the breakdown state of (2,1).

The Civil War was a clash of interests over a fundamental issue. Moreover, the differences of the two sides over slavery in 1861 were probably irreconcilable by any kind of compromise, such as occurred with the Missouri Compromise of 1821 and the Compromise of 1850.

The question worth raising is not whether the opportunity to fashion a compromise was lost but rather whether better information about the strength and determination of Lincoln to force the issue—by military means if necessary—could have induced a less belligerent response from the South and settled the conflict more quickly. Realistically, probably not, but the foregoing analysis highlights how the outcome of the conflict seems to have turned on which side possessed threat power, or thought it did.

Although "learning the hard way" was extremely costly to both sides in the Civil War, it may have had the effect of creating the conditions for a more long-term solution than—in the absence of a test of strength—trying once again to patch over differences. Without such a test, information remains incomplete about which side in fact has greater power, even when the two sides know each other's preferences and, therefore, can make the TOM calculations I have described.

As long as the balance of power remains in doubt, it is easy for one side to overestimate its capabilities and think that it can coerce the other side into submission. The decades of lower-level yet persistent conflict over slavery between the North and South, beginning in 1819 over the admission of Missouri to the Union, illustrate this point. Fortunately for both sides in the aftermath of the Civil War, the settlement that was achieved has proved sturdy—slavery was never a serious option after 1865.

8.7 Summary and Conclusions

To summarize, I began by showing that it is rational in game 28 for R at (4,1) to sacrifice its best payoff in order to induce (3,4), lest C induce (2,2)—the unique Pareto-inferior Nash equilibrium—by moving first instead. I then showed how the two-sidedness convention clarifies the application of rules 5 and 6 of TOM to give this result, which is relevant in a total of seven 2×2 games (proposition 8.1). All of these games are subsumed by the Magnanimity Game (MG) in figure 6.2, which is a generic game that comprises a total of twelve specific 2×2 games.

To introduce MG, I began by discussing two contending schools of thought on how a victor should treat a defeated party after a war or other major dispute. Instead of taking sides in this controversy, I showed that each side may be "right," based on two-sided analysis in which the defeated party as well as the victor is considered a player able to make choices. Whether magnanimity or nonmagnanimity by the victor, or cooperation or noncooperation by the defeated party, is rational depends on the specific game being played or, more generally, the class of games into which it falls.

The analysis of MG demonstrated that each of the four states of this generic game, starting at Status Quo, may be an NME. For example, sticking with the Status Quo is never rational when this state is the worst for the defeated party, but it is always rational when it is the defeated party's next-best state. Magnanimity is rational in some games, including game 28 and Prisoners' Dilemma (game 32), in which the Nash equilibria are Pareto-inferior. Noncooperation by the defeated party is a rational strategy in still other games, including a total-conflict game (11) and Chicken (game 57, in which cooperation may also be rational), with the resulting outcome either Rejected Status Quo or Rejected Magnanimity.

It was not in the Union's interest to be magnanimous in game 22, which I used to model the U.S. Civil War. But the puzzle in this conflict was not that the North refused to compromise, once war broke out, but why the South chose to provoke a war that it knew it would lose if it were prolonged.

It did so, I suggested, because it thought it could force a quick nego-tiated settlement with early victories, but it miscalculated. Although both sides, according to TOM, could potentially exercise threat power in game 22, it was the Union that was able to demonstrate its superiority in a horrific four-year test of strength.

These findings of TOM may be viewed normatively, at least insofar as they offer interpretable conditions for deciding a rational course of action after a war or other major crisis. Thus, for example, because all the rational outcomes in MG are Pareto-optimal, decision makers may use MG to try to avoid the Pareto-inferior Nash equilibria that occur in games like Prisoners' Dilemma and game 28. In addition, TOM may help decision makers look ahead and anticipate dire long-term consequences that may arise from seemingly attractive, yet shortsighted, actions.

To conclude, MG helps explicate, in a systematic fashion, the logic of strategic choices in postdispute situations. Because players' choices in these situations may critically affect the outcomes of civil and international conflicts, they need to be carefully thought through, which TOM facilitates.

More generally, the analysis of this chapter demonstrates that magnanimity after a war, or a cooperative gesture in other situations may— apart from reasons of altruism— make good strategic sense. Compromise by a victor may be rational not because it does not hurt the victor but because it heads off action by the defeated party that may hurt both players even more at a breakdown outcome.

9 Incomplete Information in Literature and History

9.1 Introduction

The classical definition of a game in extensive form (i.e., one represented by a game tree) includes the specification of the information players have about the sequence moves of the other players.[1] Although the role of information in games has always been central in game theory, it takes on special significance under the rules of TOM.

For example, because standard game theory pays little attention to possible differences in the power of players, focusing instead on player choices and the stability of outcomes, it has little to say when there is incomplete information about power differences. Yet a player's information about the power of its opponent is often as significant as its information—or lack thereof—about its opponent's preferences, as I showed in section 8.6 in the case of the Confederacy's miscalculation of President Abraham Lincoln's unwavering pursuit of, and his ability to achieve, victory in the U.S. Civil War.

In this crisis, some leaders of the Confederacy appeared to understand quite well its inferior strategic position. Nevertheless, they attempted to coerce Union leaders into believing, through both threats and actions, that the Confederacy possessed threat power. Despite early military successes, however, the Confederacy was eventually brought to its knees in a gruesome war.

In this chapter, I focus on the incomplete information that players may have about each other's preferences, which may induce them to try to

---

1. Parts of this chapter are adapted from Brams 1977 and Brams 1994b, chap. 6, with permission.

seek out additional information, misperceive an opponent's interests, or try to deceive an adversary. I also consider the circumstances when the possession of information may backfire, creating a "paradox of omniscience."

To begin the analysis, I analyze in section 9.2 another one of Shakespeare's great tragedies, *Hamlet*. As in *Macbeth* (section 7.5), its principal character is frustrated, but more from his inability to acquire information about the possible misdeeds of his uncle and new stepfather, Claudius, than from thwarted ambition. In examining the conflict between Hamlet and Claudius, I argue that, contrary to many interpretations of this play (Elster 2009, 9–11), Hamlet's apparent dithering is less a tragic flaw in his character than a rational response within a game in which sketchy information had first to be filled in and verified before a rational course of action could be plotted and then taken.

In section 9.3 I show how the effects of incomplete information in the generic Magnanimity Game (MG) (section 8.4) can be analyzed theoretically. Assuming the players have no information about the preferences of their opponents, I derive two propositions about what information each player, not knowing the type of opponent it faces, would have to acquire to make a rational strategy choice in MG.

In section 9.4 I analyze the confrontation between President Jimmy Carter and Ayatollah Ruhollah Khomeini over the release of the American hostages taken and held by Iran in 1979–1981. Several months into their captivity, Carter ordered that a rescue mission be sent to Iran, which had to be aborted. Carter bungled the crisis not because Khomeini willfully deceived him but because of erroneous assumptions he had made about Khomeini's preferences. The failed rescue mission precipitated the resignation of Carter's secretary of state, Cyrus Vance, who had vigorously opposed it, and caused considerable embarrassment to the United States.

In section 9.5 I analyze strategic moves in the Cuban missile crisis of October 1962, based on two different representations of the game that was played between the United States and the Soviet Union. I suggest that the usual representation of this crisis as a game of Chicken is problematic and propose an alternative game. Despite the lack of information each side had about the other in this game, TOM elucidates the moves of the players and shows how the exercise of different kinds of power facilitated a peaceful settlement of this crisis.

In section 9.6 I extend the analysis of this crisis to argue that Premier Nikita Khrushchev may have consciously deceived President John F. Kennedy about his preferences. Paradoxically, his deception—or perhaps a sincere change in his preferences—expedited a resolution of the crisis. Indeed, there is a set of games in which it is actually in the interest of one player to be deceived by the other.

There is another set of games, discussed in section 9.7, in which being omniscient is a curse rather than a blessing. This anomalous result can also be interpreted as illustrating the power of commitment, akin to that exercised in making a compellent threat. Here, however, I stress how a player's awareness that its omniscient opponent can anticipate its choices may, in fact, hurt the omniscient player.

I conclude in section 9.8 with some thoughts on the double-edged effects of information. Although it is usually helpful to know more rather than less about an opponent and his or her capabilities, in certain games ignorance—or at least a lack of omniscience—may be bliss.

9.2   Information Revelation in *Hamlet*

In William Shakespeare's most famous play, *Hamlet*, there are several intertwined plots, but the main conflict is between the young Danish prince, Hamlet, and Claudius, Hamlet's uncle who becomes his stepfather after the death of Hamlet's father, the king of Denmark. Hamlet and Claudius stalk each other relentlessly throughout the play, each seeking more information about the knowledge and motives of the other.

The intrigue begins when the ghost of Hamlet's father describes to Hamlet the true cause of his father's mysterious death: He was not bitten by a venomous snake in an orchard, as supposed, but was murdered by Claudius, who poured poison into the king's ear as he slept. The apparition also reveals that Claudius was engaged in an adulterous affair with Hamlet's mother, Queen Gertrude, before the king's murder. The king's ghost asks Hamlet to "revenge his foul and most unnatural murder" (I:v:30).[2]

2. This ordered triple indicates (act:scene:verse), as given in Shakespeare 1601/1958.

Although Gertrude married Claudius with undue haste after the murder, the ghost tells Hamlet to ignore his mother's act, because she will suffer in her own way:

Taint not thy mind, nor let thy soul contrive
Against thy mother aught. Leave her to heaven,
And to those thorns that in her bosom lodge
To prick and sting her. (I:v:92–95)

After the ghost vanishes, Hamlet remains doubtful of its appearance, wondering whether it might even be the devil.

Nonetheless, Hamlet vows to kill his uncle, now King Claudius, in order to avenge his father's murder. The question then is how best to carry out this deed. Should he reveal his newfound but still uncertain knowledge of the treachery of his uncle (and now new stepfather), or should he keep secret his knowledge and dispatch him quickly?

On the one hand, declaring, or even insinuating, his suspicions would invite an attempt on Hamlet's own life by Claudius, who would then be able to surmise Hamlet's intentions. On the other hand, to hide his knowledge yet murder Claudius would make killing him seem an unjustifiable act as thoroughly dishonorable as Claudius's murder of Hamlet's father. Thus, Hamlet's two strategies are to reveal (R) or not reveal ($\overline{R}$) his secret but uncertain knowledge.

Hamlet actually gives a subtle twist to his strategy of R. It involves hinting at his knowledge of the murder, in a way that would be apparent only to Claudius, to try to force Claudius to confirm, perhaps unconsciously, his evil deed. Hamlet does this by feigning madness, under the guise of an "antic disposition" (I:v:197), to avoid being killed by a suspicious Claudius and to buy more time to gather incriminating evidence against him. The pretense confuses Polonius, the king's counselor: "Though this be madness, yet there is method in't" (II:ii:222–223).

Claudius, too, tries to obtain more information about Hamlet's knowledge of the murder and Hamlet's intentions to avenge it, enlisting Hamlet's friends, Rosencrantz and Guildenstern, as spies. But Hamlet sees through them and engineers their execution.

At one point, Claudius eavesdrops on a conversation between Hamlet and Ophelia, Hamlet's lover (to whom he also feigns madness). Hamlet admits that he is "very proud, revengeful, ambitious; with more offenses at my beck than I have thoughts to put them in, imagination to give them shape, or time to act them in" (III:i:134–137).

Claudius concludes that the young prince is not acting peculiarly because he is a harmless, lovesick fool. On the contrary, Claudius worries that "madness in great ones must not unwatched go" (II:i:198–199).

As the evidence accumulates that Hamlet is a threat both to his life and his throne, Claudius must decide between killing Hamlet immediately (K), a risky strategy because of "the great love the general gender bear him" (IV:vii:20), or not killing him ($\overline{K}$), which is also risky if Hamlet indeed intends to avenge his father's murder and slays him first. In combination with Hamlet's strategies, the resulting game is shown in figure 9.1.

Claudius

	Kill (K)	Don't kill ($\overline{K}$)	
Reveal (R)	I Martyrdom for Hamlet (3,2) [3,2]	II Success for Hamlet (4,1) [3,2]	Dominant strategy
Don't reveal ($\overline{R}$)	IV Failure for Hamlet (1,3) [3,2]	III Dishonor for Hamlet (2,4) [3,2]	

Hamlet

Key: (x,y) = (payoff to Hamlet, payoff to Claudius)

[x,y] = [payoff to Hamlet, payoff to Claudius] in anticipation game (AG)

4 = best; 3 = next-best; 2 = next-worst; 1 = worst

Nash equilibrium in original game underscored

Nonmyopic equilibrium (NME) circled

Arrows show moves from state III to state I

Figure 9.1
Hamlet-Claudius Conflict (game 26)

The consequences of the players' strategy choices at the four states, moving clockwise from the upper left-hand state, are as follows:

I. RK: Martyrdom for Hamlet—(3,2)   Hamlet publicly reveals Claudius's treachery against his father but is killed as a result; Claudius is implicated in both murders and is punished.

II. R$\overline{\text{K}}$: Success for Hamlet—(4,1)   The murderer of Hamlet's father is uncovered, and Claudius is dethroned and killed.

III. $\overline{\text{R}}\overline{\text{K}}$: Dishonor for Hamlet—(2,4)   Hamlet never reveals evidence to avenge his father's murder and is disgraced; Claudius is no longer threatened.

IV. $\overline{\text{R}}$K: Failure for Hamlet—(1,3)   Hamlet is dishonored for not revealing the murderer of his father and is killed as well; Claudius faces possible punishment for Hamlet's murder.

The game commences in state (2,4), wherein Hamlet hides his knowledge of the heinous crime and Claudius receives his best payoff. As TOM predicts, Hamlet gingerly switches to R. In an imaginative attempt to confirm his suspicions, Hamlet puts on a skit for Claudius and Gertrude that reenacts the murder of his father and the clandestine affair between his mother and his uncle. Furthermore, Hamlet asks Horatio to observe Claudius's actions throughout the performance:

Observe my uncle. If his occulted guilt
Do not itself unkennel in one speech,
It is a damned ghost that we have seen,
And my imaginations are as foul
As Vulcan's stithy [forge]. (III:ii:81–85)

Horatio reports back that Claudius became pale during the performance and then, after becoming extremely agitated, walked out. Apparently guilt-stricken, Claudius was unable to bear the scene on stage. This confirms Hamlet's suspicions that the tale the ghost told was true, and that Claudius is in fact the murderer of his father.

Now the next move is Claudius's at (4,1). Even before the skit, his suspicions were aroused that Hamlet had uncovered the murder. But now his worst fears are confirmed, and he, like Hamlet, agonizes no more about what to do.

A series of events, too complex to relate here, unfolds. By the end of the play, Hamlet has revealed to Claudius his knowledge of the crime and slain him. But Hamlet himself succumbs to poison, as does his mother, a direct consequence of Claudius's actions.[3]

Thus, the players end up at the unique NME of (3,2) in game 26, which is also the Nash equilibrium associated with Hamlet's dominant strategy of R. What the Nash equilibrium fails to make apparent, however, is the rationality of the *sequence* of moves leading to it, from states III through II to I.[4]

Of course, even a move-by-move analysis does not begin to capture all the richness and subtlety of Shakespeare's play. What TOM does demonstrate, however, is that the behavior of the principal antagonists is perfectly explicable in terms of rational moves, which is a view distinctly at odds with psychological interpretations of this play.

In particular, Hamlet had good reasons for acting bizarrely: first, to cover up his intentions so as not to get killed himself; second, to try to elicit the truth from Claudius about his perfidy. (Of course, Hamlet's behavior might also be interpreted as randomizing his choices to conceal his intentions, but the figure 9.1 game, interpreted cardinally, does not have a mixed-strategy Nash equilibrium.) Claudius was no less astute in trying to ascertain how much Hamlet knew about his fratricide.

Hamlet's hesitancy to move decisively against Claudius, until the end, is perhaps harder to fathom. His irresoluteness is often attributed to a tragic flaw in Hamlet's character—his melancholy nature or suicidal personality—which are viewed as psychological abnormalities. But is it so abnormal to be grief-stricken by the murder of one's father and lethargic after such an event?

---

3. In the play, Hamlet chooses R before Claudius chooses K, which suggests that Hamlet acted first, after which Claudius made his choice, in a 2 × 4 game, wherein Claudius's strategies depend on Hamlet's prior choices. But, in fact, Claudius contemplated killing Hamlet well before the skit, so the 2 × 2 game form is appropriate.

4. Interestingly enough, moves from I to IV, and from IV back to III, are clearly infeasible (Hamlet cannot hide his knowledge of Claudius's complicity after letting it slip out, and Claudius cannot bring Hamlet back to life after killing him). But these moves would not be made, even if they were feasible, because state I is the unique NME.

Aside from inconsolable grief and possible depression, Hamlet had cogent reasons for vacillating. He could not be sure about Claudius's complicity until after Horatio had witnessed Claudius's reaction to the skit. Also, he would have jeopardized his own ascension to the throne if he had acted rashly, before the evidence of Claudius's guilt was incontrovertible.

Hamlet's planning that led up to the entrapment of Claudius is, in my opinion, nearly flawless. But Claudius is no less adroit a game player. Like Hamlet, he could not act precipitously—by killing Hamlet—lest he be discovered as the perpetrator of two murders. In effect, each of the protagonists sought to peel away layers from the mystery surrounding the other.

Polonius, who, as I indicated earlier, had a dim view of what was going on, was also involved in the attempt to ferret out the truth:

If circumstances lead me, I will find
Where truth is hid, though it were hid indeed
Within the centre. (II:ii:171–173)

But Polonius, whom Hamlet kills before he can unravel the mystery, is no match for Hamlet.

I have made Hamlet's strategy choice one of revelation or nonrevelation, in which the purpose of revelation is to evoke a telltale reaction from Claudius. Though I posit Claudius to choose between killing or not killing Hamlet, bear in mind that he, like Hamlet, is vitally concerned with gathering and exploiting any information before deciding whether to move against Hamlet.

Ultimately, of course, both players attempt to eliminate each other. Perhaps the most significant difference in their strategies is that Hamlet wants first to discover the truth, which requires revealing something about what he knows. Claudius wants to hide it but, at the same time, to discover what Hamlet knows.

Each player was slow to move against the other until he had assembled what he thought was overwhelming evidence. But once each had done so, their cat-and-mouse game turned diabolical and grim. Thus, Claudius tried to have Hamlet murdered in England, just as Hamlet plotted to kill Claudius when he returned to Denmark. In the end, tragedy befalls not only the antagonists but several other characters as well. Nevertheless, all the characters—including Hamlet—seem eminently rational in light of the informational constraints they faced.[5]

9.3   Incomplete Information in the Magnanimity Game (MG)

Although players may have no information about their opponents, it is more likely they will have some information, such as a partial ordering of their preferences. Often they endeavor to make this information more complete, as I showed occurred in *Hamlet*. However, a player may not need to fill in all the gaps in order to act rationally, as I next illustrate in the case of MG (section 8.4).

In this game, depicted in figure 8.2, V's (the victor's) preferences were restricted to two types and D's to six types, yielding twelve specific games (figure 8.3). To analyze the effects of incomplete information on the play of MG, consider V's two types of preferences: Given D (the defeated party) chooses $\overline{C}$, either V prefers $\overline{M}$ (Rejected Status Quo) over M (Rejected Magnanimity), or vice versa. Call the first type *hard* (V prefers to be tough when D is), and the second type *soft* (V prefers to be lenient when D is tough).

Assume that V knows whether it is hard or soft but does not know D's six types of preferences (I will not give them names). If V is *totally* ignorant of D's type, it is unable to make a rational choice—that is, choose a strategy that always contains an NME, given that play commences at Status Quo. However, observe in figure 8.3 that if V is soft, which it is in games 34, 29, 50, 18, 22b, and 57, its rational strategy is M in all games except 34, which defines one type of D opponent. If V is hard, which it is in games 22a, 33, 35, 28, 32, and 11, its rational strategy is $\overline{M}$ in all games except 28 and 32, which define two types of D opponent. These results can be summarized as follows:

---

5. Information, or the lack thereof, is also the key to Howard's (1996) drama-theoretic explanation of the characters' choices in *Hamlet*; the role information plays is also discussed in Elster 2007, 246–248. Orbell (1993) analyzes Hamlet from a decision-theoretic rather than a game-theoretic perspective, in which uncertainty rather than the choices of other players are decisive. Decision theory is also employed by Dalkey (1981) to analyze Hamlet's famous "to be or not to be" soliloquy.

Proposition 9.1 *If V is soft, it must rule out only one type of D (out of six) to render its strategy of M rational. If V is hard, it must rule out two types to render its strategy of $\overline{M}$ rational.*

As one would expect, a soft V will generally choose M and a hard V will generally choose $\overline{M}$.

Now reverse matters and assume that D knows which of the six types it is. However, assume that D does not know whether V is hard or soft. This means that D can narrow down the games being played to a pair, of which there are six, depending on V's type (hard, soft):

(22a, 57); (35, 50); (33, 34); (28, 29); (32, 22b); (11, 18).

D's choice of C is rational in (35, 50), (33, 34), and (28, 29), whereas $\overline{C}$ is rational in (11, 18); neither strategy is rational in *both* games of pair (22a, 57). These results can be summarized as follows:

Proposition 9.2 *Assume D knows its own preferences, of which there are six types. Four of D's six types can choose a rational strategy (either C or $\overline{C}$) without knowing whether V is hard or soft. For D's two remaining types, this knowledge is necessary for D to choose a rational strategy.*

The four games that represent the latter two types are Prisoners' Dilemma (32) and Chicken (57)—and their two counterparts, in which V has Prisoners' Dilemma preferences and D has Chicken preferences (22a) and vice versa (22b). Thus, D can determine its rational strategy if its preferences are *not* those of either Prisoners' Dilemma or Chicken. If they are, it must ascertain whether V is hard or soft (i.e., has Prisoners' Dilemma or Chicken-type preferences), which fixes one of the four specific games.

I will not attempt to apply propositions 9.1 and 9.2 to particular cases, though both might help to explain some of the different outcomes of MG that occurred in the historical examples discussed in section 8.5. These propositions may also be applicable to policy analysis—for example, in helping V or D decide its best strategy after a war.

Thus, if a country is D, and its preferences make it one of the four types in which its rational strategy (C or $\overline{C}$) is independent of V's type, then it has an optimal choice whatever type V is. But if D is one of the other two types, it would behoove it to try to gather intelligence on V's type before choosing C or $\overline{C}$. Similarly, V's rational choice does not require that it identify which of the six types it is but only ascertain that it is not one of, at most, two types.

I next present an historical example of a game of incomplete information, wherein one player had incomplete information about the preferences of its opponent. Misperceiving its opponent's preferences, it took actions that it almost surely would not have taken had its information been correct.[6]

9.4 Misperception in the Iran Hostage Crisis

In the Iranian seizure of American embassy hostages in November 1979, the military capabilities of the two sides were almost irrelevant. Although an attempt was made in April 1980 to rescue the hostages in an aborted U.S. military operation that cost eight American lives, the conflict was never really a military one. It can best be represented as a game in which President Jimmy Carter misperceived the preferences of Ayatollah Ruholla Khomeini and attempted, in desperation, to find a solution in the wrong game (Brams and Mattli 1993).[7]

Why did Khomeini sanction the takeover of the American embassy by militant students? Doing so had two advantages. First, by creating a confrontation with the United States, Khomeini was gradually able to sever the many links that remained with this "Great Satan" from the days of Mohammad Reza Pahlavi, who had ruled before being exiled. Second, the takeover mobilized support for extremist revolutionary objectives just at the moment when moderate secular elements in Iran were challenging the principles of the theocratic state that Khomeini had installed.

President Carter most wanted to obtain the immediate release of the hostages. His secondary goal was to hold discussions with Iranian religious authorities on resolving the differences that had severely strained U.S.-Iranian relations. Of course, if the hostages were killed,

---

6. Dynamic models, based on TOM, for inferring the preferences of enduring rivals in international politics are developed in Maoz and Mor 1996, 2002.

7. The importance of perceptions in applying TOM is emphasized in Malici's (2008) reconstruction of the "subjective games" of one leader who learned and changed his beliefs (the Soviet Union's Mikhail Gorbachev) and one leader who did not (North Korea's Kim Il Sung).

the United States would defend its honor, probably by a military strike against Iran.

Carter considered two strategies:

1. Negotiate (N) With diplomatic relations broken after the seizure, negotiations could be pursued through the U.N. Security Council, the World Court, or informal diplomatic channels; the negotiations might include the use of economic sanctions.

2. Intervene militarily (I) Military action could include a rescue mission to extract the hostages or punitive strikes against selected targets (e.g., refineries, rail facilities, or power stations).

Khomeini also had two strategies:

1. Negotiate (N) Negotiations would involve demanding a return of the shah's assets and an end to U.S. interference in Iran's affairs.

2. Obstruct (O) Obstructing a resolution of the crisis could be combined with feigning to negotiate.

Carter perceived the game to be game 50, which is shown in the top matrix of figure 9.2.[8] He most preferred that Khomeini choose N (4 and 3) rather than O (2 and 1), but in any case he preferred N to O, given the difficulties of military intervention.

These difficulties were compounded in December 1979 by the Soviet invasion of Afghanistan, which eliminated the Soviet Union as a possible ally in seeking concerted action for release of the hostages through the United Nations. With Soviet troops next door in Afghanistan, the strategic environment was anything but favorable for military intervention.

As for Khomeini, Carter *thought* that the Ayatollah faced serious problems within Iran because of a critical lack of qualified people, demonstrations by the unemployed, internal war with the Kurds, Iraqi incursions across Iran's western border, and a continuing power struggle at the top (though his own authority was unchallenged). Consequently,

---

8. Game 50 is one of the twelve specific MG games, shown in figure 8.3, in which Magnanimity is an NME. Because I distinguish game 50 from the "real game" (game 5) later, I do not list, as I did earlier (using Roman numerals), the four possible outcomes: They change between the "misperceived game" (game 50) and the real game (game 5), so it seems better to compare the outcomes directly rather than by two different sets of Roman numerals.

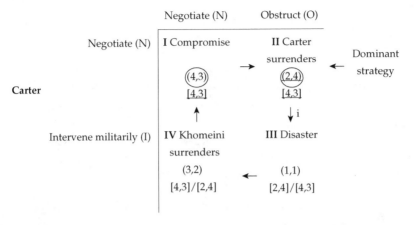

Game as misperceived by Carter (game 50)

Khomeini

Negotiate (N)   Obstruct (O)

Carter

Negotiate (N)

I Compromise   II Carter
                 surrenders

(4,3)   (2,4)
[4,3]   [4,3]

Dominant
strategy

Intervene militarily (I)

IV Khomeini   III Disaster
surrenders

(3,2)   (1,1)
[4,3]/[2,4]   [2,4]/[4,3]

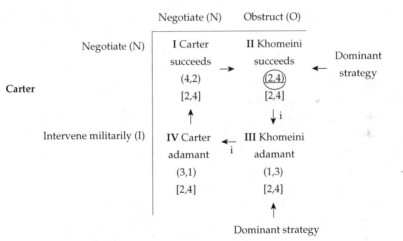

Real game (game 5)

Khomeini

Negotiate (N)   Obstruct (O)

Carter

Negotiate (N)

I Carter   II Khomeini
succeeds   succeeds

(4,2)   (2,4)
[2,4]   [2,4]

Dominant
strategy

Intervene militarily (I)

IV Carter   III Khomeini
adamant   adamant

(3,1)   (1,3)
[2,4]   [2,4]

Dominant strategy

Key : (x,y) = (payoff to Carter, payoff to Khomeini)

[x,y] = [payoff to Carter, payoff to Khomeini] in anticipation game (AG)

4 = best; 3 = next-best; 2 = next-worst; 1 = worst

i = impediment

Nash equilibria in original games and AG of game 50 underscored

Nonmyopic equilibria (NMEs) circled

Arrows in matrices indicate direction of cycling

Figure 9.2
Iran Hostage Crisis (games 50 and 5)

Carter believed that negotiations would give Khomeini a dignified way out of the difficulties that beset his regime (Carter 1982, 459–489).

One implication of this view is that while Carter thought that Khomeini most preferred a U.S. surrender at NO (4), he believed Khomeini would next most prefer the compromise of NN (3). Thus, Khomeini's two worst states (1 and 2), in Carter's view, were associated with the U.S. strategy of military intervention (I).

Carter's imputation of these preferences to Khomeini turned out to be a major misperception of the strategic situation. Khomeini wanted the total Islamization of Iranian society; the United States was "a global Shah—a personification of evil" (quoted in Saunders 1985, 102) that had to be cut off from any contact with Iran. Khomeini abjured his nation never to "compromise with any power . . . [and] to topple from the position of power anyone in any position who is inclined to compromise with the East and West" (Sick 1985a, 237).

If Iran's leaders should negotiate the release of the hostages, this would weaken their uncompromising position. Those who tried, including President Bani-Sadr and Foreign Minister Ghotbzadeh, lost in the power struggle. Bani-Sadr was forced to flee for his life to Paris, and Ghotbzadeh was arrested and later executed.

What Carter was unable to grasp was that Khomeini most preferred O (4 and 3), independent of what the United States did. Doubtless, Khomeini also preferred that the United States choose N, whatever his own strategy choice was, giving him the preferences shown in the bottom matrix of figure 9.2, which is game 5 and what I call the "real game."

Perhaps the most salient difference between Carter's game (game 50) and the real game (game 5) is that the former game contains two NMEs, (4,3) and (2,4), whereas the latter game contains only one, (2,4). In Carter's game, Carter's preferred solution of compromise at (4,3) can be reached wherever play commences, as is evident from its anticipation game (AG). In addition, (4,3) is not vulnerable to moving power (section 3.4): Whichever player possesses it, (4,3) is the outcome, making this kind of power irrelevant.

To see this, note from the arrows in game 50 in figure 9.2 (top matrix) that game 50 is cyclic in clockwise direction (an impediment, indicated by "i," is also shown). If Carter has moving power, he can force Khomeini to stop at either (4,3) or (1,1), from which the horizontal arrows, indicating Khomeini's moves, emanate. Because Khomeini prefers (4,3), Carter thought he would stop there.

By contrast, if Khomeini has moving power (section 3.4), he can force Carter to stop at either (3,2) or (2,4), from which the vertical arrows, indicating Carter's moves, emanate. Because Carter prefers (3,2), he would presumably stop there. But because (4,3), which Carter can induce, is better for both players than (3,2), which Khomeini can induce, it would be in the players' mutual interest to stop the move-countermove process at (4,3), making the possession of moving power irrelevant.

In game 50, threat power (section 7.2) is effective: Carter has a deterrent threat—threatening I, at which Khomeini prefers (3,2), to implement (4,3)—whereas Khomeini has a compellent threat—choosing O to implement (2,4) that Carter prefers to (1,1). Thus, the possessor of threat power can implement its best outcome [(4,3) for Carter, (2,4) for Khomeini], as can the possessor of order power (section 7.4), starting from either (3,2) or (1,1), the two indeterminate states in this game. Insofar as Carter believed that he had the upper hand in game 50, he would see compromise as attainable by the exercise of any of the three kinds of power.

The prospects for compromise are very different in the real game (game 5), shown as the lower matrix in figure 9.2. Not only is (2,4) the unique NME, favoring Khomeini, but Khomeini can induce it with a compellent threat by choosing and sticking with O. Carter does not have a threat strategy in this game; moreover, though game 5 is cyclic, moving power is *ineffective* (the stoppage of the game that each player can force with moving power is worse for it than what the other player can force, making its exercise futile); and order power is not defined because there are no indeterminate states. But because Carter thought he was playing game 50, in which the (4,3) NME can always be induced if play starts at either state associated with N—even without the exercise of order power—Carter would have no reason not to choose N.

Adopting this strategy from the start turned out to be a major blunder. However, in the game as he perceived it, Carter also had a deterrent threat (noted earlier) that could induce (4,3), which he pursued as well. He dispatched the aircraft carrier USS *Kitty Hawk* and its supporting battle group from the Pacific to the Arabian Sea. The carrier USS *Midway* and its battle group were already present in the area. Sick (1985b, 147) reported:

With the arrival of *Kitty Hawk*, the United States had at its disposal the largest naval force to be assembled in the Indian Ocean since at least World War II and the most impressive array of firepower ever deployed to those waters.

But this threat, like those preceding it, did not lead to any change in Khomeini's strategy because of Carter's fateful underestimation of Khomeini's willingness and ability to absorb economic, political, and military punishment in the pursuit of his revolutionary goals. In the real game, military intervention in Iran (I) leads to the (1,3) state when Khomeini chooses obstruct (O). Because of the possible execution of the hostages that this attack might provoke—the threat of which was "taken with deadly seriousness in Washington" (Sick 1985b, 147)—I rank it as worst for the United States.

After negotiations faltered and then collapsed in April 1980, Carter was forced to move to his I strategy. If the rescue operation had succeeded and the hostages had been freed, the game would have been in state (3,1), because Khomeini could in that situation no longer use the hostages as a weapon, precluding his choice of O.

The rescue's failure kept the situation in state (2,4) for another nine months. But the Iranian leadership had already concluded in August 1980, after the installation of an Islamic government consistent with Khomeini's theocratic vision, that the continued retention of the hostages was a liability (Saunders 1985, 44–45). Further complicating Iran's position was the attack by Iraqi forces in September 1980. It was surely no accident that the day of Carter's departure from the White House on January 20, 1981, 444 days after the capture of the hostages, they were set free.[9]

Although Carter's strategic acumen in this crisis can be questioned, it was less his rationality that was at fault than his misperception of

---

9. That the hostages were not released before the November 1980 presidential election, which clearly would have benefited Carter's bid for reelection, Sick (1991) attributes to a secret deal Iran made with Reagan supporters. But this allegation, at least as far as George Bush's involvement is concerned, is disputed by a bipartisan October Surprise Task Force of the U.S. House of Representatives chaired by Lee H. Hamilton (Lewis 1992). Sick's argument for and Hamilton's argument against a secret deal are joined in "Last Word on the October Surprise?" (Hamilton 1993).

Khomeini's preferences. Within a week of the American embassy seizure, analysts in the State Department had reached the conclusion that diplomatic action had almost no prospect of being successful in liberating the hostages and that no economic or other U.S. pressure on the Iranian regime, including military action, was likely to be any more successful in securing their safe release. Consequently, they concluded, the detention of the hostages could continue for some months (Sick 1985, 246).

In the first few months of the crisis, U.S. Secretary of State Cyrus Vance counseled that "we continue to exercise restraint" (Vance 1983, 408). Privately, he vehemently opposed any military action; and after the military rescue operation failed, he resigned.

But others, including secular politicians in Iran who claimed to speak for Khomeini, voiced different views. There was an abundance, rather than a dearth, of information, but the question, as always, was: What was accurate?

Carter, perhaps, should not be judged too harshly for misperceiving the situation. In fact, even if he had foreseen the real game from the start, this analysis suggests that there was little that he could have done to move the state away from (2,4), given that the military power of the United States could not readily be translated into a credible threat or helpful action.

Nevertheless, Carter's misperception gave him the hope that he could implement the compromise outcome in game 50, not only because it is an NME in that game but also because it can be induced via threat, moving, or order power. By contrast, the "Carter succeeds" outcome in game 5 is not an NME, and no kind of power can induce it.

This contrast between the two games is obscured in standard game theory, which shows (2,4), in which Carter surrenders, to be the unique Nash equilibrium, associated with Carter's dominant strategy of N, in each game. Thus, this theory makes Carter's actions inexplicable in terms of rational choice—whether he misperceived Khomeini's preferences or not—whereas TOM shows that Carter's actions were not ill founded, given his misperception.[10]

---

10. *Misperception* may be too strong. In 1997, Carter said, "My feeling for him [Khomeini] was [that I had] a lack of understanding of what he wanted" (*New York Times Magazine*, October 27, 1997, 19). Nonetheless, Carter acted on the basis of the misperception I described earlier.

I next offer an extended analysis of the Cuban missile crisis, which was suffused with incomplete information. I show this first by presenting in section 9.5 two quite different games to model this crisis, arguing that the second game provides a more realistic representation. Then I indicate in section 9.6 how, given the paucity of information about the true motives of the Soviet Union in provoking this crisis, deception might have played a role in its resolution.

9.5 The Cuban Missile Crisis: Moving, Order, and Threat Power

Before the breakup of the Soviet Union in 1991 and its demise as a superpower, the most dangerous confrontation between the super-powers ever to occur was the Cuban missile crisis. It was precipitated by a Soviet attempt in October 1962 to install in Cuba medium-range and intermediate-range nuclear-armed ballistic missiles capable of hitting a large portion of the United States. How the superpowers—or, more accurately, their leaders—managed this crisis has been described in great detail, but this scrutiny has involved little in the way of formal and systematic strategic analysis.

After the presence of such missiles was confirmed on October 14, the Central Intelligence Agency estimated that they would be operational in about ten days. A so-called Executive Committee (ExCom) of high-level officials was convened to decide on a course of action for the United States, and ExCom met in secret for six days. The comments of Theodore Sorensen, special counsel and advisor to President John F. Kennedy, on its deliberations reflect well the game-theoretic thinking of its members:

We discussed what the Soviet reaction would be to any possible move by the United States, what our reaction with them would have to be to that Soviet reaction, and so on, trying to follow each of these roads to their ultimate conclusion. (quoted in Holsti, Brody, and North 1964, 188)

Several strategies were considered, which were eventually narrowed to two.

The most common conception of this crisis is that the two superpowers were on a collision course.[11] The game of Chicken (game 57), at first

---

11. *Collision Course* is the title of one book describing the crisis (Pachter 1963).

Soviet Union (SU)

Withdrawal (W)   Maintenance (M)

		Withdrawal (W)	Maintenance (M)
	Blockade (B)	I Compromise ((3,3)) [3,3]	II Soviet victory, U.S. defeat ((2,4))[#] [4,2]/[3,3]
United States (US)			
	Air strike (A)	IV U.S. victory, Soviet defeat ((4,2))[*] [3,3]/[2,4]	III Nuclear war (1,1) [2,4]/[4,2]

Key: (x,y) = (payoff to US, payoff to SU)

$[x,y]$ = [payoff to US, payoff to SU] in anticipation game (AG)

4 = best; 3 = next-best; 2 = next-worst; 1 = worst

Nash equilibria in original game and AG underscored

Nonmyopic equilibria (NMEs) circled

* = US's compellent threat state

= SU's compellent threat state

Figure 9.3
Cuban Missile Crisis (Chicken [game 57])

blush, would seem an appropriate model of this conflict. As applied to the Cuban missile crisis, with the United States and the Soviet Union as the two players, the alternative courses of action, and a ranking of the players' states in terms of Chicken, are shown in figure 9.3.[12]

The goal of the United States was immediate removal of the Soviet missiles, and U.S. policy makers seriously considered two strategies to achieve this end:

1. A naval blockade (B), or "quarantine" as it was euphemistically called, to prevent shipment of further missiles, possibly followed by stronger

---

12. I assume that the superpowers can be considered unitary actors, though this is clearly a simplification. It is rectified in part by constructing alternative models that emphasize different features, as Allison (1971) has done. For alternative game-theoretic interpretations of the crisis, see Dixit, Skeath, and Reilly 2009, chap. 15.

action to induce the Soviet Union to withdraw those missiles already installed.

2. A "surgical" air strike (A) to wipe out the missiles already installed, insofar as possible, perhaps followed by an invasion of the island.

The alternatives open to Soviet policy makers were:

1. Withdrawal (W) of their missiles.

2. Maintenance (M) of their missiles.

Needless to say, the strategy choices and probable outcomes as presented in figure 9.3 provide only the barest structure of the crisis as it developed over a period of thirteen days. Both sides considered more than the two alternatives listed, as well as several variations on each. The Soviets, for example, demanded withdrawal of American missiles from Turkey as a quid pro quo for withdrawal of their own missiles from Cuba, a demand publicly ignored by the United States.

Furthermore, there is no way to verify that the states given in figure 9.3 were the most likely ones, or valued in a manner consistent with the game of Chicken. For example, if the Soviet Union had viewed an air strike on its missiles as jeopardizing its vital national interests, the (4,2) state may very well have ended in nuclear war between the two sides, giving it the same value as (1,1). Still another simplification relates to the assumption that the players chose their actions simultaneously, when in fact a continual exchange of messages, occasionally backed up by actions, occurred over those fateful days of October 1962.[13]

Most observers of this crisis agree that neither side was eager to take any irreversible step, such as one of the drivers in Chicken might do by defiantly ripping off his or her steering wheel in full view of the other driver, thereby foreclosing the option of swerving and communicating this to the other driver. While the United States "won," in a sense, by getting the Soviets to withdraw their missiles, Premier Nikita Khrushchev extracted from President Kennedy a promise not to invade

---

13. Books on this crisis include Abel 1966, Weintal and Bartlett 1967, Kennedy 1969, Allison 1971, Divine 1971, Chayes 1974, Dinerstein 1976, Detzer 1979, and Brune 1985. Books that take account of revelations from the Soviet side include Blight and Welsh 1989, Garthoff 1989, and Thompson 1992; for details on the use of aerial surveillance, see Brugoni 1992.

Cuba, which seems to indicate that the eventual outcome was a compromise of sorts.[14] Moreover, even though the Soviets responded specifically to the blockade and, therefore, did not make the choice of their strategy independently of the Americans' strategy choice, the fact that the United States held out the possibility of escalating the conflict to at least an air strike indicates that the initial blockade decision was not considered final—that is, the United States considered its strategy choices still open after imposing the blockade.

Truly, this was a game of sequential bargaining, in which each side did not make an all-or-nothing choice but instead considered alternatives should the other side fail to respond in a manner considered appropriate. Representing the most serious breakdown in the deterrence relationship between the superpowers that had persisted from World War II until that point, each side was carefully feeling its way, step by ominous step.

Before the crisis, the Soviets, fearing an invasion of Cuba by the United States and also driven by the need to bolster their international strategic position, concluded that it was worth the risk of installing the missiles; confronted by a fait accompli, the United States, in all likelihood, would be deterred from invading Cuba and would not attempt any other severe reprisals (Garthoff 1989). Presumably, the Soviets did not reckon the probability of nuclear war to be high in making their calculation,[15] thereby making it rational for them to risk provoking the United States.

Although this thinking may be more or less correct, there are good reasons to believe that U.S. policy makers viewed the game not to be Chicken at all, at least as far as they ranked the possible states. In figure 9.4, I offer an alternative representation of the Cuban missile crisis,[16]

14. A release of letters between Kennedy and Khrushchev, however, indicates that Kennedy's promise was conditional on the good behavior of Cuba (Pear 1992).

15. This probability seems to have been higher than initially thought, according to some disclosures, which indicate that the Soviets had four times as many troops as U.S. intelligence estimated as well as tactical nuclear weapons that they would have used in the event of a U.S. invasion (Tolchin 1992). At the height of the crisis, President Kennedy estimated the chances of war to be between one-third and one-half (Sorensen 1965, 705). For a theoretical analysis of the probability of nuclear war, see Avenhaus et al. 1989.

16. Still another 2 × 2 game is proposed in Snyder and Diesing 1977, 114–116; an "improved metagame analysis" of the crisis is presented in Fraser and Hipel 1982–1983; and a game-tree analysis is offered in Brams 1985/1989, 1985, 1990.

Key: (x,y) = (payoff to US, payoff to SU)

   [x,y] = [payoff to US, payoff to SU] in anticipation game (AG)

   4 = best; 3 = next-best; 2 = next-worst; 1 = worst

   Nonmyopic equilibrium (NME) circled

   * = state induced by moving power of US, deterrent threat of US,
         and compellent threat of SU

   # = state induced by moving power of SU

   Arrows indicate direction of cycling

Figure 9.4
Cuban Missile Crisis (game 30)

retaining the same strategies for both players as given in the Chicken representation (figure 9.3) but assuming a different ranking of states by the United States.

The resulting game is game 30, whose states may be interpreted as follows:

I. BW: (3,3)   The choice of blockade by the United States and withdrawal by the Soviet Union remains the compromise state for both players.

II. BM: (1,4)   In the face of a U.S. blockade, Soviet maintenance of its missiles leads to a Soviet victory (its best state) and U.S. capitulation (its worst state).

III. AM: (4,1)   An air strike that destroys the missiles that the Soviets were maintaining is an "honorable" U.S. action (its best state) and thwarts the Soviets (their worst state).

IV. AW: (2,2)   An air strike that destroys the missiles that the Soviets were withdrawing is a "dishonorable" U.S. action (its next-worst state) and thwarts the Soviets (their next-worst state).

Even though an air strike thwarts the Soviets in the case of both states (2,2) and (4,1), I interpret (2,2) to be a less damaging state for the Soviet Union. This is because world opinion, it may be surmised, would severely condemn the air strike as a flagrant overreaction—and hence a "dishonorable" action of the United States—if there were clear evidence that the Soviets were in the process of withdrawing their missiles anyway. However, given no such evidence, a U.S. air strike, perhaps followed by an invasion, would probably be viewed by U.S. policy makers as a necessary, if not "honorable," action to dislodge the Soviet missiles.

Before analyzing these possibilities, however, I offer a brief justification—mainly in the words of the participants—for the alternative representation given by game 30. The principal protagonists, of course, were President Kennedy and Premier Khrushchev, the leaders of the two countries. Their public and private communications over the thirteen days of the crisis indicate that they both understood the dire consequences of precipitous action and shared, in general terms, a common interest in preventing nuclear war. For the purpose of the present analysis, however, what is relevant are their specific preferences for each state.

Did the United States prefer an air strike (and possible invasion) to the blockade, given that the Soviets would withdraw their missiles? In responding to a letter from Khrushchev, Kennedy said:

If you would agree to remove these weapons systems from Cuba . . . we, on our part, would agree . . . (a) to remove promptly the quarantine measures now in effect and (b) to give assurances against an invasion of Cuba. (Allison 1971, 228)

This statement is consistent with the game 30 representation of the crisis [because (3,3) is preferred to (2,2) by the United States] but not consistent with the Chicken (game 50) representation [because (4,2) is preferred to (3,3) by the United States].

Did the United States prefer an air strike to the blockade, given that the Soviets would maintain their missiles? According to Robert F. Kennedy, the attorney general and a close adviser to his brother during the crisis, "If they did not remove those bases, we would remove them" (Kennedy 1969, 170). This statement is consistent with the game 30 representation [because (4,1) is preferred to (1,4) by the United States] but is not consistent with the Chicken representation [because (2,4) is preferred to (1,1) by the United States].

Finally, it is well known that several of President Kennedy's advisers felt very reluctant about initiating an attack against Cuba without exhausting less belligerent courses of action that might bring about the removal of the missiles with less risk and greater sensitivity to American ideals and values. As Robert Kennedy put it, an immediate attack would be looked upon as "a Pearl Harbor in reverse, and it would blacken the name of the United States in the pages of history" (Sorensen 1965, 684). This statement is consistent with the United States' ranking AW next-worst (2)—a "dishonorable" U.S. action in the game 30 representation—rather than best (4)—a U.S. victory in the Chicken representation.

If game 30 (figure 9.4) provides a more realistic representation of the participants' perceptions than does Chicken (figure 9.3), standard game theory offers little in the way of explaining how the compromise (3,3) state was achieved and rendered stable in either game. After all, as in Chicken, this state is not Nash equilibrium in game 30; but unlike Chicken, no other state in game 30 is a pure-strategy Nash equilibrium.

The instability of states in this game can most easily be seen by examining the cycle of preferences, indicated by the arrows going in a clockwise direction in game 30. Following these arrows shows that this game is "strongly cyclic" (see section 3.4), with one player always having an *immediate* incentive to depart from every state: The Soviets from (3,3) to (1,4); the United States from (1,4) to (4,1), the Soviets from (4,1) to (2,2); and the United States from (2,2) to (3,3).

Chicken, on the other hand, is noncyclic, with its Nash equilibria of (4,2) and (2,4) precluding cycling in a clockwise and a counterclockwise direction, respectively, because neither player would depart from its best state of 4 and move to its next-best state of 3. What Chicken and game 30 share is that neither player has a dominant strategy: Each player's best strategy depends on the strategy choice of the other player. In game 30, for example, the United States prefers B if the Soviets choose W, but A if they choose M.

How, then, can one explain the choice of (3,3) in either game, given its nonequilibrium status according to standard game theory? The evident answer in game 30, according to TOM, is that (3,3) is the unique non-myopic equilibrium (NME): Wherever play commences, players will move to this state if they are not there in the first place.

But this explanation is perhaps a little too glib, because it assumes that there is a prohibition on cycling, according to rules 5 and 6. As I indicated earlier, however, bargaining between the players went back and forth, suggesting that the players were willing to revisit previous states, especially if it might save them from a nuclear holocaust (more evidence on this point will be given in section 9.6, where I discuss the possible use of deception by Khrushchev in the crisis).

Because the conflict occurred in the Caribbean, within the U.S. "sphere of influence," the United States could bring to bear far greater military capabilities than the Soviet Union. Presuming that these capabilities give the United States moving power in game 30 (section 3.4), they enable it to induce the Soviets to stop at either (3,3) or (4,1), where they have the next move (see figure 9.4). Clearly, the Soviets would prefer compromise at (3,3) to being thwarted at (4,1).

Reinforcing this choice is the fact that moving power is irrelevant in this game (sections 3.4 and 9.4). If the Soviets possessed it (unlikely as this may be), they can force the United States to choose between (2,2) and (1,4) when the game cycles in a clockwise direction (see arrows in figure 9.4). But instead of inducing (2,2), it would be in the Soviets' interest to accede to (3,3). Thus, if game 30 cycles, then "compromise" is the only rational choice of the players, whichever has moving power.

In fact, the United States not only had superior military capabilities in this confrontation, but President Kennedy also was determined to show his resolve in this crisis after the 1961 Bay of Pigs debacle in Cuba.

Hence, I believe moving power offers a persuasive explanation of the outcome in this game.[17]

Moving power is undefined in Chicken because it is a noncyclic game. In this game, which has three NMEs, it is order power (section 7.4) that is crucial in singling out an outcome in all states except (3,3). If the players at the height of the crisis are at (1,1), for example, then the United States' order power induces (4,2), a U.S. victory and Soviet defeat (figure 9.4) by forcing the Soviets to back off from M and move to W.

In fact the Soviets retreated first, but they did not do so in response to a U.S. air strike, as suggested by the Chicken representation (figure 9.3). Rather, only the blockade was in effect, even at the height of the crisis, so it is reasonable to assume that the game begins at (2,4), with Soviet missiles not yet removed.[18]

Assume neither player has order power in the Chicken representation. Even without such power, as I showed in section 8.4 (figure 8.3), the NME induced in Chicken from (2,4) will always be a state associated with the strategy of magnanimity, which is W in the Cuban missile crisis. And in this game, it is rational for the Soviets to take the first step, moving from (2,4) to (3,3).

Knowing that an escalation of the conflict by the United States would have been all but certain had they not retreated first, the Soviets chose to be magnanimous. Indeed, if they had not been, it would have been rational for the United States to have induced (4,2) in Chicken by moving from (2,4) to (1,1), from which the Soviets would then move to (4,2)—unless (1,1) were catastrophic (e.g., an all-out nuclear war, preventing movement away from it).

The fact that the United States delayed an air strike suggests that it did not want to take the chance of trying to move play "through" (1,1),

---

17. Since a move by the United States from air strike to blockade was probably infeasible, the correspondence between Kennedy and Khrushchev might be interpreted as verbal moves or probings, by which both sides could back off from their threats in a feasible manner before making physical moves (for more on the their correspondence, see section 9.6).

18. In this situation, paradoxically, it is the Soviets' order power in Chicken that enables them to move to (3,3), given that the United States does not first escalate to an air strike at (1,1) to induce a subsequent move by the Soviets to (4,2). Yet it is highly unrealistic to suppose that the Soviets had order power, once their missiles had been detected and the U.S. blockade had been imposed.

which might not have been possible if escalation to nuclear war had occurred at this point. Occasionally, then, players might *not* want to exercise order power if it entails movement that, realistically, might be either risky or infeasible (section 2.6).

In game 30, on the other hand, the moving-power explanation reinforces the choice of the NME, (3,3), in this game. Chicken, by comparison, works best as a model if the Soviets are assumed, starting at (2,4) in figure 9.3, to make the rational choice of magnanimity—though not after winning a war—in this specific example of an MG game. At the same time, it was in the interest of the United States to "let" the Soviets be magnanimous so as to be able to bypass (1,1).[19]

The exercise of threat power offers an alternative explanation of the outcome in game 30. Recall from section 7.2 that threat power gives a player greater ability to endure a Pareto-inferior state than its opponent, should it need to carry out a threat that hurts both players; by prevailing, however, it can induce the choice of a Pareto-superior outcome, which is, of course, preferred by both players.

Thus in game 30 (figure 9.4), by threatening to choose strategy A, which includes the Soviet Union's two worst states (1 and 2), the United States can induce the Soviets to choose strategy W when the United States chooses strategy B, resulting in (3,3). Even though the Soviets have an incentive to move from (3,3) to (1,4), as indicated by the top horizontal arrow, they would be deterred from doing so by the threat that if they did, the United States would choose its strategy A and—by virtue of possessing threat power—stay there. Assuming the Soviets move to their preferred state in the second row, the United States would still inflict upon them (2,2), which is Pareto-inferior to (3,3).

Given that the United States has threat power, then, it is rational for the Soviets to accede to this threat, enabling the United States to

19. In effect, letting the Soviets back down by moving to (3,3) is to carry the concept of order power to one higher level. If traversing (1,1) were not so hazardous, it would clearly be in the interest of the United States to depart first from (2,4) to induce (4,2), its best state. [Notice that each player's desire to move first from (2,4) is the opposite of its desire to move second from (1,1).] But because of the danger of nuclear war at (1,1), it was rational for the United States to prescribe a different order of moves, giving the Soviets the opportunity to seek a compromise under the threat of more dire action than the blockade.

implement (3,3). If the Soviets possess threat power in game 30, the outcome would not change, because their compellent threat of choosing W would also induce (3,3).

Thus, who possesses threat power is irrelevant in this game. Although irrelevant, however, its impact is certainly salutary in allowing the players to avoid (2,2) and obtain (3,3) instead. This is significant in game 30, because neither player has a dominant strategy, there are no pure-strategy Nash equilibria, and, consequently, there is no indubitably rational choice according to standard game theory.

The two different representations of the Cuban missile crisis testify to the need to ponder strategic conflicts from different perspectives that take into account the perceptions of players, or possibly misperceptions, as in the Iran hostage crisis (section 9.4). In the fashion of *Rashomon* (a Japanese movie that portrays four different versions of a rape), each perspective gives new insights. It is especially instructive to see how sensitive outcomes are to the different reconstructions on which each is based and to consider the relationship of these to the actual outcome. In section 9.6, I explore the possibility of deception in the Cuban missile crisis.

9.6   Deception in the Cuban Missile Crisis

Define a player's *deception strategy* to be a false announcement of its preferences to induce the other player to choose a strategy favorable to itself (i.e., the deceiver).[20] I assume that the deceived

1. has no information about the deceiver's true preference ranking.[21]

The deceived, therefore, has no basis for mistrusting the deceiver. I also assume that the deceived

2. does not have a dominant strategy.

---

20. Game-theoretic models of deception, including some with applications, can be found in Brams 1977; Brams and Zagare 1977, 1981; Zagare 1979; Muzzio 1982; and Board 2002. A useful compilation of material on deception, both in theory and practice, is Daniel and Herbig 1982.

21. This was not true in the Iran hostage crisis. Although Carter misperceived Khomeini's preferences, he was correct about Khomeini's most-preferred state (4), namely NO (figure 9.2).

Otherwise, the deceived would always choose it, regardless of what the deceiver announced as its own strategy.

A deception strategy, like a threat strategy, requires prior communication, but to indicate preferences rather than threaten some action. Given such communication and that conditions 1 and 2 are met, the deceiver, by pretending to have a dominant strategy, can induce the deceived to believe that it will always be chosen. Anticipating this choice, the deceived will then be motivated to choose its strategy that leads to the better of the two states associated with the deceiver's (presumed) dominant strategy.

In the case of deception, I assume that play starts with the communication of (false) preferences by the deceiver. The players choose strategies, but play does not commence from a particular state. I will return to this point later and discuss its consistency with TOM, but first I consider the possible use of deception in the Cuban missile crisis.

As the crisis heightened, the Soviets indicated an increasing predisposition to withdraw rather than maintain their missiles if the United States would pledge not to attack Cuba and not to invade it in the future. In support of this shift in preferences, contrast two statements by Premier Khrushchev, the first in a letter to the British pacifist, Bertrand Russell, the second in a letter to President Kennedy:

If the way to the aggressive policy of the American Government is not blocked, the people of the United States and other nations will have to pay with millions of lives for this policy. (Divine 1971, 38)

If assurances were given that the President of the United States would not participate in an attack on Cuba and the blockade lifted, then the question of the removal or destruction of the missile sites in Cuba would then be an entirely different question. (Divine 1971, 47)

Finally, in an almost complete about-face, Khrushchev, in a second letter to Kennedy, all but reversed his original position and agreed to remove the missiles from Cuba, though he demanded a quid pro quo (which was ignored by Kennedy in his response, quoted in section 9.5):

We agree to remove those weapons from Cuba which you regard as offensive weapons. . . . The United States, on its part, bearing in mind the anxiety and concern of the Soviet state, will evacuate its analogous weapons from Turkey. (Divine 1971, 47)

Khrushchev, who had previously warned (in his first letter to Kennedy) that "if people do not show wisdom, then in the final analysis they will come to clash, like blind moles" (Divine 1971, 47)—which I suggested earlier (chapter 7, note 21) indicated his sense of loss of control—seemed, over the course of the crisis, quite ready to soften his original position. This is not to say that his later statement misrepresented his true preferences—on the contrary, his language evoking the fear of nuclear war has the ring of truth to it. Whether he actually changed his preferences or simply retreated strategically from his earlier pronouncements, there was a perceptible shift from a noncooperative position (maintain the missiles regardless) to a conditionally cooperative position (withdraw the missiles if the United States would also cooperate).

Perhaps the most compelling explanation for Khrushchev's modification of his position is that there was, to use Howard's (1971, 148, 199–201) apt expression, "deterioration" in his original preferences in the face of their possibly apocalyptic consequences if they were acted upon. By interchanging, in effect, 3 and 4 in the Soviet ranking of states in the figure 9.4 representation of the crisis (game 30), Khrushchev made W appear dominant, thereby inducing the United States to cooperate (choose B). The resulting (3,4) state is next-best for the United States, best for the Soviet Union, and renders BW a Nash equilibrium in this putative game.[22]

Whether Khrushchev deceived Kennedy or actually changed his preferences, the effect is the same in inducing the compromise selected by both sides. Although there seems to be no evidence that conclusively establishes whether Khrushchev's shift was honest or deceptive, this question is not crucial to the analysis. True, I have developed the analysis in terms of rational deception strategies, but it could as well be interpreted in terms of a genuine change in Khrushchev's preferences, given that preferences are not considered immutable.

Could the United States have deceived the Soviets to induce (3,3) in game 30? The answer is no: If the United States had made B appear dominant, the Soviets would have chosen M, resulting in (1,4); if the United States had made A appear dominant, the Soviets would have chosen W, resulting in (2,2). Paradoxically, because the United

---

22. This game is 21 in the appendix, and (3,4) is also the unique NME in this game.

States, as a deceiver, could not ensure an outcome better than its next worst (2)—whatever preference it announced—it was in *its* interest to be deceived (or at least induced) in order that (3,3) could be implemented.

More generally, in five of the fifty-seven 2 × 2 conflict games (29, 30, 31, 46, 47), at least one player can do better as the deceived than the deceiver, in terms of a player's comparative rankings of outcomes. Thus, it may be profitable that the deceived not know the preferences of the deceiver, and for the deceiver to know that the deceived does not know, and so on ad infinitum. For this set of five games, the strange notion that "ignorance is strength" seems well founded.[23]

Now consider the consequences for both sides if they had "played it safe" in the game 30 representation of the Cuban missile crisis by choosing their "security-level strategies." (A player's *security level* is the best payoff that it can ensure for itself, whatever contingency occurs, which in this case is the United States' next-worst payoff of 2; a player's pure strategy associated with this payoff is its *security-level strategy*.) The choice of such a strategy to avoid its worst state (1) means the United States would choose A; if the Soviets also choose their security-level strategy (W), the resulting state is (2,2), which is Pareto-inferior to (3,3).

In section 9.5 I argued that not only is (3,3) the unique NME in game 30 but also that it can be induced by the moving power of either player, by a deterrent threat of the United States, and by a compellent threat of the Soviet Union. Thus, (3,3) is a compelling solution in game 30, even though this game is strongly cyclic and has (2,2) as its security-level outcome.

Khrushchev had good reason to try to enhance (3,3)'s attractiveness to the United States by making it appear that he definitely would choose W because of its dominance. By seeming to interchange 3 and 4 in his

---

23. These five games are a subset of the "deception-vulnerable" games, which comprise a total of seventeen of the seventy-eight 2 × 2 strict ordinal games (22 percent); twenty-one games (27 percent) are "deception-proof," and forty games (51 percent) are "deception-stable" (Brams 1977). Deception-vulnerable games are the only games in which deception is both possible—because both players do not have dominant strategies (unlike deception-proof games)—and profitable—because at least one player can induce a better outcome by announcing a false preference order (unlike deception-stable games). All the 2 × 2 games that fall into these mutually exclusive categories, as well as various subcategories, are given in Brams 1977.

preference ordering, he transformed game 30 into game 21 (see appendix), which entirely robs him of any incentive to depart from W.

This explanation for Khrushchev's about-face, grounded in standard game theory, makes a good deal of sense. But there is an alternative explanation, based on TOM, which seems to me equally plausible.

At the start of the crisis, the state was (1,4) in game 30: The Soviets were in the process of installing their missiles, and the United States announced that it would blockade further shipments. According to TOM, the migration from (1,4) to the NME of (3,3) in game 30 must proceed through the two other states, (4,1) and (2,2), as shown in figure 9.4. By contrast, in game 21, it is rational for the Soviets to move directly from (1,3) to the NME of (3,4).

Thus, the compromise state is, in a sense, more efficiently achieved in game 21 than game 30, according to TOM. This efficiency-based explanation of why Khrushchev sought to change the game offers an alternative way of viewing, within the TOM framework, the rationality of deception in this crisis.

I will not analyze the efficiency of moves in games generally. But it is certainly related to the feasibility of moves discussed in section 2.6, where I argued that certain moves might be impossible. Even when moves are possible, there may be more than one path to an NME, in which case players will presumably prefer to make fewer moves to reach it.

Changing the appearance of a game through deception may contribute to this greater efficiency. When it does, it is reasonable to suppose that players will use deception, especially if it can go undetected in games of incomplete information.[24]

9.7 The Paradox of Omniscience

Hamlet well illustrates a game in which information is at a premium. Throughout the play, each of the antagonists tries to learn more about

---

24. The game-theoretic models cited in note 20 distinguish between "tacit" deception, which is undetected, and "revealed" deception, which is detected. This distinction is illustrated by the 1954 Geneva negotiations over the future of the two Vietnams, which involved three players and are analyzed in Zagare 1979; see also Brams 1990, chap. 8.

the other's plans. As they perfect their information about each other, however, they draw closer and closer to the looming tragedy.

One wonders whether players, either in *Hamlet* or in real-life games, might sometimes do better by knowing less. Assume, for concreteness, that Claudius is *omniscient*, by which I mean that he can predict Hamlet's strategy choice before he actually makes it. That would seem to give Claudius an advantage.

Now suppose that Hamlet is *aware* of Claudius's omniscience. Then Hamlet can ascertain, assuming he has complete information about Claudius's preferences as well as his own, that

• if he chooses R in game 26 (figure 9.1), Claudius will predict this choice and, as a best response, choose K, giving (3,2);

• if he chooses $\overline{R}$, Claudius will predict this choice and, as a best response, choose $\overline{K}$, giving (2,4).

Obviously, Hamlet prefers (3,2) and so will choose R. Claudius, because he is omniscient, will predict this choice and therefore choose K. Note that, in terms of the comparative rankings of the two players, Hamlet receives his next-best payoff and Claudius his next-worst. Relatively speaking, then, the omniscient player does worse than the nonomniscient one.

This comparison, however, can be challenged on two grounds. First, it involves an interpersonal comparison of utilities (or ranks in the ordinal case), and theorists have persuasively argued that such comparisons cannot be made. Who is to say that Hamlet's next-best payoff is better than Claudius's next-worst payoff unless there is a standard for making such a comparison, shared by both players? In fact, both players die in the end, in part because once Hamlet chooses R and Claudius's treachery is unmasked, Hamlet opts to kill his antagonist, just as Claudius chooses the same strategy against his opponent. Is it really possible to say who does better in death?[25]

---

25. The fact that I label Hamlet a "martyr" at the (3,2) state is meant to reflect Hamlet's presumed willingness to sacrifice his own life to avenge his father. But this ranking in no way implies that this is a better outcome for Hamlet than is death for Claudius, who ranks only one other state lower—not killing Hamlet after his revelation. The rankings by each player reflect *their own* assessment of each state relative to the other states, not how these assessments compare with those of the other player.

The second challenge to the result that the omniscient player does worse is that omniscience is less the issue than Hamlet's dominant strategy of R. In a game of complete information, Claudius hardly has to be omniscient to predict that Hamlet will choose R, which contains Hamlet's two best states (3 and 4). Thus, as long as information is complete, omniscience is beside the point: A nonomniscient player could as well predict that Hamlet will choose R, though not perhaps that Hamlet would try to cover up his knowledge by hiding it under the cloak of madness.

The omniscience of a player, coupled with an opponent's awareness of this omniscience, is more paradoxical in a game like Chicken (game 57), given in figure 9.3, divorced from the interpretation in the Cuban missile crisis. (Assume the United States is Row and the Soviet Union is Column, and that Column is omniscient.) Consider the consequences of Row's choices:

• if Row chooses B (cooperate), Column will predict this choice and choose M (not cooperate), giving (2,4).

• if Row chooses A (not cooperate), Column will predict this choice and choose W (cooperate), giving (4,2).

Because Row prefers (4,2), it will choose A (not cooperate), forcing an omniscient Column to back down, receiving only its next-worst payoff (2), whereas the nonomniscient Row obtains its best payoff (4).

Because the latter payoff cannot be improved on, whereas Column's payoff most definitely can, there is more justification for saying that omniscience hurts Column. More generally, a *paradox of omniscience* occurs when it is better to be nonomniscient than omniscient, given that the nonomniscient player is aware of its opponent's omniscience.[26]

This is not true in game 26 (figure 9.1). If Hamlet were omniscient rather than Claudius, and Claudius were aware of this fact, then the outcome would be (3,2) if Claudius chose K and (4,1) if he chose $\overline{\text{K}}$. Clearly, it is in Claudius's interest to choose K against an omniscient Hamlet and receive (3,2). Thus, neither player does better or worse

---

26. Note that this definition avoids interpersonal comparisons, because it makes the standard not how well one does vis-à-vis an opponent but how well one does vis-à-vis oneself in the opposite role.

by being omniscient—the outcome remains (3,2), which is both the unique Nash equilibrium and the NME in this game, whichever player is omniscient.

Besides Chicken, there are five 2×2 games (51–55 in the appendix) in which there is a paradox of omniscience (Brams 1981, 1982a, 1982b, 1983/2007). Neither player in any of these games has a dominant strategy, and each game has two Nash equilibria, which are also its NMEs. These are also games in which threat power is effective.

To have omniscience in a game is equivalent to a player's moving second, giving it the opportunity to observe the prior choice of its opponent and respond to it. Omniscience simply eliminates the necessity of having to move second: It enables the omniscient player to anticipate its opponent's choice, without actually having observed it beforehand. But the nonomniscient player, aware that omniscient player will rationally respond to its prediction, can capitalize on this fact in games vulnerable to the paradox of omniscience.

The resolution that TOM provides to the paradox of omniscience is that it enables players to depart from a state that the paradox initially induces. In Chicken, for example, the paradox induces (2,4) or (4,2), depending on whether Row or Column is omniscient (see figure 9.3). Yet from each of these states the NME of (3,3) can be reached if Column or Row, respectively, has order power.

Unfortunately for the players in Prisoners' Dilemma (game 32 in the Appendix), there is no such resolution to another problem tied to the possession of omniscience. If either player is omniscient in PD, it is easy to show that the state induced is (2,2), from which there is no escape because it is an NME. Fortunately, PD is the only 2×2 game with a Pareto-inferior NME.[27]

I conclude that one player's omniscience, and the other player's awareness of it, is not always a blessing for the omniscient player. In fact, the omniscient player will prefer to be the nonomniscient player if (1) there is a paradox of omniscience, or (2) only the other player can, by its omniscience, induce a Pareto-optimal outcome. On the other hand, with

---

27. Although one player's omniscience induces a Pareto-inferior state in six other games, the other player's omniscience always leads to a Pareto-superior state. In these games, which are 27–31 and 48 in the appendix, it is therefore in *both* players' interest for one player—and never the other—to be omniscient (Brams 1982b).

the exception of Prisoners' Dilemma, players can always escape a Pareto-inferior initial state and move to a Pareto-superior NME, although there may be a conflict over which NME, if there is more than one, will be chosen.

9.8 Summary and Conclusions

I began this chapter by analyzing in section 9.2 how the main characters in *Hamlet* sought to acquire information on the actions and future intentions of their antagonists. That their stalking game ended in tragedy does not impugn their rationality—either Hamlet or Claudius might have been killed sooner, without having killed his opponent, if he had not been so assiduous in his information-gathering efforts.

Hamlet seemed particularly cunning in not killing Claudius until he had incontestable evidence of his guilt. Once Hamlet did, he moved swiftly against him, so the accusation that Hamlet was indecisive and procrastinated is ill founded. Indeed, if Hamlet had killed Claudius prematurely, his rash action could have cost him not only his life but also his reputation.

In section 9.3 I showed how players who have no information about the preferences of an opponent in the Magnanimity Game (MG) can infer the circumstances under which they should choose one or another of their strategies. It turns out that they do not need complete information about an opponent's preferences to make rational choices for themselves. Instead, they need only rule out one or two games.

Incomplete information, especially when compounded by misperceptions, is a major problem for players in real-life games, as I illustrated in the case of the Iran hostage crisis in section 9.3, in which President Carter misperceived Ayatollah Khomeini's preferences with disastrous consequences. Nevertheless, there are games in which not only a lack of information, but also the deception of one player by another, can redound to the benefit of both, as I illustrated in the Cuban missile crisis (section 9.6). To be sure, the overwhelming power of the United States in the Caribbean also played a role in its peaceful resolution, as I argued in section 9.5.

My overview of some effects of different levels of information in games shows how information may influence both their play and the choice of an outcome. More information is not necessarily good for players, as the paradox of omniscience demonstrated (section 9.7), nor is being deceived necessarily bad, illustrating some of information's nonobvious consequences.

Generally speaking, however, having only incomplete information about an opponent's preferences complicates the difficulties players have in making rational choices. When information is incomplete about the relative powers of players, as may have been the case in both the U.S. Civil War (section 8.6) and the several wars between Egypt and Israel between 1948 and 1973, there is likely to be a wrenching test of strength, which benefits neither player, at least in the short run.

In the longer run, however, the results of this test may instill a painful awareness of the limits of using force. This may induce both sides to seek a peaceful resolution of their conflict, as Israel and some of its Arab neighbors (notably, Egypt and Jordan) have successfully done. The resolutions achieved in some of the historical cases studied here—including the U.S. Civil War and the Cuban missile crisis—have been fairly robust, suggesting that hard lessons, caused in part by incomplete information, may not be easily undone.

10 Catch-22s in Literature and History

10.1 Introduction

In his classic novel, *Catch-22* (1961, 52), Joseph Heller describes the thoroughly frustrating situation a U.S. combat pilot faced in World War II: "If he flew them [more missions] he was crazy and didn't have to; but if he didn't want to he was sane and had to."[1] Unlike the frustrating situations I described in chapter 7, in which a player in an unsatisfactory state could initiate a series of moves to extricate itself, this strategy will not work if the game can cycle back to the initial state, whence the frustration and attendant anger returns.

In this chapter, I allow such cycling, generalizing the pilot's predicament in *Catch-22* to a class of situations that can be modeled by the following generic 2×2 game: Whatever strategy the column player C chooses (c_1 or c_2), the best response of the row player R (r_1 or r_2) inflicts on C a worst or next-worst outcome, and possibly vice versa.[2] This game can be characterized by the following four properties, based on TOM (Brams 1994b):

1. Cyclicity The game is cyclic (section 3.4): There is one and only one direction—clockwise or counterclockwise—in which neither player, when it has the next move, ever departs from its best outcome as the

---

1. This chapter is adapted from Brams and Jones 1999 with permission.

2. The novel offers a specific realization of the generic game, which seems roughly to fit the following dictionary definition of a catch-22: "A supposed law or regulation containing provisions which are mutually frustrating ...; a set of circumstances in which one requirement, etc., is dependent on another, which is in turn dependent upon the first" (*Oxford English Dictionary*, 2nd ed., 1989).

players alternately move and countermove around the matrix. Because each player must always move to try to attain this outcome, cycling in this direction is rational.

2. Frustration for C   When it is R's turn to move during this cycling (by switching from r_1 to r_2 or from r_2 to r_1), these moves induce C's two worst outcomes. If forced to choose between them, it is rational for C to choose its next-worst outcome (call this outcome x).

3. Incentive of R to Frustrate C   R prefers x to either of the outcomes when it is its turn to move, giving R an incentive always to move to try to attain x.

4. Power of R to Frustrate C   R has moving power—it can continue the move-countermove process when C no longer has the wherewithal or will to continue and must, consequently, stop—forcing C to choose x (section 3.4).

Of the fifty-seven 2×2 conflict games in which there is no mutually best outcome,[3] thirty-six are cyclic, and twelve of the thirty-six are *catch-22 games.* In four of these games, C can also induce a catch-22 if it, rather than R, has moving power.

The catch-22 games illustrate how frustration can arise in a setting different from those that I discussed in chapter 7, wherein Lysistrata and Lady Macbeth were frustrated by men in their lives. Each exploded in anger, which I modeled by specific frustration and self-frustration games. Lysistrata was able to induce the men of Athens, and Lady Macbeth was able to shame Macbeth, to move in a way that benefited each woman.

Instead of moving to nonmyopic equilibria (NMEs), as in the frustration and self-frustration games, each player in catch-22 games find itself caught in a cycle from which it is difficult if not impossible to escape. In sections 10.2 and 10.3, I show how the exercise of moving power can help the frustrated player, and sometimes the other player as well.

In section 10.4, I apply TOM to the specific catch-22 game in Heller's novel, which involves a pilot trying to avoid combat duty and a doctor

---

3. If the twenty-one games with a mutually best outcome are included, there are a total of seventy-eight 2×2 games (Rapoport and Guyer 1966; Rapoport, Guyer, and Gordon 1976; Robinson and Goforth 2005).

who may declare him to be sane or not sane to fly. I then extend this analysis to all games that satisfy the aforementioned four conditions, showing that they are a subset of games in which moving power is effective: Each player can induce a better outcome when it possesses moving power than when its opponent possesses it, which turns out to imply cyclicity (proposition 10.1).

In section 10.5, I show that medieval witch trials can be conceptualized as a catch-22 game different from the game in *Catch-22*. In these trials, men and women who were accused of consorting with the devil were condemned (and often executed) if they confessed to being witches, and tortured if they did not confess.

Somewhat less frustrating than the catch-22 games are four other cyclic games in which moving power is effective. These are *king-of-the-mountain games*, in which the player that has moving power can induce its best outcome, forcing on the other player its next-best outcome (instead of its next-worst outcome, as in catch-22 games).

After defining these games in section 10.6, I briefly discuss the conflicts that king-of-the-mountain games seem best to model and show that they, together with the twelve catch-22 games, exhaust the 2×2 cyclic games in which moving power is effective (proposition 10.1). These sixteen games, which constitute 28 percent of all conflict games and 44 percent of the cyclic games, are precisely the games in which each player has a clear incentive to continue the cycling—if it thinks it has moving power—in order to try to come out on top.

Ten of the sixteen games have a unique pure-strategy Nash equilibrium, but it may not prevail if one player has moving power. The fact that plausible dynamic rules of play, based on TOM, can undermine such equilibria—fueled by the frustration of players, who continually move to try to escape inferior outcomes—illustrates how static equilibria may be dynamically unstable.[4]

In section 10.7 I discuss possible ways of stabilizing outcomes by showing how players, caught in catch-22 or king-of-the-mountain games,

---

4. A "Surprise Game," which subsumes six specific 2×2 games (two of these games, 48 and 56, are also catch-22 games) also illustrates the dynamic instability of some Nash equilibria, but the Surprise Game is based on rules 5 and 6 instead of rules 5' and 6', discussed in section 10.2 (Brams 1997b).

might reach mutually satisfactory settlements. Indeed, I offer a few examples in which they seem to have done just that.

10.2   TOM: Cyclic Games

The rules of TOM that I described in section 2.5 preclude cycling and the return of play to the initial state. They include two so-called rationality rules: a termination rule (rule 5), and a two-sidedness rule (rule 6), which lead, based on backward induction, to a definition of NMEs. In section 8.2, I introduced the two-sidedness convention (TSC), which modifies the backward-induction calculation when it would otherwise produce a Pareto-inferior outcome.

These rules do not capture the cyclicity of catch-22 and king-of-the-mountain games. To do so, I define a different solution concept, based on alternative rules 5' and 6'; rule 5' permits players to cycle in a matrix, and rule 6' enables one player, if it possesses moving power, to force the other player to terminate the cycling. I previously illustrated these rules in the case of the Revelation Game (section 3.4), the Iran hostage crisis (section 9.4), and the Cuban missile crisis (section 9.5), but I did not formally specify them, which I do next.

Because cycling can occur for an indefinite number of moves, a game has no definite endpoint. Technically, the games are finite but unbounded, which precludes using backward induction to solve them.

To try to model the cyclic aspect of certain conflicts, and give players the ability to make choices in which they repeat themselves (why they may do so will be considered shortly), I define a class of games in which cycling is possible by precluding a class of games in which it is not. Rule 5' provides a sufficient condition for cycling *not* to occur:

5'. If, at any state in the move-countermove process, a player whose turn it is to move next receives its best payoff (4), it will not move from this state.

Rule 5', which says that a player will never move from a best state, precludes cycling in forty-two of the seventy-eight distinct 2×2 ordinal games, twenty-one of which contain a mutually best (4,4) state. Excluding the latter games, there are fifty-seven conflict games, thirty-six of which are cyclic, as defined by property 1 in section 10.1.

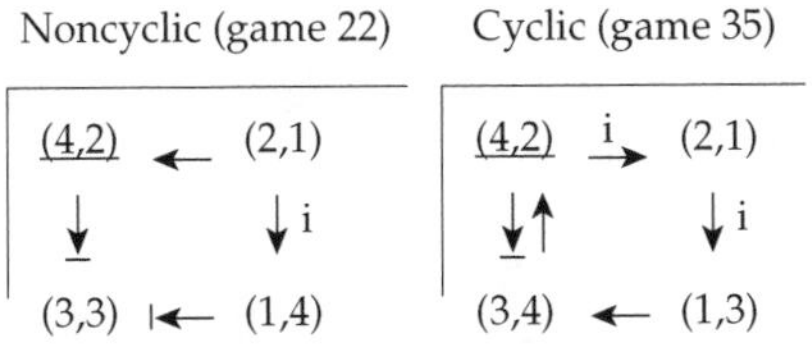

Noncyclic (game 22)   Cyclic (game 35)

Key: (x,y) = (payoff to R, payoff to C)

    4 = best; 3 = next-best; 2 = next-worst; 1 = worst

    i = impediment (not shown when there is blockage)

    Nash equilibria underscored

    Unblocked arrows indicate direction of cycling in game 35

Figure 10.1
Cyclicity of two games

Because only twelve of the cyclic games (33 percent) are catch-22 games, properties 2 and 3 have bite—they confer catch-22 status on only a minority of cyclic games. In these games, as I will show, the incentive that players have to cycle to try to attain their best outcomes creates frustration when the player with moving power uses it to force the other player to choose between its two worst outcomes.

As an illustration of one game that does not cycle and one game that does, consider the two games shown in figure 10.1 (these are games 22 and 35 in the appendix). Starting from (4,2) in each of these games, neither player has an incentive to move, according to both standard game theory (it is a Nash equilibrium) and TOM (it is an NME).[5]

But, in fact, there is a significant difference between these two games: Game 35 is "cyclic," whereas game 22 is not. To illustrate this distinction, first consider game 22. Cycling will not occur—in either a clockwise or counterclockwise direction—in this game, because moves starting from any state eventually bring the process to a state where the player who moves next receives its best payoff of 4, making a move from this state irrational, according to rule 5'. Thus, for example,

---

5. I do not show NMEs in this figure or other figures in this chapter, because I focus on rules of play (5' and 6') that may yield different outcomes from NMEs if one player has moving power (section 10.3). But the NMEs of all 2×2 conflict games are shown in the appendix.

• in a clockwise direction, the move by R from (2,1) to (1,4) gives C its best payoff, so C will not move from (1,4), as shown by the blocked arrow emanating from (1,4); and

• in a counterclockwise direction, the move by C from (2,1) to (4,2) gives R its best payoff, so R will not move from (4,2), as shown by the blocked arrow emanating from (4,2).

Now consider game 35 in figure 10.1. Because a counterclockwise move by R from (4,2) to (3,4) is blocked, cycling cannot occur in a counterclockwise direction—as shown by the blocked arrow emanating from (4,2). By contrast, moves in a clockwise direction never give a player its best payoff when it has the next move: R at (2,1), C at (1,3), R at (3,4), and C at (4,2) never receive payoffs of 4, making cycling in a clockwise direction possible, according to rule 5', as shown by the clockwise arrows in figure 10.1.

The fact that clockwise moves around the payoff matrix of game 35 do not violate rule 5' renders this game *cyclic*. In cyclic games, it turns out, cycling can occur in only one direction—either clockwise or counterclockwise, but not both (Brams 1994, Theorem 4.1, 90–91)—so which player moves first from any state in a cyclic game is dictated by the direction of cycling.[6]

Game 22 is *noncyclic*, because moving either clockwise or counterclockwise, one player, when it has the next move, receives its best payoff and, consequently, would not move. The forty-two 2 × 2 noncyclic games include all twelve *symmetric games* (e.g., Prisoners' Dilemma and Chicken), wherein the payoffs of the players can be arranged so that their ranks along the main diagonal are the same and those on the off-diagonal are mirror images of each other (Brams 1994b, Corollary 4.1, 91).

To summarize, no symmetric game is cyclic; if an asymmetric game is cyclic, cycling can go in only one direction. As I will illustrate in section 10.6, cyclic games can be divided into three classes—strongly cyclic, moderately cyclic, and weakly cyclic—but first I analyze the effects of moving power in these games.

6. Recall that rules 5 and 6 make the first mover a function of the players' backward-induction analysis and, in some games, which player possesses order power (sections 7.4, 9.4, and 9.5). For related approaches in which players make nonmyopic calculations, see Greenberg 1990, Chwe 1994, and Xue 1997.

10.3   Moving Power in TOM

In cyclic games, under what circumstances would players have an incentive to cycle to try to outlast an opponent? By *outlasting* I mean that one (stronger) player can force the other (weaker) player to stop the move-countermove process at a state where the weaker player has the next move.

Forcing stoppage at such a state involves the exercise of moving power. One player (P1) has *moving power* if it can force the other player (P2) to stop, in the process of cycling, at one of the two states at which P2 has the next move. The state at which P2 stops is that which P2 prefers. Hence, while it is P1 that can force stoppage, it is P2 that chooses at which of the two states it will stop.

Recall that rule 5' specified what players would *not* do—namely, move from a best (4) state when it was their turn to move. However, this rule did not say anything about *where* cycling would stop, which the exercise of moving power determines by enabling the player who possesses it (I assume there is at most one player who does) to break the cycle of moves.

Rule 6' ensures that there will be termination:

6'. At some point in the cycling, P1 can force P2 to stop.

This is not to say that P1 will always exercise its moving power. In some games, it is rational for P1 to terminate play, even though it can always force P2 to stop first.

Moving power is *effective* if the outcome that a player can induce with this power is better for it than the outcome that the other player can induce. To illustrate when moving power is effective, consider game 56 in figure 10.2a. The arrows shown in figure 10.2a (ignore for now the distinction between the single and double arrows) illustrate the cyclicity of game 56 in a counterclockwise direction: Starting in the upper right-hand state,

• C benefits by moving from (4,2) to (2,4);

• R does worse by moving from (2,4) to (1,1), because of an impediment (i) (section 3.4), but it departs from a 2, not a 4, state so does not violate rule 5';

2a. Moving power is effective in game 56

R has moving power   C has moving power

(2,4) ← (4,2)^r	(2,4) ⇐ (4,2)
i⇓ ⇑	i↓ ↑
(1,1) → (3,3)	(1,1) ⇒ (3,3)^c

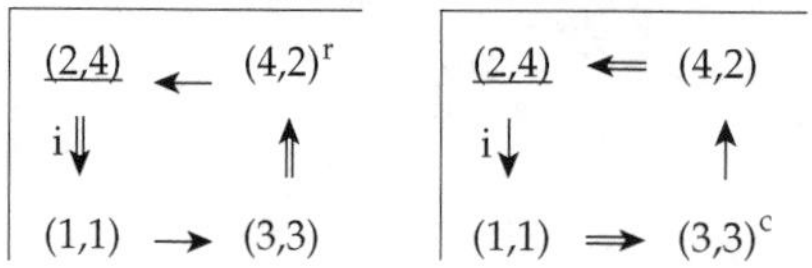

2b. Moving power is irrelevant in game 49

R has moving power   C has moving power

(2,4) ← (4,1)	(2,4) ⇐ (4,1)
i⇓ ⇑	i↓ ↑
(1,2)^r → (3,3)	(1,2) ⇒ (3,3)^c

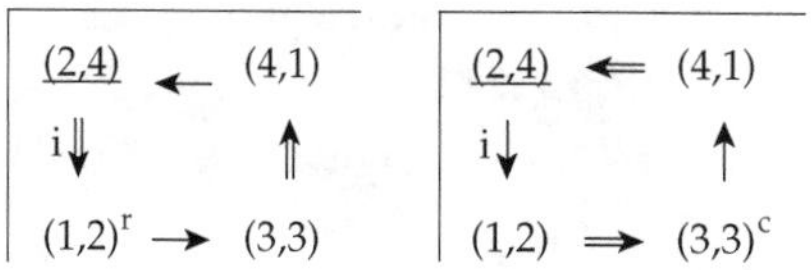

Key: (x,y) = (payoff to R, payoff to C)

4 = best; 3 = next-best; 2 = next-worst; 1 = worst

i = impediment

Double arrows indicate moves of player with moving power

Single arrows indicate moves of player without moving power

Nash equilibria underscored

r = state that R can induce with moving power

c = state that R can induce with moving power

Figure 10.2
Moving power in two cyclic games

- C benefits by moving from (1,1) to (3,3); and
- R benefits by moving from (3,3) to (4,2).

Because neither player, when it is its turn to move, ever departs from its best state of 4 (C departs from 2 or 1, R from 2 or 3), game 56 is cyclic.

To show what outcome R can induce if it has moving power, which might be thought of as greater stamina or endurance—in the sense that R can continue moving when C must eventually stop—let R's moves (vertical, as illustrated on the left side of figure 10.2a) be represented by double arrows. C, whose (horizontal) moves are represented by single arrows, must stop in the cycling at either (1,1) or (4,2), from where its single arrows emanate that indicate it has the next move. Since C would prefer to stop at (4,2) rather than (1,1), R can induce its best state of (4,2) as the outcome if it has moving power.

By contrast, if C has moving power (right side of figure 10.2a), it can force R to stop at either (2,4) or (3,3), from where its single arrows emanate, indicating that it has the next move. Since R would prefer to stop at (3,3) than (2,4), C can induce its next-best outcome of (3,3) if it has moving power. Thus, the possession of moving power benefits the player who possesses it—compared with the other player's possession of it—so it is effective in game 56.

This is not the case in a game in which C's payoffs of 1 and 2 in game 56 are interchanged, which defines game 49 in figure 10.2b. Applying the foregoing reasoning to game 49, on the one hand, if R has moving power, it can induce (1,2), because C prefers this state to (4,1), the other state from which it can move.

On the other hand, if C has moving power, it can induce (3,3), because R prefers this state to (2,4), the other state from which it can move. Hence, moving power is not effective in game 49: R *cannot* induce a better outcome when it has moving power than when C has it. Instead, moving power in game 49 is "irrelevant," because it would be in R's interest to stop at (3,3), even if it has moving power, rather than to force C to stop at (1,2). More generally, moving power is *irrelevant* when the outcome induced by one player is better for both.[7]

In many real-world conflicts, there may be no clear recognition of which, if either, player has moving power. In fact, there may be a good deal of uncertainty or misinformation. For example, if both players believe they can hold out longer in a game in which moving power is effective, cycling is likely to persist until one player succeeds in demonstrating its greater endurance, or both players are exhausted by the repeated cycling, which is a subject I will return to later.

---

7. There is a third possibility: Moving power is *ineffective* for a player when the outcome its opponent can induce is better than the outcome the player can induce with this power. Moving power is ineffective in only four of the thirty-six cyclic games (5, 6, 25, and 26), whereas it is irrelevant in sixteen games and effective in sixteen games. As I will show later, twelve of the sixteen games in which moving power is effective are catch-22 games; the remaining four games are king-of-the-mountain games.

10.4 The Original Catch-22 Game and the Generic Game

In *Catch-22*, pilot John Yossarian and the other men who fly combat missions in World War II have two strategies for avoiding combat duty: They can ask the doctor in their unit, Doc Daneeka, for psychiatric leave or not ask him. Doc Daneeka can declare each man to be either sane or insane; a declaration of insanity would exempt a man from combat duty.

Yossarian has two goals. His top priority is to survive the war, so he works hard to avoid combat duty. But once put on a combat mission, he does his best to avoid being shot down; as "the best man in the group at [taking] evasive action" after bombing runs (Heller 1961, 56), Yossarian is well equipped to escape unharmed.

At the same time, Yossarian wishes to act honorably. When given a chance to escape the war by Colonels Cathcart and Korn, he says, "That's a pretty scummy trick I'd be pulling on the men of the squadron, isn't it?" (Heller 1961, 393). Translating these thoughts into action, Yossarian declares, "I'm not making any deals with Colonel Korn . . . I'm breaking the agreement [with them to avoid combat duty], . . . which is best for Cathcart, Korn, and me, not for everyone" (Ibid., 405–406).

Evidently, the pull of "everyone" overrides the pull of "me," however, so a conscience-stricken Yossarian prefers not to bail out (figuratively speaking). In the end, Yossarian, searching desperately for a way out of his predicament, finds one—desertion.[8]

Doc Daneeka "was a very warm, compassionate man, who never stopped feeling sorry for himself" (Heller 1961, 42). Lamenting his own bad luck, the doctor preferred not to have to render any medical judgment. If he had to make a judgment, he preferred to render the easiest one, which was not to buck the system. After all, "The system worked fine for everybody, especially for Doc Daneeka. . . . The only time Doc Daneeka went to the medical tent was when he began to feel that he was a very sick man" (Ibid., 40).

I model the conflict between Yossarian (Y) and Doc Daneeka (D) by game 47, shown in figure 10.3. This game is cyclic in a counterclockwise

8. As I show in section 10.5, some accused witches chose confession after being tortured, which they had previously not considered as an option. A catch-22, it seems, may change people's opinions, or stimulate the search for new options, thereby providing an escape from the very dilemma it creates.

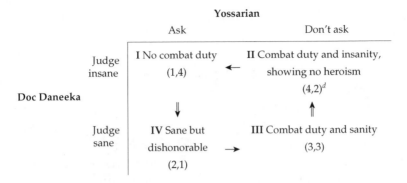

Key: (x,y) = (payoff to Doc Daneeka, payoff to Yossarian)

    4 = best; 3 = next-best; 2 = next-worst; 1 = worst

    Double arrows indicate moves of player (Doc Daneeka) with moving power

    Single arrows indicate moves of player (Yossarian) without moving power

    d = state that player with moving power (Doc Daneeka) can induce

Figure 10.3
Catch-22 in the novel (game 47)

direction, as indicated by the arrows in the figure (I will justify shortly why I give Doc Daneeka the double arrows). Y either can ask to be relieved of combat duty or not ask. D either can judge him insane or judge him sane.

The rankings of the players for the four possible states, starting in the upper left-hand cell and moving clockwise, are based on the following considerations:

I. Y asks, D judges insane: (1,4) This is the best state (4) for Yossarian, because he gets out of combat duty. Moreover, because Doc Daneeka certifies him as truly insane, leaving the squadron is not dishonorable. It is the worst state (1) for Doc Daneeka, because it requires him to render an opinion, and to file official papers, declaring Yossarian insane.

II. Y does not ask, D judges insane: (4,2) This is the next-worst state (2) for Yossarian, who, while not getting out of combat duty, at least acts honorably. Because he is declared insane, however, he is no hero when he goes willingly into battle. It is the best state (4) for Doc Daneeka, because he can show compassion without filing papers (since no request was made).

III. Y does not ask, D judges sane: (3,3)   This is the next-best state (3) for Yossarian, because even though he must go into combat, a sane man who willingly risks death is a hero. Doc Daneeka is also quite happy (3), because, though he does not render a compassionate judgment, he does not have to file papers (since no request was made).

IV. Y asks, D judges sane: (2,1)   This is the worst state (1) for Yossarian, because he does not get out of combat duty and, in addition, he acts dishonorably by attempting, deceptively, to get psychiatric leave. It is the next-worst state (2) for Doc Daneeka, because he must respond negatively to Yossarian's request, although he need not file papers declaring him insane.

I assume that military regulations endow Doc Daneeka with moving power, as shown by the vertical double arrows in figure 10.3. Thus, he can induce Yossarian to stop at either (4,2) or (2,1)—when it is Yossarian's turn to move—which are Yossarian's two worst states (II and IV).

Yossarian makes the rational choice of II, but the process by which he reasons his way to this outcome requires him to understand Doc Daneeka's motives. These are revealed in two exchanges that Yossarian has (Heller 1961, 51–52), which provide further justification of Doc's ranking:

[Yossarian asks] "Can't you ground someone who's crazy?"
[Doc Daneeka replies] "Oh sure. I have to. There's a rule saying I have to ground anyone who's crazy . . ."
"Then ask the others, they'll tell you how crazy I am."
"They're crazy."
"Then why don't you ground them?"
"Why don't they ask me to ground them?"
"Because they're crazy, that's why."

In other words, if Yossarian chooses not to ask for psychiatric leave, Doc Daneeka concludes that he is crazy; hence, he will judge him insane, consistent with Doc's preferences in figure 10.3. Yet this state (II) is the next-worst (2) for Yossarian.

If, on the other hand, Yossarian asks for psychiatric leave, he faces a quandary (Heller 1961, 52):

"Is Orr crazy?"

"He sure is," Doc Daneeka said.

"Can you ground him then?"

"I sure can, but first he has to ask me to, that's part of the rule."

"And then you can ground him?"

"No, then I can't ground him."

"You mean there is a catch?"

"Sure, there is a catch," Doc Daneeka replied. "Catch-22. Anyone who wants to get out of combat duty isn't really crazy."

. . .

"That's some catch, that catch-22," he [Yossarian] observed.

"It's the best there is," Doc Daneeka agreed.

Thus, anytime Yossarian asks for psychiatric leave, Doc Daneeka will conclude that he is sane and judge him so, consistent with Doc's preferences in figure 10.3. Yet this state (IV) is worst (1) for Yossarian, so Yossarian's better option is not to ask for psychiatric leave and receive a payoff of 2 in state II. Because this is Doc Daneeka's best state (4), he prefers it to either of the states (I and III) at which he could halt the cycling; hence, Doc has no desire to halt the cycling.[9]

Game 47 satisfies the four properties given in section 10.1 and, in my view, accurately models the dilemma posed in *Catch-22*. But there are eleven other 2×2 games that also satisfy these conditions, which are given in figure 10.4.

I next show that these twelve games, along with four others, exhaust all games in which moving power is effective. Surprisingly, if moving power is effective, a game is automatically cyclic, making condition 1 (cyclicity) in section 10.1 redundant:

Proposition 10.1 *If moving power is effective, a 2×2 ordinal game is cyclic. There are exactly sixteen specific games in which moving power is effective, twelve of which are catch-22 games that satisfy the four properties given in section 10.1.*

Proof Consider the generic game in figure 10.4. Assume moves are clockwise, as shown, but that the game is not necessarily cyclic. If R has moving power, it can induce either (x_{11}, y_{11}) or (x_{22}, y_{22}); without loss of generality, assume that C prefers (x_{11}, y_{11}), so

9. The cycling is largely mental in this game, in contrast to the often physical moves in the witch trials analyzed in section 10.5.

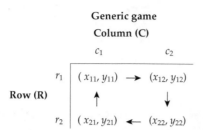

Generic game

Column (C)

c_1 c_2

Row (R)

r_1 (x_{11}, y_{11}) → (x_{12}, y_{12})

r_2 (x_{21}, y_{21}) ← (x_{22}, y_{22})

Twelve specific games subsumed by generic game

Class I (eight games): R can induce a catch-22 with moving power

38			39			40			41	
$(3,4)^c$	$(4,2)^r$		$(3,4)^c$	$(4,2)^r$		$(3,3)^c$	$(4,2)^r$		$(3,3)^c$	$(4,2)^r$
$(2,1)$	$(1,3)$		$(1,1)$	$(2,3)$		$(2,1)$	$(1,4)$		$(1,1)$	$(2,4)$

46			47			48			56	
$(3,4)^c$	$(2,1)$		$(3,3)^c$	$(2,1)$		$(2,3)$	$(4,2)^r$		$(2,4)$	$(4,2)^r$
$(4,2)^r$	$(1,3)$		$(4,2)^r$	$(1,4)$		$(1,1)$	$(3,4)^c$		$(1,1)$	$(3,3)^c$

Class II (four games): R and C can each induce a catch-22 with moving power

42			43			44			45	
$(2,4)^c$	$(4,1)$		$(2,4)^c$	$(3,1)$		$(2,3)^c$	$(4,1)$		$(2,3)^c$	$(3,1)$
$(3,2)^r$	$(1,3)$		$(4,2)^r$	$(1,3)$		$(3,2)^r$	$(1,4)$		$(4,2)^r$	$(1,4)$

Key: (x,y) = (payoff to R, payoff to C)

4 = best; 3 = next-best; 2 = next-worst; 1 = worst

Nash equilibria underscored

Arrows indicate the direction of cycling

r = state that R can induce with moving power

c = state that C can induce with moving power

Figure 10.4
Generic Catch-22 Game and twelve specific games it subsumes

$$y_{11} > y_{22}. \tag{10.1}$$

If C has moving power, it can induce either (x_{21}, y_{21}) or (x_{12}, y_{12}); without loss of generality, assume that R prefers (x_{21}, y_{21}), so

$$x_{21} > x_{12}. \tag{10.2}$$

Moving power will be effective if R prefers the state it can induce, (x_{11}, y_{11}), to that which C can induce, (x_{21}, y_{21}), or

$$x_{11} > x_{21}; \tag{10.3}$$

and C prefers the state it can induce, (x_{21}, y_{21}), to that which R can induce, (x_{11}, y_{11}), or

$$y_{21} > y_{11}. \tag{10.4}$$

Combining inequalities (10.2) and (10.3) yields

$$x_{11} > x_{21} > x_{12}, \tag{10.5}$$

which gives rise to four different preference orderings of R:

(i) $x_{11} = 3, x_{21} = 2$, and $x_{12} = 1 \Rightarrow x_{22} = 4$
(ii) $x_{11} = 4, x_{21} = 2$, and $x_{12} = 1 \Rightarrow x_{22} = 3$
(iii) $x_{11} = 4, x_{21} = 3$, and $x_{12} = 2 \Rightarrow x_{22} = 1$
(iv) $x_{11} = 4, x_{21} = 3$, and $x_{12} = 1 \Rightarrow x_{22} = 2.$

Analogously, combining inequalities (10.1) and (10.4) yields

$$y_{21} > y_{11} > y_{22},$$

which gives rise to four different preference orderings of C:

(i) $y_{21} = 3, y_{11} = 2$, and $y_{22} = 1 \Rightarrow y_{12} = 4$
(ii) $y_{21} = 4, y_{11} = 2$, and $y_{22} = 1 \Rightarrow y_{12} = 3$
(iii) $y_{21} = 4, y_{11} = 3$, and $y_{22} = 2 \Rightarrow y_{12} = 1$
(iv) $y_{21} = 4, y_{11} = 3$, and $y_{22} = 1 \Rightarrow y_{12} = 2.$

Altogether, then, there are $4 \times 4 = 16$ games in which moving power is effective.

Notice in these games that when it is R's turn to move (lower left-hand and upper right-hand states in the generic game), neither x_{21} nor x_{12} is R's best state (4); and when it is C's turn to move (upper left-hand and lower right-hand states in the generic game), neither y_{11} nor y_{22} is C's best state (4). Hence, the sixteen games in which moving power is effective are necessarily cyclic (but, as I showed earlier, there are cyclic games in which moving power is not effective).

The easiest way to show that twelve of the sixteen games are catch-22s is to single out the four games that are not. These are the games in which the moving-power outcome that R can induce, (x_{11}, y_{11}), as well as that which C can induce, (x_{21}, y_{21}), are at least next-best (3) for both players. They are defined by the aforementioned (iii) and (iv) orderings for R, and the aforementioned (iii) and (iv) orderings for C, which yield $2 \times 2 = 4$ games that I analyze in section 10.6.

For the remaining twelve games, property 2 in section 10.1 (frustration for C, but it could be either player) in the generic game is satisfied: The player with moving power (say, R) inflicts on C its two worst outcomes ($y_{11} = 2$ and $y_{22} = 1$), leading C to choose (x_{11}, y_{11}) that gives C its next-worst state. Property 3 in section 10.1 [incentive of R to frustrate C by forcing the choice of (x_{11}, y_{11})] is also satisfied: That this outcome, (x_{11}, y_{11}), is better for R than the two outcomes that C can induce, (x_{21}, y_{21}) and (x_{12}, y_{12}), or

$x_{11} > x_{21}$ and $x_{11} > x_{12}$,

is implied by inequality (10.5). Property 1 (cyclicity) in section 10.1, as I showed earlier in the proof, is implied by moving power's being effective, and property 4 in section 10.1 (power of R to frustrate C) is satisfied whenever R has moving power. Q.E.D.

In figure 10.4, I distinguish the eight games in which R can induce a catch-22 if it has moving power (class I) and the four games in which either player can induce a catch-22 if it has moving power (class II). In the class I games—which includes game 47 used to model *Catch-22*—R inflicts on C its next-worst state (2) when it exercises moving power, whereas C inflicts on R its next-best state (3) when it exercises moving power.[10]

---

10. Note that six of these eight games have unique pure-strategy Nash equilibria, but R's moving power undermines all of them, resulting in a different outcome. C's moving power induces the Nash equilibrium in four games (38–41) but not two others (48 and 56). None of the four class II games has a pure-strategy Nash equilibrium.

By contrast, in the class II games, each player inflicts on its opponent its next-worst state (2) when it exercises moving power.[11] In section 10.5 I model the witch trials by a class II game, although I argue that only one player in this game (the accusers) possesses moving power.

The twelve games in figure 10.4 are not the only games in which moving power is effective (as proved in proposition 10.1): There are four games (the "king-of-the-mountain games"), to be analyzed in section 10.5, in which *each* player, when it exercises moving power, inflicts on its opponent its next-best (3) state. In these latter games, the player exercising moving power invariably enjoys its best state (4), whereas this is not always true in either the class I or the class II catch-22 games.

10.5 The Witch Trials

In Europe during the Middle Ages, those accused of practicing witchcraft were placed in a judicial catch-22. In brief, if they confessed, they were executed; if they denied the charges, they were tortured to death (I note some exceptions to this later).

The alleged witches' accusers had a paramount goal: to accumulate wealth by accusing people of witchcraft, executing them, and then confiscating their property.

So far, at length, did the madness of the furious population go in this thirst for blood and booty that there was scarcely anybody who was not smirched by some suspicion of this crime. . . . Meanwhile notaries, copyists, and innkeepers grew rich. The executioner . . . went clad in gold and silver. (Burr 1971, 13, quoting from *Gesta Trevirorum*, 1473)

Not only did the accusers desire to kill the person accused of witchcraft in order to confiscate his or her property, but they also wished to provide

---

11. Class I and class II games can be defined in terms of the orderings in the proof of proposition 10.1. The eight class I games match orderings (iii) and (iv) for R against orderings (i) and (ii) for C, which lead to C's two worst outcomes when R has moving power (four games); and orderings (iii) and (iv) for C against orderings (i) and (ii) for R, which lead to R's two worst outcomes when C has moving power (four games). (In the latter four games, however, I have reversed the roles of R and C in figure 10.4 so that in *all* class I games it is R that inflicts on C its two worst outcomes.) The four class II games match orderings (i) and (ii) for R against orderings (i) and (ii) for C, which lead to each player's two worst outcomes when the other player has moving power.

themselves with future opportunities—usually by getting the accused to implicate others in his or her alleged crime.[12]

The accused individuals had three goals. First, they preferred to live rather than die at the hands of their accusers. Second, most preferred to die honorably rather than to besmirch their names by confessing to witchcraft while being killed anyway. (I discuss the third shortly.)

Knowing they would probably die, many were willing, at least at the outset, to endure torture rather than confess to their alleged crimes:

> Then [the torturer] asks me, "Kinsman, how come you here" . . . I said, "I am no witch" . . . [Then] the executioner . . . put the thumb-screws on me . . . so that the blood ran out at the nails and everywhere. . . . Thereafter they first stripped me, bound my hands behind me. . . . Eight times did they draw me up and let me fall again, so that I suffered terrible agony. (Burr 1971, 26, quoting from *Beiträge zur Geschichte des Hexenwesen in Franken*, 1883, on events that occurred in Bamberg, Germany, in 1628)

Manifestly, persons accused of witchcraft would have no reason to undergo such excruciating pain unless they placed high value on their honor.

As a third goal, the accused preferred not to implicate others, whom they knew to be innocent, even though they were often pressed to do so by their accusers:

> For not only is there in general no . . . escape, but she is also compelled to accuse others, of whom she knows no ill, and whose names are not seldom suggested to her by her examiners or by the executioner. These in their turn are forced to accuse others, and these still others, and so it goes on. (Burr 1971, 35, quoting Friedrich Spee, *Cautio Criminalis*, 1631)

To model the conflict between the accused witches and their accusers, consider first the strategies of each player. A person, once accused of witchcraft, could either confess (C) or deny the charge and not confess ($\overline{C}$). This person's accusers, whom I treat as a single player, could either

---

12. Confiscation of property was not the principal force driving the Salem witch trials in Massachusetts in 1632 (Konig 1979, 174) but, rather, the perceived "survival of society," especially "at a time of profound insecurity" (Ibid., 177) caused by, among other things, challenges to the church and French and Indian raids that threatened to erupt into war. Of the twenty-six people convicted of witchcraft in Salem in 1632, nineteen were executed (Weisman 1984, 118), compared with the thousands who were killed in witch hunts in Europe beginning in the fifteenth century. For popular accounts of the Salem witch trials, see Hill 1995 and Hoffer 1997.

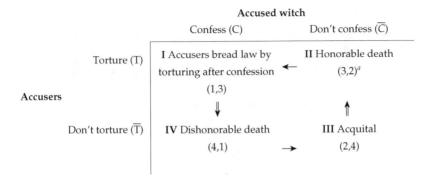

Key: (x,y) = (payoff to accusers, payoff to accused witch)

4 = best; 3 = next-best; 2 = next-worst; 1 = worst

Double arrows indicate moves of player (accusers) with moving power

Single arrows indicate moves of player (accused witch) without moving power

a = state that player with moving power (accusers) can induce

Figure 10.5
The Witch's Game (game 45)

torture (T) or not torture ($\overline{\text{T}}$) the accused, yielding the game shown in figure 10.5.

The rankings of the players for the four possible states, starting in the upper left-hand cell and moving clockwise, are based on the following considerations (I consider a different ranking for the persons accused of witchcraft in note 15):

1. TC: Accusers torture, Accused confesses—(1,3) Despite the accused's confession, the accusers continue to torture him or her. Because this action would break medieval law, which had strict rules about the use of torture,[13] it would bring punishment down on the accusers, making this

---

13. When torture is carried out, "the notary must write down everything in his record of the trial—how the prisoner is tortured, on what points he is questioned, and how he answers" (Burr 1971, 12, quoting from *Malleus Maleficarum*, 1486). Later I discuss how accused witches, who confessed during torture, were later required to verify that the confession "is not due alone to the force of the torture." These "safeguards" for the accused, as will be seen later, were quite empty, but they at least suggest that torturers would be penalized if they tortured a suspect after he or she had confessed. (The torturers and accusers may well be different people, but because the accusers directed the actions of the torturers, I consider them to be the same player.)

their worst state (1). It is the next-best state (3) for the accused: Whether this person lives or dies, he or she knows the accusers will suffer too.

II. T$\overline{\text{C}}$: Accusers torture, Accused does not confess—(3,2) This is the next-best state (3) for the accusers, because their torture is "justified" by a recalcitrant suspect. It is the next-worst state (2) for the alleged witch, who at least dies honorably without implicating others.

III. $\overline{\text{T}}\overline{\text{C}}$: Accusers do not torture, Accused does not confess—(2,4) This is the next-worst state (2) for the accusers, because they do not execute the suspect, despite his or her denial, and hence are unable to confiscate the accused's property. It is the best state (4) for the accused—tantamount to acquittal—because this person continues to live with his or her honor intact and keeps his or her possessions.

IV. $\overline{\text{T}}$C: Accusers do not torture, Accused confesses—(4,1) This is the best state (4) for the accusers, because their allegations appear to have been justified and execution can occur immediately. It is the accused witch's worst state (1), because he or she dies dishonorably, implicating himself or herself as well as others without even being under duress.

Note that the game given in figure 10.5 is game 45 in figure 10.4 (with the roles of R and C reversed), which is a class II catch-22 game. I presume that only the accusers have moving power, in which case they can implement (3,2), which is quite unfortunate for the accused.

Evidence suggests that the players moved in cyclical fashion, as TOM predicts.[14] These dynamics were buttressed by medieval law, which required that confessions obtained under torture be "verified" later without torture. But, ironically, torture was allowed to resume if someone who confessed changed his or her mind:

And note that, if he confesses under the torture, he must afterward be conducted to another place, that he may confirm it and certify that it was not due alone to the force of the torture.

But, if the prisoner will not confess the truth satisfactorily, other sorts of tortures must be placed before him. (Burr 1971, 12, quoting from *Malleus Maleficarum*, 1486)

---

14. TOM does not make this prediction if there is a clear recognition that one player has moving power, in which case the other player should submit immediately. That this was not the case—because a "forced" confession was not acceptable, as I will next explain—is why the exercise of moving power and a testing of wills often occurred.

Thus, the accused might confess in order to escape torture, but then he or she could revert to denial once the torture ceased. The torture would subsequently resume, however, yielding a cycle of physical moves.

The Jesuit poet, Friedrich Spee, who was a confessor of those sentenced to death for witchcraft, recognized the catch-22 nature of the accusers' moving power:

> So, whether she confesses or does not confess, the result is the same. If she confesses . . . , she is executed. If she does not confess, the torture is repeated—twice, thrice, four times. . . . There is no limit of duration or severity or repetition of the tortures. (Burr 1971, 34, quoting from Friedrich Spee, *Cautio Criminalis*, 1631)

Thus, the accused can never do better than his or her next-worst state, (3,2), because the accusers can move indefinitely—leaving "no stone unturned" (Burr, 1971, 33, quoting from Friedrich Spee, *Cautio Criminalis*, 1631)—through the states which the accused prefers.[15]

Interestingly, the witch persecutions usually ended with confession rather than death by torture, even though those accused of witchcraft preferred denial to confession *before the torture*. There seem to be two possible explanations for this. First, the accused might have changed their minds after enduring some torture, caring less about honor and more about a quick death and, possibly, a reprieve, as some were led to believe (Burr 1971, 111, quoting from *Malleus Maleficarum*, 1486).[16] Second,

---

15. If 2 and 3 are interchanged for the accused in game 45—under the presumption that he or she prefers "honorable death" to "accusers break law" (and are, therefore, punished)—then the resulting game is 40 in figure 10.4. With moving power, the accuser can again induce "honorable death," which is now (3,3) instead of (3,2). Consequently, the accused does better according to this interpretation, but the moving-power outcome that the accuser can induce is the same.

16. Game 45 reflects this preference on the part of the accused being tortured: (1,3) when the accused confesses is better than (3,2) when the accused does not. What game 45 does not capture is the fact that once the confession is extracted—in the manner suggested by the aforementioned quotation of Friedrich Spee—and torture ceases, the outcome is not "dishonorable death," yielding (4,1) in figure 10.5. Instead, the outcome is more like a (3,3) "compromise," in which both players get something of what they want (the accused survives with his or her dignity partially intact for having endured some torture before succumbing; the accusers get their confession, and perhaps some new names, but at a cost if the inquisition takes long). In effect, the exercise of moving power in game 45 may change the choices of the players and their preferences over time—leading to a new game—but the *process* by which this new game evolves is, I would argue, well modeled by the TOM moving-power rules. Finally, it is worth noting that when the accused witches remain steadfast in their honor, the predicted outcome—their martyrdom at (3,2)—is accurate.

even if they continued to recognize that denial would produce an outcome they preferred, they nonetheless might have lost their ability to resist under the pain of torture, even though "it was all a lie" (Ibid., 27, quoting from *Beiträge zur Geschichte des Hexenwesen in Franken*, 1883, on events that occurred in Bamberg, Germany, in 1628).

10.6 King-of-the-Mountain Games

The four games I call *king-of-the-mountain games* are given in the bottom half of figure 10.6.[17] Observe that in each game there is a (3,4) state that C can induce with moving power and a (4,3) state that R can induce with moving power. While the outcome predicted by standard game theory is the unique Nash equilibrium, (3,4)—associated with the dominant strategy of R and the best response of C—TOM predicts (4,3) as the outcome if R has moving power.

Instead of giving an extended example of a king-of-the-mountain game, and the exercise of moving power in it, I next consider the class of situations that these games seem best to model and cite some historical examples that reflect struggles for supremacy. As depicted in the generic game in the top half of figure 10.6, R can choose to cooperate or not cooperate with C. C, in turn, can choose to hold out or not hold out against R.

If R is noncooperative, the outcomes are bad for both players (i.e., never better than next-worst, or 2), whereas if R is cooperative, the outcomes are good for both (3 or 4). Following standard game theory, this game is easy to solve: R will choose its dominant strategy of cooperation; anticipating this choice, C will hold out for its preferred state, resulting in the Nash equilibrium, (3,4).

But if R has moving power, according to TOM, it can force C to stop at (4,3), just as C can force R to stop at (3,4) if it has moving power. In other words, which one of the Pareto-optimal outcomes that occurs depends on which, if either, player can continue the move-countermove

---

17. The appellation "king of the hill" is also used for these games, which are defined to be games "in which each person attempts to climb to the top of some point, as a mound of earth, and to prevent all others from pushing or pulling him off the top" (*Random House Dictionary of the English Language*, 1979). Note that game 33 was used to define the hypothetical 2 × 4 Caring Game that I suggested might have been played between Abraham and God (section 2.3).

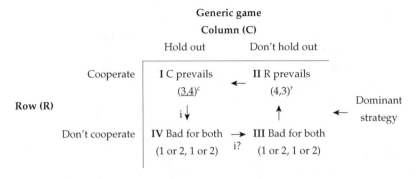

Four specific games subsumed by generic game

33	34	36	37
$(3,4)^c$ $(4,3)^r$ $(1,2)$ $(2,1)$	$(3,4)^c$ $(4,3)^r$ $(2,2)$ $(1,1)$	$(3,4)^c$ $(4,3)^r$ $(2,1)$ $(1,2)$	$(3,4)^c$ $(4,3)^r$ $(1,1)$ $(2,4)$

Key: (x,y) = (payoff to R, payoff to C)

    4 = best; 3 = next-best; 2 = next-worst; 1 = worst

    i = impediment (question mark indicates impediment a possibility)

    Nash equilibria underscored

    Arrows indicate the direction of cycling

    r = state that R can induce with moving power

    c = state that C can induce with moving power

Figure 10.6
Generic King-of-the-Mountain Game and four specific games it subsumes

process when the other player is forced to "throw in the towel." In game 37, for example, the latter player was North Vietnam after repeated bombing campaigns by the United States toward the end of the Vietnam war (Brams 1994b, chap. 4), and Saddam Hussein after the air and ground attacks by the United States and its allies in the 1990–1991 Persian Gulf war (Massoud 1998).

These conflicts were rife with misperception and were also vulnerable to threats.[18] But, as I indicated in section 10.3, a simple lack of

18. In game 37 in particular, R can threaten C's two worst outcomes, assuming it has threat power (sections 7.3 and 9.4), to try to induce its preferred (4,3) outcome instead of the Nash equilibrium, (3,4).

information as to which player has moving power may by itself lead to cycling, as each player strives to demonstrate—by continuing the move-countermove process—that it can prevail (i.e., be the "king").

There are some subtle differences among the four games. Recall from section 3.4 that there is an impediment if a move involves a player's moving from a better to a worse state, as is the case in all the king-of-the-mountain games when R moves from the upper left-hand state to the lower left-hand state (i.e., from 3 to either 2 or 1). In games 36 and 37, this is the only impediment, making these games *moderately* cyclic. In games 33 and 34, by comparison, there is a second impediment when C moves from the lower left-hand state to the lower right-hand state (i.e., from 2 to 1), making these games *weakly* cyclic.[19] By contrast, strongly cyclic games have no impediments.

Notice in the king-of-the-mountain games that the players must move through *two* states in which the players suffer their worst (1) or next-worst (2) outcomes, which is never the case in catch-22 games. Presumably, when a parent tells a child being punished that "it hurts me as much as it hurts you," he or she is suffering at one of these states.

It is well known, of course, that such punishment does not always lead to the best outcome for the parent, nominally the more powerful figure. Likewise, such prepossessing historical figures as Julius Caesar, Napoleon Bonaparte, Adolf Hitler, Winston Churchill, Charles de Gaulle, and Margaret Thatcher each fell from grace abruptly and, sometimes, ignominiously when their power fizzled out. As I suggested in section 3.4, even God seems to lose His immediacy, and potency as a commanding figure, at certain times.

10.7   Summary and Conclusions

The twelve catch-22 games, when combined with the four king-of-the-mountain games, constitute 28 percent of the fifty-seven 2×2 conflict

---

19. Of the twelve catch-22 games, six are moderately cyclic (38–41, 48, and 56) and none is weakly cyclic; the remaining six games (42–47) are strongly cyclic (no impediments), making these games "frictionless." It would seem that players would have the most incentive to cycle in the latter games, because a move always brings a player to an immediately better state.

games. To be sure, this theoretical percentage says nothing about the empirical relative frequency of these games. However, the fact that people often speak sadly of being in catch-22s suggests that these unfortunate situations are by no means rare.[20]

The TOM perspective I offer in this chapter is that of cyclic games (thirty-six in all), in which moves in either a clockwise or a counterclockwise direction—but not in both directions—are never from the moving player's best state. But more than being cyclic, what the twelve catch-22 and four king-of-the-mountain games share is that moving power in them, and only in them, is effective. That is, a player does better if it possesses moving power than if its opponent possesses it in 44 percent of the cyclic games (moving power is irrelevant or ineffective in the remainder), so there is good reason for each player to try to outlast its opponent as the players alternately move and countermove around the matrix.

Such cycling can lead to endless frustration on the part of the players, but occasionally they may recognize the futility of cycling and resolve their differences. This seems to have occurred in the Egyptian-Israeli conflict between 1948 and 1978 as well as similar long-standing conflicts (e.g., between France and Germany after World War II, and within South Africa and Northern Ireland more recently). Although Egypt and Israel fought five wars in this period (1948, 1956, 1967, 1969–1970, and 1973) at great cost to both sides, it still required considerable pressure from the United States to achieve the 1978 Camp David accords that paved the way for the signing of a peace treaty between Egypt and Israel in 1979 (Brams and Togman 1996, Brams and Taylor 1999, and Brams 2008, describe a dispute-resolution procedure that might have led to a quicker resolution of this conflict).

---

20. Several of these games have been used to model conflicts in Brams 1994b, including the exodus of the Israelites from Egypt, which involved twelve broken promises by Pharaoh about freeing the Israelites from bondage, each of which was followed by a plague visited on the Egyptians by Moses and God. Moving power has also been applied to the analysis of a series of sanctions continually imposed, lifted, and reimposed by the United States on Haiti in the 1980s and early 1990s (Simon 1996). Also at the international level, mobilization decisions that escalate from crises into wars have been modeled as catch-22 games (Brams 1998).

Likewise, similar outside pressure was exerted successfully in the South African and Northern Ireland conflicts.[21] However, it required the intervention of a major UN military force to persuade the warring sides in the former Yugoslavia to sign a peace treaty in November 1995, but only after four years of bitter fighting that cost some 250,000 lives.

Enduring international and national rivalries, in which learning can also be modeled using TOM (Maoz and Mor 1996, 2002), take more poignant form at the organizational and personal level, as I illustrated in the fictional case of *Catch-22* and the real case of medieval witch trials. Great frustration can build up, and destruction may occur, unless there is a recognition that

• one side has moving power and, therefore, it is in the other side's interest to acquiesce in the more powerful player's preferred state; or

• neither side has a clear advantage, and some compromise can work to their mutual advantage.

In the former case, the settlement is likely to be one-sided, but this is simply a reflection of the one-sidedness of the conflict—the two players are unequally matched.

In the latter case, it is harder to define what, if any, compromise will be achieved, because each side presumably wants to hold out as long as possible if there is still some reasonable chance that, by persisting, it can wear down the other side and thereby achieve a better outcome. Outcomes that are mutually advantageous [e.g., (4,3) and (3,4) in king-of-the-mountain games] may be destroyed if the players' continually strive to come out on top (by getting 4 rather than 3 in these games).

I see no ready solution to this problem, short of the mutual exhaustion of the players after long travail. Because cycling is rational in games in which moving power is effective, one must, to prevent cycling and its attendant frustration, deprive the players of the wherewithal that fuels

---

21. A TOM analysis of the latter conflict, based on threat power, is given in Brams and Togman 1998. Moving power, threat power, and NMEs have all been applied to the analysis of conflicts between donor and recipient countries over the disposition of refugees, some of which also involved the United Nations as a player (Zeager and Bascom 1996; Zeager 1998, 2002, 2005; Zeager and Williams 2004).

the cycling. Limiting their resources by embargoes, sanctions, outside intervention, ostracism, and the like are obvious tools for this purpose, but they have not always been successful.

A less obvious means for bringing such conflicts to a halt is to cast doubt that either player will "win" in the end. The more clouded victory appears, the more the will of the combatants to continue fighting will be sapped. Undermining the players' faith in victory, especially if this victory is likely to be Pyrrhic, may well bring the two sides to a settlement.

11 Summary and Conclusions

Most of the applications I have made of game theory and the theory of moves (TOM) to the humanities alternate between fictional narratives and historical reconstructions. While they occur in two different worlds—made up and real—they share common ground: The players in them act *rationally*, in accordance with their goals.

• If Abraham's faith in God wavers, he still can anticipate that God will renege on his command that he sacrifice Isaac, affording Abraham the opportunity to save Isaac by heeding God's command (chapter 2).

• If, hypothetically, Abraham had refused to offer Isaac for sacrifice, he would have benefited from taking a morally defensible position and, most likely, not have been severely punished by God for doing so (chapter 2).

• In telling Delilah the secret of his strength after much cajoling, Samson gains relief from being harassed by the woman he loves, though he recognizes that his revelation is not without risk (chapter 2).

• In Pascal's wager, a person derives a higher expected payoff from believing in God than not believing or, in one variation, keeping an open mind if the answer may be indeterminate (chapter 3).

• In the Revelation Game, believing depends on whether the Superior Being (SB) or the Person (P) has moving power. If SB does, it is rational to believe, but if P does—perhaps because he or she changes over time and so may not apprehend the presumed superiority of SB—it is rational not to believe, which makes the game thoroughly unstable and helps to explain periods of religious revival and decline (chapter 3).

• The fair division of indivisible goods among two or more players may not simultaneously satisfy properties like efficiency and envy-freeness, but this does not impugn the rationality of players trying to achieve such a division, because certain trade-offs among desirable properties are unavoidable (chapter 4).

• In providing for public goods, illustrated by a referendum on the renovation of a park and a referendum on Moses's leadership, voting can transform difficult games like Prisoners' Dilemma into games in which the cooperative outcome is the product of dominant strategies of the voters (chapter 5).

• In confrontations that Richard Nixon and Franklin Roosevelt had with their Supreme Courts, the presidents and members of the Court acted rationally, even though the outcomes in each case were not always favorable to the players (chapter 6).

• Jury selection can be viewed as a game of incomplete information in which the optimal choices of prosecution and defense may not result in an impartial jury, but there is a procedure that can ensure impartiality (chapter 6).

• Rallying the women of Athens to abstain from sex is costly to Lysistrata and other women, causing the men to suffer as well. But the resulting crisis triggers a reconciliation, which benefits both players when the men stop fighting and sex is resumed (chapter 7).

• Lady Macbeth, by humiliating her husband, induces him to murder King Duncan. She clearly benefits from his change of mind, as does Macbeth when Lady Macbeth's wrath subsides and Macbeth's hope of accession to the throne rises (chapter 7).

• The games of Lysistrata and Lady Macbeth are examples, respectively, of a generic Frustration Game and a generic Self-Frustration Game. The frustration each woman experiences gives rise to anger—causing the players to threaten their antagonists to the point of breakdown and even, in the case of Lysistrata, to carry out her threat—demonstrating how expressing emotions may best satisfy the goals of players (chapter 7).

• The generic Magnanimity Game (MG) shows that it may be rational after a war (1) for the victor to be magnanimous and (2) for the defeated player to be cooperative, but not always. Historical examples provide empirical support for the occurrence of the game's four possible outcomes, each of which may be a nonmyopic equilibrium (NME) for different preferences of the players (chapter 8).

• The U.S. Civil War shows how the Confederacy attempted to use a deterrent threat to force the Union into negotiations. The Union prevailed because it not only persevered but also was able to implement the unique NME, with a compellent threat, by holding out longer at the breakdown state. This does not negate the rationality of the Confederacy's attempt to assert its threat power at the beginning of the war, though it was unable to sustain it in the end (chapter 8).

• Hamlet, deeply suspicious of his uncle, Claudius, after his father is murdered and his mother hastily marries his uncle, seeks to gather incriminating evidence on Claudius's complicity in his father's murder. Hamlet does not vacillate once he has obtained this information, contrary to his reputation for being indecisive. Claudius acts with equal dispatch and cunning, but the stalking game they play turns into a deadly game of pursuit, ending in tragedy not only for Hamlet and Claudius but also for several other characters in the play (chapter 9).

• Because Jimmy Carter lacked accurate information on the preferences of Ayatollah Khomeini in the Iran hostage crisis, he chose a rational strategy in the wrong game. Consequently, his attempt to use the military power of the United States to threaten Khomeini failed, but his failure does not call into question his rationality in the misperceived game (though his intelligence gathering may be faulted) (chapter 9).

• Although John F. Kennedy and Nikita Khrushchev were both encumbered by incomplete information in the Cuban missile crisis, they eventually reached a peaceful settlement. Threats, and possibly deception, played a salutary role in achieving this settlement, in part because each player moved with considerable caution during the crisis (chapter 9).

• Caught in a catch-22 in Joseph Heller's novel, *Catch-22*, John Yossarian deals with his predicament as best he can. The specific game he plays with Doc Daneeka generalizes to a generic Catch-22 Game, in which moving power is effective, enabling the player who possesses it to do better than if the other player possesses it (chapter 10).

• A different specific catch-22 game models medieval witch trials, in which the accused, when they act honorably by not confessing and not implicating others, face death. Many of the accused chose this course of action, despite its dire consequences; the resulting outcome, in which they are tortured, is reinforced by the moving power of the accusers (chapter 10).

• To gain the upper hand in the generic King-of-the-Mountain Game, moving power is effective, but it does not cause the extreme frustration or damage that it does in the generic Catch-22 Game (chapter 10).

The pervasive rationality of players in all these games has several implications. Let me suggest three:

1. The world is not as irrational as some people suppose, rendering choices in it coherent and explicable.

2. There *are* circumstances in which it is rational to initiate a dispute, escalate a conflict, or go to war.

3. It may not be in one's interest to keep a cool head, especially if one is frustrated. Threatening an opponent, or exploding in anger, may facilitate achieving one's goals.

The last implication, especially, highlights the human side of the humanities. Emotions and rational choice are inextricably linked. Doubtless, there is calculation behind many of our actions, but we are also emotional creatures, hard-wired by our genetic makeup to express a variety of spontaneous feelings, both happy and sad.

As cases in point, the anger that Lysistrata and Lady Macbeth vent appears quickly, only to dissipate after it helps each character implement her preferred outcome. As well, we may express impetuous feelings of joy or love when some unexpectedly happy event occurs. Although I have applied game theory and TOM mainly to analyze the negative emotions of frustration and anger, positive emotions may be equally rational in demonstrating attraction, joy, or love.

Hard-wired emotions support strategies that have worked in the past—if not personally for us, then for our species. Game theory has been used to model the learning of such strategies, including the evolution of coping and survival strategies—such as fleeing or fighting in a threatening situation—in both animal populations and human societies. In selecting an optimal strategy in the game at hand, our choices are also conditioned by our personal experiences and the more ancient past, including what is built into the DNA of homo sapiens.

The humanities describe and explain human experiences, but they may be viewed through different theoretical lenses. This is true of the social sciences and the natural sciences as well (in physics, consider particle and wave theories of light).

While the social sciences are surely more subject to a unified explanation via game theory than the humanities (Gintis 2009 makes this case for social and behavioral sciences), I do not claim there is a single coherent way of thinking about all the humanities. Nonetheless, I believe TOM provides an excellent start in analyzing texts, both literary and historical. At the same time, standard game theory also offers key insights into, for example, how indivisible goods may be divided fairly (chapter 4), how voting can encourage cooperative choices in public-goods games (chapter 5), and how voting power is distributed among players who coalesce in certain ways (chapter 6).

Game theory and TOM will not, and should not, replace other modes of inquiry in the humanities. Like logic in philosophy, they provide rigorous tools for analyzing and interpreting behavior. They are especially useful, and sometimes even indispensible, in elucidating the strategic role that conflict and cooperation play in human affairs.

Appendix

There are seventy-eight structurally distinct 2×2 ordinal games in which the two players, each with two strategies, can strictly rank the four states from best to worst.[1] These games are "distinct" in the sense that no interchange of the column player's strategies, the row player's strategies, the players, or any combination of these can transform one game into any other. That is, these games are structurally different with respect to these transformations.

Of the seventy-eight games, twenty-one are no-conflict games with a mutually best (4,4) state. These states are always both Nash and nonmyopic equilibria (NMEs) in these games; no kind of power—moving, order, or threat—is needed by either player to implement them as outcomes.

I list here the remaining fifty-seven games (figures A.1, A.2, and A.3), in which the players disagree on a most-preferred state. The numbers used in the appendix of Brams (1994b) are shown for each game.[2] The

---

1. For a complete listing of the seventy-eight games, see Rapoport and Guyer 1966, Rapoport, Guyer, and Gordon 1976, and Brams 1977, in which the games are divided into three categories based on their vulnerability to deception. Fraser and Kilgour (1986, 1988) enumerate the 726 2×2 games in which preferences are not necessarily strict (i.e., there may be ties in the ranks). Fishburn and Kilgour (1990) simplify preferences further by making only a binary distinction in preferences, and Robinson and Goforth (2005) provide a sophisticated mathematical analysis of 2×2 games, giving what they call a "new periodic table."

2. The moving-power outcomes identified in the fifty-seven conflict games listed in Brams 1982a, 1983/2007 differ somewhat from those given here because of changes I have made in the rules of play of TOM. Threat-power outcomes were previously identified in Brams 1983/2007, 1990 and Brams and Hessel 1984. Order power was first used in Brams 1994b, which was previously called "staying power" (Brams 1983; Brams and Hessel 1983; a different concept of staying power is defined in Kilgour, De, and Hipel 1987).

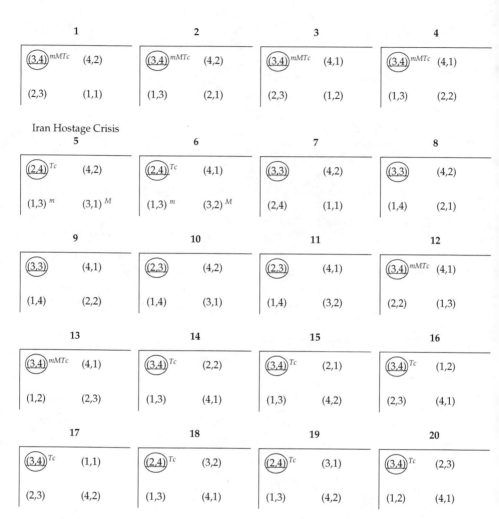

Figure A.1
Thirty-one games with one NME

Union-Confederacy

	21		22		23		24

| $(3,4)^{Tc}$ | $(1,3)$ | $(2,4)^{Tc}$ | $(3,3)^{td}$ | $(3,3)^{mMTc}$ | $(4,1)$ | $(3,3)^{mMTc}$ | $(4,1)$ |
| $(2,2)$ | $(4,1)$ | $(1,2)$ | $(4,1)$ | $(2,2)$ | $(1,4)$ | $(1,2)$ | $(2,4)$ |

Hamlet-Claudius   White House Tapes

	25		26		27		28

| $(3,2)^{M}$ | $(4,1)$ | $(3,2)^{M}$ | $(4,1)$ | $(2,3)$ | $(4,1)$ | $(2,2)$ | $(4,1)$ |
| $(2,3)^{m}$ | $(1,4)$ | $(1,3)^{m}$ | $(2,4)$ | $(1,2)$ | $(3,4)^{mMtcTd}$ | $(1,3)$ | $(3,4)^{mMtcTd}$ |

Cuban Missile Crisis

	29		30		31

| $(3,2)$ | $(2,1)$ | $(2,2)$ | $(4,1)$ | $(2,2)$ | $(3,1)$ |
| $(4,3)^{mMtdTc}$ | $(1,4)$ | $(3,3)^{mMtdTc}$ | $(1,4)$ | $(4,3)^{mMtdTc}$ | $(1,4)$ |

Figure A.1
(continued)

fifty-seven games are divided into three main categories: (1) those with one NME (thirty-one games), (2) those with two NMEs (twenty-four games), and (3) those with three NMEs (two games).

I have grouped together at the end of the list the nine games with indeterminate states—seven of which fall in category 2 and two of which fall in category 3—in which order power is effective when play starts at an indeterminate state. Indeterminate states show two NMEs in the anticipation game (AG), separated by a slash.

Moving power outcomes that the row and column players can induce are indicated by superscripts in the key given below. If the outcomes induced by moving power are different, then this power is effective if the player who possesses it can implement a better outcome for itself than if the other player possessed it; otherwise, it is irrelevant or ineffective. The latter two categories are distinguished in Brams (1994b, chap. 4), which also distinguishes cyclic games that are strongly cyclic (no

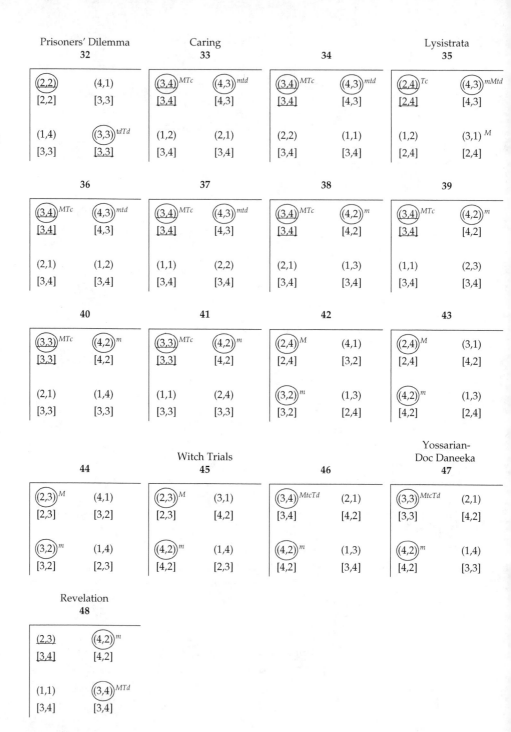

Figure A.2
Twenty-four games with two NMEs

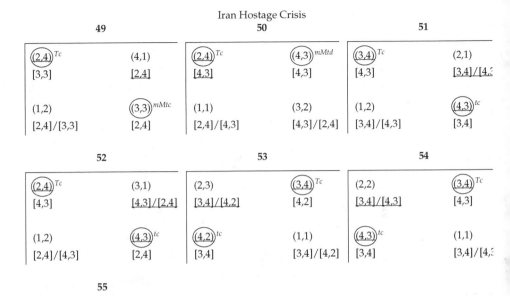

Iran Hostage Crisis

49

(2,4) ^{Tc}	(4,1)
[3,3]	[2,4]
(1,2)	(3,3) ^{mMtc}
[2,4]/[3,3]	[2,4]

50

(2,4) ^{Tc}	(4,3) ^{mMtd}
[4,3]	[4,3]
(1,1)	(3,2)
[2,4]/[4,3]	[4,3]/[2,4]

51

(3,4) ^{Tc}	(2,1)
[4,3]	[3,4]/[4,3
(1,2)	(4,3) ^{tc}
[3,4]/[4,3]	[3,4]

52

(2,4) ^{Tc}	(3,1)
[4,3]	[4,3]/[2,4]
(1,2)	(4,3) ^{tc}
[2,4]/[4,3]	[2,4]

53

(2,3)	(3,4) ^{Tc}
[3,4]/[4,2]	[4,2]
(4,2) ^{tc}	(1,1)
[3,4]	[3,4]/[4,2]

54

(2,2)	(3,4) ^{Tc}
[3,4]/[4,3]	[4,3]
(4,3) ^{tc}	(1,1)
[3,4]	[3,4]/[4,3

55

(2,2)	(4,3) ^{tc}
[3,4]/[4,3]	[3,4]
(3,4) ^{Tc}	(1,1)
[3,4]	[3,4]/[4,3]

Figure A.2
(continued)

Samson-Delilah
Macbeth
56

Chicken
Cuban Missile Crisis
57

(2,4) ^{Tc}	(4,2) ^{m}
[3,3]	[4,2]
(1,1)	(3,3) ^{Mtc}
[2,4]/[3,3]	[2,4]

(3,3)	(2,4) ^{Tc}
[3,3]	[4,2]/[3,3]
(4,2) ^{tc}	(1,1)
[3,3]/[2,4]	[2,4]/[4,2]

Figure A.3
Two games with three NMEs

impediments), moderately cyclic (one impediment), and weakly cyclic (two impediments).

Threat power outcomes are indicated by superscripts in the key given below, with compellent threat outcomes distinguished from deterrent threat outcomes. Threat power is always effective when the row and column players can induce different outcomes; when they induce the same outcome, threat power is irrelevant.

Certain games are further identified by their descriptive names or by the conflicts modeled by them in the text. These include Caring (game 33), Samson and Delilah (game 56), Revelation (game 48), Prisoners' Dilemma (game 32), Chicken (game 57), White House Tapes (game 27), Union-Confederacy (game 22), Lysistrata (game 35), Macbeth (game 56), Hamlet-Claudius (game 26), Iran Hostage Crisis (games 5 and 50), Cuban Missile Crisis (games 30 and 57), Yossarian-Doc Daneeka (game 47), and Witch Trials (game 45).

The key to the symbols is as follows:

(x,y) = (payoff to row, payoff to column)

$[a,b]$ = [payoff to row, payoff to column] in anticipation game (AG)

$[w,x]/[y,z]$ = indeterminate state in AG, where $[w,x]$ is the NME induced if row has order power, $[y,z]$ if column has order power, from corresponding state in original game

4 = best; 3 = next-best; 2 = next-worst; 1 = worst

Nash equilibria in original game and in AG underscored (except when there is only one NME in AG)

NMEs in original game circled

m/M = moving-power outcome row/column can induce

t/T = threat-power outcome row/column can induce

c/d = compellent/deterrent threat outcome

Glossary

This glossary contains definitions of the more technical concepts used in this book. Illustrations of these concepts can be found in the text.

Anticipation game (AG) An anticipation game is described by a payoff matrix, whose entries, given in brackets, are the nonmyopic equilibria (NMEs) into which each state of the original game goes.

Approval voting Approval voting is a voting system in which individuals can vote for as many alternatives as they like or consider acceptable, and the alternative with the most votes wins.

Backtracking Backtracking occurs when a player moves first in one direction and then reverses the direction of its move.

Backward induction Backward induction is a reasoning process in which players, working backward from the last possible move in a game, anticipate each other's choices in order to make a rational choice.

Banzhaf index The Banzhaf index, a measure of the relative voting power of a player, is the number of a player's critical defections divided by the total number of critical defections of all players.

Blockage Blockage occurs when it is not rational, based on backward induction, for a player to move from a state.

Borda maximin allocation In the fair division of indivisible items, a Borda maximin allocation is an allocation that maximizes the minimum modified Borda score that any player receives.

Borda maxsum allocation In the fair division of indivisible items, a Borda maxsum allocation is one that maximizes the sum of modified Borda scores of all players.

Breakdown strategy/state A breakdown state is the Pareto-inferior state that a threatener threatens to implement, by choosing its breakdown strategy, unless the threatenee accedes to the threat state.

Cardinal utility *See* **Utility**

Characteristic-function form The characteristic-function form describes a cooperative game in which each subset of players can ensure itself of specified portion of some good, such as money.

Chicken A two-person variable-sum symmetric game in which each player has two strategies: to cooperate or defect. Neither player has a dominant strategy; the compromise outcome, in which both players cooperate, is not a Nash equilibrium, but the two outcomes in which one player cooperates and the other defects are Nash equilibria (game 57 in the appendix).

Common knowledge   Players in a game have common knowledge when they share certain information, know that they share it, know that they know that they share it, and so on ad infinitum.

Compellent threat   In repeated play of a two-person game, a threatener's compellent threat is a threat to stay at a particular strategy to induce the threatened player to choose its (as well as the threatener's) best state associated with that strategy.

Complete information   A game is one of complete information if each player knows the rules of play, the rationality rules, the preferences or payoffs of every player for all possible states, and which player (if either) has moving, order, or threat power. When this is not the case, information is incomplete.

Condorcet alternative   A Condorcet alternative is an alternative that defeats every other alternative, based on majority rule, in separate pairwise contests.

Condorcet paradox   A Condorcet paradox occurs when no alternative can defeat all other alternatives in separate pairwise contests.

Configuration   *See* **Game configuration**

Conflict game   A conflict game is a 2×2 ordinal game in which there is no mutually best (4,4) state; a no-conflict game is one in which there is such a state.

Constant-sum (zero-sum) game   A constant-sum (zero-sum) game is a game in which the utility payoffs to the players at every outcome sum to some constant (zero); if the game has two players, what one player gains the other player loses.

Contingency   A contingency is the set of strategy choices made by players other than the one in question.

Cooperative game theory   In a game, players can make binding and enforceable agreements, usually with respect to how the payoffs will be split among them.

Critical defection   A defection from a wining coalition is critical if the defecting player causes the coalition to be losing.

Cyclic game   A 2×2 ordinal game is a cyclic if moves either in a clockwise or a counterclockwise direction never give a player its best payoff when it has the next move. A cyclic game is strongly cyclic (no impediments) if each player always does immediately better by moving; otherwise, it is either moderately cyclic (one impediment) or weakly cyclic (two impediments).

Deception strategy   In a two-person game of incomplete information, a deception strategy is a player's false announcement of a preference order to induce the other player to choose a strategy favorable to the deceiver.

Decision   *See* **Game against nature (one-person game)**

Decision theory   Decision theory is a mathematical theory for making optimal choices in situations in which the outcome does not depend on the choices of other players but rather on states of nature that arise by chance.

Deterrent threat   In repeated play of a two-person game, a threatener's deterrent threat is a threat to move to another strategy to induce the threatened player to choose a state, associated with the threatener's initial strategy, that is better for both players than the states threatened.

Differential game   A differential game is a dynamic game in which the strategies of the players are given by differential equations, which model their continuous choices over time.

Difficult game A difficult game is one in which there is only one cooperative outcome, which is not a Nash equilibrium but is at least next-best for each player, and the noncooperative outcome is Pareto-inferior to the cooperative outcome.

Dominant strategy A dominant strategy is a strategy that leads to outcomes at least as good as those of any other strategy in all possible contingencies, and a better outcome in at least one contingency. A strongly dominant strategy is a dominant strategy that leads to a better outcome in every contingency, whereas this is not the case for a weakly dominant strategy.

Dominated strategy A dominated strategy is a strategy that leads to outcomes no better than those of any other strategy in all possible contingencies, and a worse outcome in at least one contingency. A strongly dominated strategy is a dominated strategy that leads to a worse outcome in every contingency, whereas this is not the case for a weakly dominated strategy.

Effective power Power is effective when possessing it induces a better outcome for a player in a game than when an opponent possesses it; when the opposite is the case, power is ineffective.

Efficiency An allocation is efficient if there is no other allocation that is better for one player and at least as good for all the other players.

Envy-freeness An envy-free allocation is one in which each player thinks it receives at least a tied-for-largest portion, so it does not envy the allocation of another player. If an allocation is not envy-free, it may be envy-possible (envy is possible but not guaranteed to occur) or envy-ensuring (envy is sure to occur).

Equal division An equal division is one in which all players receive the same number of items.

Equilibrium *See* **Nash equilibrium; Nonmyopic equilibrium (NME)**

Expected payoff/utility A player's expected payoff/utility is the weighted sum of the payoff that it receives from each outcome multiplied by the probability of its occurrence.

Extensive form A game in extensive form is represented by a game tree, in which the players make sequential choices but do not necessarily know all the prior choices of the other players.

Feasibility A move is feasible if it can plausibly be interpreted as possible in the situation being modeled.

Final state A final state is the state induced after all rational moves and countermoves (if any) from the initial state have been made, according to the theory of moves, making it the outcome of the game.

Free rider A free rider is a player who obtains the benefit of a public good without contributing to its provision.

Game A game is an interdependent decision situation, whose outcome depends on the choices of all players. It is described by rules of play.

Game against nature (one-person game) A game against nature (one-person game) is a game in which one player is assumed to be "nature," whose choices are neither conscious nor based on rational calculation but instead on chance.

Game configuration A game configuration is a payoff matrix, in which the initial state is not specified.

Game of conflict A game of conflict is one in which there is no mutually best outcome.

Game of partial conflict A game of partial conflict is a variable-sum game, in which the players' preferences for outcomes are not diametrically opposed.

Game of total conflict   A game of total conflict is a constant-sum game in which in which the players' preferences for outcomes are diametrically opposed: The best outcome for one player is the worst for the other, the next-best outcome for one player is the next-worst for the other, and so on. *See also* **Constant-sum (zero-sum) game**

Game theory   Game theory is a mathematical theory of rational strategy selection used to analyze optimal choices in interdependent decision situations; the outcome depends on the choices of two or more players, and each player has preferences for the possible outcomes. See also *Cooperative game theory*; *Noncooperative game theory*.

Game tree   A game tree is a symbolic tree, based on the rules of play of a game, in which the vertices or nodes of the tree represent choice points, and the branches represent courses of action that can be selected by the players.

Generic game   A generic game is a game in which the preferences of the players are partially ordered; it subsumes several specific games in which the preferences of the players are strictly ordered.

Impediment   An impediment in a cyclic game occurs when the player with the next move does immediately worse by moving in the direction of the cycling.

Indeterminate state   A state is indeterminate if the outcome induced from it depends on which player moves first (in which case order power is effective).

Information   *See* **Complete information**

Initial state   An initial state is the state in a payoff matrix where play commences.

Irrelevant power   Moving power is irrelevant when the outcome induced by one player in a game is better for both players than the outcome that the other player can induce; threat power is irrelevant when either player's possession of it leads to the same outcome.

Lexicographic decision rule   A lexicographic decision rule enables a player to rank states on the basis of a most important criterion (primary goal), then a next most important criterion (secondary goal), and so on.

Magnanimity   A player is magnanimous when it moves from its best state to its next-best state.

Maximin allocation   In the fair division of indivisible items, a maximin allocation maximizes the minimum rank of items that any player receives; such an allocation is sometimes referred to as "Rawlsian" after philosopher John Rawls.

Minimax theorem   In a two-person constant-sum game, the minimax theorem guarantees that each player can ensure at least a certain expected value, called the value of the game, which does not depend on the strategy choice of the other player.

Mixed strategy   A mixed strategy is a strategy that involves a random selection from two or more pure strategies, according to a particular probability distribution.

Modified Borda score   In the fair division of indivisible items, the modified Borda score scores items the same as the Borda count, except that the scoring begins with 1 instead of 0 for a worst-ranked item.

Move   In a normal-form game, a move is a player's switch from one strategy to another in the payoff matrix.

Moving power   In a cyclic game, moving power is the ability to continue moving when the other player must eventually stop; the player possessing it uses it to try to induce a preferred outcome.

Nash equilibrium   A Nash equilibrium is a state—or, more properly, the strategies associated with a state—from which no player would have an incentive to depart unilaterally because its departure would immediately lead to a worse, or at least not a better, state.

Noncooperative game theory In a game, players cannot make binding or enforceable agreements but can choose strategies and can move to and from states.

Nonmyopic equilibrium (NME) In a two-person game, a nonmyopic equilibrium is a state from which neither player, anticipating all possible rational moves and countermoves from the initial state, would have an incentive to depart unilaterally because the departure would eventually lead to a worse, or at least not a better, outcome.

Normal (strategic) form A game is represented in normal (strategic) form when it is described by a payoff matrix in which the players independently choose their strategies. The possible states of the game correspond to the cells or entries of the matrix.

Omniscience In a two-person game, an omniscient player is one who can predict the nonomniscient player's strategy before the nonomniscient player chooses it.

Order power In a two-person game, order power is the ability of a player to dictate the order of moves in which the players depart from an indeterminate initial state in order to ensure a preferred outcome for itself.

Ordinal game An ordinal game is a game in which each player can order or rank the states but not necessarily assign numerical payoffs or cardinal utilities to them; when there are no ties in the ranking, the ordering is strict.

Outcome An outcome in the theory of moves (TOM) is the final state of a game, from which no player chooses to move and at which the players receive their payoffs.

Outcome matrix In a game in normal (strategic) form, the entries of an outcome matrix indicate the outcomes to the players resulting from their strategy choices.

Paradox of omniscience In a two-person game, a paradox of omniscience occurs when it is in a player's interest to be nonomniscient rather than omniscient.

Pareto-dominance/domination In the fair division of indivisible items, allocation X Pareto-dominates allocation Y for a player if, for every item in X that is not in Y, there is a different item in Y that the player ranks lower.

Pareto-inferior state A state is Pareto-inferior if there exists another state that is better for all players, or better for at least one player and not worse for any other players.

Pareto-optimal/superior state A Pareto-optimal state is one that is not Pareto-inferior. A state is Pareto-superior to a Pareto-inferior state if it is better for all players, or better for at least one player and not worse for any other players.

Pareto-optimality *See* **Efficiency**

Payoff A payoff is a measure of the value that a player attaches to a state in a game; usually payoffs are taken to be cardinal utilities, but here they are assumed to be ordinal (i.e., ranks from best to worst).

Payoff matrix In a game in normal (strategic) form, the entries of a payoff matrix indicate the payoffs to the players resulting from their strategy choices.

Payoff termination Payoff termination occurs when one player receives its best payoff in the move-countermove process and, if it has the next move, terminates play.

Player *See* **Rational player**

Plurality voting Plurality voting is a voting procedure in which voters can vote for only one alternative; the alternative with the most votes wins.

Power *See* **Effective power; Irrelevant power; Moving power; Order power; Threat power**

Preference Preference is a player's ranking of states from best to worst.

Prisoners' Dilemma A two-person variable-sum symmetric game in which each player has two strategies, cooperate or defect. Defect dominates cooperation for both players, even though the mutual-defection outcome, which is the unique Nash equilibrium in the game, is worse for both players than the mutual-cooperation outcome (game 32 in the appendix).

Public good A public good is a good that cannot be withheld from any player, whether or not this player contributes to its provision.

Pure strategy A pure strategy is a single specific strategy. *See also* **Mixed strategy**

Rational choice A rational choice is a choice that leads to a preferred outcome, based on a player's goals.

Rationality rules Rationality rules specify when players will stay at, or move from, states, taking into account the rational moves of the other players.

Rational outcome *See* **Nash equilibrium**; **Nonmyopic equilibrium (NME)**

Rational player A rational player is an actor with free will who makes rational choices, in light of the presumed rational choices of other players in a game or the states of nature that may arise in a decision.

Rational termination Rational termination is a constraint, assumed in the definition of a nonmyopic equilibrium (NME), that prohibits a player from moving from an initial state unless it leads to a better outcome before cycling.

Repeated game A repeated game is a game in which play of some game is repeated again and again.

Rules of play The rules of play of a game describe the possible choices of the players at each stage of a game.

Saddlepoint In a two-person game of total conflict, a saddlepoint is an entry in a payoff matrix at which the row player receives the minimum payoff in its row and the maximum payoff in its column.

Security level The security level of a player is the best payoff that it can ensure for itself whatever contingency arises.

Sequential game A sequential game is one in which players can move and countermove after their initial strategy choices according to the theory of moves (TOM).

Signaling game A signaling game is a game of incomplete information, in which a sender sends a message to a receiver, which may or may not identify the signaler's true type in equilibrium.

State A state is an entry in a payoff matrix from which the players may move. Play of a game starts at an initial state and terminates at a final state, or outcome.

Strategy In a game in normal (strategic) form, a strategy is a complete plan that specifies the course of action a player will follow in every contingency.

Stoppage Stoppage occurs when blockage occurs for the first time from some initial state.

Survivor A survivor is the state that is selected at any stage as the result of backward induction.

Symmetric game A symmetric game is a two-person normal (strategic)-form game, in which the payoff ranks along the main diagonal are the same for each player and the payoff ranks along the off-diagonal are mirror images of each other.

Theory of moves (TOM) The theory of moves describes optimal strategic calculations in normal-form games, in which the players can move and countermove from an initial state.

Threat power In a two-person game that is repeated, threat power is the ability of a player to threaten a mutually disadvantageous outcome in the single play of a game to deter untoward actions in the future play of this or other games. *See also* **Compellent threat**; **Deterrent threat**

Threat state/strategy   A threat state is the Pareto-superior state that a threatener promises to implement, by choosing its threat strategy, if the threatened party also agrees to its choice. *See also* **Breakdown state**

Two-sidedness convention (TSC)   The two-sidedness convention describes the conditions under which one player will be magnanimous by moving from a state, even though this move leads to an outcome with a worse payoff for that player. *See also* **Magnanimity**; **Rationality rules**; **Rules of play**

Two-sidedness rule   The two-sidedness rule describes how players determine whether or not to move from a state on the basis of the other players' rational choices as well as their own.

Undominated split   An undominated split is a division of items between two players such that each allocation might be preferred by a player.

Undominated strategy   An undominated strategy is a strategy that is neither a dominant nor a dominated strategy.

Utility   Utility is the numerical value, indicating degree of preference, which a player has for an outcome.

Value   In two-person constant-sum games, the value is the amount that the players can ensure for themselves by choosing their optimal strategies (which may be mixed).

Variable-sum game   A variable-sum game is a game in which the sum of the payoffs to the players in different states is not constant but variable, so the players may gain or lose simultaneously in different states.

Zero-sum game   *See* **Constant-sum (zero-sum) game**

References

Abel, Elie. 1966. *The Missile Crisis*. Philadelphia: Lippincott.

Abraham, Henry J. 1975. *The Judicial Process*, 3rd ed. New York: Oxford University Press.

Ackerlof, George A., and Robert J. Shiller. 2009. *Animal Spirits*. Princeton, NJ: Princeton University Press.

Allison, Graham T. 1971. *Essence of Decision: Explaining the Cuban Missile Crisis*. Boston: Little, Brown.

Alpern, Steve, Shmuel Gal, and Eilon Solan. 2010. A Sequential Selection Game with Vetoes. *Games and Economic Behavior* 68 (1): 1–14.

Amir, Rabah. 1995. Endogenous Timing in Two-Player Games: A Counterexample. *Games and Economic Behavior* 9 (2): 234–237.

Anchor Bible: Genesis. 1964. New York: Doubleday.

Aristophanes. 411 BCE/1973. *Aristophanes: Lysistrata and Other Plays*, tr. with an introduction by Alan H. Sommerstein. London: Penguin.

Aron, Raymond. 1966. *Peace and War*. New York: Doubleday.

Arrow, Kenneth J. 1951/1963. *Social Choice and Individual Values*. New Haven, CT: Yale University Press.

Aumann, Robert, and Mordecai Kurz. 1977. Power and Taxes. *Econometrica* 45 (July): 522–539.

Avenhaus, Rudolf, Steven J. Brams, John Fichtner, and D. Marc Kilgour. 1989. The Probability of Nuclear War. *Journal of Peace Research* 26 (1): 91–99.

Axelrod, Robert. 1984. *The Evolution of Cooperation*. New York: Basic.

Banzhaf, John F., III. 1965. Weighted Voting Doesn't Work: A Mathematical Analysis. *Rutgers Law Review* 19 (2): 337–343.

Bates, Robert H., Avner Greif, Margaret Levi, Jean-Laurent Rosenthal, and Barry R. Weingast. 1998. *Analytical Narratives*. Princeton, NJ: Princeton University Press.

Ben-Ze'ev, Aaron. 2000. *The Subtlety of Emotions*. Cambridge, MA: MIT Press.

Binmore, Ken. 2009. *Rational Decisions*. Princeton, NJ: Princeton University Press.

Blight, James G., and David A. Welch. 1989. *On the Brink: Americans and Soviets Reexamine the Cuban Missile Crisis*. New York: Hill and Wang.

Board, Oliver. 2002. The Deception of the Greeks: Generalizing the Information Structure of Extensive Form Games. Preprint, Department of Economics, University of Oxford.

Brams, Steven J. 1975. Newcomb's Problem and Prisoners' Dilemma. *Journal of Conflict Resolution* 19 (4): 596–612.

Brams, Steven J. 1975/2004. *Game Theory and Politics*. New York and Mineola, NY: Free Press and Dover.

Brams, Steven J. 1976. *Paradoxes in Politics: An Introduction to the Nonobvious in Political Science*. New York: Free Press.

Brams, Steven J. 1977. Deception in 2 × 2 Games. *Journal of Peace Science* 2 (Spring): 171–203.

Brams, Steven J. 1979. Faith versus Rationality in the Bible: Game-Theoretic Interpretations of Sacrifice in the Old Testament. In *Applied Game Theory: Proceedings of a Conference, Vienna, 1978*, ed. S. J. Brams, A. Schotter, and G. Schwödiauer, 430–445. Würzburg, Germany: Physica-Verlag.

Brams, Steven J. 1980/2003. *Biblical Games: Game Theory and the Hebrew Bible*. Cambridge, MA: MIT Press.

Brams, Steven J. 1981. Mathematics and Theology: Game-Theoretic Implications of God's Omniscience. *Mathematics Magazine* 53 (November): 277–282.

Brams, Steven J. 1982a. Omniscience and Omnipotence: How They May Help—or Hurt—in a Game. *Inquiry* 25 (2): 217–231.

Brams, Steven J. 1982b. A Resolution of the Paradox of Omniscience. In *Reason and Decision, Bowling Green Studies in Applied Philosophy*, vol. 3, ed. Michael Bradie and Kenneth Sayre, 17–30. Bowling Green, OH: Department of Philosophy, Bowling Green State University.

Brams, Steven J. 1983/2007. *Superior Beings: If They Exist, How Would We Know? Game-Theoretic Implications of Omniscience, Omnipotence, Immortality, and Incomprehensibility*. New York: Springer.

Brams, Steven J. 1985/1989. *Rational Politics: Decisions, Games, and Strategy*. Washington, DC, and New York: CQ Press and Academic.

Brams, Steven J. 1985. *Superpower Games: Applying Game Theory to the Superpower Conflict*. New Haven, CT: Yale University Press.

Brams, Steven J. 1990. *Negotiation Games: Applying Game Theory to Bargaining and Arbitration*. New York: Routledge.

Brams, Steven J. 1993. Theory of Moves. *American Scientist* 81 (6): 562–570.

Brams, Steven J. 1994a. Game Theory and Literature. *Games and Economic Behavior* 6 (1): 32–54.

Brams, Steven J. 1994b. *Theory of Moves*. Cambridge, UK: Cambridge University Press.

Brams, Steven J. 1997a. Game Theory and Emotions. *Rationality and Society* 9 (1): 91–124.

Brams, Steven J. 1997b. The Rationality of Surprise: Unstable Nash Equilibria and the Theory of Moves. In *Decisionmaking on War and Peace: The Cognitive-Rational Debate*, ed. Alex Mintz and Nehemia Geva, 103–129. Boulder, CO: Lynne Reinner.

Brams, Steven J. 1999a. To Mobilize or Not to Mobilize: Catch-22s in International Crises. *International Studies Quarterly* 43 (4): 621–640.

Brams, Steven J. 1999b. Modeling Free Choice in Games. In *Topics in Game Theory and Mathematical Economics: Essays in Honor of Robert J. Aumann*, ed. Myrna H. Wooders, 41–62. Providence, RI: American Mathematical Society.

Brams, Steven J. 2001. Response to Randall Stone: Heresy or Scientific Progress? *Journal of Conflict Resolution* 45 (2): 245–256.

Brams, Steven J. 2006. Fair Division. In *Handbook of Political Economy*, ed. Barry Weingast and Donald Wittman, 425–437. New York: Oxford University Press.

Brams, Steven J. 2008. *Mathematics and Democracy: Designing Better Voting and Fair-Division Procedures*. Princeton, NJ: Princeton University Press.

Brams, Steven J., Paul J. Affuso, and D. Marc Kilgour. 1989. Presidential Power: A Game-Theoretic Analysis. In *The Presidency in American Politics*, ed. Paul Brace, Christine Harrington, and Gary King, 55–74. New York: New York University Press.

Brams, Steven J., and Morton D. Davis. 1976. A Game-Theory Approach to Jury Selection. *Trial* 12 (December): 47–49.

Brams, Steven J., and Morton D. Davis. 1978. Optimal Jury Selection: A Game-Theoretic Model for the Exercise of Peremptory Challenges. *Operations Research* 26 (6): 966–991.

Brams, Steven J., Paul H. Edelman, and Peter C. Fishburn. 2001. Paradoxes of Fair Division. *Journal of Philosophy* 98 (6): 300–314.

Brams, Steven J., Paul H. Edelman, and Peter C. Fishburn. 2003. Fair Division of Indivisible Goods. *Theory and Decision* 55 (2): 147–180.

Brams, Steven J., and Peter C. Fishburn. 1983/2007. *Approval Voting*. Cambridge, MA, and New York: Birkhäuser Boston and Springer.

Brams, Steven J., and Peter C. Fishburn. 2000. Fair Division of Indivisible Items between Two People with Identical Preferences: Envy-Freeness, Pareto-Optimality, and Equity. *Social Choice and Welfare* 17 (2): 247–267.

Brams, Steven J., and Marek P. Hessel. 1983. Staying Power in 2 × 2 Games. *Theory and Decision* 15 (3): 279–302.

Brams, Steven J., and Marek P. Hessel. 1984. Threat Power in Sequential Games. *International Studies Quarterly* 28 (1): 15–36.

Brams, Steven J., and Christopher B. Jones. 1999. Catch-22 and King-of-the-Mountain Games: Cycling, Frustration, and Power. *Rationality and Society* 11 (2): 139–167.

Brams, Steven J., and Todd R. Kaplan. 2004. Dividing the Indivisible: Procedures for Allocating Cabinet Ministries in a Parliamentary System. *Journal of Theoretical Politics* 16 (2): 143–173.

Brams, Steven J., and D. Marc Kilgour. 2001. Competitive Fair Division. *Journal of Political Economy* 109 (2): 418–443.

Brams, Steven J., and D. Marc Kilgour. 2009. How Democracy Resolves Conflict in Difficult Games. In *Games, Groups, and the Global Good*, ed. Simon Levin, 229–241. Berlin, Germany: Springer.

Brams, Steven J., D. Marc Kilgour, and Christian Klamler. 2009. The Undercut Procedure: An Algorithm for the Envy-Free Division of Indivisible Items. Preprint, Department of Politics, New York University.

Brams, Steven J., and Daniel L. King. 2005. Efficient Fair Division: Help the Worst Off or Avoid Envy? *Rationality and Society* 17 (4): 387–421.

Brams, Steven J., and Walter Mattli. 1993. Theory of Moves: Overview and Examples. *Conflict Management and Peace Science* 12 (2): 50–54.

Brams, Steven J., and Ben D. Mor. 1993. When Is It Rational to Be Magnanimous in Victory? *Rationality and Society* 5 (4): 432–454.

Brams, Steven J., and Douglas Muzzio. 1977a. Game Theory and the White House Tapes Case. *Trial* 13 (May): 48–53.

Brams, Steven J., and Douglas Muzzio. 1977b. Unanimity in the Supreme Court: A Game-Theoretic Explanation of the Decision in the White House Tapes Case. *Public Choice* 32 (Winter): 67–83.

Brams, Steven J., and Philip D. Straffin, Jr. 1979. Prisoners' Dilemma and Professional Sports Drafts. *American Mathematical Monthly* 86 (2): 80–88.

Brams, Steven J., and Alan D. Taylor. 1996. *Fair Division: From Cake-Cutting to Dispute Resolution*. New York: Cambridge University Press.

Brams, Steven J., and Alan D. Taylor. 1999. *The Win-Win Solution: Guaranteeing Fair Shares to Everybody*. New York: W. W. Norton.

Brams, Steven J., and Jeffrey M. Togman 1996. Camp David: Was the Agreement Fair? *Conflict Management and Peace Science* 13 (3): 99–112.

Brams, Steven J., and Jeffrey M. Togman. 1998. Cooperation through Threats: The Northern Ireland Case. *PS: Political Science and Politics* 31 (1):32–39.

Brams, Steven J., and Donald Wittman. 1981. Nonmyopic Equilibria in 2×2 Games. *Conflict Management and Peace Science* 6 (1): 39–62.

Brams, Steven J., and Frank C. Zagare. 1977. Deception in Simple Voting Games. *Social Science Research* 6 (September): 257–272.

Brams, Steven J., and Frank C. Zagare. 1981. Double Deception: Two against One in Three-Person Games. *Theory and Decision* 13 (March): 81–90.

Brenner, Saul. 1980. Game Theory and Supreme Court Decision Making: A Bibliographic Overview. *Law Library Journal* 72:470–475.

Broome, John. 1991. *Weighing Goods*. Oxford, UK: Basil Blackwell.

Brugoni, Dina A. 1992. *Eyeball to Eyeball: The Inside Story of the Cuban Missile Crisis*. New York: Random House.

Brune, Lester H. 1985. *The Missile Crisis of October 1962: A Review of Issues and References*. Claremont, CA: Regina.

Buber, Martin. 1958. *I and Thou*, tr. Ronald Gregor Smith, 2nd ed. New York: Scribner's.

Bueno de Mesquita, Bruce. 1996. Counterfactuals and International Affairs: Some Insights from Game Theory. In *Counterfactual Thought Experiments in World Politics: Logical, Methodological, and Psychological Perspectives*, ed. Philip E. Tetlock and Aaron Belkin, 211–229. Princeton, NJ: Princeton University Press.

Burr, George L., ed. 1971. The Witch Persecutions. In *Translations and Reprints from the Original Sources of European History*, vol. 3, no. 4. New York: AMS Press. Originally published by the Department of History, University of Pennsylvania, 1907.)

Carter, Jimmy. 1982. *Keeping Faith: Memoirs of a President*. New York: Bantam.

Chami, Ralph. 1996. King Lear's Dilemma: Precommitment and the Last Word. *Economics Letters* 52 (2): 171–176.

Chayes, Abram. 1974. *The Cuban Missile Crisis: International Crises and the Role of Law*. New York: Oxford University Press.

Chimenti, Frank A. 1990. Pascal's Wager: A Decision-Theoretic Approach. *Mathematics Magazine* 63 (5): 321–325.

Chwe, Michael Suk-Young. 1994. Farsighted Coalitional Stability. *Journal of Economic Theory* 63:299–325.

Chwe, Michael Suk-Young. 2001. *Rational Ritual: Culture, Coordination, and Common Knowledge*. Princeton, NJ: Princeton University Press.

Chwe, Michael Suk-Young. 2009. Rational Choice and the Humanities: Excerpts and Folktales. *Occasion: Interdisciplinary Studies in the Humanities* 1 (October 15). http://occasion.stanford.edu/node/9.

Clark, Michael. 2002. *Paradoxes from A to Z*. London: Routledge.

Clausewitz, Karl von. 1832/1966. *On War*, ed. Anatol Rapoport. New York: Penguin.

Clinton, Robert Lowry. 1994. Game Theory, Legal History, and the Origins of Judicial Review: A Revisionist Analysis of *Marbury v. Madison*. *American Journal of Political Science* 38 (2):285–302.

Cohen, Raymond. 1991. *Negotiating across Cultures*. Washington, DC: U.S. Institute of Peace.

Condorcet, Marquis de. 1785. *Essai sur l'application de l'analyse à la probabilité des décisions rendues à la pluralité des voix*. Paris.

Cowley, Robert, ed. 2000. *What If?: The World's Foremost Military Historians Imagine What Might Have Been*. New York: Berkley.

Cowley, Robert, ed. 2003. *More What If?: Eminent Historians Imagine What Might Have Been*. New York: Pan.

Cowley, Robert, ed. 2004. *What Ifs? of American History*. New York: Berkley.

Crain, Caleb. 2009. Bootylicious. *The New Yorker*, September 7, 72–78.

Dalkey, Norman C. 1981. A Case Study of a Decision Analysis: Hamlet's Soliloquy. *Interfaces* 11 (5): 45–49.

Damasio, Antonio R. 1994. *Descartes' Error: Emotion, Reason, and the Human Brain*. New York: Grosset/Putnam.

Damasio, Antonio. 1999. *The Feeling of What Happens: Body and Emotion in the Making of Consciousness*. San Diego, CA: Harcourt.

Daniel, Donald C., and Katherine L. Herbig, eds. 1982. *Strategic Military Deception*. New York: Pergamon.

Dawkins, Richard. 2006. *The God Delusion*. Boston: Houghton Mifflin Harcourt.

Davis, Morton D. 1970. *Game Theory: A Nontechnical Introduction*. New York: Basic.

Davis, Morton D. 1990. Private communication (September 6).

de Ley, Herbert 1988. The Name of the Game: Applying Game Theory in Literature. *Substance* 17, no. 1 (issue 55): 33–46.

Dennett, Daniel C. 2006. *Breaking the Spell: Religion as a Natural Phenomenon*. New York: Viking.

Dershowitz, Alan M. 2000. *The Genesis of Justice: Ten Stories of Biblical Injustice That Led to the Ten Commandments and Modern Law*. New York: Warner.

de Sousa, Ronald. 1987. *The Rationality of Emotion*. Cambridge, MA: MIT Press.

Detzer, David. 1979. *The Brink: Story of the Cuban Missile Crisis*. New York: Crowell.

Dimand, Robert, and Mary Ann Dimand. 1992. The Early History of the Theory of Strategic Games from Waldegrave to Borel. In *Toward a History of Game Theory (Annual Supplement to History of Political Economy, 24)*, ed. E. Roy Weintraub, 15–27. Durham, NC: Duke University Press.

Dinerstein, Herbert. 1976. *The Making of the Cuban Missile Crisis, October 1962*. Baltimore: Johns Hopkins University Press.

Divine, Robert A., ed. 1971. *The Cuban Missile Crisis*. Chicago: Quadrangle.

Dixit, Avinash K. 1990. Private communication (December 18).

Dixit, Avinash, and Barry Nalebuff. 1991. *Thinking Strategically: The Competitive Edge in Business, Politics, and Everyday Life*. New York: W. W. Norton.

Dixit, Avinash K., and Barry J. Nalebuff. 2008. *The Art of Strategy*. New York: W. W. Norton.

Dixit, Avinash, Susan Skeath, and David Reilly. 2009. *Games of Strategy*, 3rd ed. New York: W. W. Norton.

Edelman, Paul H., and Peter C. Fishburn. 2001. Fair Division of Indivisible Items among People with Similar Preferences. *Mathematical Social Sciences* 41 (3): 327–347.

Elster, Jon. 1979. *Ulysses and the Sirens: Studies in Rationality and Irrationality*. Cambridge, UK: Cambridge University Press.

Elster, Jon. 1991. Envy in Social Life. In *Strategy and Choice*, ed. Richard J. Zeckhauser, 49–82. Cambridge, MA: MIT Press.

Elster, Jon. 1994. Rationality, Emotions, and Social Norms. *Synthese* 98 (1): 21–49.

Elster, Jon. 1999. *Alchemies of the Mind: Rationality and the Emotions*. Cambridge, UK: Cambridge University Press.

Elster, Jon. 2007. *Explaining Social Behavior: More Nuts and Bolts for the Social Sciences*. Cambridge, UK: Cambridge University Press.

Elster, Jon. 2009. Interpretation and Rational Choice. *Rationality and Society* 21, no. 1 (February): 5–33.

Emotions and Rational Choice. 1993. Special issue of *Rationality and Society* 5 (2).

Evans, Richard, and Robert Novak 1974. Mr. Nixon's Supreme Court Strategy. *Washington Post*, June 12, A29.

Faulkner, William. 1950. *Light in August*. New York: Random House.

Fehr, Ernst, and Simon Gächter. 2000. Fairness and Retaliation: The Economics of Reciprocity. *Journal of Economic Perspectives* 14 (3):159–181.

Felsenthal, Dan S., and Moshé Machover. 1998. *The Measurement of Voting Power: Theory and Practice, Problems and Paradoxes*. Cheltenham, UK: Edward Elgar.

Fishburn, Peter C. 1974a. Lexicographic Orders, Utilities and Decision Rules: A Survey. *Management Science* 20 (11):1442–1471.

Fishburn, Peter C. 1974b. Paradoxes of Voting. *American Political Science Review* 68 (3):537–546.

Fishburn, Peter C., and Steven J. Brams. 1983. Paradoxes of Preferential Voting. *Mathematics Magazine* 56 (4): 207–214.

Fishburn, Peter C., and D. Marc Kilgour. 1990. Binary 2 × 2 Games. *Theory and Decision* 29 (3): 165–182.

Fisher, Philip. 2002. *The Vehement Passions*. Princeton, NJ: Princeton University Press.

Fowler, James W. 1981. *Stages of Faith: The Psychology of Human Development and the Quest for Meaning*. San Francisco: Harper and Row.

Frank, Robert H. 1988. *Passions within Reason: The Strategic Role of the Emotions*. New York: W. W. Norton.

Fraser, Niall M., and Keith W. Hipel. 1982–1983. Dynamic Modeling of the Cuban Missile Crisis. *Conflict Management and Peace Science* 6 (2): 1–18.

Fraser, Niall M., and D. Marc Kilgour. 1986. Non-Strict Ordinal 2 × 2 Games: A Comprehensive Computer-Assisted Analysis of the Possibilities. *Theory and Decision* 20 (2): 99–121.

Fraser, Niall M., and D. Marc Kilgour. 1988. A Taxonomy of All Ordinal 2 × 2 Games. *Theory and Decision* 24 (2): 99–117.

Frijda, Nico H. 1986. *The Emotions*. Cambridge, UK: Cambridge University Press.

Garthoff, Raymond L. 1989. *Reflections on the Cuban Missile Crisis*, rev. ed. Washington, DC: Brookings.

Geanakoplos, John, David Pearce, and Ennio Stacchetti. 1989. Psychological Games and Sequential Reality. *Games and Economic Behavior* 1 (1): 60–79.

Gelernter, David. 1994. *The Muse in the Machine: Computerizing the Poetry of Human Thought*. New York: Free Press.

Gilboa, Itzhak, and David Schmeidler. 1988. Information Dependent Games: Can Common Sense Be Common Knowledge? *Economics Letters* 27:215–221.

Gilboa, Itzhak, and David Schmeidler. 2001. *A Theory of Case-Based Decisions*. Cambridge, UK: Cambridge University Press.

Gintis, Herbert. 2009. *The Bounds of Reason: Game Theory and the Unification of the Behavioral Sciences*. Princeton, NJ: Princeton University Press.

Greenberg, Joseph. 1990. *The Theory of Social Situations: An Alternative Game-Theoretic Approach*. Cambridge, UK: Cambridge University Press.

Haldeman, H. R., with Joseph DiMona. 1978. *The Ends of Power*. New York: Times Books.

Hamilton, Jonathan H., and Steven M. Slutsky. 1993. Endogenizing the Order of Moves in Matrix Games. *Theory and Decision* 34 (1): 47–62.

Hamilton, Lee. 1993. Last Word on the October Surprise? *New York Times*, January 24, E17.

Hanson, Norwood Russell. 1971. *What I Don't Believe and Other Essays*, ed. Stephen Toulmin and Harry Woolf. Dordrecht, Holland: D. Reidel.

Hardin, Russell. 1971. Collective Action as an Agreeable *n*-Person Prisoners' Dilemma. *Behavioral Science* 16 (5): 472–481.

Harmgart, Heike, Steffen Huck, and Wieland Müller. 2008. Tannhäuser's Dilemma: A Counterfactual Analysis. Preprint, Department of Economics, University College London.

Harmgart, Heike, Steffen Huck, and Wieland Müller. 2009. The Miracle as a Randomization Device: A Lesson from Richard Wagner's Romantic Opera *Tannnäuser und de Sängerkrieg auf Wartburg*. *Economics Letters* 102:33–35.

Hassner, Ron E. 2003. The Trial and Crucifixion of Jesus: A Modest Proposal. *Theory and Decision* 34 (1): 1–32.

Headley, J. T. 1863. *The Great Rebellion: A History of the Civil War in the United States*, vol. 1. Hartford, CT: Hulburt, Williams and Company.

Heller, Joseph. 1961. *Catch-22*. New York: Simon and Schuster.

Herreiner, Dorothea, and Clemens Puppe. 2002. A Simple Procedure for Finding Equitable Allocations of Indivisible Goods. *Social Choice and Welfare* 19 (2): 415–430.

Higgins, George V. 1985. *Cogan's Trade*. New York: Carroll & Graf.

Hill, Frances. 1995. *A Delusion of Satan: The Full Story of the Salem Witch Trials*. New York: Doubleday.

Hirshleifer, Jack. 1987. On the Emotions as Guarantors of Threats and Promises. In *The Latest on the Best: Essays on Evolution and Optimality*, ed. John Dupré, 305–326. Cambridge, MA: MIT Press.

Hirshleifer, Jack. 1994. The Dark Side of the Force. *Economic Inquiry* 32 (1): 1–10.

Hirshleifer, Jack. 2000. *The Dark Side of the Force: Economic Foundations of Conflict Theory*. Cambridge, UK: Cambridge University Press.

Hitchens, Christopher. 2008. *God Is Not Great: How Religion Poisons Everything*. New York: Hachette.

Hoffer, Peter Charles. 1997. *The Salem Witchcraft Trials: A Legal History*. Lawrence: University of Kansas Press.

Hoffman, Robert. 2001. Mixed Strategies in the Mugging Game. *Rationality and Society* 13 (2): 205–212.

Holler, Manfred J., and Barbara Klose-Ullmann. 2008. Wallenstein's Power Problem and Its Consequences. *AUCO Czech Economic Review* 2:197–218.

Holsti, Ole R., Richard A. Brody, and Robert C. North. 1964. Measuring Affect and Action in International Reaction Models: Empirical Materials from the 1962 Cuban Missile Crisis. *Journal of Peace Research* 1:170–189.

Howard, Nigel. 1971. *Paradoxes of Rationality: Theory of Metagames and Political Behavior*. Cambridge, MA: MIT Press.

Howard, Nigel. 1988. The Plot of Dr. Zhivago. *CONAN Newsletter* 2 (4): 2–4.

Howard, Nigel. 1990. Private communication (August 15).

Howard, Nigel. 1994. Drama Theory and Its Relation to Game Theory. Part I: Dramatic Resolution vs. Rational Solution; Part 2: Formal Model of the Resolution Process. *Group Decision and Negotiation* 3 (2): 187–206, 207–235.

Howard, Nigel. 1996. Negotiation as Drama: How "Games" Become Dramatic. *International Negotiation* 1 (1): 125–152.

Howard, Nigel, Peter G. Bennett, Jim W. Bryant, and Morris Bradley. 1993. Manifesto for a Theory of Drama and Irrational Choice. *Journal of the Operational Research Society* 6 (4): 429–434.

Huang, Peter H., and Ho-Mou Wu. 1992. Emotional Responses in Litigation. *International Review of Law and Economics* 12 (1): 31–44.

Huck, Steffen. 2008. Why Elsa Asks from When He Came: An Epistemological Analysis of Richard Wagner's *Lohengrin*. Preprint, Department of Economics, University College London.

Hurly, S. L. 1994. A New Take from Nozick on Newcomb's Problem and Prisoners' Dilemma. *Analysis* 54 (2): 65–72.

James, William. 1902/1967. *The Writings of William James*, ed. John J. McDermott. Chicago: University of Chicago Press.

Jaworski, Leon. 1976. *The Right and the Power: The Prosecution of Watergate*. New York: Reader's Digest Press.

Jordan, Jeff. 2006. *Pascal's Wager: Pragmatic Arguments and Belief in God*. Oxford, UK: Oxford University Press.

Kaminski, Marek M. 2004. *Games Prisoners Play: The Tragicomic World of Polish Prisons*. Princeton, NJ: Princeton University Press.

Karsh, Efraim. 1989. Military Lessons of the Iran-Iraq War. *Orbis* 33 (2): 209–223.

Kennedy, Robert F. 1969. *Thirteen Days: A Memoir of the Cuban Missile Crisis*. New York: W. W. Norton.

Kierkegaard, Søren. 1954. *Fear and Trembling*, tr. Walter Lowrie. Princeton, NJ: Princeton University Press.

Kilgour, D. Marc. 1984. Equilibria for Far-Sighted Players. *Theory and Decision* 16 (2): 135–157.

Kilgour, D. Marc, Mitali De, and Keith W. Hipel. 1987. Conflict Analysis Using Staying Power. In *Proceedings of the 1986 IEEE International Conference on Systems, Man, and Cybernetics.* Atlanta, GA.

Kilgour, D. Marc, and Frank C. Zagare. 1987. Holding Power in Sequential Games. *International Interactions* 13 (2): 321–347.

King, Stephen. 1987. *Misery.* New York: Viking Penguin.

Kissinger, Henry A. 1964. *A World Restored.* New York: Grosset and Dunlap.

Kolakowski, Leszek. 1982. *Religion.* New York: Oxford University Press.

Konig, David Thomas. 1979. *Law and Society in Puritan Massachusetts: Essex County, 1629–1692.* Chapel Hill: University of North Carolina Press.

Küng, Hans. 1980. *Does God Exist? An Answer for Today*, tr. Edward Quinn. New York: Doubleday.

Lalu, Iolanda. 1977. Richard III: Balance and Games in the Study of Theatre. *The Formal Study of Drama*, special issue of *Poetics* 6 (3/4): 339–350.

Landsberg, P. T. 1971. Gambling on God. *Mind* 80 (317): 100–104.

Lazarus, Richard S., and Bernice N. Lazarus. 1994. *Passion and Reason: Making Sense of Our Emotions.* Oxford, UK: Oxford University Press.

Ledwig, Marion. 2006. *Emotions: Their Rationality and Consistency.* New York: Peter Lang.

Leeson, Peter T. 2009. *The Invisible Hook: The Hidden Economics of Pirates.* Princeton, NJ: Princeton University Press.

Leeson, Peter T. 2010. Rational Choice, Round Robin, and Rebellion: An Institutional Solution to the Problems of Revolution. *Journal of Economic Behavior & Organization* 73 (3): 297–307.

Lewis, David. 1985. Prisoners' Dilemma Is a Newcomb Problem. In *Paradoxes of Rationality and Cooperation*, ed. Richmond Campbell and Lanning Sowden, 251–255. Vancouver: University of British Columbia Press.

Lewis, Michael. 1995. Self-Conscious Emotions. *American Scientist* 83 (1): 68–78.

Lewis, Neil A. 1992. Panel Rejects Theory Bush Met Iranians in Paris in '80. *New York Times*, July 2, A16.

Lewis, Neil A. 1993. House Inquiry Finds No Evidence of Deal on Hostages in 1980. *New York Times*, January 13, A1, A19.

Livingston, Paisley. 2001. *Literature and Rationality: Ideas of Agency in Theory and Fiction.* Cambridge, UK: Cambridge University Press.

Luce, R. Duncan, and Howard Raiffa. 1957. *Games and Decisions: Introduction and Critical Survey.* New York: Wiley.

Lukas, J. Anthony. 1976. *Nightmare: The Underside of the Nixon Years.* New York: Viking.

Mailath, George J., Larry Samuelson, and Jeroen Swinkels. 1993. Extensive Form Reasoning in Normal Form Games. *Econometrica* 61 (2): 273–302.

Mailath, Geroge J., Larry Samuelson, and Jeroen Swinkels. 1994. Normal Form Structures in Extensive Form Games. *Journal of Economic Theory* 64:325–371.

Malici, Akan. 2008. *When Leaders Learn and When They Don't: Mikhail Gorbachev and Kim Il Sung at the End of the Cold War.* Albany: State University of New York Press.

Mandler, George. 1994. Emotions and the Psychology of Freedom. In *Emotions: Essays on Emotion Theory*, ed. Stephanie H. M. van Gooozen, Nanne E. Van de Poll, and Joseph A. Sergeant. Hillsdale, NY: Lawrence Erbaum Associates.

Maoz, Zeev. 1984. Peace by Empire? Conflict Outcomes and International Stability, 1816–1979. *Journal of Peace Research* 21 (3): 227–241.

Maoz, Zeev. 1990. *Paradoxes of War: On the Art of National Self-Entrapment*. Boston: Unwin Hyman.

Maoz, Zeev, and Ben D. Mor. 1996. Enduring Rivalries: The Early Years. *International Political Science Review* 17 (2): 141–160.

Maoz, Zeev, and Ben D. Mor. 2002. *Bound by Struggle: The Strategic Evolution of Enduring International Rivalries*. Ann Arbor: University of Michigan Press.

Marcus, Solomon. 1977. Editorial Note. *The Formal Study of Drama*, special issue of *Poetics* 6 (3/4): 203–207.

Marcus, Solomon. 1990. Private communication (December 19).

Massoud, Tansa George. 1998. Theory of Moves and the Persian Gulf War. In *The Political Economy of War and Peace*, ed. Murray Wolfson, 247–265. Amsterdam: Kluwer.

McCart, Samuel W. 1965. *Trial by Jury*. Philadelphia: Chilton.

McKenna, Marian C. 2002. *Franklin Roosevelt and the Great Constitutional War: The Court-Packing Crisis of 1937*. New York: Fordham University Press.

Mehlman, Alexander. 1990. Private communication (December 19).

Mehlmann, Alexander. 2000. *The Game's Afoot! Game Theory in Myth and Paradox*, tr. David Kramer. Providence, RI: American Mathematical Society.

Meydani, Assaf, and Shlomo Mizrahi. 2010. The Relationship between the Supreme Court and Parliament in Light of the Theory of Moves: The Case of Israel. *Rationality and Society* 22 (1): 55–82.

Miles, Jack. 1995. *God: A Biography*. New York: Vintage.

Mongin, Phillippe. 2009. A Game-Theoretic Analysis of the Waterloo Campaign and Some Comments on the Analytic Narrative Project. Preprint, Ecole HEC School of Management, France.

Mor, Ben D. 1993. *Decision and Interaction in Crisis: A Model of International Crisis Behavior*. Westport, CT: Praeger.

Morgenstern, Oskar. 1928. *Wirtschaftsprognose, Eine Untersuchung ihrer Voraussetzungen und Möglichkeiten (Economic Prediction: An Examination of Its Conditions and Possibilities)*. Vienna: J. Springer.

Morgenstern, Oskar. 1935. Volkommene Voraussicht und Wirtschaftliches Gleichgewicht. *Zeitschrift für Nationalökonomie* 6, part 3 (August): 337–357. (Translated as "Perfect Foresight and Economic Equilibrium," in *Selected Writings of Oskar Morgenstern*, ed. Andrew Schotter, 169–183. New York: New York University Press, 1976.)

Moulin, Hervé. 2003. *Fair Division and Collective Welfare*. Cambridge, MA: MIT Press.

Muzzio, Douglas. 1982. *Watergate Games: Strategies, Choices, Outcomes*. New York: New York University Press.

New York Times staff. 1974. *The End of a Presidency*. New York: Bantam.

Nowak, Martin A. 2007. *Evolutionary Dynamics: Exploring the Equations of Life*. Cambridge, MA: Harvard University Press.

Nurmi, Hannu. 1999. *Voting Paradoxes and How to Deal with Them*. Berlin: Springer.

O'Neill, Barry. 1990. Private communication (October 1).

O'Neill, Barry. 1991. The Strategy of Challenges: Two Beheading Games in Medieval Literature. In *Game Equilibrium Models IV: Social and Political Interaction*, ed. Reinhard Selten. Berlin, Germany: Springer-Verlag.

O'Neill, Barry. 1994. Game Theory Models of Peace and War. In *Handbook of Games with Economic Applications*, vol. 2, ed. Robert J. Aumann and Sergiu Hart, 996–1053. Amsterdam: Elsevier Science.

O'Neill, Barry. 1999. *Honor, Symbols, and War*. Ann Arbor: University of Michigan Press.

O'Neill, Barry. 2007. Game Models of Peace and War: Some Recent Results. In *Diplomacy Games: Formal Models and International Negotiations*, ed. Rudolf Avenhaus and I. William Zartman, 25–44. Berlin: Springer.

Orbell, John. 1993. Hamlet and the Psychology of Rational Choice under Uncertainty. *Rationality and Society* 5 (1): 127–140.

Oren, Nissan. 1982. Prudence in Victory. In *Termination of Wars*, ed. Nissan Oren, 147–163. Jerusalem: Magnes.

Ostrom, Elinor, Roy Gardner, and James Walker. 1994. *Rules, Games, and Common-Pool Resources*. Ann Arbor: University of Michigan Press.

Pachter, Henry M. 1963. *Collision Course: The Cuban Missile Crisis and Coexistence*. New York: Praeger.

Parrott, W. Gerrod, and Rom Harré 1996. Overview. In *The Emotions: Social, Cultural, and Biological Dimensions*, ed. Rom Harré and W. Gerrod Parrott, 1–20. London: Sage.

Pascal, Blaise. 1670/1950. *Pensée*, tr. H. F. Stewart. New York: Pantheon.

Pear, Robert. 1992. The Cuba Missile Crisis: Kennedy Left a Loophole. *New York Times*, January 7, A5.

Pinker, Steven. 2007. The Discover Interview. *Discover* 71 (September): 48–52, 71.

Posner, Richard A. 1998. *Law and Literature*, rev. ed. Cambridge, MA: Harvard University Press.

The Prophets—Nevi'im (1978). Philadelphia: Jewish Publication Society.

Rabin, Matthew. 1993. Incorporating Fairness into Game Theory and Economics. *American Economic Review* 83 (5): 1281–1302.

Rapoport, Anatol. 1960. *Fights, Games, and Debates*. Ann Arbor: University of Michigan Press.

Rapoport, Anatol. 1962. The Use and Misuse of Game Theory. *Scientific American* 207 (6): 108–118.

Rapoport, Anatol. 1990. Private communication (August 28).

Rapoport, Anatol, and Melvin J. Guyer. 1966. A Taxonomy of 2 × 2 Games. *General Systems: Yearbook of the Society for General Systems Research* 11:203–214.

Rapoport, Anatol, Melvin J. Guyer, and David G. Gordon. 1976. *The 2 × 2 Game*. Ann Arbor: University of Michigan Press.

Rasmusen, Eric. 1989. *Games and Information: An Introduction to Game Theory*. Oxford, UK: Basil Blackwell.

Rasmusen, Eric. 1990. Private communication (August 30).

Rawls, John. 1971. *A Theory of Justice*. Cambridge, MA: Harvard University Press.

Rescher, Nicholas. 1985. *Pascal's Wager: A Study of Practical Reasoning in Philosophical Theology*. South Bend, IN: University of Notre Dame Press.

Rescher, Nicholas. 2001. *Paradoxes: Their Roots, Range, and Resolution*. Chicago: Open Court.

Riker, William H. 1962. *The Theory of Political Coalitions*. New Haven, CT: Yale University Press.

Riker, William H. 1986. *The Art of Political Manipulation*. New Haven, CT: Yale University Press.

Riker, William H. 1990. Private communication (September 28).

Robertson, Jack, and William Webb. 1998. *Cake-Cutting Algorithms: Be Fair If You Can*. Natick, MA: A K Peters.

Robinson, David, and David Goforth. 2005. *The Topology of 2 × 2 Games: A New Periodic Table*. New York: Routledge.

Roemer, John. 1996. *Theories of Distributive Justice*. Cambridge, MA: Harvard University Press.

Rosenthal, Robert W. 1991. A Note on Robustness of Equilibria with Respect to Commitment Opportunities. *Games and Economic Behavior* 3 (2): 237–242.

Roth, Arthur, Joseph B. Kadane, and Morris H. DeGroot. 1977. Optimal Peremptory Challenges in Trials by Juries: A Bilateral Sequential Approach. *Operations Research* 25 (6): 901–919.

Saari, Donald G. 2008 *Deposing Dictators, Demystifying Voting Paradoxes: Social Choice Analysis*. Cambridge, UK: Cambridge University Press.

Sachar, Howard M. 1979. *A History of Israel: From the Rise of Zionism to Our Time*. New York: Knopf.

Saks, Michael J. 1976. The Limits of Scientific Jury Selection: Ethical and Empirical. *Jurimetrics Journal* 17: 3–22.

Saunders, Harold. 1985. Diplomacy and Pressure, November 1979–May 1980. In *American Hostages in Iran: The Conduct of a Crisis*, ed. Warren Christopher, 72–144. New Haven, CT: Yale University Press.

Schelling, Thomas C. 1960. *The Strategy of Conflict*. Cambridge, MA: Harvard University Press.

Schelling, Thomas C. 1966. *Arms and Influence*. New Haven, CT: Yale University Press.

Schelling, Thomas C. 1978. *Micromotives and Macrobehavior*. New York: W. W. Norton.

Schelling, Thomas C. 1991. Private communication (September 28).

Schubert, Glendon A. 1958. The Study of Judicial Decision Making as an Aspect of Political Science. *American Political Science Review* 52 (4): 1007–1025.

Schulman, J., P. Shiver, R. Colman, B. Enrich, and R. Christie. 1973. Recipe for a Jury. *Psychology Today* 6 (May): 37–44, 77–84.

Schwartz, Bernard. 1996. *Decision: How the Supreme Court Decides Cases*. New York: Oxford University Press.

Scigliano, Robert. 1971. *The Supreme Court and the Presidency*. New York: Free Press.

Shakespeare, William. 1601/1958. *The Tragedy of Hamlet, Prince of Denmark*, Folger Library Shakespeare. New York: Pocket Books.

Shakespeare, William. 1606/1994. *Macbeth*, ed. Nicholas Brooke. Oxford, UK: Oxford University Press.

Shapley, L. S., and Martin Shubik. 1984. A Method of Evaluating the Distribution of Power in a Committee System. *American Political Science Review* 48 (3): 787–792.

Shesol, Jeff. 2010. *Supreme Power: Franklin Roosevelt vs. the Supreme Court*. New York: W. W. Norton.

Sick, Gary. 1985a. *All Fall Down*. New York: Penguin.

Sick, Gary. 1985b. Military Options and Constraints. In *American Hostages in Iran: The Conduct of a Crisis*, ed. Warren Christopher, 144–172. New Haven, CT: Yale University Press.

Sick, Gary. 1991. *October Surprise: America's Hostages in Iran and the Election of Ronald Reagan*. New York: Random House.

Simon, Marc V. 1996. When Sanctions Can Work: Economic Sanctions and the Theory of Moves. *International Interactions* 21 (3): 203–228.

Skyrms, Brian. 1996. *The Evolution of the Social Contract*. Cambridge, UK: Cambridge University Press.

Skyrms, Brian. 2004. *The Stag Hunt and the Evolution of Social Structure*. Cambridge, UK: Cambridge University Press.

Snyder, Glenn H., and Paul Diesing. 1977. *Conflict among Nations: Bargaining, Decision Making, and Systems Structure in International Crises*. Princeton, NJ: Princeton University Press.

Solomon, Dorf. 2009. *FDR v. the Constitution: The Court-Packing Fight and the Triumph of Democracy*. New York: Walker.

Solomon, Robert C. 1993. *The Passions: Emotions and the Meaning of Life*. Indianpolis, IN: Hackett.

Sorensen, Theodore C. 1965. *Kennedy*. New York: Harper and Row.

Stampp, Kenneth M. 1950. *And the War Came: The North and the Secession Crisis, 1860–61*. Baton Rouge: Louisiana State University Press.

Staudenraus, P. J., ed. 1963. *The Secession Crisis, 1860–61*. Chicago: Rand McNally.

Stephenson, D. Grier, Jr. 1975. 'The Magistry of the Law': U.S. v. Richard Nixon. *Intellect* 103 (February): 288–292.

Steriadi-Bogdan, Mariana. 1977. The Evolution of the Plot and Problems of Strategy in a Detective Play. *The Formal Study of Drama*, special issue of *Poetics* 6, nos. 3/4 (December): 375–382.

Stone, Randall W. 2001. The Use and Abuse of Game Theory in International Relations: The Theory of Moves. *Journal of Conflict Resolution* 45 (2): 216–244.

Swinburne, Richard. 1981. *Faith and Reason*. Oxford, UK: Clarendon.

Swirski, Peter. 1996. Game Theory in the Third Pentagon: A Study in Strategy and Rationality. *Criticism* 88 (2): 303–370.

Swirski, Peter. 2007. *Of Literature and Knowledge: Explorations in Narrative Thought Experiments, Evolution, and Game Theory*. New York: Routledge.

Taylor, Alan D., and Allison M. Pacelli. 2008. *Mathematics and Politics: Strategy, Voting, Power and Proof*, 2nd ed. New York: Springer.

Taylor, Gabrielle. 1996. Guilt and Remorse. In *The Emotions: Social, Cultural and Biological Dimensions*, ed. Rom Harré and W. Gerrod, 57–73. Parrott. London: Sage.

Teodorescu-Brinzeu, Pia. 1977. A Systemic Approach to the Theatre. *The Formal Study of Drama*, special issue of *Poetics* 6 (3/4) (December): 351–374.

Tetlock, Philip E., and Aaron Belkin, eds. 1996. *Counterfactual Thought Experiments in World Politics: Logical, Methodological, and Psychological Perspectives*. Princeton, NJ: Princeton University Press.

Thompson, Robert Smith. 1992. *The Missiles of October: The Declassified Story of John F. Kennedy and the Cuban Missile Crisis*. New York: Simon and Schuster.

Tolchin, Martin. 1992. U.S. Underestimated Soviet Force in Cuba During '62 Missile Crisis. *New York Times*, January 15, A11.

The Torah: The Five Books of Moses, 2nd ed. 1967. Philadelphia: Jewish Publication Society.

Totenberg, Nina. 1975. Behind the Marble, Beneath the Robes. *New York Times Magazine* (March 16): 15ff.

Vance, Cyrus. 1983. *Hard Choices: Critical Years in America's Foreign Policy*. New York: Simon and Schuster.

van Damme, Eric, and Sjaak Hurkens. 1996. Commitment Robust Equilibria and Endogenous Timing. *Games and Economic Behavior* 5 (2): 290–311.

von Neumann, John. 1928. Zur Theorie de Gesellschaftssiele. *Mathematische Annalen* 100: 295–300. (Translated as "On the Theory of Games of Strategy," *Contributions to the Theory of Games* 4, *Annals of Mathematics Studies* 40 [1959]: 13–42.)

von Neumann, John, and Oskar Morgenstern. 1944/1953. *Theory of Games and Economic Behavior*. Princeton, NJ: Princeton University Press.

Vorob'ev, Nikolai. 1968. Khudozhestvennoe Modelirovanie Konflickty i Teoria Igr (Literary Conflict Modeling and the Theory of Games). In *Socruzhestvo Nauk i Tainy Tvorchestva (The Close Relationship of the Sciences and the Secrets of Artistic Creation)*, ed. B. S. Meilakh. Moscow: Izkustvo.

Weingast, Barry R. 1996. Off-the Path Behavior: A Game-Theoretic Approach to Counterfactuals and Its Implications for Political and Historical Analysis. In *Counterfactual Thought Experiments in World Politics: Logical, Methodological, and Psychological Perspectives*, ed. Philip E. Tetlock and Aaron Belkin, 230–243. Princeton, NJ: Princeton University Press.

Weintal, Edward, and Charles Bartlett. 1967. *Facing the Brink: An Intimate Study of Crisis Diplomacy*. New York: Scribner.

Weisman, Richard. 1984. *Witchcraft, Magic, and Religion in 17th-Century Massachusetts*. Amherst: University of Massachusetts Press.

Williams, John D. 1954/1966. *The Compleat Strategyst: Being a Primer on the Theory of Games of Strategy*. New York: McGraw-Hill and Dover.

Willson, Stephen J. 1998. Long-Term Behavior in the Theory of Moves. *Theory and Decision* 45 (3): 201–240.

Woerdman, Edwin. 2000. Rationality and Stability in the Theory of Moves. *Rationality and Society* 12 (1): 67–86.

Wollheim, Richard. 1999. *On the Emotions*. New Haven, CT: Yale University Press.

Woodward, Bob, and Scott Armstrong. 1979. *The Brethren: Inside the Supreme Court*. New York: Simon and Schuster.

Wright, Richard. 1945. *Black Boy*. New York: Harper & Brothers.

Xue, Licun. 1997. Nonemptiness of the Largest Consistent Set. *Journal of Economic Theory* 73: 453–459.

Young, H. Peyton 1994. *Equity in Theory and Practice*. Princeton, NJ: Princeton University Press.

Zagare, Frank C. 1979. The Geneva Conference of 1954: A Case Study of Tacit Deception. *International Studies Quarterly* 23 (3): 390–411.

Zagare, Frank C. 1984. Limited-Move Equilibria in 2 × 2 Games. *Theory and Decision* 16 (1): 1–19.

Zagare, Frank C. 2011. *The Games of July: Explaining the Great War*. Ann Arbor: University of Michigan Press.

Zagare, Frank C., and D. Marc Kilgour. 2000. *Perfect Deterrence*. Cambridge, UK: Cambridge University Press.

Zeager, Lester A. 1998. Negotiations for Refugee Repatriation or Local Settlement: A Game-Theoretic Analysis. *International Studies Quarterly* 42 (2): 367–384.

Zeager, Lester A. 2002. The Role of Strategic Threats in Refugee Resettlement: The Indochinese Crisis of 1978–79. *Rationality and Society* 14 (2): 159–191.

Zeager, Lester A. 2005. Strategic Interaction in the 1994 and Earlier Cuban Refugee Crises. *International Interactions* 31 (4): 327–348.

Zeager, Lester A., and Jonathan Bascom. 1996. Strategic Behavior in Refugee Repatriation: A Game-Theoretic Analysis. *Journal of Conflict Resolution* 40: 460–485.

Zeager, Lester A., and John H. P. Williams. 2004. Macedonian Border Closings in the Kosovo Refugee Crisis: A Game-Theoretic Perspective. *Conflict Management and Peace Science* 21 (4): 233–254.

Ziegler, David W. 1987. *War, Peace, and International Politics*, 4th ed. Glenview, IL: Scott, Foresman.

Index